D1605473

Immigrants in Tudor
and Early Stuart England

Immigrants in Tudor and Early Stuart England

Edited by

Nigel Goose and Lien Luu

sussex
ACADEMIC
PRESS

BRIGHTON • PORTLAND

Organization of this volume
© Nigel Goose and Lien Luu, 2005. Text © Sussex Academic Press, 2005.

2 4 6 8 10 9 7 5 3 1

First published in 2005 in Great Britain by
SUSSEX ACADEMIC PRESS
P.O. Box 2950
Brighton BN2 5SP

and in the United States of America by
SUSSEX ACADEMIC PRESS
920 NE 58th Ave.   Suite 300
Portland, Oregon 97213-3786

British Library Cataloguing in Publication Data
A CIP catalogue record for this book is available from the British Library.

Library of Congress Cataloging-in-Publication Data
Immigrants in Tudor and early Stuart England / edited by Nigel Goose and
Lien Luu.
    p. cm.
    Includes bibliographical references and index.
    ISBN 1-903900-14-X (pbk. : alk. paper)
    1. England—Ethnic relations—History—16th century.
    2. England—Emigration and immigration—History—16th century.
    3. England—Emigration and immigration—History—17th century.
    4. England—Ethnic relations—History—17th century. 5. Immigrants—
England—History—16th century. 6. Immigrants—England—History—
17th century. 7. Great Britain—History—Stuarts, 1603–1714.
    8. Great Britain—History—Tudors, 1485–1603. I. Goose, Nigel.
II. Luu, Lien, 1967–
DA125.A1I46 2005
942.05′086′91—dc22   2004007293
                                                      CIP

Typeset and designed by G&G Editorial, Brighton
Printed by MPG Books, Bodmin, Cornwall.
This book is printed on acid-free paper.

Contents

Contributors

Dr. **Raingard Esser** is Senior Lecturer in History at the University of the West of England in Bristol. She is the author of *Niederländische Exulanten im England des 16. und frühen 17. Jahrhunderts* (Berlin, 1996), and an authority of the immigrant community in Norwich. She teaches early modern social and cultural history and is particularly interested in the Low Countries in the 17th century.

Professor Dr Raymond Fagel is Lecturer in Early Modern History at the University of Leiden and specializes in relations between Spain and the Netherlands and emigration from the Low Countries during the Renaissance. He currently also occupies a special chair at the Free University of Brussels called 'The Low Countries in the World'.

Nigel Goose is Professor of Social and Economic History at the University of Hertfordshire. He has published widely in the fields of early modern urban, economic and demographic history, and has a particular interest in the Dutch immigrant community in sixteenth- and seventeenth-century Colchester. He also writes on nineteenth century local history, and is editor of the journal *Local Population Studies.*

Charles Littleton completed his Ph.D. on the French and Walloon immigrant community in Elizabethan London in 1966, summarising its main points in *Archiv für Reforationsgeschichte*, Vol. 92 (2001). He has since worked on a project to digitize the 'workdiaries' of Robert Boyle and is currently a Research Fellow for the History of Parliament. In 2000 he convened the conference which resulted in the publication of *From Strangers to Citizens: the Integration of Immigrant Communities in Britain, Ireland and Colonial America, 1550–1750* (Sussex Academic Press, 2001).

Dr Lien Luu is Senior Lecturer in History at the University of Hertfordshire. She is the author of a number of articles on the impact and reception of immigrants in early modern England and her book, *Immigrants and the Industries of London*, is shortly to be published by Ashgate.

Dr Andrew Spicer is Lecturer in Early Modern European History at Oxford Brookes University. He is the author of *The French-speaking Reformed Community and their Church in Southampton*, and co-editor of *Society and Culture in the Huguenot World, 1559–1685* and *Sacred Space: the Redefinition of Sanctity in Post-Reformation Europe.*

His current research focuses upon the impact of the Reformation and its theology on church architecture.

Dr David J. B. Trim is Lecturer in History at Newbold College and Honorary Research Fellow at the University of Reading. A Fellow of the Royal Historical Society, he is the author of a number of scholarly essays, and editor of *The Chivalric Ethos and the Development of Military Professionalism* (Brill, 2003) and *Cross, Crown and Community: Religion, Government and Culture in Early-Modern England* (Peter Lang, 2004).

Joseph P. Ward is an Associate Professor of History at the University of Mississippi. He is the author of *Metropolitan Communities: Trade Guilds, Identity, and Change in Early Modern London* (Stanford University Press, 1997); a co-editor of *The Country and the City Revisited: England and the Politics of Culture, 1550–1850* (Cambridge University Press, 1999) and of *Protestant Identities: Religion, Society, and Self-fashioning in Post-Reformation England* (Stanford University Press, 1999); and the editor of *Britain and the American South: From Colonialism to Rock and Roll* (University Press of Mississippi, 2003).

Tables and Maps

Tables

Map

Abbreviations

―――――――

APC	*Acts of the Privy Council of England,* J. R. Dasent (ed.), 32 vols (London, 1890–1907)
BL	British Library
BN	Bibliothèque Nationale, Paris
CRO	County Record Office
CSPD	*Calendar of State Papers Domestic,* J. Bruce *et al.* (eds), 22 vols (London, 1858–93)
CSP Foreign	*Calendar of State Papers Foreign*
CSP Spanish	*Calendar of State Papers Spanish*
CSPV	*Calendar of State Papers Venetian*
DNB	*Dictionary of National Biography*, ed. L. Stephen and S. Lee, 21 vols (Oxford, 1921–2)
FPC 3	French Protestant Church of London, MS 3 (consistory minutes 1578–88)
FPC 4	French Protestant Church of London, MS 4 (consistory minutes 1589–1615)
Hessels	J. H. Hessels (ed.), *Ecclesiae Londino-Batavae Archivum. Epistulae et Tractatus*, 4 Vols. (Cambridge, 1887–97)
HMC	Historical Manuscripts Commission
Kirk & Kirk	R. E. G. and E. F. Kirk (eds), *Returns of Aliens Dwelling in the City and Suburbs of London, Huguenot Society of London*, vol. 10, parts 1–4 (1900–8)
KL	*Relations politiques des Pays-Bas et de l'Angleterre, sous le règne de Philippe II*, ed. Kervyn de Lettenhove, 11 vols (Brussels, 1882–1900)
JHC	*Journals of the House of Commons*
PCC	Prerogative Court of Canterbury
PRO	Public Record Office, Kew
SP	State Papers

Immigrants in Tudor and Early Stuart England

1

Immigrants in Tudor and Early Stuart England

NIGEL GOOSE

It is now over 100 years since William Cunningham published his *Alien Immigrants to England*, in which he brought together the material that underpinned his view that skilled immigrants from continental Europe had exerted a decisive impact upon the English economy.[1] It was a book that spanned the centuries, beginning with the Norman invasion and extending into the late eighteenth century, and no historian writing since has attempted a similarly wide-ranging analysis of the impact of alien settlers. That said, the main focus of the book is upon the later Middle Ages and the early modern period up to the middle of the seventeenth century: earlier settlers are considered quite briefly, while the Huguenot diaspora that is associated with the Revocation of the Edict of Nantes in 1685 also gets but cursory treatment. The heart of the book is devoted to the sixteenth and early seventeenth centuries, to those immigrants who fled from Spanish persecution in the southern Netherlands from the middle of the sixteenth century forwards, successive waves of Dutch, Flemish and Walloons escaping from religious persecution, warfare and economic dislocation, many of whom gravitated towards the northern Netherlands, Germany and other destinations in continental Europe, but considerable numbers of whom also found their way across the North Sea to England.[2] With the exception of the Moriscos expelled from Spain in 1609 and the Huguenots who fled Louis XIV's France during the 1680s, this was the largest uprooting experienced in early modern Europe, and their number has been estimated at a total of *ca.* 180,000.[3] Of these, it has been suggested that perhaps 10,000 were to be found in England by the 1570s, the number peaking at roughly 15,000 in the 1590s before falling back again to around 10,000 a generation later.[4] These estimates, which will be re-examined below, relate to the number of aliens resident in England at specific points in time.[5] Were it possible to trace all those who – either as new immigrants or as the family of immigrants – had experience of English life at one point or another across the later sixteenth and early seventeenth centuries, the number would be considerably higher, for migration to England in this period came in successive waves, with evidence of considerable return migration too.[6] The alien population was thus somewhat more fluid than that associated with the persecution of the Huguenots in France in the late seventeenth century, commonly described as the "second refuge", and it is this that makes it so difficult to calculate the number of these immigrants of the "first refuge" with precision.

There has been a great deal of work on alien immigrants to England since Cunningham wrote, particularly in the last 30 years or so, but it would be fair to say that while the Huguenots have found their modern historian, the immigrants of the first refuge still await theirs.[7] The remark made by Andrew Pettegree in 1986 still holds true: "For a view of the general significance of the immigration one is still forced to turn back to William Cunningham's *Alien Immigrants to England* . . . ".[8] That said, considerable progress has been made towards an understanding of the organization and influence of immigrant communities in both the capital and the provinces, for – while considerable scope for further research remains – all of the larger immigrant communities, and some of the smaller ones, have now been the subject of modern scrutiny.[9] The small foreign communities in Kentish and East Anglian towns such as Maidstone, Dover, Rye, Great Yarmouth and Canvey Island have yet to attract detailed, modern attention, but for these too at least a start has been made towards an outline of their history and significance.[10] This work provides the basis for a reassessment of some of the issues relating to immigrants explored by Cunningham a century ago, in particular their status and social organization, the manner in which they were regulated by local and national governments, and their economic influence. In each of these areas new research has made it possible to go beyond the assessment Cunningham was able to offer, particularly in terms of quantitative analysis and through more detailed consideration of their economic impact, but also in terms of a fuller appraisal of the multi-faceted nature of their reception and the process of assimilation. New areas of interest have emerged too, most notably in the form of more precise analysis of the backgrounds and origins of immigrants, their cultural impact, their religious discipline and the role of their churches, as well as their ongoing relationship with the wider international community. All of these topics are represented in the present volume, by leading scholars in the field of English immigration history, and they are offered as a first step towards a modern reappraisal of the immigrants and their impact in Tudor and early Stuart England. To properly understand this impact, however, requires an appreciation of the wider political and religious, economic and social contexts.

The Political and Religious Context

Religion and politics were intimately connected throughout this period, an association symbolized by the royal supremacy over the English church, established first in 1534 and re-established following the Marian reaction in the Elizabethan Settlement of 1559, when the queen adopted the title "supreme governor" of the Church of England, her jurisdiction in ecclesiastical affairs "annexed to the imperial crown of this realm by the authority of Parliament".[11] Neither the relationship between Crown and Church nor between Crown and Parliament in this respect was wholly unproblematic, and historians have spent a great deal of ink in probing these issues.[12] The Vestiarian controversy that emerged during the 1560s epitomized the ongoing difficulties, in this instance Elizabeth at least appearing to get her way in insisting upon the wearing by the clergy of cap and surplice. But with regard to the basic issue of who controlled the church, the theoretical authority of the Crown did not always translate into practice, for Elizabeth relied upon the ecclesiastical hierarchy to enforce compliance, and enforcement was frequently less than fully effective. The clergy themselves had to negotiate in practice with a range of interest groups, the strength of which increased as the century wore on and Protestantism gained a firmer hold. If the English Reformation shared features in common with that on the continent, notably in the break with Rome and the adoption of Calvinist theology, it combined this with a far more traditional form of organization and church discipline, to produce an Anglican church "but halfly reformed".[13] That organization was not strong enough to ensure that the will of the Crown was imposed at every turn, and the English *via media* left scope for a range of views that necessarily included those of the 'hotter sort' of Protestants, who in fact performed an important evangelical role in accommodating committed Protestants to the national church.[14]

Where Puritanism went to separatist extremes, however, it was quickly crushed: the "Brownists" were exiled in 1581, the separatists Barrow, Greenwood and Penry tried and executed in 1593, while Dutch Anabaptists also paid the ultimate sanction in being put to the flames – in 1538, in the reign of Edward VI, and again in 1575.[15] Toleration had its limits, therefore, and the fact that the churches established in England by the exile communities stood far closer to the Calvinist churches of the continent than did the English parish churches provides essential context for an understanding of the attitude of the monarchy and Privy Council towards them. If, as Andrew Spicer suggests below, Elizabethan Puritans "viewed these churches as beacons of the True Religion", then it was crucial for the crown to ensure that their practices remained the correct side of the line that separated more ardent Protestantism from separatism.[16] It is not surprising, therefore, to find the Privy Council in 1573 firing warning shots across the bows of the Dutch Church in London, insisting that they suppress all "tumultuous and disquiet people" within their congregation, drawing a very clear connexion indeed between subversion in religion and in the state.[17] Giving succour to co-religionists was one thing; tolerating potential subversion by a Trojan horse from within was a very different matter indeed. Not surprisingly, while they formed national colloquies and attended overseas synods, the foreign churches consistently claimed that they were not subject to continental authority.[18]

At the local level the religious commitment and complexion of the populace is often difficult to gauge. A. G. Dickens has argued that England was already well prepared to accept Protestantism by the third decade of the sixteenth century, as a result of the prevalence of neo-Lollardy at the popular level, the negative opinions held of the contemporary clergy, as well as via the positive influence of Christian humanism in smoothing the path to acceptance of Lutheranism.[19] The evidence of the religious preambles employed in the writing of wills, however, suggests considerable variation in the speed with which the new religion was adopted, as well as a degree of diplomatic pragmatism in response to the changing religious opinions of both the monarch and local bishops, which caused a reversion to Catholic formulations during the short reign of Mary.[20] If some parts of Nottinghamshire and Yorkshire appear to show early acceptance of the Protestant faith, in a number of other areas it was not until the last 20 years or so of the sixteenth century that traditional preambles disappeared completely and Protestant ones gained the ascendancy. Such evidence sits well with Patrick Collinson's conclusion that "it is only with the 1570s that the historically minded insomniac goes to sleep counting Catholics rather than Protestants, since only then did they begin to find themselves in a minority situation", a conclusion that provides important context for the reception afforded to Protestant immigrants.[21]

Most immigrants, of course, settled in towns, and in some counties, such as Sussex, religious change proceeded fastest in urban areas, even if the example of the city of York shows that this was not invariably true.[22] In many towns in southern and eastern England, however, where proximity to the continent had provided a haven for foreign Protestants as well as an entry point for more radical religious ideas, Protestantism made more rapid progress, as it did in Colchester. Here Lollardy, strong in the early fifteenth century, experienced an early sixteenth-century revival, and despite the opposition of some members of the local clergy to the royal supremacy and a degree of ambivalence on the part of the leading townsmen, Protestantism was quite rapidly embraced in the town as a whole, which became a focal point of opposition to Mary's Catholic regime in the 1550s – so much so that Dickens was to remark that "if the Battle of Waterloo was won on the playing fields of Eton, the English Reformation was secured in the pubs of Colchester".[23] As early as 1561 a borough preachership was established in the town, "to the increase of God's glory and maintenance of his word", and during the 1560s and 1570s a string of talented preachers in the vanguard of reformed opinion, in alliance with the Colchester assembly, set about creating a godly civic commonwealth.[24] The reformers did not have it all their own way, however, and from the later 1570s a division emerged between extremists and moderates in the town, while even here Catholicism retained a foothold, Thomas Audley's house at Berechurch emerging as an important centre of recusancy.[25] Towns like Colchester also included their share of "ungodly persons", as the town bailiffs complained in 1583, as well as those who were only nominally religious, but at least a majority of the middling and upper echelons of Colchester society were predisposed by religious affiliation to welcome their Dutch co-religionists.[26]

Colchester was by no means alone in its Protestant precocity, which was shared by other East Anglian and Kentish towns such as Ipswich, Bury St Edmunds, Kings Lynn, Norwich, Sandwich and Canterbury. Even when all the important qualifications have been made, it does appear to be at least generally true that Protestantism was embraced more readily in the south and east of the country than in the north and west, and that the counties of Essex and Kent stood in the vanguard, their towns decidedly to the fore.[27] Leadership, however, was the prerogative of London. London retained its importance as a Lollard centre in the early sixteenth century and if – as heretics and anti-social elements – they often stood outside of London society, far from all the "scripture men" were Lollards.[28] The tracts of Martin Luther were being imported without restriction by 1518, and although they were outlawed three years later, his ideas were spread by an underworld of "evangelical brethren" who successfully infiltrated the Inns of Court and – when persecuted – fled to the continent from where they provided inspiration and a steady flow of smuggled books and tracts. Early Protestantism in London had all the appeal of a protest movement, and appears to have been particularly attractive to radical youth, while it also appealed to a long tradition of anti-clericalism and even brought Lollardy within its more respectable fold.[29]

The oppression orchestrated by Thomas More in the early 1530s was largely halted by the political reformation from above of 1534–6 which, even if Henry professed his rejection of Lutheranism, required that it was now the conservative opponents of the

Supreme Head of the Church who were hunted down rather than the heretics, with London as the prime hunting ground.[30] The tide was soon to turn, the latter years of Henry's reign witnessing renewed persecution of the evangelists, but the fact that in the 1540s 13 per cent of London testators prefaced their bequests with undeniably Protestant preambles suggests that inroads had already been made.[31] The tide was to turn again with the accession of Edward in 1547, which signalled both the start of concerted reform and the hasty return of the evangelical exiles, while it was just three years later that the King granted the Austin Friars to the stranger communities.[32] By the early 1550s Londoners rarely demonstrated adherence to the old faith in their wills, while distinctly Protestant convictions were found in one-third of the Commissary Court wills and fully one-half of those proved in the PCC in 1551.[33] The Marian interlude may have won some Londoners back to the Catholic faith, and their wills in the last years of her reign betray an uneasy co-existence of belief in both justification by faith and the intercessionary power of the saints, but it created martyrs too. In the 1560s London remained the undoubted centre of radical Protestantism, the godly looked to the stranger churches within their midst as a model for further reformation while some even became actively involved in their affairs. Whatever the true religious persuasion of the mass of the London populace, there is little to indicate that the stranger churches were widely resented on religious grounds, concerns over economic competition from their membership notwithstanding, and they were certainly distinctly welcomed by the godly minority.[34]

The other side of the coin of support for Protestantism, of course, was hostility to Catholicism, which developed most forcefully when combined with political animosity between England and the counter-Reformation power of Spain. From the 1560s many of Elizabeth's advisers feared the threat of an international Catholic league, a fear encouraged by the arrival in the Netherlands of the Duke of Alva's army, particularly when he made incursions into Germany and France too. Anti-Catholicism in parliament was further fuelled by a series of plots which focused upon the claims of Mary Queen of Scots to the English throne, notably the Northern Rebellion of 1569 which, for all its incoherence and lack of success, offered an early warning of the possibilities that could arise through a combination of political dissatisfaction and religious conservatism.[35] A serious breach between England and Spain developed through a sequence of relatively petty disputes between 1569 and 1573 but, despite the advice of senior councillors such as Walsingham and Leicester, Elizabeth retained her position of neutrality through to 1578, partly because of her doubts over rebellion against a legitimate sovereign.[36] This was to change when the peace forged by the Pacification of Ghent in 1576 broke down just two years later, and when the States-General again found their offer to Elizabeth of sovereignty in exchange for military aid rejected they turned to the French Duke of Anjou. Following abortive attempts to secure first a marriage and subsequently a military alliance with France, in September 1585 Elizabeth signed the Treaty of Nonsuch with the States-General, agreeing to provide the Dutch with £126,000 a year to pay an English force of 6,400 soldiers and 1,000 horse. This sum amounted to half the queen's ordinary peacetime revenue: actual expenses for the two years 1585–7 were estimated by the Privy Council at £313,000. In return, the Dutch were to deliver to her the two "cautionary" towns of the Brill and Flushing as insurance for the repayment of English war expenses, their garrisons to be maintained at English expense. Despite early recriminations over pay on the one side and the quality of the troops supplied on the other, the alliance survived. English opposition to the claim to leadership by the States of Holland was withdrawn in April 1588 in the face of the growing threat from the Spanish Armada, against which Elizabeth needed Dutch naval cooperation. By the 1590s the troops were more professional and better paid. Alongside the Scots volunteers who had been active since the early 1570s, they formed perhaps one-third of Maurice of Nassau's army, and to this must be added the garrisons at Flushing and the Brill.[37] Estimates of the size of English garrisons in the Dutch republic vary and clearly fluctuated over time, but a return dated August 1588 suggests a nominal strength in eight garrisons of 7,867, and an actual strength of 5,660.[38] *A Declaration of the Causes moving the Queen of England to give aid to the Defence of the People afflicted and oppressed in the Low Countries*, probably written by Walsingham, declared "that they were otherwise more straitly knit in ancient friendship to this realm than to any other country", but also emphasized "our own danger at hand by the overthrow and destruction of our neighbours, and access and planting the great forces of the Spaniards so near to our countries, with precedent arguments of many troublesome attempts against our realm".[39] The latter consideration also eventually led to military support for the Huguenot leader in France, Henry of Navarre, when it looked like France might fall to the Catholic League, itself allied to Spain. Military action was largely limited to securing the ports of Brittany, and ended in 1595 once Henry IV had reasserted his position and the Spanish threat was effectively over. But between 1589 and 1595 nearly 20,000 English troops had been sent to France, in addition to the 8,500 or so active in the Netherlands, with the result that "on the defensive side, Elizabethan England had done a great deal to frustrate a Spanish domination of western Europe, to secure the survival of the Dutch republic, and to re-establish the independence of the French monarchy".[40]

While the threat from Catholicism from within declined over the last 20 years of the sixteenth century, therefore, the fear of its threat from without continued unabated and was fuelled by a whole sequence of events – the threat from the Armada in 1588, the Spanish invasions of Ireland, the Gunpowder Plot of 1605, invasion scares and the proposed Spanish match in the 1620s.[41] It was, of course, Spanish Catholic oppression that had brought many of the Dutch immigrants to England, rendering them natural objects of sympathy to many ministers and magistrates, while in turn French Protestants fled from native oppression, the blood that was shed in events such as the St Bartholomew's Day Massacre of 1572 only serving to underline the by now self-evident association of the Pope with the Antichrist. The image created by William Haller of John Foxe, through his *Book of Martyrs*, as the architect of the notion of "God's Englishmen" may well have been overstated, ignoring the internationalist leaning of Foxe and other English Protestants. But this is not to deny this as a possible, albeit selective, reading, and anyway Protestant nationalism and internationalism were not mutually exclusive.[42] Nineteen years of hostilities between England and Spain, from 1585 to the Anglo-Spanish Treaty of London in 1604, and six years of intervention in Brittany, battling to prevent the resumption of Spanish overlordship across the Netherlands as well as to thwart the designs of Philip II upon France, could only serve to underline the congruence of religious and political allegiance. For if direct intervention was limited and concern for national security paramount, both passive and active assistance at both home and abroad also reflect a determination to resist the Catholic threat and to offer support for European co-religionists.

Under the Stuarts the focus of attention once again turned to the possibility of a Catholic threat from within, not so much from a resurgent indigenous Catholicism, but from the apparently increasing influence of Catholicism at court.[43] If the Anglo-Spanish Treaty of 1604 raised eyebrows in some quarters, the Gunpowder Plot of 1605 rang alarm bells. The influence of the crypto-Catholic Howard group at court, who accepted Spanish pensions, and after 1614 the apparent influence of the Spanish ambassador Gondomar upon James I – "arch Enemy to the flourishing Estate of our England" according to a pamphlet of 1626 – were further causes for concern.[44] The fact that Gondomar was subjected to an assault by London apprentices in 1621 provides ample testimony to the depth of popular feeling, as well as again raising the intriguing notion of radical youth standing in the vanguard of Protestantism.[45] James's attempt to negotiate a Spanish match for his son Charles to balance the marriage in 1613 of his daughter Elizabeth to Frederick, Elector Palatine, and his failure to offer more concerted support when Spain attacked the Palatinate, added fuel to the flames, while the discussions at the Synod of Dort in 1618–19 sharpened the differences between the Calvinist and the Arminian factions within the Anglican Church.[46] Neither war with Spain (1625–30) nor with France (1627–9) could distract from the rise of Arminianism at home and particularly the growing influence of Bishop William Laud, while the marriage of Charles to the devout French Catholic Henrietta Maria and her conduct of Catholic services at court raised fears of a Catholic conspiracy. In 1634 Laud, now Archbishop of Canterbury, launched his attack on the foreign congregations in England, requiring them to conduct their services in English and for second-generation immigrants to use their parish churches: it was an attack that was not forgotten when he was eventually indicted.[47] This is not the place to enter the debate over the causes of the English Civil War, but there can be little doubt that religion was a factor of great importance, and the continued anti-popery that was further excited by the activities of Charles and his close advisers, and exploited by Pym in parliament, found immediate expression in the attacks upon Catholic recusants in Essex in 1640–1, as well as in occasional assaults in the early 1640s upon French and Spanish immigrants – for their Catholic associations – in London.[48]

Anti-popery survived the Civil War and Interregnum, and revived later in the century in the context of the Exclusion Crisis at home, the growing power of Louis XIV's France abroad and the oppression of French Protestants which led to the Huguenot immigration of the "second refuge" – all clear indications of the perception of Catholicism as a political as well as a religious threat.[49] But in the meantime the politics of economic rivalry had generated new conflicts, which no appeal to international Protestant solidarity had been able to quell, which surfaced in the Naval Wars against the Dutch.[50] In the late sixteenth and early seventeenth century the Dutch had established themselves as pre-eminent in the European carrying trade, particularly during their 12-year truce with Spain after 1609. Dominance in European traffic created a springboard for the development of their oriental and colonial trade which, along with the incursions that the Dutch herring fleet made into British coastal waters, created a further theatre of competition.[51] Resentment against the Dutch was not new: Walter Raleigh was among those who had expressed his objection to the manner in which they had continued to trade with their Spanish enemy in the later sixteenth century, as well as to their fishing exploits, during a Commons debate of 1593 over whether or not aliens should be allowed to sell in England by retail:

The nature of the Dutchman is to fly to no man but for his profit, and they will obey no man long, now under Spain, now under Mounfort, now under the Prince of Orange, but under no governour long. The Dutchman by his policy that gotten trading with all the world into his hands, yea he is now entering into the trade of Scarborough fishing, and the fishing of the New-found-Lands, which is the stay of the West Countries. They are the people that maintain the King of Spain in his greatness. Were it not for them he were never able to make out such armies and navies by sea . . . [52]

The early seventeenth century witnessed a number of clashes and disputes which remained unresolved, and neither the Dutch prohibition on English cloth exports during the abortive Cockayne Project nor the advantage they took of James's financial difficulties to regain the cautionary towns on favourable terms in 1616, did anything to endear them to those in England who increasingly feared and resented their economic strength. In 1623 a number of English merchants were tortured and killed on the Dutch East Indian island of Amboyna for an alleged conspiracy, creating a further focus for resentment which provided propaganda for decades to come, and although in 1625 common cause was made once more in war with Spain, they again continued to trade with the enemy.[53] In 1630 Charles deserted the Dutch once again, and even entered into private negotiations with Spain for the possible partitioning of the United Provinces. Whatever Charles's personal predilections, the English more generally faced a dilemma: on the one hand there was ever-growing economic rivalry with and resentment against the Dutch, and on the other the Dutch retained both their anti-Spanish and Protestant credentials, not forgotten through to the early 1640s.[54] It was a dilemma that remained unresolved in 1642 when the mounting crisis at home reached breaking point.

By 1649 both England and the United Provinces were Protestant republics; by 1652 they were at war. England's commerce had benefited considerably from a long period of neutrality while much of Europe remained embroiled in the Thirty Years War, a conflict brought to an end by the Treaty of Westphalia in 1648, renewing the prospect of intensified competition.[55] English privateering exploits against the Dutch had also proceeded apace during the preceding decade, and none of the long-standing disputes over jurisdiction over the seas had been settled. Abortive negotiations in 1651 provided the trigger for the instigation of the English Navigation Acts, which were uncompromisingly aimed at Dutch supremacy in the carrying trade and racked up the existing ill-will between the two nations, to the extent that a dispute over the rights of search in the following May ushered in the First Dutch War. It lasted from 1652 to 1654, and resulted in the seizure of at least as many Dutch ships as the English already had in their entire merchant navy: it was to be followed by two further – less successful – conflicts, in 1665–7 and 1672–4. During each conflict anti-Dutch propaganda was rife, but such views were not necessarily typical of English opinion during the seventeenth century, and expressions of admiration for both its economy and the openness of its society co-existed with jealousy and resentment.[56] For all the growing competition during the first half of the century, and the conflicts that erupted in the third quarter, the United Provinces remained a natural ally, as the political developments of the late seventeenth century were to prove, and those who resided in London and the provincial towns of southern and eastern England continued in a state of (more or less) peaceful co-existence, with little sign that economic, political or even military rivalry impacted upon relationships at home.

This brief outline of some of the key religious and political developments of the period which incorporates the "first refuge" will, it is hoped, provide some useful context for an appreciation of the status, reception, assimilation and international connexions of the English immigrant communities, topics which are all represented in the essays in this volume. In each of these respects there was a degree of ambivalence or even contradiction: privileges and restrictions, welcome and resentment, religious affinity and fear of radicalism, endogamy and assimilation, commitment to the new home and loyalty to the old. In all of this religion was a crucial consideration, but it was not invariably the dominant one. At home the desire to give succour to fellow co-religionists could at times be over-ridden by economic self-interest, and in this context it raises once again the difficult question of the extent to which the reformed religion ever really penetrated the lower echelons of the social structure, from whence the most fierce resentment of immigrants invariably came. Exactly how the London apprentices should be characterized in this context – as early modern adolescents or as the popular Protestant vanguard – remains problematic. In international terms policy was clearly strongly shaped by religion affiliation, but these policies were also tempered by considerations of national self-interest, while in this sphere too issues of economic rivalry could at times take precedence, as they did in the third quarter of the seventeenth century. Throughout all of the conflicts and controversies of the period London remained notably cosmopolitan, accommodating not only Dutch and French, but also small communities of Spanish, Italians, Germans and other nationalities, while there is little to indicate that – except for brief periods of national crisis or in relatively isolated incidents – foreign conflict ever translated into concerted action against the immigrants in our midst. For as Edmund Howes noted in 1615, the influx of Dutch and French refugees,

> . . . together with the encrease of our owne Nation, who from that time, have infinitely conjoyned in marriage with straungers, and the great freedome of Traffique, and commerce into France, Spaine, Italy and Turky, & c. that then, and for many years after, this land enjoyed, was, and is the maine cause of our encrease of wealth . . . [57]

It is to the economic and social context of the immigrant contribution that we can now turn.

The Economic and Social Context

There can no longer be any doubt that the English economy made considerable progress during the early modern period. For an earlier generation of economic historians, the fashion for de-bunking purported "revolutions" in industry, agriculture, commerce or social relations, revolutions associated with names such as Nef, Kerridge, Davis and Tawney, resulted in a tendency to underplay the changes that occurred, in the sixteenth and early seventeenth centuries in particular: only the financial revolution of the late seventeenth century appears to have survived largely, if not entirely, unscathed.[58] The conundrum that this tendency produced is a simple one: if only limited changes had occurred in each of these areas during the preceding two centuries, then why was the English economy, and English society, so palpably different in 1700 compared to 1500? Instead of standing on the periphery of the European economy or, at the very least, clearly trailing behind nations such as Spain and Portugal, Italy and the southern Netherlands in commercial and industrial terms, why did England now stand in the vanguard of European economic progress, admired and feared by all its continental rivals?[59]

It may be that the backwardness of England in 1500 has been exaggerated. Numerous foreign observers around the turn of the sixteenth century remarked very favourably upon various aspects of English economic life: its considerable trade in woollen cloth, its lead, tin and other metal industries, the vitality of London and the luxury trades to be found there, its pasture lands replete with sheep and the advantages of a temperate climate.[60] England had also by this date freed itself of the shackles of a feudal system of land tenure, while the favourable relationship between population and resources produced by successive plagues in the later medieval period had reshaped the English social structure and laid the foundations for a more productive agriculture.[61] Furthermore, England had already made the transition from an exporter of primary products to an exporter of manufactured woollen cloth, and had developed a market economy articulated through some 600 market towns, large and small. Even granted all of this, however, there can be no doubt that England by 1700 had experienced a further and fundamental shift in its economic complexion, that both industry and commerce featured far more prominently than they had done two centuries earlier, that there were considerably more large towns, that agriculture was more efficient and productive and – perhaps more controversially – that the idea of progress had already instilled itself into the English psyche.

In his recent discussion of the "divergence of England", setting it on the road towards the first industrial revolution in human history, Wrigley writes:

> A first point to stress is that the relative advance was in train long before the period which has conventionally been assigned to the industrial revolution. The change was cumulative and progressive rather than abrupt. It was largely the product of developments within the period often termed pre-industrial . . .[62]

For Wrigley, the progress of the agricultural sector was a key factor in these developments.[63] Wrightson too has recently offered a highly positive interpretation of England's economic progress in the pre-industrial period. More chronologically precise than Wrigley, Wrightson focuses upon the period between the early sixteenth century and the mid-eighteenth century, to argue that "the early modern period was indeed a turning point in British economic and social development", the key to which was the emergence of a market economy that "became increasingly a capitalist economy", involving "a quickening of economic activity, significant increases in agricultural and industrial output and rising percapita income and consumption for at least part of the population, at least some of the time".[64] For Wrightson agricultural developments were also important, but here the emphasis is less upon one economic sector or another and more on the general advance of commercialization and the developing habits of mind that accompanied this process.[65]

When, exactly, did these developments take place? Here too there has been a shift of emphasis in recent literature towards a greater appreciation of the changes that occurred in the sixteenth and early seventeenth centuries, even if the subsequent century saw greater progress in terms of growth, specialization and productivity. In his classic characterization of "Tawney's century", the period between the Dissolution of the Monasteries and the English Civil War, Fisher wrote that "the late sixteenth and early seventeenth centuries constitute perhaps the last period in English history in which economic appetites were remarkably vigorous but in which economic expansion was still slow".[66] He went on to outline the obstacles to growth he perceived: problems on the supply side underpinned by the numerous competing claims upon land, and on the demand side the absence of a wide enough market to encourage growth and specialization, both of which served to create conservatism in economic thought and a restrictive economic policy. As a further consequence, Fisher argued, there was a struggle for the ownership and occupancy of land and an enthusiasm for a professional career that diverted resources away from industry and commerce, reflecting the relative unattractiveness of these alternative employments for capital and skill, operating as both cause and effect.[67]

Fisher's characterization has been enormously influential, and remains unchallenged in some key respects: the twin forces of population growth and inflation in this period served to discourage the search for increases in productivity, as labour was abundant and relatively cheap and the size of the home market for industrial goods was kept in check by a substantial decline in real wages. Government, at both local and national levels, tended towards a defensive economic policy – insofar as its pragmatic and piecemeal responses could be described as a policy as such – prioritizing social stability over economic growth. But research in the 40 years since Fisher wrote has also revealed far more dynamism than he allowed, and it is increasingly clear that he exaggerated the obstacles to economic growth and underplayed the opportunities. In agriculture, there is no doubt that rampant inflation reflected limited achievements in terms of productivity, but there were at least modest improvements in the form of increased manuring, enclosure and the adoption of convertible husbandry, to produce a more intensive agriculture and a higher degree of specialization. There is no doubt too that many of the larger landowners, and at least some of the smallholders, profited considerably from these trends. Urban growth, in both London and the provinces, stimulated this process, while the profits of agriculture enhanced the market for the goods and services of the towns and for the products of rural industry. Industry spread considerably across the English countryside, complementing rather than competing with urban production. Demand was found among the prospering landowners, the gentry great and small and the expanding yeomanry, whose increasing wealth is reflected in the evidence of enhanced material possessions and the "great rebuilding" of rural England that characterized these years. And while it may be true that declining real wages meant that the mass of the population of necessity spent a high proportion of their incomes on the basic necessities of life, one must remember that it was these very basic necessities that the English economy, for the most part, produced. The result of this increasingly symbiotic relationship between industry and agriculture, town and countryside, was a considerable intensification of internal trade, a notable feature of the period that was further enhanced by an expansion and re-orientation of international commerce, for the goods laded and landed at English ports had first to get there, and from thence be transported to their final destination. After the London-Antwerp axis, which had dominated English trade, collapsed in the mid-sixteenth century, English commerce diversified, both in search of the luxury imports previously supplied via Antwerp, and in search of new markets for English cloth, increasingly found in southern Europe once the New Draperies had become established, while the increasing exploitation of the Newfoundland fisheries and early expeditions to the New World pointed the way to the future.[68] For Wrightson, if change accelerated in the later seventeenth century, "It was in the later decades of the sixteenth and the opening decades of the seventeenth centuries that the conception of a society of estates defended by the commonwealthsmen crumbled in a tide of economic expansion and commercial intensification."[69]

It would be surprising if these developments had not been accompanied by significant social change, and the period between the early sixteenth and mid-seventeenth centuries has been characterized as one of "social polarization". In an economy within which economic activity was clearly quickening, the population was expanding and becoming more mobile, the land market was growing more active due to royal confiscation and sale of monastic land, and within which the long-term inflationary trend placed a premium upon individual ability and efficiency, it is not surprising to find that this was a period of enhanced individual social mobility.[70] But it has also been characterized as a period of structural change in English society, as the landed classes – both as rentiers and substantial farmers – took advantage of their control over the means of production to profit disproportionately from rising rents and food prices engendered by population growth and inflation, and substantial merchants and at least some trade and craftsmen prospered on the back of expanding external and internal trade and growth in industrial consumption. Conversely, at the other end of the social scale, small farmers struggled to cope with higher rents and threats to common rights in the context of harvests that were highly variable in quality, while the lack of a deep mass market, rising raw material costs and continued economic instability prevented the benefits of industrial development from being spread too widely. Further down the social scale still, the wage-earning class grew in size at the same time as its real earnings were being dramatically eroded by inflation, while poverty and vagrancy increased in extent and intensity to become a major preoccupation of government at national and local level. The net result was a significant exacerbation of the inequalities that had for so long existed in the English social hierarchy – an increasing polarization between rich and poor that was expressed in cultural, educational and normative, as well as in economic, terms.[71] Within this process the "middling sort", it is argued, often had a crucial role to play at the local level, for they were among the beneficiaries of change as well as instrumental in imposing the regulatory framework through which those changes were expressed. The precise nature of this differentiation may have varied from community to community, but in the words of the leading exponent of this thesis:

> It was a polarization that took different forms in different localities, in accordance with the particular structure of the local economy. But it was everywhere an inescapable fact . . . Differentiation of values and a shattering of shared attitudes and understandings added a new dimension to the existing polarization of wealth.[72]

The social polarization thesis is not one that commands universal acceptance, at least not without qualification. It is clear, for instance, that smallholding farmers were not forced from the land in their droves in this period, particularly in the predominantly pastoral areas of the country: if they had been, their persistence as an element in English social structure through into the nineteenth century would be difficult to explain.[73] Indeed, some were able to profit from inflated food prices just as were their social superiors, and they were often also quite capable of taking advantage of mano-rial custom to protect their rights.[74] Qualifications need also to be made to the most pessimistic interpretations of the plight of wage-earners, whose fortunes are not wholly encapsulated by the price and wage indices of building workers constructed by economic historians during the 1950s. These may not have been typical of wage trends generally, they fail to reflect payments in kind and customary perquisites, ignore the benefits that rural labourers may have gained from smallholdings, gardens or common rights, and fail to take account of changes in family incomes.[75] As for the poor, extant relief lists – unfortunately mostly urban – appear to indicate that in normal years only approximately 5–7 per cent of the population were dependent paupers, even if the proportion in need of relief could rise dramatically in years of economic dislo-cation, while crises of subsistence were diminishing in their frequency and impact by the early seventeenth century in stark contrast to some other parts of Europe.[76] The situation of the middle orders of society, often described by historians (if rarely by contemporaries) as the "middling sort", has proved particularly problematic: they are difficult to define and identify with precision, their number before the mid-seven-teenth century may have been exaggerated, and the role that has been attributed to them as critical arbiters of the process of change within local communities has been questioned.[77]

To define the changing social order of Tudor and early Stuart England in terms of social polarization may, therefore, be a simplification of a more complex reality, but as a broad outline of the general impact of the prevailing economic and social forces of the day upon the English social structure it is one that is difficult to reject entirely. Nowhere is this clearer than in English towns and cities, particularly those in the more economically advanced south and east of England, and it is to those towns and cities that the vast majority of foreign immigrants gravitated. There is no doubt that London – the one truly European city that England possessed – shared fully in the demographic and economic expansion that the sixteenth and early seventeenth century witnessed. It grew virtually continuously, from a population of perhaps 50,000 in 1500, to 80,000 in 1550, 200,000 in 1600 and 400,000 by the mid-seventeenth century.[78] Uniquely, London incorporated all of the roles of a great city, as the overwhelmingly dominant focus of international trade, the most important hub of internal commerce, the largest concentrated manufacturing centre, as a key provider of social services and centre of conspicuous consumption and as the seat of national government and justice. The fate of English provincial towns during the sixteenth and early seventeenth centuries has been the subject of more controversy, a case having been made for urban economic and demographic contraction through to the third quarter of the sixteenth century, and another which highlights continued demographic, economic and social instability through to the mid-seventeenth century. But the thesis of extended and widespread urban decline across much of the sixteenth century is at the very least unproven and, indeed, can be refuted for many towns, while for the later period a wealth of demo-graphic and economic evidence makes it quite clear that provincial towns shared in the expansion in industrial activity, internal trade and international commerce that was experienced by the economy as a whole. The condition of provincial urban economies towards the mid-sixteenth century remains unclear, and there is evidence in some towns of at least short-term difficulty, and in others of readjustment, which may well explain the alacrity with which they welcomed – indeed petitioned for – foreign settlers. Some may indeed have been in difficulties, though it is hard to accept that this was by any means the universal experience. For the later years of the sixteenth and the early seventeenth centuries, few would now challenge the view that the English urban sector – albeit with a degree of regional variation – shared fully in the economic growth experienced by the wider economy in these years, with provincial towns functioning as essential hubs in an increasingly integrated economic system.[79]

If both the capital city and the majority of provincial towns shared in the demographic and economic expansion of the later sixteenth and early seventeenth centuries, however, they also shared fully in the impact of that growth upon their social structures. Indeed, the process of social polarization may have impacted in its starkest form in towns. Urban growth was fuelled partly by natural increase and partly by immigration, the balance between the two varying substantially between towns and often also over time, but few major centres failed to attract substantial numbers of incomers in search of opportunity or relief. Concern over this influx echoes through the records of urban corporations in the late sixteenth and early seventeenth centuries, for urban trades and craftsmen were jealous of their economic privileges, for which they had often paid a redemption or served a long apprenticeship, and their representatives on urban corporations were particularly concerned that poor incomers would add to the burden of urban poor relief.[80] For if London and most large provincial towns experienced economic growth in this period and many of their merchants, craftsmen and traders prospered, their wage-earning populations also increased substantially at the same time as real wages fell, while the economic vicissitudes that could result from trade slumps, plague or harvest failure periodically exposed the vulnerability of the poorer independent craftsmen.[81] It is this polarization in English urban society, often reflected in topographic and demographic as well as in economic and social terms, that provides the essential backdrop to the regulatory framework that was imposed upon foreign immigrants, as well as to the ambivalent reception afforded them and to the different attitudes that were exhibited both over time and by social class.[82]

An Immigrant Panorama

The start of the "first refuge" can be dated from July 1550, when the "Strangers' Church" of London was founded by Edward VI under the leadership of the Polish reformer Jean à Lasco, establishing an ecclesiastically independent congregation for the benefit of the various Protestant refugees in London.[83] This was by no means the first time that aliens had settled in London: for several centuries they had been established there either in enclaves such as the Hanse Steelyard dedicated to serving the needs of particular groups of alien merchants, or as individual merchants and craftsmen who had settled in the English capital to conduct their trades and businesses.[84] The numbers of aliens found among national taxation lists in the fifteenth century, and those among the London taxpayers in the Exchequer Lay Subsidies of the early sixteenth century, provide eloquent testimony to this presence.[85] But the establishment of an independent church dedicated to their needs is undoubtedly an important milestone in the history of immigration to England, marking recognition of the permanence of the foreign communities as well as the succour that the English crown felt moved to extend to foreign Protestants. The church was soon to divide along linguistic lines, with the former Augustinian priory of Austin Friars serving the Dutch and Flemish speaking exiles, the French Church in St Anthony's Hospital on Threadneedle Street ministering to those who spoke French, and the small Italian congregation meeting in the Chapel of the Mercers' Company on Cheapside.[86] Despite temporary disbandment during the reign of Mary, and a challenge to their authority thrown down by Archbishop Laud during the 1630s, the stranger churches in London flourished throughout the later Tudor and early Stuart periods, catering to the spiritual needs of the substantial immigrant communities that settled there, and taking responsibility too for many aspects of their ecclesiastical and moral discipline, and social well-being.[87]

When the first Strangers' Church was established in 1550 the foreign population in the capital was growing rapidly, numbering perhaps 5,000–6,000 at the end of the reign of Henry VIII and possibly as many as 10,000 by the time that Mary took the throne. Most of them settled in the poorer areas of the city, where they were thus particularly noticeable, their growth and visibility fuelling a rumour in 1551 that there were as many as 40,000 of them "besides women and children", in which year "500 or 600 men waited on the Mayor and Aldermen of London, complaining of the late influx of strangers".[88] Despite the closure of the French and Dutch churches under Mary and the subsequent proclamation of 17 February 1554 ordering the departure of all foreign residents without denizen status, as many as 40–50 per cent of the alien community appear to have remained in the capital, either because they had acquired denizen status or were granted exemption through membership of one of the city companies, or because they simply laid low, the Privy Council receiving precious little help from the city authorities in its campaign against foreigners.[89] With the accession of Elizabeth I in 1558, the religious impediment to their presence was again removed, and as early as June 1559 Philip II's special envoy in London was reporting the movement of large numbers of people from the Low Countries to England.[90] A survey of 1562 counted 4,534 alien men, women and children in the City of London and its various liberties and suburbs.[91]

Mounting religious tension in the mid-1560s produced a particularly heavy influx, which is reflected in the fact that numerous returns of aliens were ordered after 1566. An enumeration made in 1568 lists 6,704 in London and its Liberties, indicating a substantial increase since 1562, while a further survey of 1571 of the City, its Liberties and suburbs gives a total of 6,603 (4,631 in the city and 1,972 in the suburbs) and another of 1573 lists 7,143.[92] Numbers clearly fluctuated, and in a letter dated 28 March 1577 the consistory of the Dutch in London was complaining that "many are leaving us", but such fluctuations appear to have had only a temporary effect at this date.[93] The returns of the 1580s are very difficult to interpret, their coverage being even more obscure than usual. The year 1583 lists 4,141 within the City of London (including "exempted places"), but it is noted that "There wantes certificates from Westminster, Sowthwarcke, Horseydowne, Newington, Lambeth" where there were apparently "great nombers of Strangers inhabitinge".[94] Given that the number residing in the suburbs is unlikely to have grown more slowly than the number within the city, there is little to suggest any significant decline since the preceding decade. And if there was a decline numbers had recovered by 1593, when a detailed list dated 4 May that year records 5,259 inhabiting within the city alone, while another dated 15 May gives 5,545 in the city, Blackfriars and St Martins Le Grande, and a total including various outlying areas of 7,113.[95]

Although they frequently convey an impression of careful preparation, all of these enumerations are likely to underestimate the number of aliens. There were questions of definition, problems of accidental under-recording or positive evasion, difficulties in identifying alien servants living with English masters, in addition to the uncertainties involved in establishing exactly what areas the various returns covered.[96] Imperfect recording is occasionally identified in the returns themselves, as in 1573 when it was noted that "of housholders, as by the presentmente, from the Wardes appearethe, the trewe nomber is not certified, for that many of their bookes be unperfecte".[97] Even the most detailed 1593 return may exclude part of Westminster.[98] It is likely, therefore, that figures of the order of 6,500–7,000, which recur in the various surveys discussed above, represent a true alien population of perhaps 8,000–10,000.[99] On the other hand, as detailed surveys tended to coincide with periods of escalating immigration, and were often employed by the authorities to calm the growing fears among the populace, they are also likely to represent peak figures, with a somewhat lower regular presence in between. An Elizabethan "norm" in the region of 8,000 would therefore be a sensible estimate, this figure rising periodically (but also repeatedly) as high as 10,000.[100]

In the early seventeenth century the size of the alien population appears to have fallen back, no doubt the product of the truce between the United Provinces and Spain signed in 1609 and the Edict of Nantes in France.[101] At the same time, increasing numbers integrated into the indigenous community, either losing their alien identity or becoming harder to define as such. In the difficult economic conditions of the second decade it was suggested that the number of foreigners was again increasing, to which the Church Council of the Austin Friars replied in 1616 that this was simply not the case, claiming that they were in fact fewer in number than they had been 30 years previously.[102] In 1619 the Council submitted statistics claiming there were 1,613 foreigners, 77 denizens and 882 persons who had been born in England of Dutch parents.[103] If this indicates, as it appears to, a Dutch population of 2,572, unless there has been a substantial shift in balance between Dutch and French aliens between the late sixteenth century and 1619, their number would indeed appear to have declined significantly. On the other hand, it is not clear whether this enumeration refers only to members of the Dutch Church or to all the Dutch in the capital, while as it was intended to quell fears concerning the number of resident aliens it is likely to have minimized that number. This view is supported by a survey of 1621, which claimed that there were 10,000 strangers in London alone, carrying out 121 different trades.[104] Increasing numbers in the early 1620s might be explained by the arrival of more refugees from France, primarily from Normandy in 1621, forced into exile by the beginning of the second phase of the religious wars.[105]

We have to wait until the 1635 for the next extant return, which enumerated 3,622 foreigners in the City, Liberties and suburbs. If this figure were accurate it would certainly indicate a significant decline, but it has been argued that "the information afforded by this Return is so spasmodic its absolute validity is questionable".[106] Another source for the 1630s is the numbers provided by John Bulteel, Minister of the French Church in Canterbury, on behalf of the foreign churches when their privileges and immunities were called into question by Laud.[107] In 1635 he claimed that the French and Walloon Communicants in the capital numbered 1,400, and the Dutch just

840, a total of 2,240, which included "men, women and children, men-servants and maid-servants, both strangers and native-borne . . . nothing so many as they were presupposed to be".[108] To convert communicants to total population we can apply the ratio between church membership and the full number of aliens that pertained in 1593, when 48 per cent of the total were recorded as members of the Dutch, French, Italian and English churches (plus the small number, presumably eligible for church membership, recorded as of "no church").[109] This would give a total for 1635 of 4,667 communicants and their families, members of the Dutch and French Churches in London. It would still, however, exclude those who were now members of the English church, or of no church at all, and if the ratio between membership of the French and Dutch churches alone and the total listed in 1593 is applied to the figures for 1635, the total rises to 5,895.[110] It is also clear that Bulteel was concerned to minimize the number of aliens, and was rather smug when he appeared to have done so, claiming that although with regard to foreigners in London "the royal *Exchange* seemeth to swarme with them . . . they are not all French and Dutch, there are Spaniards, Italians, Portugals, and others, and a great number of such Papists live in the suburbs and skirts of that City"; indeed, in London, he claimed, "there were five French Papists to one French Protestant . . . and in part because of the Queens Court".[111] The figure given for the Colchester congregation, just 700, is also revealing, for it is less than half the number listed in total in 1622, and less than half the number in the congregation calculated from baptismal figures for the 1640s.[112] Numbers in London, therefore, may have fallen somewhat by the 1630s, but they had clearly not collapsed, particularly if allowance is made for those who by now had assimilated into the English population and had joined the English church, not to mention the "papists" with which, Bulteel claimed, the London suburbs were now swarming.[113]

We can be more certain that by the 1630s there had been a considerable change in the balance of membership between the Dutch and French Churches, the latter now coming to predominate. Nor were they any longer composed of first-generation immigrants: by the early seventeenth century around 40 per cent had been born in England, being either children or grandchildren of the original refugees.[114] Within the French Church there was also a change in composition. From its establishment until the St Bartholomew's Day Massacre in 1572 (which brought the first significant number of French refugees to London), the French community had consisted almost entirely of Walloons from the southern Netherlands. With a steady inflow of new French refugees in London in the 1620s, the French began to outnumber the Walloon members of the Threadneedle Street congregation.[115]

All of the more significant provincial immigrant settlements are to be found in the south and east of England, in the towns of Norwich, Canterbury, Colchester, Sandwich, Maidstone, Southampton, Great Yarmouth, Dover, Thetford, Kings Lynn, Stamford, Halstead, Rye, Winchelsea, and later also on Canvey Island in Essex and in the fens of Lincolnshire and Cambridgeshire, at Sandtoft and Thorney respectively.[116] Their foundations, with the exceptions of the fenland and Canvey Island communities, date from between 1561 and 1576. Many of them were very small, some (such as Halstead) were only transitory, still others rose in importance in the late sixteenth century only to decline in the early seventeenth, all of which makes it difficult to estimate with precision their collective number at any point in time. Nevertheless, addition of the various counts or estimates of their sizes from the 1570s and 1580s, by when they had become fully established, produces a total of approximately 13,750, at which date the communities in Colchester and Canterbury had yet to reach their peak.[117] In other words, it is very likely that collectively the provincial immigrant communities outnumbered those in London in the late sixteenth century, and in total there may have been as many as 23,000–24,000 aliens in England by the 1590s, a figure substantially higher than the 15,000 suggested by Robin Gwynn.[118] If we turn to the 1630s and consider the figures that Bulteel provided for communicants of the foreign churches in 1635, those listed for Canterbury, Colchester, Norwich, Maidstone, Sandwich, Yarmouth and Southampton again outnumber those in London, collectively totalling 2,973 compared with the 2,240 recorded for the London churches.[119] By 1631, a complaint from the Dutch Church at Norwich suggests that, here at least, the more established among them – denizens or natives – were already withdrawing from their congregations to join their parish churches, a similar complaint having been heard from the Walloon church in the town ten years previously.[120] Allowing for non-communicants, those who by now had joined the English churches or were of no church at all, and remembering that Bulteel's purpose was to dispel fears by mini-mizing the foreign presence, the full total may have been as high as 7,800 at this date, indicating that – just as in the capital – many of these provincial communities were proving remarkably resilient 60 or 70 years after their foundation.

The largest of the provincial immigrant communities in the late sixteenth century was in Norwich. The process began when Norwich authorities approached the Duke of Norfolk for assistance in establishing an alien community to arrest the "decay" of the town precipitated by the decline of its worsted manufacture.[121] They hoped to revive the economy by introducing the manufacture of "Flanders commodities made of wool" and for this purpose asked to receive 30 master workmen with up to ten servants each, or 330 people, to introduce the skills.[122] As the Duke already had contacts with a leading figure in the Dutch Church, Jan Utenhove, the process moved speedily and in November 1565 Norwich obtained its letters patent at the Duke of Norfolk's expense.[123] Most newcomers to Norwich came from Sandwich, with the London churches assisting in the resettlement of the initial 30 households, but the Norwich immigrant population soon expanded far beyond its original quota.[124] By 1571 it numbered as many as 3,999 (Dutch and Walloon), and 4,679 by 1583 despite the death of 2,482 strangers in the plague of 1579–80.[125] On the eve of the plague it has been estimated that there were perhaps 6,000 aliens in Norwich out of a total popula-tion of 14–15,000, and by the early 1590s roughly 4,000 out of ca. 11,000, falling back to less than 3,000 by the end of the decade while the city's population continued to expand.[126] At its peak, therefore, the alien community in Norwich accounted for over 40 per cent of its population. Already by September 1574 the Mayor had warned the Dutch in Norwich that the town would receive no more strangers, but the continued growth in numbers shows this was wholly ineffective.[127] Ten years later a similar order was issued: on 11 August 1584 the consistory of the Dutch Church at Norwich explained to the Dutch Church in London that "Our magistracy published on the 21st of last month an ordinance that henceforth they would receive no more foreigners in this town", a message the London church conveyed to the various foreign churches both in England and overseas.[128] Reinforcement was necessary the following year when an order was issued commanding Henry Fond and Thomas Weavers not to bring any more aliens to dwell in Norwich on pain of imprisonment, and the late 1580s may well have marked the peak of the alien settlement.[129] In a list of 1624 only 999 Dutch men, women and children were recorded as living in Norwich, and another a decade later lists only 678.[130] In 1635, however, Bulteel records 396 communicants in the Walloon Church in Norwich, and 363 in the Dutch Church, giving a total of 759, which would convert to a minimum of 1,500 individuals and, using the formula applied above for London, to a maximum of nearly 2,000.[131] Assimilation was clearly taking place, no doubt encouraged by the fact that from 1598 aliens could be admitted to the freedom of the city on the same terms as natives, but although the stranger community had diminished from its late sixteenth-century heyday it remained a substantial presence in the city 60 years after its foundation.[132]

Next in importance in terms of size among the provincial settlements was that at Canterbury. Established in 1575, it was probably the most resilient of the sixteenth-century planted communities, surviving into the eighteenth century. Its longer life-span was in part due to reinforcement – first from a new wave of migrants from the Calais region in the early 1640s and subsequently from the Huguenot immigration of the later seventeenth century – and in part due to its success in developing a silk industry.[133] Although the Mayor, Aldermen and Commonalty of Canterbury agreed to accept a group of strangers to settle in their city as early as 1567, there occurred long delays for reasons unknown, and it was not until 1575 that the major settlement began. This was the result of determined efforts made by Cobham, Lord Warden of the Cinque Ports, to reduce the number of immigrants at Sandwich.[134] Continued immigration, largely of French-speaking Walloons into Sandwich, led not only to the doubling of the immigrant population there but also generated diplomatic problems due to the piracy they engaged in against Spanish ships in the Channel.[135] It was against this background that Cobham suggested to the Crown that the Walloons should move from Sandwich to Canterbury, where there were already 18 French refugees from Winchelsea, and to give them permission to manufacture new draperies there.[136] Although Canterbury initially agreed to take only 100 families, that number was again quickly exceeded. By 1582 there were already 1,679 strangers in the town; the same year it was ordered that no more were to be admitted without the permission of the mayor and three aldermen, while those already in the city who had "not come for theire Consciences as protestants", and for whom the elders of the congregation would not vouch, were to be sent away.[137] Nevertheless, a count made in 1597 gives a total of 2,068, while calculations based upon the annual average number of baptisms among the Walloon congregation suggests that their number may have approached 1,000 in the first half of that decade, and averaged more than 3,000 across the decade as a whole.[138] As the latest estimate of the town's population suggests a total of ca. 5,200 English in the 1590s, the Walloon community by this time may have accounted for over a third of its total population.[139] Initially, the aliens in Canterbury, like those at Norwich, concentrated on manufacture of the new draperies, making "Florence serges, Orleans serges, Bays, Mauntes", but this gave way to silkweaving by the 1590s, laying the foundations of an important industry after 1675.[140] The Canterbury colony was on the whole very successful, the aliens bringing industry, employment and prosperity to the city, providing the corporation with tax, rental and retail income, and serving as a "catalyst for economic rejuvenation".[141] In 1635, the Walloon Church there, with 900 communicants according to Bulteel, was the largest of the provincial churches, even exceeding the Dutch Church of London in size.[142] At this date, therefore, the community probably numbered between 1,800 and 2,400, retaining a highly significant presence, a presence soon to be reinforced by further arrivals.

The first of the official provincial settlements, that in Sandwich, was partly a response to fears of overcrowding in London. A small number of Flemish emigrant families had already settled there when, in May 1561, they petitioned for official recognition of their community, prompting negotiations between the Sandwich Corporation, the Privy Council and the Dutch Church in London regarding further settlement to relieve pressure in the capital. On 6 July 1561 Elizabeth I signed the letters patent, permitting the town to house an alien community of 20–25 households, or 200–300 persons.[143] The patent cost £50, £20 of which was contributed by the settlers themselves.[144] Between 1561 and 1566 some 150 persons moved to Sandwich from the capital.[145] To qualify for resettlement, migrants had to possess the skills demanded by the corporation in the manufacture of bays, says and other cloths new to England. The selection process was carried out by ministers of the Dutch Church in London and one of them, Peter Delenus, also made a brief trip to Sandwich to assist in the setting up of a community church.[146] The availability of accommodation was one possible reason for making the move from London to Sandwich. While housing in the capital was overcrowded and expensive – Stow reporting that strangers living on waterfront wards were willing to pay £20 for a house previously let for four marks in the 1560s – it was rumoured that 200 homes were available for the foreign community in Sandwich.[147] Political reasons provided another motivation, for at least 32 of the 150 people who moved to Sandwich were Calvinist militants, and geographical proximity to Flanders was important because it meant they could cross the English Channel to fight for their cause there when necessary.[148]

Continued immigration from the continent led to the rapid expansion of the Sandwich settlement. In 1561 the Minister of the Flemish community counted a total of 406 refugees.[149] Calculation of its exact size thereafter depends upon the conversion of lists of names, which are assumed to be householders, or lists of rate-payers, to total population, and the rather erratic year-on-year totals offered by Backhouse using these procedures must either reflect the problematic nature of such calculations, or indicate a highly mobile community, or both.[150] These difficulties notwithstanding, by the early 1570s the Flemish community in Sandwich numbered a minimum of ca. 1,000 and a maximum approaching 2,000.[151] In addition there were an estimated 279 Walloons in 1571 and 460 in 1574. [152] The total immigrant presence was thus in the region of 1,500–2,500 in the early 1570s, and it has been suggested that this represented as much as 53 per cent of the total population of the town.[153] This calculation, however, depends upon further estimates of the number of the native population based upon baptismal data, where there is again room for error. Annual average numbers of baptisms for the 1570s suggest a native population of ca. 2,500: as the number of baptisms was growing towards the end of the decade, it may indeed be true that the combined foreign communities in Sandwich in the early 1570s temporarily exceeded the indigenous population, which may well explain why the town made such determined efforts to reduce their number after 1575.[154] Despite the resettlement of some Sandwich strangers – in 1565 to Colchester and Norwich, and a further 100 Walloon households to Canterbury in 1575 – the influx had clearly exerted an enormous strain on local resources.[155] It was the overwhelming size of the foreign immigrant community in Sandwich that led to the imposition of particularly severe economic restrictions in

1582, as well as the enforced removal of 45 stranger families who did not belong to the foreign congregations. By then the Flemish community may already have passed its peak, for the tax list of 1582 suggests a population of just 1,053.[156] It has also been suggested that in the 1580s "the baize-making industry was in decay", but 2,000–5,000 cloths were made annually in Sandwich during the 1570s and 1580s, while export figures for the early seventeenth century show that the industry was anything but moribund, at least until the onset of trade depression in the mid-1620s, and it survived through to the start of the eighteenth century.[157] Some Sandwich aliens, however, did return to the Dutch Republic. Leiden, with its thriving textile industry, inevitably attracted the greatest number, where 289 Sandwich strangers settled between 1576 and 1625, and a handful in other towns.[158] Their number may have recovered in the early seventeenth century, by which time they accounted for just over one-third of the number of probate inventories which survive for the town, providing some indication of their economic success.[159] Periodic difficulties beset them and the indigenous inhabitants, and in the depression of 1631 they were complaining to the London Dutch Consistory of the "bad trade and dearness which impoverish nearly every one of us ... ", claiming that "If we receive no help we will have to break up ... ".[160] They clearly survived this crisis, however, for Bulteel's figures for 1635, while confirming the disappearance of the Walloon community, show that with 500 communicants the Dutch community in Sandwich remained a substantial presence, reflecting a population of at least 1,000, and possibly as many as 1,300, at this date.[161] The history of the Sandwich community in the seventeenth century remains to be written, but despite some difficulties towards mid-century it proved to be among the more long-lived of the provincial congregations, remaining in existence through into the eighteenth century.[162]

The Dutch community in Colchester never quite achieved the size of that in Sandwich, but nor did it suffer the late sixteenth-century setbacks that appear to have been experienced in the Kent town. Late in 1561 the Corporation of Colchester agreed that Benjamin Clere, one of the bailiffs, should treat with the Privy Council for the taking in of Dutch refugees.[163] Dutch settlers arrived in 1565 – as noted above via Sandwich in Kent – numbering 55 people in 11 households. Their numbers grew slowly at first, producing a foreign community of 185 by 1571, of whom 177 were Dutch. Two years later this had more than doubled to 431, no doubt a product of the economic dislocation that afflicted the Low Countries in the early 1570s, but the real influx was yet to come, for by 1586 a total of 1,291 Dutch settlers were present in the town. As in late sixteenth-century London, some individuals returned home, some new settlers arrived, and it is impossible to trace detailed fluctuations in the size of the community over time. Nevertheless, a return of 1616 records 1,271, another of 1622 lists 1,535, while the average number of baptisms in the Dutch Church during the mid-seventeenth century suggests, on a conservative estimate, a total population of around 1,500.[164]

Foreign settlers had long been active in Colchester, – in the brewing industry, as gardeners, shoemakers and in a range of other trades, – accounting for as many as 103 of the 996 taxpayers included in the Exchequer Lay Subsidies of 1524–5.[165] But, as in the other provincial communities discussed above, it was the benefits to be drawn from immigrant skills in cloth production that provided the *raison d'être* for the larger community established after 1565, and it was new drapery production that underpinned their contribution to the town's economy. This is discussed in more detail below, but it is worth noting here that although their economic integration in the town proceeded rapidly, involvement in borough politics remained marginal to their interests until the eighteenth century.[166] Between 1576 and 1713 the Corporation of Colchester comprised either two bailiffs or (from 1635) a mayor, 8–12 aldermen and 32–6 subordinate officers, the latter constituting the two tiers of the common council.[167] The first Dutch representative was Wynken Grenerice, "cordiner", listed in 1571 as a denizen resident in Colchester for about 46 years, who served the town as a common councillor on the first tier of the council from 1577 until his death in 1585.[168] There were no further Dutch representatives until Hugh de Lobell in October 1599, who served for five years to September 1604, an unusually short term.[169] After de Lobell, there was no Dutch representation for over 50 years, until the appointment of Andrew Fromanteel in 1659, which coincided with the issue of a new charter, serious parliamentary interference in the town's government, and a shake out of all of those deemed to have neglected their duties. Fromanteel became an assistant in July 1659, the first tier of the common council, but was quickly elevated to alderman by January 1660.[170] Also in January 1660 Francis Pollard appears as a common councillor, only to disappear again after 29 July 1662, another year in which there was a considerable shake up of the corporation's membership.[171] Andrew Fromanteel junior became a common councillor in August 1663, graduating to the position of assistant by August 1667, just two months before his father was elected mayor. After his term of office as mayor, Andrew Fromanteel senior remained an alderman until his death in 1672/3, while his son was never promoted above the level of assistant, a position he held until 1684.[172] No further Dutch representative can be found until the turn of the century, and it is only then, almost 140 years after their original settlement, that they begin to appear more regularly. Political assimilation, therefore, was remarkably slow. The Dutch, occasional exceptions notwithstanding, appear to have shown little interest in participating in local governance until well over a century after their arrival. It was only as the Congregation itself waned in the later seventeenth century, and they gradually also lost control over the bay trade, that they turned to alternative hierarchies of power and influence.[173]

Norwich, Canterbury, Sandwich and Colchester: these were the four immigrant communities of significance in terms of their size and longevity. That at Southampton, founded in 1567, was considerably smaller, but – unusually among the smaller congregations – has been the subject of detailed scholarly attention. Prior to their arrival the town's economy relied largely upon overseas trade and, despite several attempts to establish textile production in the late fifteenth and early sixteenth centuries, Southampton had not developed a substantial manufacturing base.[174] Its trade was in the doldrums early in the sixteenth century, but it has been argued that its economy was in good health when the immigrants arrived, the welcome extended to them reflecting the willingness of the corporation to take advantage of a new opportunity rather than an attempt to counteract economic decline.[175] Alien communities of French and Italians had brought prosperity to the city in earlier periods, and it was against this background that the city hoped to revive a foreign community there, on this occasion looking to the establishment of new drapery production in the town.[176]

There is no evidence to suggest that Southampton directly petitioned for permission to establish a foreign community: in fact, the letters patent were granted probably as a result of the immigrants' own initiatives. On 16 May 1567 refugees from the Low Countries sent a letter to Cecil and petitioned the queen for permission to settle in England. The queen directed these refugees to Southampton, presumably in response to its informal enquiries about establishing an alien community there. Two months after the request a patent was granted, allowing 40 households with up to 12 per household, or a total of 480 persons, to settle in Southampton.[177] In marked contrast to the experience elsewhere, however, the Southampton community did not quickly expand beyond its quota: in 1584 there were only 186 communicants, and by 1596 only 297 aliens in total in the city.[178] Southampton's relative geographical remoteness from the Low Countries, as well as removal by those who initially settled there to London, provide two possible reasons why the community remained small. The size of the community, however, resulted in greater cohesion. The refugees were largely French-speaking, with a prominent group from Valenciennes who had established familial and business ties between themselves, and with others from Tournai and Antwerp, before moving to Southampton.[179] Their economic contribution was twofold, involving both new drapery manufacture and overseas trade. In 1573–4 Southampton exported 334 pieces of say and 140 bays and, although such quantities are insignificant in comparison to levels of production at Norwich or Colchester, the manufacture of the new draperies did "make a significant contribution to the town's economic life and overseas trade".[180] By the early seventeenth century, however, they had already relinquished their domination of new drapery production. The immigrant population itself declined rapidly after 1604 as a result of assimilation, the devastating effects of the plague, and the return of some exiles to the continent. Its church was constantly dogged by financial problems after 1610 and by 1635 could count only 36 communicants, indicating of a population of just 70–95.[181] Despite increasing social integration with the host community in the early seventeenth century, as in Colchester political assimilation was slow, and it was not until 1630 and 1634 that the first two burgesses of refugee stock were sworn.[182] By the 1650s the congregation appeared to be in terminal decline, and it was only the renewed influx of French Huguenots from the 1660s that saved it from extinction.[183]

The only other formal congregations mentioned by Bulteel in 1635 were those of the Dutch churches at Maidstone and Yarmouth, with 50 and 28 communicants respectively.[184] In June 1567 the corporation of Maidstone had petitioned the queen for a licence by letters patent to settle 60 families in the town skilled in production of the new draperies, as well as in an array of other crafts "which are not knowen being both necessary and proffitable for the common wealthe".[185] In the event a licence was issued for 30 households of no more than 12 persons each, "as well for the helpe, repair and amendment of our towne of Maidston . . . as also for the relief and convenient placing of certaine Duchemen aliens now residing within our Citie of London and ells where . . . being very skilfull in divers Arts, occupations, handycrafts and faculties which may tende to the commodities of our Realme . . . ".[186] Some, at least, had arrived by December 1568, and in 1585 115 Dutch adults were enumerated, living in 43 families, indicating a population of *ca.* 250.[187] At first they concentrated upon new drapery production, but by the early seventeenth century had turned to the manufacture of linen thread, which gradually assumed greater importance as a component of the town's economy.[188] The community clearly remained small, frequently complaining of its financial difficulties and seeking support from the Dutch Church in London. As early as 1574 the consistory there was writing to the London church concerning its difficulty in maintaining a ministry, as "many of our members have departed, though we expect others in their place, so that we trust you will send us one of your ministers".[189] It fluctuated in size, its consistory explaining in 1583 that "Our community is increasing a little, but as far as we can see, only two or three of those who have lately arrived have any means, and we see that our Minister is unable to live on £16 . . .", and again in 1586: "our Community has a little increased, though our income is not materially augmented". In response to these difficulties, in 1574 the Dutch Church in London gave a contribution of £3 per annum towards the cost of maintaining a minister, which had risen to £6 per annum by 1583, and also provided help in supplying suitable candidates for the position.[190] By the end of 1600 Maidstone lacked a minister altogether, and still in January 1604 the "overseers of the Community of Christ at Maidstone" were writing to the minister and elders of the London church requesting that "you send to us one of your Ministers to preach to us the word of God, and especially to administer the Lord's Supper to us about 2 February . . .".[191] By 1617 they appear to have been in better straits, for although there was a question mark over the orthodoxy of their new minister Daniel de Nielles and the permanence of his residence there, it was noted that he was receiving a generous stipend, the church in London refusing to assist the community in raising it further.[192] By 1631 they were also significantly involved in agriculture activity, explaining in August that year that they could only send one representative to the *colloque* in London "as our number is very small, and we are in the midst of our harvest, so that we cannot conveniently leave home."[193] In 1622 when the mayor and recorder submitted a list to the government of "strangers borne and theire children as use handycrafts within this towne", it included only 23 names, but this would of course have excluded second generation immigrants, and by 1635, as we have seen, the congregation still included 50 communicants, suggesting a population in the region of 100–30.[194] Through into the 1630s they continued to importune the Dutch Church in London for aid for "our weak community whose means are decreasing from year to year", but formal support was withdrawn in February 1634, although at least one more £10 payment was received. Despite their claims that "as the old members of our community die off, and no new ones take their places, nay some of them leave us . . .", they could still claim "more than forty communicants" in February 1640, when their pastor Enoch Surtijnes promised to remain with them for one final year.[195] Their problems with securing and retaining a ministry, familiar to all of the smaller congregations, continued through the 1640s, as did their requests for assistance from the Dutch Church in London, which was again regularized into a "quarterly donation" in the 1640s.[196] The Maidstone Congregation limped on into the 1650s. In 1655, however, it claimed to be "totally decayed", and although later that year it was noted that it retained its Elders despite having no minister, a further report that it was "entirely decayed" in January 1656 seems to mark its final demise, for from that date there is no further record of formal correspondence between the Maidstone Church and the Dutch Church in London.[197]

The Dutch community in Great Yarmouth differed from all the others by concentrating upon fishing rather than cloth production, building upon a long tradition of Dutch herring fishing off the East Anglian coast. They formed part of the exodus precipitated by the arrival of the Duke of Alva in the Netherlands in 1568, and in June 1570 letters patent were granted for 30 families from Flanders, Holland and Zeeland, each of up to 10 persons, to settle in the town, "where diverse of them being fishermen, have used the feat and trade of fishing of herrings, codd, mackrell and other fish, according to the season of the year, after the manner of their country".[198] The town provided testimonial that "the said strangers do there live godly and orderly, and towards our people do behave themselves quietly, and that sundry of them do apply their fishing to the benefit of that town, and instruct our subjects there in the manner of their fishing." They were to be allowed to hire and inhabit houses and shops "in as ample a manner as any of our lieges or subjects naturally born", to fish freely in their own boats or in the boats of others, to "prepare, pack and brand the herrings, which they shall take, after the manner of the Low Countries", and to sell them either in England or in foreign parts "being in league and amity with us", any statute, law or custom to the contrary notwithstanding. Those who were not fishermen were to be allowed to practice trades "which are not at this time used in the said town".[199] Just a year later, in 1571, there were as many as 104 alien households in the town – indicating a population of *ca.* 500 – 74 of these families coming from the Low Countries, 80 per cent of them from Zeeland. More than half were fishermen, or drove trades connected with the sea.[200] In February 1574 the town sought to limit their number, passing an order that there were to be no more than in the queen's grant, all of them members of the Dutch Congregation, that the number of vessels (or pinks) they used be restricted to ten, three English sailors to be employed on each, and with further restrictions upon their ability to buy corn in the market or to make provision for flesh, butter and victuals other than to satisfy the needs of their own households.[201] Whether it was due to these new restrictions or to adverse trading conditions, for the majority of aliens residence in Yarmouth was only a temporary recourse, and by 1575 the Dutch church was writing to the Austin Friars in London complaining that "we are few in number and bear already great burden, while every day some of us depart".[202] A dispute across the years 1626–32 concerning Mr Brinsley, the town preacher, reveals that the Dutch chapel there was a converted warehouse which remained unconsecrated, and in 1632 the King and Privy Council ruled that it be reconverted to its former use.[203] The 28 communicants remaining in Yarmouth in 1635 represent a community of just 50–75, and in the 1630s and 1640s it was even more importunate upon the Dutch Church in London than was Maidstone. Repeated requests were made for assistance, complaining of the death or departure of leading members, the difficult conditions for fishing, their minister's losses at sea, his age and weakness and his charge of children. In 1634–5 the church there provided lists of contributing members, enumerating 46 in August 1633, but just 28 the following February, the latter figure no doubt providing the basis for Bulteel's estimate.[204] The position of Yarmouth as a "frontier town" was also emphasized, relieving not only its own poor but those who were shipwrecked or had been taken by Dunkirkers, besides other fishermen who came for the season and "would probably go to the public houses instead of to our place of worship" should the ministry be lost. In July 1633 guaranteed assistance was withdrawn from here too, having been provided for "about twenty-four years" previously although, as in Maidstone, less regular payments continued to be elicited.[205] In April 1639 the Yarmouth consistory announced that it had secured £5 per annum for two years from Colchester and the promise of a similar sum from Norwich, and with further support from the town corporation and continued assistance from the Dutch Church in London it survived until its final demise in 1681.[206]

More temporary still was the French community in Rye, which flowered briefly between the 1560s and 1580s. Over 500 French refugees had fled to the town by November 1562, shortly after the Protestant massacre perpetrated by the Duke of Guise. Most quickly returned home, but a further influx followed when renewed religious conflict erupted in France in July 1568, producing an alien community of *ca.* 300 by March 1569.[207] Two years later their number had fallen to just 20 households (*ca.* 100 individuals), 13 of these described as being of the French Church.[208] The largest influx was yet to come, however, and followed the St Bartholomew's Day Massacre in August 1572, for between 27 August and 4 November of that year as many as 641 new refugees – many of them very poor – arrived in Rye. An uncorroborated source suggests there were as many as 1,534 French refugees in the town by 1582, and through a combination of new arrivals and departures *ca.* 1,500 remained in 1586, by which year the town was complaining to the Privy Council about their excessive number.[209] But such high numbers were again only temporary, and as early as 1590 the minister of the Rye congregation, Lewis Morrell, was reporting to the Canterbury colloquy that the congregation had dwindled.[210] For a generation, however, the town had played host to an immigrant community that – while fluctuating markedly in size – reached as many as 1,500 at its peak, and this in a town of just *ca.* 4,000 inhabitants in 1580 and *ca.* 2,000 by the end of the century.[211]

Of most of the other small or transitory immigrant communities less is known. The case of Halstead, however, has been documented because of the controversy that arose, for of 30 families transplanted here from Colchester in 1576, 20 of them left again less than four years later in the face of local jealousy and harassment. Baymaking slumped in the town in consequence, and local officials petitioned the Privy Council, with success, to order them to return, but the strangers refused.[212] The community survived, but by 1587 was without a minister and seeking help from the Dutch Church in London in persuading Jacobe de Hont to stay and serve them.[213] In May the following year they wrote again to London, now complaining that Jan Bertholf, despite exhortation from the community, had joined the English church, as a result of which "all our Discipline, both of the Church and Polity, is lost", and bemoaning "the loss of this privilege, which otherwise might have served as a refuge for the Christians who still come over daily in great numbers". Departure, it seemed, was necessary, although they were "very sorry to leave here, and would remain if we could do so without great loss", implicating also "the actions of the English baize-makers", but their further request for funds to enable them to settle their debts and "depart with honour" fell on deaf ears.[214] The community duly foundered; by 1589 its members had all returned to Colchester.[215] In April 1590 the Privy Council wrote to the minister and elders of the Dutch Church in London ordering them to send some of their members who were "baize-makers" to Halstead to replace the former community, but there is no evidence that they complied.[216]

At Dover, the immigrant presence was particularly erratic and precarious. A return of 1571 lists 277 men, women and children, most of whom were engaged in textile manufacture.[217] In February 1575 the Consistory of the Dutch Church there declined to send representatives to the synod at Flushing on the grounds that "we are few in number, and it seems that most of us will depart, wherefore we leave every one free to conform to or join the Churches across the sea, or to assemble in London", while less than a month later they declined to attend the London assembly "as we have heard that Letters have arrived forbidding us to remain here".[218] A Flemish congregation still existed in the town in 1576, however, though it was again pleading poverty and paucity of numbers by 1578, and continued to do so in 1586. Although it has been suggested that it may have ceased to exist shortly after 1589, it was still limping along in 1597, despite complaining in May 1595 that it had lost more than half its membership in the past year, amongst them the most opulent.[219] A French congregation met there briefly at the close of the reign of James I, numbering approximately 100 in total in July 1621, 272 by October the same year, but just 92 some seven or eight months later. The church may have folded soon thereafter, and by 1638 the community there was seeking permission to establish a new ministry, and was searching for a minister who could speak both French and Dutch, noting that "there had formerly been a Dutch community in the place . . . [but now there were] more than a hundred Dutchmen residing in Dover with their wives and children, but who, having no exercise of the Reformed Religion, and, not understanding English, can derive no satisfaction from the ordinary places of worship . . . ".[220] There is no record of any immediate outcome, but a further re-foundation took place in April 1646, though this community, too, remained small in size.[221]

At Glastonbury a community of French and Walloon clothworkers was established by the Duke of Somerset in 1550, but as early as 1554 their minister, Valerandus Pollanus, was attempting to establish a church at Frankfurt for the benefit of the French of Glastonbury, and hence this may have been another short-lived venture.[222] Little is known of the progress of the community at King's Lynn, which numbered 226 men, women, children and servants in 1570, and even less about the other small communities at Stamford, Thetford and Winchelsea.[223] Although the Thetford church did manage to send their minister to the Colloque of the Anglo-Dutch Churches held in London in 1575, it explained to the consistory of the Dutch Church in London the following year that "we are unable to be present, as our Community, being so small, is unable to bear the expenses . . . ".[224] In 1578 the Dutch Consistory in London wrote to the various Dutch churches in England complaining that there was little prospect of holding a colloque next year, "seeing that last year two of the largest Communities remained away, and some of the ministers have now departed, while some of the Communities are broken up . . . ".[225] Which communities are here referred to is unclear, but the one at Thetford was still functioning in April 1584, when it complained that its poverty prevented it from sending representatives to either the ecclesiastical synod or the colloque.[226] This may have been a reference to Ipswich. The existence of the small Dutch congregation at Ipswich is rarely noticed, and it was clearly precarious and short-lived, its minister writing in 1571 that it rested "only on the verbal and temporary permission of the magistrate without any written license of Her Majesty", consisted of just 10 or 12 families, and with little hope of increase, as the strangers there "cannot occupy themselves with any established trade". There is tentative evidence of the existence of a Dutch church in the town in the early 1570s, but by 1575 it may well have already folded, for by then its minister, Michael Ephippius, was minister to the Dutch Reformed Church at Norwich.[227] The subsidy rolls for 1568 and 1576 include, respectively, 31 and 39 apparently Dutch names, but as only six are common to both it would appear that the alien population was highly transient.[228] A letter from Karle van Stavele to the Dutch consistory in London dated July 1588 advocated the re-establishment of a congregation at Ipswich, a place he described as "more fit for establishing a Community than any other place in England". He had tried to convince those about to leave Halstead to settle there, enlisting the aid of "some of our brethren here of the old Community, especially the Ministers", one of whom had informed him that "one of the Bailiffs had told him that the people would be welcome".[229] His efforts, however, appear to have been to no avail. The same may be true of the efforts of Jaen Heindrickxsn to secure a ministry for Plymouth in 1631 to cater for the needs "not only of those who reside here, but a great many mariners, skippers & c., who daily arrive, and on Sundays wander around like sheep without a shepherd . . . [for] There are often between 50 and 60, even more, Dutch ships here at a time . . . ".[230] The extent of the Dutch and French presence in the ports of south-western England, already evident in the early sixteenth century, is a subject that deserves closer scrutiny.[231]

By the start of the seventeenth century there had clearly been a shake-out among the foreign communities in England, although it is clearly possible that an informal presence continued even after the demise of their churches, as it appears to have done at Ipswich. During the 1620s, however, there were a small number of new plantations – the various communities engaged in drainage projects – and, although these might not strictly be regarded as refugees, they will close our consideration of the first refuge. At Canvey Island, Essex, in 1622, an agreement was signed between Cornelius Vermuydden and a group of Canvey landowners for the protection of the island from the incursions of the sea, in exchange for one-third of the enclosed land. When the wall was completed, a number of Dutch workmen engaged on the project settled on the island as farmers, 200 of them petitioning the king for permission to hold services in the Dutch language in 1628.[232] They remained a close-knit enclave that was never fully absorbed into the life of the neighbourhood, maintaining their own chapel through to 1704.[233] The cause of the demise of the community in the early eighteenth century is a mystery: the notion of a mass exodus seems unlikely, and it is more plausible that the ravages of disease combined with eventual anglicization explains the disappearance of distinctive Dutch names.[234] In the fens of Cambridgeshire and Lincolnshire Vermuydden was again active, signing an agreement to drain the waste areas of the Isle of Axholme (including Hatfield Chase) in 1626, which led to the establishment of a Dutch chapel and community at Sandtoft, and eventually the settlement of perhaps 200 foreign farming families in the area, both Dutch and French. Despite intense local opposition the Sandtoft church survived into the late seventeenth century, though as a result of a drift inland to other parts of Lincolnshire and the anglicization of second-generation migrants it appears to have been in decline from the 1650s.[235] Once work in the Isle of Axholme had been completed Vermuydden turned his attention to an even larger project – the drainage of the vast area of fenland known as the Bedford Level – resulting in the establishment of a foreign church at Thorney in Cambridgeshire in 1639, the services at which were to be conducted either in French or Dutch. Again foreign settlement followed reclamation, the settlers receiving a far better reception here than at Sandtoft, and quickly beginning to marry into the indigenous English community. At Thorney the community was thus more stable, although again destined for long-term decline and fragmentation.[236]

These, then, are the various immigrant communities with which this volume is concerned. Collectively, even at their peak, they comprised only a tiny proportion of the national population, certainly less than one per cent.[237] Their concentration in the south and east, however, rendered them a far more significant influence there, while their urban presence, in both London and the provinces, was of particular importance – overwhelmingly so in the case of a number of towns in Norfolk, Essex and Kent. But their influence cannot simply be measured in terms of size alone, and there is no doubt that their impact, through their own contributions and as a catalyst of change, considerably outweighed their numerical presence, extending well beyond the physical confines of the communities in which they lived. That contribution was diverse, though there is no doubt that it was in the realm of textile production that it was felt most strongly. They were diverse in origins too (if within circumscribed limits), with heavy concentrations coming from particular regions within the Low Countries and France. They came to a society with which they were not wholly unfamiliar, where their compatriots had previously settled and with which they had traded for generations. They arrived in successive waves, "for their conscience sake", to escape both religious and political oppression, to take advantage of the economic opportunities that England had to offer, and to escape from the economic degradation that so often accompanied the European wars of religion. Their reception was shaped by the very fact of their Protestantism, but also by the perception of the economic benefits they could bring on the one hand, and the economic competition that they posed within the context of an increasingly polarized society on the other. Many common threads run through their relationships, with national and local governments, and with indigenous communities, mainly in towns and (more marginally) in the countryside but particular local circumstances shaped those interactions too. Their success or otherwise was also dependent upon propitious local circumstances, and it may have been these – in conjunction with the unfolding of events in their homelands – that determined the size and longevity of their various settlements. Where they established themselves in numbers – in London, Norwich, Canterbury, Colchester and Sandwich in particular – there is little to suggest that they viewed their new home as merely a temporary refuge: in the words of a petition of 1599, many of them they had "abandoned and left all together with their native Countries, and betaken themselves to handy labours according to Gods word, under the wings of her Majesties most gracious protection . . . ".[238] If some drifted back to the continent as circumstances improved, and if the small settlements at Maidstone and Yarmouth succumbed in 1656 and 1681 respectively, the larger communities in England and the churches around which they were founded retained considerable strength through to the later seventeenth century, by when the process of assimilation, while by no means yet complete, was well underway. By the late seventeenth century their churches were in decline, their task complete, and the multi-faceted process of assimilation began to extend into the political realm, quite early in London, somewhat later in the provinces. It was then that the Huguenot diaspora erupted, to produce in England the "second refuge", opening another chapter in the history of English immigration just as the previous one was drawing towards its close.

Notes

1   Cunningham, *Alien Immigrants*; see also Cunningham, *Growth of English Industry*.
2   For a summary of the key developments and the importance of a religious motivation see Chapter 9 below, pp. 177–8.

NIGEL GOOSE

3   This estimate is from van Houtte, *Economic History*, p. 135. The start of the large, religiously inspired waves of migration can be dated to the 1540s when the Counter-Reformation got underway: Pettegree, "Protestant Migration", pp. 441–58. For background on European diasporas see Kamen, *Iron Century*, pp. 419–21. Gwynn estimates 180,000–190,000 Huguenots left France in the late 1670s and 1680s, although others have suggested higher figures: Gwynn, *Huguenot Heritage*, pp. 29–31.

4   Gwynn, *Huguenot Heritage*, pp. 39–41.

5   Pettegree suggests perhaps as many as 40,000–50,000 arrivals between 1550 and 1585 alone: *Foreign Protestant Communities*, p. 299.

6   See Chapter 10 below, pp. 200–6.

7   I mean, of course, Robin Gwynn, most notably in *Huguenot Heritage*.

8   Pettegree, *Foreign Protestant Communities*, p. 5.

9   Pettegree, *Foreign Protestant Communities*; Grell, *Dutch Calvinists*; Littleton, "Geneva on Threadneedle Street"; Backhouse, *Flemish and Walloon Communities*; Eßer, *Niederländische Exulanten im England*; Spicer, *French-Speaking Reformed Community*; Durkin, "Civic Government and Economy"; Goose, "The 'Dutch' in Colchester"; Goose, "The Dutch in Colchester in the 16th and 17th Centuries"; Luu, "Immigrants and the Diffusion of their Skills"; Luu, *Immigrants and the Industries of London* (Ashgate, 2004).

10 Chalklin, *Seventeenth Century Kent*, pp. 123–9; Mayhew, *Tudor Rye*, pp. 81–90; Clark and Murfin, *History of Maidstone*, pp. 47–8, 81–2; Zell (ed.), *Early Modern Kent*, pp. 115–24; Roker, "Dutch Fishing Community"; Cracknell, *Canvey Island*, pp. 20–8.

11 This contrasts with the title "supreme head" previously taken by her father, and was adopted in order to get the legislation relating to the Supremacy through the House of Lords in 1559: see Elton, *Tudor Constitution*, pp. 364–5, 372–7.

12 See, for instance, Heal and O'Day (eds), *Church and Society*, pp. 44–122.

13 Collinson, *Elizabethan Puritan Movement*, pp. 29–44; Bellamy *et al.*, *Culture and Belief in Europe*, p. 8.

14 Collinson, *Religion of Protestants*, pp. 242–83; Collinson, *Birthpangs of Protestant England*, pp. 36–47; Sheils, "Religion in Provincial Towns".

15 Guy, *Tudor England*, p. 306; Haley, *British and the Dutch*, pp. 28, 30.

16 See Chapter 5 below, p. 93; this echoes Collinson, "Europe in Britain", p. 63. See also his important seminal essay, "Elizabethan Puritans and the Foreign Reformed Churches".

17 See Chapter 6 below, pp. 125–6.

18 For fuller discussion see Chapter 9 below, pp. 184–6.

19 Dickens, *English Reformation*, Chapters 2–5; see also Dickens, *Lollards and Protestants*, esp. pp. 171–2, 215–18.

20 The evidence of will preambles and formularies is discussed in Goose and Evans, "Wills as an Historical Source", pp. 54–7.

21 Collinson, *Birthpangs of Protestant England*, p. ix.

22 Mayhew, "Progress of the Reformation", pp. 46–8; Goring, "Reformation and Reaction", pp. 141–54; Palliser, *Tudor York*, pp. 248–54.

23 Goose and Cooper, *Tudor & Stuart Colchester*, pp. 121–2; Ward, "Reformation in Colchester", pp. 84–5; Higgs, "Wills and Religious Mentality", pp. 87–100. Dickens's unpublished remark is quoted in Collinson, *Birthpangs of Protestant England*, p. 38.

24 Colchester Record Office, Liber Ordinacionum, fo. 83; Goose and Cooper, *Tudor & Stuart Colchester*, p. 125.

25 Byford, "Price of Protestantism", esp. pp. 259–68, 277–8. For the development of Protestantism in Colchester see also Byford, "Birth of a Protestant Town", pp. 23–47; Ward, "Reformation in Colchester".

26 Higgs, *Godliness and Governance*, pp. 340–6.

27 Palliser, "Popular Reactions to the Reformation", pp. 40–6; Clark, *English Provincial*

Society, pp. 34–98, 149–52; Collinson, *Birthpangs of Protestant England*, pp. ix–x, 38, 40.

28 Lollardy was not, of course, exclusively urban, and was also well established in the Chilterns along the Buckinghamshire/Hertfordshire border.

29 Brigden, *London and the Reformation*, pp. 82–128.

30 Brigden, *London and the Reformation*, pp. 179–255.

31 Brigden, *London and the Reformation*, pp. 277–384.

32 Brigden, *London and the Reformation*, pp. 421–67.

33 Brigden, *London and the Reformation*, pp. 485–6.

34 Brigden, *London and the Reformation*, pp. 628–39; Collinson, 'Elizabethan Puritans and the Foreign Reformed Churches', pp. 257–72; and see Chapter 11 below, p. 214. For consideration of the significance of testamentary provision in London wills over and above their preambles see Hickman, "From Catholic to Protestant", *passim*.

35 Solt, *Church and State*, pp. 99–111; Fletcher, *Tudor Rebellions*, pp. 91–106.

36 For a succinct summary of these developments see Doran, *England and Europe*, pp. 69–72.

37 Doran, *England and Europe*, pp. 72–5; Haley, *British and the Dutch*, pp. 34–45; Israel, *Dutch Republic*, pp. 234–8. For English volunteers see Chapter 11 below, pp. 211–19.

38 Calculated from Israel, *Dutch Republic*, table 6, p. 238. Haley suggests figures of 850 and 650 men respectively for Flushing and the Brill by the start of the 17th century, compared to an actual strength of 1,445 and 852 in 1588.

39 Haley, *British and the Dutch*, p. 39.

40 Wernham, *After the Armada*, pp. 564–5.

41 Maltby, *The Black Legend*; Lake, "Anti-Popery", esp. p. 80; Cogswell, "England and the Spanish Match", pp. 107–33.

42 Collinson, *Birthpangs of Protestant England*, pp. 12–16

43 For the following see Russell, *Crisis of Parliaments*, pp. 256–316; Tyacke, "Puritanism, Arminianism and Counter-Revolution", pp. 119–143; Clifton, "Fear of Popery", pp. 144–67; Cust and Hughes (eds), *Conflict in Early Stuart England*; Solt, *Church and State*, pp. 164–205.

44 Anon., *Sir Walter Raleigh's Ghost*, p. 53. It continues, "the Fox, whose stench hath not cured the Palsy, but rather impoisoned and brought into an Apoplexy many noble, and sometimes well deserving, English Hearts."

45 See above, p. 4 and below, Chapter 4, pp. 82–4

46 Solt, *Church and State*, pp. 158–63.

47 It featured as item 12 of his impeachment: *Accusation and Impeachment*, p. 546; Grell, *Dutch Calvinists*, pp. 224–48.

48 Hunt, *Puritan Moment*, Chapter 11; Manning, *English People*, pp. 72–83.

49 Miller, *Popery and Politics*, *passim*; Sharp, "Popular Political Opinion".

50 For the following section see especially Haley, *British and the Dutch*, pp. 50–106; Wilson, *England's Apprenticeship*, pp. 53–65, 160–73; Jones, *Britain and Europe*, pp. 38–66.

51 Gentleman, *Englands Way to Win Wealth*, pp. 379–90.

52 D'Ewes, *Compleat Journal*, p. 509.

53 For the impact of these strained relations on the form of Dutch participation in the procession planned to mark the coronation of Charles I see Chapter 8, below, p. 168.

54 Anon., *Wicked Plots and Perfidious Practices of the Spaniards* (c. 1642), *passim*.

55 Taylor, "Trade, Neutrality and the 'English Road' ".

56 As an example of virulent anti-Dutch at times of war, and the re-interpretatin of history that often accompanied it, see De Britaine, *Dutch Usurpation* (1672), *passim*; see also below, Chapter 6, p.115.

57 Howes (ed.), *Annales*, p. 868.

58 Nef, "Progress of Technology"; Kerridge, *Agricultural Revolution*: Davis, *Commercial Revolution*; Tawney, "Rise of the Gentry"; Tawney, *Agrarian Problem*. For a few of the

key pieces of de-bunking see: Coleman, "Industrial Growth"; Thirsk (ed.), *Agrarian History of England and Wales, Vol. 4*; Mingay, "Dr Kerridge's Agricultural Revolution"; Kerridge, *Agrarian Problems*; Hexter, *Reappraisals in History*, Chapters 5 and 6. The notion of a "commercial revolution", rather than being rejected wholesale, has been modified and played down, the phrase being retained in quotation marks, quietly dropped or noted to be an exaggeration: Coleman, *Economy of England*, pp. 131–50; Clay, *Economic Expansion and Social Change*, Vol. 2, pp. 177, 181; Wrightson, *Earthly Necessities*, p. 236. This is perhaps why one distinguished English economic historian used to assert that "nothing of any consequence happened in the English economy in early modern history": cited in Wilson, *England's Apprenticeship*, p. 376.

59   For relative English "backwardness" at the end of the Middle Ages see, for example, Cipolla, *Before the Industrial Revolution*, p. 256; Cipolla (ed.), *Fontana Economic History of Europe*, p. 413; Palliser, *Age of Elizabeth*, p. 1; Coleman, *Economy of England*, p. 2. For an interesting recent discussion of the relative economic strength of "north" and "south" Europe see Musgrave, *Early Modern European Economy*, Chapters 5 and 6.

60   *CSPV 1527–33*, pp. 292–301; *CSPV 1534–54*, pp. 338–62; Cramer (ed.), *Second Book of the Travels*, pp. 9, 21; Sneyd (ed.), *A Relation*, pp. 8–11, 28–9, 42–3; Barrington, "Venetian Secretary in England", pp. 176–7; Palliser, *Age of Elizabeth*, pp. 4–5.

61   Bridbury, *Economic Growth*, pp. 39, 55, 91–2; du Boulay, *Age of Ambition, passim*; Postan, *Medieval Economy and Society*, pp. 139–42; Hatcher, *Plague*, p. 43.

62   Wrigley, 'Divergence of England', pp. 119–20.

63   Wrigley, 'Divergence of England', pp. 120–4.

64   Wrightson, *Earthly Necessities*, pp. 22–3

65   Wrightson, *Earthly Necessities*, pp. 331–6 and *passim*.

66   Fisher, "Tawney's Century", p. 2.

67   Fisher, "Tawney's Century", pp. 3–11.

68   For a fuller summary of these developments, see Wrightson, *Earthly Necessities*, pp. 159–81. For a useful bibliography to much of the relevant specialist literature, too extensive to cite here, see Clay, *Economic Expansion and Social Change*.

69   Wrightson, *Earthly Necessities*, p. 333.

70   The seminal article on this topic is Stone, "Social Mobility", *passim*; For greater emphasis on diversity within this process, and the firm hand of continuity within change, see Everitt, "Social Mobility", pp. 56–73.

71   The most general outline of this thesis is in Wrightson, *English Society*, while economic developments feature more fully in his *Earthly Necessities*. Other key works include Thirsk (ed.), *Agrarian History of England and Wales Vol. 4*, particularly the chapters by Everitt, "Farm Labourers" and Bowden, "Agricultural Prices, Farm Profits, and Rents", pp. 396–465, 593–695; Spufford, *Contrasting Communities*; Skipp, *Crisis and Development*; Wrightson and Levine, *Poverty and Piety*; Slack, *Poverty and Policy*; Levine and Wrightson, *Making of an Industrial Society*; Sharpe, *Population and Society*. Apart from Wrightson's work, the best general survey of economic and social change in the period is Clay, *Economic Expansion and Social Change*, and there is some incisive interpretation (though within a shorter time-frame) in Palliser, *Age of Elizabeth*. A handy, short summary of many of the key issues, which contains a useful bibliography, is Coward, *Social Change and Continuity*.

72   Wrightson, *English Society*, pp. 223–4, 226.

73   Clay, *Economic Expansion and Social Change*, Vol. 1, pp. 91–101; Reed, "Peasantry of Nineteenth-Century England"; Winstanley, "Industrialization and the Small Farm"; Shepherd, "Small Owner in Cumbria".

74   Hindle, "Persuasion and Protest"; Falvey, "Crown Policy".

75   For a good, brief discussion of these and other problems with these indexes, see Palliser, *Age of Elizabeth*, pp. 157–9.

76 Slack, *Poverty and Policy*, pp. 71–2; Goose, "In Search of the Urban Variable", p. 181; Palliser, *Age of Elizabeth*, pp. 189–92; Outhwaite, *Dearth, Public Policy and Social Disturbance*, pp. 22–34.

77 See the discussion by Wrightson in "Postscript: Terling Revisited", in the second edition of Wrightson and Levine, *Poverty and Piety*, pp. 197–220. Also French, "Social Status, Localism and the 'Middle Sort of People' "; French, "Search for the 'Middle Sort of People'". For the "middling sort" as beneficiaries compared with the wage earning classes see Muldrew, *Economy of Obligation*, p. 16.

78 Estimates of London's population vary, but none contradict the picture of continuous growth. For a recent discussion see Harding, "Population of London".

79 Key contributions to the debate include Phythian-Adams and Slack, "Urban Crisis or Urban Change?"; Phythian-Adams, "Urban Decay", pp. 159–69; Dyer, "Growth and Decay"; Phythian-Adams, "Dr Dyer's Urban Undulations"; Clark and Slack, *English Towns in Transition*; Clark, "Introduction", to Clark (ed.), *Country Towns*, pp. 2–15; Goose, "In Search of the Urban Variable"; Dyer, *Decline and Growth*; Slack, "Great and Good Towns".

80 For London see also Chapter 3 below, pp. 63–8.

81 Clark, "Migrant in Kentish Towns"; Clark and Slack, *English Towns in Transition*, pp. 82–125; Beier, "Social Problems in Elizabethan London"; Goose, "Household Size and Structure", esp. pp. 349–58, and sources cited therein; Goose, "In Search of the Urban Variable", p. 179; Slack, *Poverty and Policy*, pp. 67–85; Slack, *Impact of Plague*, pp. 188–92; Galley, *Demography of Early Modern Towns*, esp. ch. 1, pp. 3–30; Griffiths *et al.*, "Population and Disease" , pp. 203–8; Slack, "Great and Good Towns", pp. 353–5.

82 See below, Chapters 4 and 6.

83 Lindeboom, *Austin Friars*, pp. 7ff; Strohm, "Discipline and Integration".

84 Pettegree, "Foreign Community Before 1547", in *Foreign Protestant Communities*, pp. 9–22; Bratchel, "Alien Merchant Colonies", pp. 44–62.

85 Thrupp, "Survey of the Alien Population"; Thrupp, "Aliens in and Around London"; Bolton (ed.), *Alien Communities*, pp. 1–40; Kirk & Kirk, Part 1 1523–71, pp. 4–15.

86 Scouloudi, "Stranger Community in London", p. 435.

87 Pettegree, "Stranger Community in Marian London"; Grell, *Dutch Calvinists*, pp. 224–48; Pettegree, *Foreign Protestant Communities*, pp. 182–214 ; Littleton, "Ecclesiastical Discipline in the French Church"; see also Chapter 5 below.

88 *CSPV 1547–1553*, pp. 119–20; Pettegree, *Foreign Protestant Communities*, pp. 171–8, 78, 145; Pettegree, "Foreign Population of London in 1549", pp. 141–6.

89 Pettegree, "Stranger Community in Marian London", pp. 395–7.

90 Pettegree, *Foreign Protestant Communities*, p. 236.

91 Kirk & Kirk, Part 1, p. 293.

92 Kirk & Kirk, Part 3, p. 439, Part 2, pp. 139, 154, 156.

93 Hessels, Vol. 3, Part 1, p. 428.

94 Kirk & Kirk, Part 2, pp. 376–78.

95 Kirk & Kirk, Part 2, p. 443; Huntingdon Library, San Marino: Ellesmere MS 2514. This return is also analysed in Scouloudi, *Returns of Strangers*, pp. 73–93. For discussion of the three extant 1593 lists see Littleton, "Social Interaction".

96 Yungblut, *Strangers Settled Here Amongst Us*, p. 14.

97 Kirk & Kirk, Part 2, p. 156.

98 Scouloudi, *Returns of Strangers*, p. 74.

99 See also Pettegree, *Foreign Protestant Communities*, pp. 78, 279–80, 292–3, 299 fn. 7.

100 Cf. Yungblut, *Strangers Settled Here Amongst Us*, p. 21, who gives a considerably lower estimate.

101 Gwynn, *Huguenot Heritage*, p. 39. See also Chapter 10 below.

102 Lindeboom, *Austin Friars*, p. 119.
103 Lindeboom, *Austin Friars*, p. 122.
104 See Chapter 10 below, p. 194.
105 Grell, "French and Dutch Congregations", p. 363.
106 Scouloudi, *Returns of Strangers*, p. 100.
107 Bulteel, *Relation of the Troubles*.
108 Bulteel, *Relation of the Troubles*, p. 22.
109 Huntingdon Library, San Marino: Ellesmere MS 2514; Scouloudi, *Returns of Strangers*, p. 90.
110 In 1593 there were 1,344 members of the French Church and 1,376 of the Dutch – 38 per cent of the total population of 7,113.
111 Bulteel, *Relation of the Troubles*, p. 22.
112 Goose, "The 'Dutch' in Colchester", p. 263.
113 Grell compared lists of members of the Austin Friars for 1617 and 1635, and found that the number of adult males had decreased from just over 500 to 359, but adds "whether the decrease was as great as the figures suggest must remain an open question": Grell, *Dutch Calvinists*, pp. 44–5.
114 Grell, "French and Dutch Congregations", p. 363.
115 Grell, "French and Dutch Congregations", pp. 362–3.
116 The transitory community at Glastonbury, planted by the Duke of Somerset, constitutes a rare exception: see below, p. 27.
117 Calculated from the figures usefully collected by Spicer: *French-Speaking Reformed Community*, table VI, p. 161. Spicer excludes Maidstone from his list, and an allowance of 250 has been made for the 43 families living in the town in 1585: Morant, "Settlement of Protestant Refugees in Maidstone", p. 212.
118 Gwynn, *Huguenot Heritage*, p. 39.
119 Bulteel, *Relation of the Troubles*, p. 22.
120 Hessels, Vol. 3, Part 1, pp. 1490–1.
121 See also Chapter 7 below, pp. 141–2.
122 "Introduction of Strangers from the Low Countries to Norwich, 1564", in Tawney and Power (eds), *Tudor Economic Documents*, Vol. 1, pp. 298–9. A request for the names of those licensed in 1567 gives their number as 300: Hudson and Tingey, *Records of the City of Norwich*, Vol. 2, p. 183.
123 Pettegree, *Foreign Protestant Communities*, p. 263; Williams, "The Crown and the Provincial Immigrant Communities", p. 122.
124 Eßer, "Norwich Strangers".
125 Pettegree, *Foreign Protestant Communities*, p. 263; Hudson and Tingey, *Records of Norwich*, Vol. 2, pp. lxxxiii, 184, 192; Moens, *Walloons and their Church*, pp. 25–38: Vane, "Walloon Community in Norwich", pp. 130, 132.
126 Miller, "Town Governments and Protestant Strangers ", p. 580 and fn. 24; Pound, *Tudor and Stuart Norwich*, p. 28.
127 Hessels, Vol. 3, Part 1, p. 268.
128 Hessels, Vol. 3, Part 1, pp. 768–9.
129 Hudson and Tingey, *Records of The City of Norwich*, Vol. 2, p. 193.
130 Martin, "New Draperies in Norwich", p. 255.
131 Bulteel, *Relation of the Troubles*, p. 22; and see above, p. 17.
132 Vane, "Walloon Community in Norwich", pp. 132–3.
133 Miller, "Town Governments and Protestant Strangers", p. 580; Gwynn, *Huguenot Heritage*, pp. 47–8.
134 Williams, "The Crown and the Provincial Immigrant Communities ", p. 122.
135 Oakley, "Canterbury Walloon Congregation", pp. 57–8.

136 Williams, "The Crown and the Provincial Immigrant Communities", p. 122.
137 Spicer, *French-Speaking Reformed Community*, p. 161; Durkin, "Civic Government and Economy", p. 28.
138 Cross, *History of the Walloon and Huguenot Church*, p. 36. Baptism figures given in Oakley, "Canterbury Walloon Congregation", table 4.1, p. 63: approximate population was calculated using the standard 'rule of thumb' assumption of a baptismal rate of 33 per 1,000, and hence a multiplier of 30. Cross's own method, of calculating a baptismal rate based upon the single year 1597, has been rejected, as single years are unlikely to be representative. Durkin's far lower estimates (just 480 immigrants in 1577, 840 in 1587 and 780 in 1595), based upon aliens assessed in the subsidy returns, have also been rejected: Durkin, "Civic Government and Economy", pp. 27–34. Not only do they produce numbers considerably out of line with the counts made in 1582 and 1597, but the example of Colchester – for which a number of enumerations are extant – suggests that subsidy returns represent a dramatic undercount. In 1598 401 aliens paid tax in Colchester, which (using Durkin's multiplier) would produce a total alien population of just 483, compared with an enumeration of 1,291 in 1586 and of 1,271 in 1616: PRO, E179/111/532 and see below, p. 21. Evasion may be partly to blame, but the very low number of children listed also suggests that many who were supposed to be taxed (all aged 7 or over) were omitted, while those aliens taxed on goods (68) most probably incorporate their wives and children, and hence should be converted to total population using a household multiplier. Later subsidies are even less reliable: only 78 alien taxpayers are recorded in 1628 (PRO E179/112/643). Nor is the argument that the Walloon registers *must* include areas lying outside of the city sufficiently proven for this baptismal data to be dismissed. It must be recognized, however, that the impact of plague and severe dearth during the 1590s does render use of baptism registers as a basis for calculation of population size particularly hazardous.
139 Durkin, "Civic Government and Economy", pp. 30, 32–3. A recent alternative estimate gives 6,000 for Canterbury as a whole in 1600, but the basis of this figure is not explained: Bower, "Kent Towns", table 10, p. 160.
140 Williams, "The Crown and the Provincial Immigrant Communities", p. 130, Oakley, "Canterbury Walloon Congregation", p. 59; Cross, *History of the Walloon and Huguenot Church*, pp. 184–5.
141 Oakley, "Canterbury Walloon Congregation", p. 70; Durkin, "Civic Government and Economy", pp. 36, 144–4. And see Chapter 7 below, pp. 142–3.
142 Bulteel, *Relation of the Troubles*, p. 22. An alternative estimate gives 1,100 communicants in the 1630s, perhaps underlining the fact that Bulteel was concered to minimize their number: Durkin, "Civic Government and Economy", p. 35.
143 "Settlement of Alien Craftsmen in Sandwich, 1561", in Tawney and Power (eds), *Tudor Economic Documents*, Vol. 1, p. 297.
144 Williams, "The Crown and the Provincial Immigrant Communities", p. 122.
145 Backhouse, *Flemish and Walloon Communities*, p. 20.
146 Pettegree, *Foreign Protestant Communities*, pp. 141–2.
147 For a discussion of overcrowding, see Pettegree, *Foreign Protestant Communities*, pp. 283–5; Backhouse, *Flemish and Walloon Communities*, p. 17.
148 Backhouse, *Flemish and Walloon Communities*, p. 20; see also Chapter 11 below, pp. 212–16.
149 Backhouse, *Flemish and Walloon Communities*, p. 25.
150 Backhouse, *Flemish and Walloon Communities*, pp. 25–7. For example, his calculations give 980 in 1570, 1,868 in 1571, 1,044 in 1572, 1,845 in 1573 and 2,304 in 1574.
151 I have ignored Backhouse's estimate of 2,304 for 1574, as it involves multiplying up the number found in just three wards to allow for those missing in the remaining nine: Backhouse, *Flemish and Walloon Communities*, p. 27, fn. 58.

152 Backhouse, *Flemish and Walloon Communities*, p. 31.

153 Backhouse, "Strangers at Work", p. 78.

154 The revised figure of 2,500 is based upon the application of a crude birth rate of 33 per 1,000 to the decadal average of baptisms, calculated from table 1, p. 21, This c.b.r. is adopted from Wrigley and Schofield, *Population History of England*, table A3.1, p. 528.

155 Goose, "The 'Dutch' in Colchester", p. 263; Pettegree, *Foreign Protestant Communities*, p. 263; Backhouse, *Flemish and Walloon Communities*, p. 35.

156 Backhouse, *Flemish and Walloon Communities*, p. 27. This may be an underestimate, given that there were approaching double that number less than a decade earlier, and a similar tax list for 1585 produces as total of just 510.

157 Backhouse, "Strangers at Work", p. 94; Andrewes, "Industries in Kent", p. 118; Stephens, "Cloth Exports of the Provincial Ports", p. 245; Chalklin, *Seventeenth-Century Kent*, p. 124.

158 Backhouse, *Flemish and Walloon Communities*, p. 36; Backhouse, "Strangers at Work", p. 92 (the number given here who arrived in Leiden is 281).

159 Andrewes and Zell, 'Population of Sandwich', pp. 88–91.

160 Hessels, Vol. 3, Part 1, p. 1500.

161 Bulteel, *Relation of the Troubles*, p. 22.

162 Hessels, Vol. 3, Part 2, p. 2769.

163 Colchester Record Office, Liber Ordinacionum, f. 92, 24 Nov. 4 Eliz.

164 For sources for these totals see Goose, "The 'Dutch' in Colchester", p. 263; for 1616, Morant, *History and Antiquities*, Vol. 1, p. 78. Bulteel gives 700 communicants in 1635, and the Dutch congregation claimed there were 600 communicants "as well strangers as of all descents, Men and Women, single-men and maids" in April 1637: Bulteel, *Relation of the Troubles*, p. 22; Hessels, Vol. 3 Part 2, p. 1747.

165 PRO, E179/108/147; E179/108/162; E179/108/169.

166 For their economic contribution, see Chapter 7 below, pp. 140–1.

167 CRO, D/B 5 Gb1–6, Assembly Books 1576–1712.

168 Moens (ed.), *Register of Baptisms in the Dutch Church*, p. 95; CRO, D/B 5, Gb1, Assembly Book 1576–99.

169 CRO, D/B 5 Gb1–2, Assembly Books 1576–99 and 1600–20. When he wrote his will in 1621, aged about 72, de Lobell showed his continued attachment to the Dutch congregation in a bequest of £2 to the Dutch poor, and through reference to Jonas Proost, then its minister: CRO, D/A CW 9/69, Archdeaconry of Essex, will of Hugh de Lobell, merchant, St Giles, Colchester, drawn 1621.

170 CRO, D/B 5 Gb4, Assembly Book 1646–66, July 1659–Jan. 1660.

171 CRO, D/B 5 Gb4, Assembly Book 1646–66, Jan. 1660–Aug. 1662.

172 CRO, D/B 5 Gb4–5, Assembly Books 1646–66, 1666–92.

173 For fuller details see Goose, "The Dutch in Colchester in the 16th and 17th Centuries", pp. 92–4.

174 Spicer, *French-Speaking Reformed Community*, p. 71. In the 15th century there were schemes to introduce cloth-finishers and dyers to Southampton, and in the 16th century silk-weaving, see Williams, "The Crown and the Provincial Immigrant Communities", p. 118.

175 Spicer, *French-Speaking Reformed Community*, pp. 24, 35–6.

176 Spicer, *French-Speaking Reformed Community*, pp. 28, 31, 72ff.

177 Spicer, *French-Speaking Reformed Community*, pp. 29–30.

178 Spicer, *French-Speaking Reformed Community*, p. 161.

179 Spicer, *French-Speaking Reformed Community*, p. 159.

180 Spicer, *French-Speaking Reformed Community*, pp. 89, 164.

181 Spicer, *French-Speaking Reformed Community*, p. 164; Bulteel, *Relation of the Troubles*, p. 22.

182 Spicer, *French-Speaking Reformed Community*, pp. 146–8. See also Spicer, "Process of Gradual Assimilation", pp. 186–98.

183 Spicer, *French-Speaking Reformed Community*, p. 165.

184 Bulteel, *Relation of the Troubles*, p. 22.

185 Morant, "Settlement of Protestant Refugees in Maidstone", p. 211. These included, *inter alia*, manufacturers of Spanish leather, pottery, tile and brickmakers, brasiers, papermakers, armourers and makers of gunpowder.

186 Morant, "Settlement of Protestant Refugees in Maidstone", pp. 211–12.

187 Morant, "Settlement of Protestant Refugees in Maidstone", p. 212.

188 See Chapter 7 below, p. 143.

189 Hessels, Vol. 3, Part 1, p. 252.

190 Hessels, Vol. 3, Part 1, pp. 262, 358, 428–9, 721–2, 811.

191 Hessels, Vol. 3, Part 1, pp. 1056, 1125.

192 Hessels, Vol. 3, Part 1, pp. 1266–7.

193 Hessels, Vol. 3, Part 2, pp. 1514–15.

194 Morant, "Settlement of Protestant Refugees in Maidstone", p. 214; Bulteel, *Relation of the Troubles*, p. 22.

195 Hessels, Vol. 3 Part 2, pp. 1515, 1542, 1545, 1659, 1678, 1722, 1727, 1743, 1756, 1794, 1805.

196 For example, Hessels, Vol. 3 Part 2, pp. 2046, 2126, 2142, 2150, 2175.

197 Hessels, Vol. 3 Part 2, pp. 2272, 2312, 2325ff.

198 Swinden, *History and Antiquities*, p. 943; Roker, "Dutch Fishing Community", p. 306.

199 Swinden, *History and Antiquities*, pp. 942–6.

200 Roker, "Dutch Fishing Community", p. 306. Spicer gives a figure of 390 for the same date: *French-Speaking Reformed Community*, p. 161.

201 Swinden, *History and Antiquities*, pp. 947–8.

202 Roker, "Dutch Fishing Community", p. 307.

203 Swinden, *History and Antiquities*, pp. 843ff.

204 Hessels, Vol. 3 Part 2, pp. 1615–18, 1678–9.

205 Hessels, Vol. 3 Part 2, pp. 1505–6, 1537, 1569–70, 1610, 1615–18, 1636, 1641, 1645, 1654, 1678–9, 1726, 1730, 1734, 1748, 1754, 1768–9, 1798.

206 Hessels, Vol. 3 Part 2, pp. 1792, 2126, 2157; Roker, "Dutch Fishing Community", p. 308.

207 Mayhew, *Tudor Rye*, p. 81.

208 Mayhew, *Tudor Rye*, p. 82.

209 Mayhew, *Tudor Rye*, p. 82; Hessels, Vol 3, Part 1, p. 819. Cf. Spicer, *French-Speaking Reformed Community*, p. 161, which gives much lower figures.

210 Mayhew, *Tudor Rye*, pp. 88–9.

211 Mayhew, *Tudor Rye*, p. 23.

212 Hardy, "Foreign Settlers at Colchester and Halstead", pp. 194–6; Yungblut, *Strangers Settled Here Amongst Us*, pp. 57–8.

213 Hessels, Vol. 3, Part 1, pp. 852–3.

214 Hessels, Vol. 3, Part 1, pp. 871, 875.

215 Yungblut, *Strangers Settled Here Amongst Us*, p. 58.

216 Hessels, Vol. 3, Part 1, p. 906.

217 Overend, "Strangers at Dover, Part 1", pp. 111, 159–62.

218 Hessels, Vol. 3, Part 1, pp. 287, 290.

219 Overend, "Strangers at Dover, Part 1", pp. 122–3, 128–9; Hessels, Vol. 3, Part 1, pp. 792, 1008.

220 Hessels, Vol. 3, Part 2, pp. 1773–6.

221 Overend, "Strangers at Dover, Part 1", pp. 131, 134, 138; Gwynn, *Huguenot Heritage*, pp. 43–4; Burn, *History*, pp. 97–8, 220; Firth and Rait, *Acts and Ordinances*, Vol. 1, pp. 845–6; Overend, "Strangers at Dover, Part 2", pp. 307–9.

222 Burn, *History*, pp. 90–4.

223 Spicer, *French-Speaking Reformed Community*, p. 161; Thirsk, "Stamford", pp. 315–16; Burn, *History*, pp. 96–7, 219–19.

224 Hessels, Vol. 3, Part 1, pp. 300, 368.

225 Hessels, Vol. 3, Part 1, pp. 505–6. In March the previous year the Dutch consistory was also complaining, in a letter to the Maidstone church, that "several of them are already breaking up, and are likely to decrease still further (as you report about your own) . . . ": Hessels, Vol. 3, Part 1, p. 428.

226 Hessels, Vol. 3, Part 1, pp. 749–50.

227 Redstone, "Dutch and Huguenot Settlements of Ipswich", pp. 185–6, 200–1.

228 Hessels, Vol. 1, p. 388, Vol. 3, Part 1, p. 148; see also Redstone, "Dutch and Huguenot Settlements of Ipswich", pp. 185–7.

229 Hessels, Vol. 3, Part 1, p. 877. This letter is mistakenly attributed by Hessels to "The Consistory of the Dutch Community, Ipswich".

230 Hessels, Vol. 3 Part 2, p. 1520.

231 Stoate (ed.), *Devon Lay Subsidy Rolls*, pp. xii (table 1), 9–10, 13, 21–2, 190–1, 195–6.

232 *CSPD 1627–1628*, p. 557; Hessels, Vol. 3, Part 1, p. 1354.

233 Cracknell, *Canvey Island*, pp. 20–2.

234 Cracknell, *Canvey Island*, p. 28.

235 Burn, *History*, pp. 101–5; Tsushima, "Melting into the Landscape", pp. 107–8.

236 Tsushima, "Melting into the Landscape", pp. 108–11.

237 Assuming 24,000 immigrants in 1590 and a national population of 4 million: Wrigley and Schofield, *Population History of England*, table A3.1, p. 528.

238 Hessels, Vol. 3, Part 1, p. 1037.

Part I

Immigrant Communities in England

Immigrant Roots: The Geographical Origins of Newcomers from the Low Countries in Tudor England

RAYMOND FAGEL

────────────

Immigrants from the Low Countries were the dominant group among the newcomers from the European continent to Tudor England during the sixteenth century. Recent research claims that in 1567 almost 75 per cent of the alien population of London and Westminster originated from the Netherlands.[1] The letters of denization and the acts of naturalization reflect this same tendency for the whole of England, as well as for the whole of the sixteenth century.[2] The inhabitants of the Low Countries, generally called Flemings in contemporary documents and sources, even appeared as early as 1554–7 in Tudor drama. The best known example is Hance Berepot, who "divided his time between drinking and job hunting".[3]

The presence of these Flemings has drawn much attention from scholars, both in the past and in more recent years. However, most studies have focused on these immigrants as inhabitants of one English city or as members of one particular immigrant organization, such as the Dutch Church at Austin Friars in London. The intention of this chapter is to focus on the position of these Flemings as emigrants. In this way, my subject could be described as a search for the geographical roots of the newcomers from the Low Countries to England during the reign of the Tudor monarchs. In order to accomplish this search, it is necessary to combine the available information on the different host cities and institutions with the information derived from denizations and naturalizations.

The Low Countries in the Sixteenth Century: State Formation and Disintegration

In order to be able to understand the emigration process, it is necessary to have at least some knowledge of the historical and geographical development of the Netherlands during the course of the sixteenth century.[4] The most important observation that has to be made concerns the fact that the Low Countries in the sixteenth century were a state in a process of genesis, of early modern state formation. The Dutch Revolt that broke out during the late 1560s would, however, change this again into a process of disintegration. As such, the highlight of the Low Countries as a coherent state may be found in the 1548–9 Pragmatic Sanction, when the Low Countries were declared an independent state, only loosely tied to the Holy Roman Empire as its "Burgundian Circle".

During the late Middle Ages most of the relatively small, but mostly fairly independent, feudal states in the north-western part of the European continent fell under the high lordship of either the French king or the Emperor of the Holy Roman Empire.[6] The duchies, counties and other lordships that were to form the Low Countries were no exception to this. At the end of the fifteenth century, some of these territories had already been united under the sovereignty of the Habsburg family. After the death of Mary of Burgundy in 1482, her husband Maximilian of Habsburg would rule these lands in the name of their son, Philip the Fair. In 1494 Philip started his independent reign that would last until his premature death in 1506.

The core states of the Low Countries, as possessed by the Habsburg family around 1500, were the Duchy of Brabant and the Counties of Flanders, Holland and Zeeland. In the following discussion, according to the historical tradition in the Netherlands, we shall refer to these smaller entities as provinces. We must, however, remember that in reality they were separate states only joined together within a personal union. The four above-mentioned coastal provinces exhibited a high degree of urbanization and they played an important part in international trade and commerce. These central provinces were adjacent to other more rural provinces to the east, such as the Duchies of Limburg and Luxembourg, and the Counties of Artois, Namur and Hainaut. The Habsburg government at the time was furthermore zealously trying to incorporate the Lordship of Friesland and the Duchy of Gelderland (Guelders) into its state complex.[5]

Some independent ecclesiastical states, officially belonging to the Holy Roman Empire and the French kingdom, stretched out their territories over the border regions of the Low Countries as possessed by the Habsburgs. As far as ecclesiastical power was concerned, the Bishoprics of Utrecht, Liège and Tournai even controlled the whole of the Habsburg territory. In order to influence the secular and ecclesiastical power of these independent church states, the Habsburg rulers, like their predecessors from the House of Burgundy, tried to control the election of new bishops within these bishoprics, a policy in which they often, but not invariably, succeeded.

During the reign of Emperor Charles V (1515–55), son of Philip the Fair and heir to the Spanish kingdom and all its further dependencies, as well as to all the Habsburg possessions within the Holy Roman Empire, the Low Countries would continue to grow as an independent state complex. Charles V succeeded in this process of state formation both by incorporating more small territories into his state, as well as by diminishing the influence of France and the Holy Roman Empire. As noted above, the Pragmatic Sanction of 1548–9 declared the Low Countries to be an independent state. By that time, the Bishoprics of Tournai (1421), Utrecht together with Overijssel (1528) and Cambrai (1529), had also been incorporated. The same had happened with the Lordships of Friesland (1524) and Groningen with the so-called "Ommelanden"(1536), the Duchy of Gelderland and the County of Zutphen (1543).[6]

It is this union of small provinces, to some degree cemented in 1548–9, that is generally called the Low Countries or, to give them an alternative title, the Seventeen

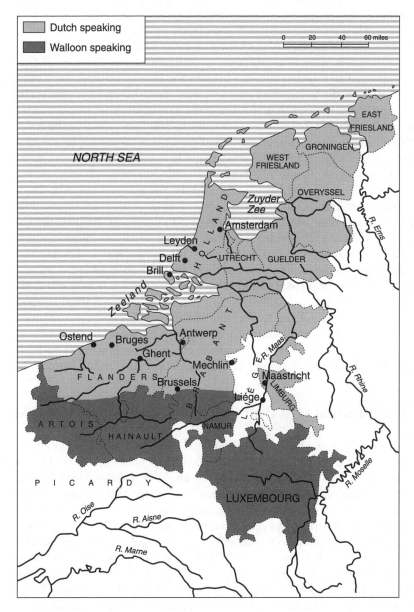

Map 2.1 The Low Countries in the Mid-Sixteenth Century

Provinces of the Netherlands. Only the Prince-Bishop of Liège remained as an independent lord in the region, with his territories intermingled with those of the Habsburgs, and still in possession of his part of ecclesiastical influence within the lands of Charles V. Because of the difficulty of separating Liège from the Low Countries, I have included the emigrants coming from Liège as if they were inhabitants of the Netherlands. However, officially they were never a part of the Low Countries. Other small territories on the fringe of the Low Countries have also been taken into consideration, as frontiers were often difficult to distinguish. The Duchies of Cleves and Jülich are particularly closely connected with the history of the Low Countries. In 1559 the union of the Seventeen Provinces was strengthened by a new ecclesiastical division into 18 bishoprics that converted the Low Countries into an independent ecclesiastical union. Mechelen was to become the religious capital of the state.

This political and religious union of the Low Countries would, however, prove to be short-lived. During the reign of Philip II, Charles's son and successor, the union would fall into pieces, finally resulting in the division into two separate states: the Republic of the Seven United Provinces, and the Spanish Netherlands. The political division lines within the Low Countries often changed during the reign of Philip II as a result of the rebellion and the king's attempts to control it. At first, the Unions of Arras and Utrecht in 1579 divided the country into a rebellious Flemish-speaking and a loyal French-speaking part. But as a result of the ongoing war, and especially because of the campaigns of the Duke of Parma, these divisions changed again. Around 1589, only Holland, Zeeland, Friesland and Utrecht were completely supporting the rebellion. The next ten years, probably the most heroic decade in national Dutch history, again altered the division lines. At the time of King Philip's death in 1598, most of the northern parts of the Low Countries were again in the hands of the rebels. By then, the frontier between the two state complexes could be found somewhere in the north of the Duchy of Brabant, alongside the east–west flowing rivers of the country.

The Inhabitants of the Low Countries: Multiple Identities

As a result of this historical and geographical background, the emigrants from the Netherlands who came to England could describe themselves, or could be described by others, in a variety of ways. At the highest level of generality we find terminology such as "from the dominions of the Emperor", or "from the dominions of the King of Spain". Especially in the letters of denization and the acts of naturalization, this manner of speech almost always refers to inhabitants from the Low Countries, respectively as governed by Charles V and Philip II. An even older way of describing the Flemish was the use of "German" or "Theotonicus". This was the case, for example, in the 1483–4 subsidy rolls for London.[7] Although we have seen that in 1548–9 the Netherlands became more or less independent of the Holy Roman Empire, this denomination sometimes remained in use after this date, for the emigrants from the eastern provinces, in particular, could easily be 'mistaken' for "Germans".

Probably the most common and enduring descriptions used were those of "Dutch" and "Flemish", both referring to a general group that in the sixteenth century could mean anybody coming from within the Low Countries, or even from regions directly adjacent. During the course of the Dutch Revolt, "Dutch" became more and more limited to people coming from the rebel provinces, while "Flemish" would refer more commonly to emigrants from the Spanish Netherlands. Of course, "Flemish" could also be used to describe the inhabitants of the County of Flanders only. Another general way of describing a whole group is the use of the description "Walloon", referring to the French-speaking inhabitants of the Low Countries but often also including people from the north of France. In this sense, this denomination could also be used to differentiate between the French-speaking and the Dutch- or Flemish-speaking immigrants.

Geographical denomination also took place at a lower level using, for example, the province or the diocese of origin of the emigrant. This is generally the easiest to understand, but difficulties can arise when we are not certain whether a denomination refers to a province, a city or a diocese. Just one of the possible examples is that of Utrecht. With this we arrive at the lowest level – the city, or village, of origin. Here a problem arises from the fact that often more places than one existed with the same name. A last consideration concerning the geographical names is the fact that it is not uncommon for people to be referred to as coming from the city where they were last living, which was often not their place of origin. Especially in the case of large commercial cities like Antwerp, we find many people mentioned as coming from Antwerp while in reality their origins may be found somewhere else in the Netherlands, or even outside of it. Another example is the situation of emigrants who had already emigrated somewhere else before coming to England: they may be described as coming from a city like Emden in East Frisia, while their true origin is to be found in the Low Countries.

Naturalization and Denization: A Chronological Comparison

A study of the denizations and naturalizations of emigrants from the Low Countries in England during the period between 1509 and 1603 makes it possible to construct a general overview of this migration, and this is presented in table 2.1.[8] The most common denominations used in this type of sources to describe these emigrants are the general "subject of the dominion of the Emperor" and "subject of the dominion of the King of Spain". Chronologically dividing the number of denizations and naturalizations of the subjects of both the Emperor and King of Spain, we can clearly distinguish the influence of the religious troubles in the Low Countries during the 1560s and 1570s. After that turbulent episode, the number of naturalizations and denizations fell back to the pre-revolt level.

In his edition of the sources, dating from 1893, William Page concluded that there existed an almost direct correlation between the number of people asking for naturalization and denization, and the number of recent immigrants from the Low Countries: for example, the great explosion of denizations and naturalizations in 1562 had to reflect a great influx of migrants. However, the frequent use of the description "subject of the Emperor" should warn us against this idea. In 1562 almost 80 applicants described themselves in this manner, although the Emperor had ceased to rule the Low Countries in 1555. Why did these people still call themselves his subjects? The most probable explanation is that they emigrated before the abdication of the Emperor, and that these people mentioned the lord ruling in the year of their emigration from the

Netherlands. If we could explain the denomination the emigrants used in this way, it is possible to distinguish between an old and a new group of applicants. For the period between 1561–70 this would mean a number of 141 old emigrants against a more recently arrived group of 419, this last group consisting of persons that had left the country after 1555.[9]

Table 2.1 Letters of Denization and Acts of Naturalization, 1509–1603

Date	Subjects of the Emperor	Subjects of the King of Spain	Total	Annual Average
1509–20	0	0	0	0
1521–30	11	0	11	1.1
1531–40	143	0	143	14.3
1541–50	398	0	398	39.8
1551–60	90	0	90	9.0
1561–70	141	419	560	56.0
1571–80	74	246	320	32.0
1581–90	10	70	80	8.0
1591–1603	0	0	0	0
Total	867	735	1602	16.9

It also seems more likely that the petitions for denization and naturalization were mostly a reaction to the situation in the host country, not to that of the country of origin. What terrible things occurred in 1562 in the Netherlands? What we do know is that a new alien subsidy was advertised in England. It seems much more probable that the emigrants wanted to change their status in order to try to avoid taxation as aliens. The large number of petitions in 1541 and 1544 might be explained in the same manner, as being the result of English government policy towards aliens.[10] The high numbers of 1571 and 1572 can also be related to the special acts against aliens during these years. The numbers do not seem to reflect a high level of immigration, as in 1571 almost as many petitioners claimed to come from the lands of the Emperor as stated that they were subjects of the King of Spain.[11]

What do the denizations and naturalizations tell us about the geographical origin of the newcomers? In order to be able to contrast the period of the refugees with the general movement, I have adopted two sub-periods – 1509–60 and 1561–1603. The data is presented in table 2.2.[12] The immigrants' geographical origins up to 1560 can be explained in a few statements.[13] The Duchy of Brabant (including Antwerp) was the most important province as far as emigrants is concerned, followed by Gelderland, Flanders and Holland, in that order. These four provinces were the only ones with a reasonable amount of applicants. If one should make an anachronistic division between the territories of the later Republic and the Spanish Netherlands, up to 1560 the northern Netherlands provided for a small majority of the migrants. However, Antwerp was clearly the most mentioned city as place of origin. On the whole, migrants from Brabant often came from the larger cities within the duchy, while those from Flanders generally came from smaller places.

The possibility of making a reliable comparison between the two periods is undermined by the fact that after 1560 the information on geographical origins in the naturalizations and denizations is less detailed. For the period up to 1560 we have 171 migrants located, while for the larger numbers during the period 1561–1603 we only have detailed geographical information on 99. For the period between 1569 and 1590 we find little geographical evidence at all. Comparing the two periods, the importance of both the Duchy of Gelderland and the Prince-Bishopric of Liège stands out in both periods, while the core provinces of Brabant, Flanders and Holland seem to have lost their importance over time. Did their migrants stop applying for denization and naturalization, or did they just need less specific geographical description in the registers? The Archbishopric of Cologne and the Duchy of Cleves, adjacent to the Low Countries, show a similar pattern to Gelderland and Liège, albeit that after 1560 the number of migrants that claimed to come from Cleves grew spectacularly, to 233 migrants.

Table 2.2 Denizations and Naturalizations by Place of Origin, 1509–1603

	1509–1560	1561–1603
Brabant	42	13
Gelderland	31	22
Flanders	28	10
Holland	26	0
Liège	23	46
Utrecht	8	2
Zeeland	5	0
Friesland	4	3
Hainaut	2	2
Tournai	2	0
Artois	0	1
Total	171	99

A special group of applicants consisted of some 80 children born abroad to an English father and a mother from the Low Countries. This information can, however, only be found for certain years.[14] The majority of the women came from the commercial city of Antwerp (49 children), while Zeeland was also well represented as a result of the English military presence (16 children), and a smaller number came from Holland (six children). Of further interest is the existence in 1573 of two emigrants from "the dominions of the Prince of Orange". They are the first applicants, and strangely enough also the last, who seem to have considered the rebel provinces as an autonomous state under William of Orange.[15]

Though it is difficult to draw general conclusions from the denizations and naturalizations, we could say that they highlight the importance of the regions on the eastern fringes of the Low Countries, like Cleves, Gelderland and Liège. The core province of Brabant, and to a lesser extent Flanders, played a particularly important role before 1560, and even after then they remained clearly ahead of the other provinces except Gelderland. Up to 1560 Holland could still match Flanders, but after that Holland lost importance. Strangely enough we do find Holland and Zeeland as places of origin among the women with an English partner.

The London Refugee Community: The Special Relationship with Antwerp

London has always been the major focal point for aliens in England. Using Page's edition of the denizations and naturalizations up to 1560, it can be shown that at least two-thirds of the migrants must have lived in London.[16] With the immigration of the refugees from the Low Countries during the second part of the century, the city kept this very special position. Of course, in 1550 it was among the first cities to establish a separate stranger church. Andrew Pettegree estimates the membership of the Dutch and French protestant churches in the beginning as high as some 700 male members. The total group of adherents of both communities must have numbered by that time between 3,000 and 4,000. During the reign of Elizabeth I, the male membership probably rose to about twice that number. Notwithstanding these impressive numbers, Pettegree reminds us that a large group of migrants from the Low Countries would never join these stranger churches and that the numbers can probably be doubled for the whole immigrant community from the Low Countries.[17]

Table 2.3   Geographical Origins of Elders and Deacons of the Dutch Church, 1567–1585

Antwerp	20	Ronse	1	Turnhout	1	Cleves	1
Ghent	13	Wervik	1	Menin	1	Bremen	2
Bruges	6	Ipres	1	England	2/3	Cologne	1
Roeselare	3	Messines	1	Geldermalsen	1	Aix-La-Chapelle	1
Courtrai	2	Den Bosch	1	Amsterdam	1	Vreden	1
Oudenaarde	2	Meteren	1	Eugies (Hainaut)	1	Liège	2/3

Table 2.4   Geographical Origins of Elders and Deacons of the French Church, 1567–1585

France	25	Antwerp	13	Armentières	1	Lessines	1
Paris	5	Tournai	12	Laventie	1	Buzet	1
Rouen	3	Valenciennes	9	Douai	1	Liège	2/3
England	1	Lille	7	Trazegnies	1	Artois	1
Spain	1	Nivelles	3	St Sauveur	1	Zutphen	1
Italy	1	Mons (Hainaut)	3	St Vaast	1	Cleves (Roermond)	1

Table 2.5   Geographical Origins of Elders and Deacons of the Italian Church, 1568–1591

Italy	3/4	Antwerp	3	Mons (Hainaut)	1
England	3	Ghent	2	Liège	1
		Bruges	2		

Of this last group we hardly know anything about their geographical origin, and even on the members of the refugee churches in London the information is hardly explicit. According to Boersma, most of its members came from the larger cities in Flanders and Brabant. Furthermore, he estimates that only some 5 per cent came from the provinces that would later form the Republic of the United Provinces. Boersma also stresses the importance within the Dutch Church of immigrants from Germany, many of them coming from the Duchy of Cleves and the Archdiocese of Cologne. These figures thus only partly coincide with the evidence from the denizations and naturalizations. Still, according to Boersma, one-third of the members of the French Church came from the Kingdom of France and not from the Low Countries. Of the foreign members of the protestant Italian Church in London, some 60 per cent also came from the Low Countries.[18]

In order to offer a more detailed insight into the origin of these migrant groups in London, I shall use three sets of data: the prosopography of Boersma on the Elders and Deacons of the stranger churches for the early period,[19] the information available from the marriage registers of the Dutch Church between 1571 and 1603,[20] and the 1593 returns of the strangers in the Metropolis.[21]

From tables 2.3–2.5 we can see that, apart from the domination of Antwerp in all three churches, within the Dutch and Italian Churches, Flemish cities such as Ghent and Bruges were important in the same way as were Tournai, Valenciennes and Lille within the French Church. In general, the Elders and Deacons were textile artisans and merchants, but within the Italian Church the free trades, such as lawyers and notaries, were dominant. A comparable picture can be derived from another study by Boersma and Jelsma on the members of the Italian Church, as shown in table 2.6. Again Brabant is dominant, only at a distance followed by Flanders, and with the other provinces hardly possessing any importance at all. It is also clearly an urban phenomenon. Antwerp accounts for 21 members, Ghent and Bruges seven each, followed by Oudenaarde, Middelburg and Brussels with three members each.[22]

Table 2.6 Geographical Origins of Members of the Italian Church from the Low Countries, 1567–1593

Brabant	36	Liège	3	Cleves	1
Flanders	22	Hainaut	2		
Zeeland	4	Gelderland	2	Dutch	11
Holland	3	Artois	1		

In order to be able to compare these figures with the members of the Dutch Church, I have studied the marriage register of that church for the period between 1571 and 1603.[23] Although the places of origin are not always mentioned, we can identify those of some 2,000 brides and grooms, who came from a total of almost 400 different places.

However, I have focused on those places with at least three brides and grooms mentioned within this period. This provides us with a list of 84 cities and villages in the Low Countries, the adjacent German territories and England, and these results are presented in table 2.7. If we leave out London (146) as a place of origin, we find the same cities dominating as for the Deacons and Elders of the Dutch Church. The importance of Antwerp, followed by Ghent, is quite clear. Very striking, however, is the fact that Brussels never provided for any Elder or Deacon between 1567 and 1585, but that it did occupy an important place as the origin of the brides and grooms. To a lesser extent the same is true for Enghien (31) and Mechelen (16). The fact that members from the cities of the interior of Brabant did not come to occupy important positions within the church might be due to the domination of these positions by rich merchants and textile entrepreneurs from Antwerp and Flanders.

A total of 19 cities each provided more than 15 brides and grooms, including almost 60 per cent of the whole population. Apart from the above mentioned cities, we find Ipres (33), Turnhout (24), Bois-Le-Duc (22), Maaseik (22), Utrecht (20), Menin (19), Emden (18), Courtrai (17), Roeselare (17) and Sandwich (17). Below this level we find 65 places with between 3 and 15 brides and grooms. The most important ones are Amsterdam, Maastricht, Nieuwkerke and Venlo with 13 each, Messines with 12, Norwich with 11, Hondschoote with 10, and Bergen-op-Zoom and Breda with 9 each. The domination of the cities of Flanders and Brabant within the immigrants from the Low Countries is thus obvious. Outside these two provinces we only find some cities on the river Maas/Meuse (Maastricht, Maaseik and Venlo) and, further north, only Utrecht and Amsterdam.

Table 2.7 Geographical Origins of Deacons and Elders, Brides and Grooms in the Dutch Church, 1571–1603 – Top Six Places

Deacons and Elders		Brides and grooms	
Antwerp	20	Antwerp	310
Ghent	13	Ghent	175
Bruges	6	Brussels	131
Roeselare	3	Bruges	80
Courtrai	2	Oudenaarde	66
Oudenaarde	2	Ronse	35

When we consider the whole group of 85 places with at least three brides and grooms, the same pattern arises of Flemish and Brabantine dominion.[24] However, in the north-eastern parts we find cities like Harlingen, Deventer, Oldenzaal, Arnhem and Zwolle. The county of Holland shows, besides Amsterdam, the cities of Hoorn, Naarden, Delft, The Hague, Haarlem, Dordrecht, Gouda, Gorcum and Leiden, but all of these cities together only account for less than 50 persons. More or less the same number can be found for the cities east of the Low Countries in this group, coming from Aix-la-Chapelle, Solingen, Heinsberg, Bremen, Düsseldorf, Geel, Neuss, Wesel and Emmerich. When we look at the whole group of all 2,000 brides and grooms, the importance of the adjacent regions is clearly marked, albeit that Cologne and Cleves are much less important than the county of Jülich, which presents us with almost 60 persons. The large group of more-than 300 places with one or two brides or grooms shows that migration was not strictly an urban phenomenon. It seems logical that the most important, and richest, migrants are to be found in the cities, but still a large number comes from smaller villages. We also find migrants from as far away as Danzig, Geneva, Nürnberg and Rouen.

Our last set of data in relation to London comes from the 1593 returns of strangers for the city and the adjacent territories. Out of almost 1,400 geographical denominations (887 from the Low Countries), again Antwerp is clearly the single most important city. Interesting, however, is the large number of migrants coming from Tournai, even ahead of Ghent and Bruges. Brussels is the fifth city within the Low Countries to be found. Another interesting feature is the presence of Middelburg, outnumbering the immigrants from the city of Amsterdam. Other cities from Holland and Zeeland did not even reach five persons. So in the 1593 returns Brabant and Flanders are again the most important provinces of origin. The border regions between the Low Countries and the Holy Roman Empire, such as Cleves, Jülich and Cologne, can also be identified as the origin of a whole group of migrants.[25]

Table 2.8 Cities of Origin in the 1593 Returns for the London Metropolis with Five or More Persons Mentioned

Antwerp	169	Douai	11
Tournai	81	Arras	10
Ghent	78	Ipres	9
Bruges	41	Oudenaarde	9
Brussels	38	Liège	8
Lille	29	Amsterdam	8
Valenciennes	28	Malines	6
Middelburg	18	Cambrai	6
Armentières	16	Tiel	5
Maastricht	13		

The most striking conclusion is the enormous importance of Antwerp for London. People from one metropolis probably preferred to go to another large metropolis. The city alongside the Thames and the one along the Scheldt were directly linked to one another, and until the mid-sixteenth century the London–Antwerp axis had dominated English trade.[26] As in the information derived from the naturalizations and denizations, we find the same importance of the eastern fringes of the Low Countries, and within the Seventeen Provinces a clear domination of Brabant and Flanders over Holland, Zeeland and all the others. Finally, the numeral importance of Brussels in both the marriage registers and the 1593 returns highlights a rather unknown phenomenon. As the migrants from this city never occupied any function as Elder or Deacon in the Stranger Churches in London, their presence has been underestimated.

An Overview of Other Refugee Communities: Links between Cities

In addition to London there were large refugee communities in Norwich, Sandwich and Canterbury, but there were also smaller immigrant communities elsewhere. We may mention above all Dover, Colchester,[27] Maidstone,[28] Rye,[29] Southampton, Stamford, King's Lynn, Winchelsea, Ipswich, Thetford, Glastonbury,[30] and Halstead. And even this long list is not complete, as we also find immigrants from the Low Countries in places like Manchester, Birmingham, Yarmouth, Hythe, Boston and Mortlake.[31] It is unfortunately impossible to examine here the origins of the Low Countries' immigrants found in all of these places.

Andrew Spicer has recently shown how immigrants from certain regions or cities in the Low Countries ended up at the same destination. In his study of Southampton he provides us with a small list of correspondences between geographical origin and host community.[32] In the beginning Southampton attracted migrants from

Valenciennes, much the same as the cities of Frankfurt and Canterbury. Other examples have to do with the special relationship between England and the western parts of Flanders: between Norwich and Ieper,[33] between Hondschoote and Leiden,[34] and between the whole of the Flemish "Westkwartier" and Sandwich.[35] The same author also points to the relationship between Maastricht and Aix-la-Chapelle, and the ties between Dieppe and Rouen and Rye. The explanation for this phenomenon must be found in a mixture of chain migration and specialization in trade or specific kinds of manufacture.

The small port of Sandwich, which even has its own historical name in Dutch – "Zandwijk" – became one of the leading communities of migrants from the Low Countries. This happened mostly as a result of the sending of migrants from London in 1561.[36] Marcel Backhouse, who has studied this community in various publications, has been able to establish the origin of 575 Dutch-speaking immigrants who came to Sandwich between 1561 and 1603. Almost all came from the County of Flanders and the Duchy of Brabant. This seems no different to the picture that has emerged for the London community itself. However, in this case most of the migrants, some 88 per cent, came from the smaller "Westkwartier" and the "Pays de l'Alleu". Ipres was the largest city within these territories, but the region was full of smaller towns and villages, being one of the main production areas of the Flemish textile industry. Belle (Bailleul) was the main place of origin, followed by Nieuwkerke, Hondschoote, Ipres and Messines.[37]

Backhouse has found three reasons for this regional dominance. Firstly, this Flemish region seems to have been one of the most influenced by Calvinism, resulting in a large exodus for fear of persecution. Secondly, the English government particularly tried to promote the growth of new textile industries in Sandwich when sending these migrants away from London. A last explanation may be the direct proximity between the "Westkwartier" and Sandwich, which made it possible to maintain direct contact.[38] Apart from this Dutch-speaking community, Sandwich also received Walloon-speaking migrants. They partly came from the same region as their Dutch-speaking countrymen, to where they must have emigrated at an earlier stage from the Walloon-speaking counties of Hainaut and Artois, as well as from Walloon Flanders and the Pays de l'Alleu.[39] The Dutch-speaking community started in 1561 with some 400 migrants, growing rapidly to about 2,000 in the early 1570s. By that time they made up more than half of the population of the city. The Walloon-speaking community numbered some 300 persons by 1571.[40]

An even larger community of migrants from the Low Countries found its way to Norwich. Starting with a small group of 24 Flemish and six Walloon artisans, they came from London and Sandwich, together with their family and servants. Most of these immigrants were Dutch-speaking. The community reached some 4,000 in 1571, and 4,678 in 1582. By that time, they formed almost one-third of the population of the city.[41] Again the County of Flanders was the main province of origin, followed by Brabant. Besides this there were 26 families from Zeeland, few compared to 313 families from Flanders, but quite a significant number compared to their scarcity among the community in London. The Walloons mostly came from Lille in Flanders, but also from Hainaut, Artois, Cambrai and Brabant, while we even find two of them coming from Utrecht.

A third community of which we possess details on the geographical origin is

Southampton. Andrew Spicer has been able to identify the origins of two-thirds of the 166 persons of the French-speaking community between 1567 and 1591. Almost one-third (51) came from Valenciennes, 13 from Tournai, another ten from the region around Armentières and seven from Antwerp. This points to a very large presence of migrants from Hainaut compared to Flanders. After the first influx of migrants from the Low Countries, immigrants from the French Kingdom started to become more numerous, especially after the massacre of St Bartholomew's day. Trade, not textile production, was the most important occupation of these migrants.[42]

Of another French-speaking church, founded in Canterbury, Beate Magen found the geographical origin of 1,943 brides and grooms between 1590 and 1644. Here we find a totally different picture compared to Southampton. The French-speaking parts of Flanders, not Hainaut, were dominant in Canterbury, and hence the colony in Canterbury looked more like the Dutch-speaking communities in Norwich and Sandwich. Due to the fact that we are talking of a later period, already 40 per cent came from other places within England. Another 30 per cent came from Flanders, 9 per cent from Hainaut, 6 per cent from Artois, and only some 9 per cent came from France. The most important cities were St Amand, Lille, Tourcoing, Valenciennes and Armentières.[43]

Conclusion

Though we have found migrants from all parts of the Low Countries, it is clear that some provinces played a much more important role than others. The populous and highly developed provinces of Brabant and Flanders clearly dominated. Nonetheless, while the larger Duchy of Brabant had already done so during the first half of the century, the prominence of Flanders was of a later date. Compared to Flanders, the county of Holland and other northern provinces clearly lost their position as an emigration area for England. This was probably the most direct result of the political turmoil within the Low Countries.

The large group of emigrants from the county of Flanders gravitated mainly towards textile centres like Norwich, Sandwich and Canterbury. Within the London metropolis migrants from the large cities of Brabant still came first, especially those from Antwerp. In the same manner as Spicer stated that some of the settlements had a specific character and a relation to a centre in the Low Countries, Antwerp and London were also clearly linked. Another group, though generally not a very visible one, consisted of the migrants from Brussels who made up a relatively large part of the Dutch Church in London. Another important discovery has been the importance of the eastern fringes, both the territories within the Seventeen Provinces as well as those just outside of it, above all the Duchies of Gelderland, Cleves and Jülich. This demonstrates that the early modern history of the Low Countries cannot be understood without including these border regions.

Although large numbers of immigrants from the Low Countries in England generally can be found in the sources with only a mere description as "Dutch", "Flemish" or "Walloon", I hope to have made clear that behind these descriptions we can find a whole range of different provinces, not even stopping at the borders of the Low Countries. It may be that they made up 75 per cent of the alien population of London and Westminster in 1567, but their roots were as diverse as the different English settlements they went to. Early modern migration was not so much a process between countries or nations, but between regions, cities and villages.

Notes

1 Yungblut, *Strangers Settled Here Amongst Us*, p. 14.
2 Page (ed.), *Letters of Denization and Acts of Naturalization*, pp. lii–liii.
3 Hoenselaars, *Images of Englishmen and Foreigners*, pp. 40–1.
4 Of course there is abundant literature available on the subject in Dutch. However, the best modern introduction to the history of the Low Countries during the early modern period is Israel, *Dutch Republic*. Other important recent contributions in English: Blockmans and Prevenier, *Burgundian Netherlands*; Koenigsberger, *Monarchies, States Generals and Parliaments*; De Schepper, "The Burgundian-Habsburg Netherlands" and Darby (ed.), *Origins and Development of the Dutch Revolt*.
5 For the sake of clarity, the special status of some smaller territories within the Low Countries will not be discussed here: Mechelen, for example, formed an independent territory within Brabant.
6 The County of Lingen followed in 1548, but generally this is not considered to be a part of the Low Countries.
7 Bolton (ed.), *Alien Communities of London*, pp. 28–30.
8 Page (ed.), *Letters of Denization*. In an earlier contribution to the history of the migration from the Low Countries, I made an error in the table concerning the denizations and naturalizations. The period 1541–1550 had 398 applicants, not 98. The total of 642 remains the same. Fagel, "Netherlandish Presence", p. 9.
9 See also Yungblut, *Strangers Settled Here Amongst Us*, p. 18.
10 Page (ed.), *Letters of Denization*, pp. xxiv–xxv.
11 Yungblut, *Strangers Settled Here Amongst Us*, pp. 18–19. She counted 4,534 aliens in the 1562–3 survey in London, the Liberties, Southwark and Westminster, of which 2,860 had come to England before the reign of Elizabeth I. The 40 per cent of immigrants arriving after 1558 more often stated religion as their motive for emigration.
12 1560 rather than 1558 is used as a dividing line because this research is part of a project studying the emigration of inhabitants from the Low Countries throughout Europe between 1480 and 1560.
13 Fagel, "Netherlandish Presence", pp. 9–12.
14 1562–63: 8; 1575–76: 50; 1580–81: 19; 1592–93: 2; 1596–97: 4, and 1600–01: 3.
15 As one of them is called Cornelius Johnson, it does not seem probable that the reference is to the principality of Orange within the French Kingdom.
16 Fagel, "Netherlandish Presence", pp. 11–12.
17 Pettegree, *Foreign Protestant Communities*, pp. 77–9 and Boersma, *Vluchtig Voorbeeld*, pp. 39–45. In a London survey of 1568, of 9,302 some 77 per cent was Dutch: Yungblut, *Strangers Settled Here Amongst Us*, pp. 19–21. In 1590 estimates for London are some 10,000 refugees from the Low Countries; for England in total some 20,000 reformed refugees including the French: Grell, *Calvinist Exiles*, p. 5. The 1593 returns for the metropolis (London and adjacent areas) give 776 names from the Low Countries, 352 from France, and 107 from Germany: Scouloudi, "Stranger Community", p. 44. For revised estimates see Chapter 1, pp. 16–18, above.
18 Boersma, *Vluchtig Voorbeeld*, pp. 55–9.
19 Boersma, *Vluchtig Voorbeeld*, pp. 64–5, 70–1 and 74. The author found the geographical origin of 65 of the 93 Elders and Deacons of the Dutch Church, of 87 of the 96 of the French Church, and of all 16 of the Italian Church.

20 Moens (ed.), *Marriage, Baptismal, and Burial Registers*, pp. 88–147.

21 Scouloudi, *Returns of Strangers*.

22 Boersma and Jelsma, *Unity and Multiformity*, pp. 209–59.

23 Moens (ed.), *Marriage, Baptismal, and Burial Registers*, pp. 88–147.

24 With 8: Aalst; Belle; Heinsberg; Izegem; Louvain; Tielt. With 7: Cassel; Deventer; Eeklo; Hasselt; Solingen; Valkenburg. With 6: Aix-la-Chapelle; Arnhem; Bremen; Horne/Hoorne; Middelburg; Naarden; Oldenzaal; Poperinge; Sittard; Sint-Truiden (Saint-Trond). With 5: Armentières; Delft; The Hague; Steenvoorde; Zwolle. With 4: Arendonk; Colchester; Deinze; Düsseldorf; Geel; Geraardsbergen (Grammont); Haarlem; Hazebrouck; Neuss; Valenciennes; Wesel. With 3: Ardooie; Comines; Diest; Dordrecht; Dover; Dunkirk; Eindhoven; Emmerich; Gorcum; Gouda; Harlingen; Leiden; Lier; Méteren; Oostende; Pittem; Tournai, and Vlissingen. Horne is both used for Hoorn in Holland as for Horn in Limburg; the name Middelburg is used both for a city in Zeeland and for a smaller village in Flanders.

25 Scouloudi, *Returns of Strangers*, pp. 84–5 and 92–3. Cleves 34, Jülich 18, Cologne 12, Emden 7, Wesel 6. Scouloudi provides the complete list of cities and villages with fewer persons involved.

26 See Chapter 1 above, p. 11.

27 Goose, "The 'Dutch' in Colchester", p. 263. 1571: 177 Dutch; 1573: 431; 1586: 1,297. Nieuwkerke and Ipres seem to have been important places of origin for the immigrants in Colchester.

28 Morant, "Settlement of Protestant Refugees in Maidstone", p. 212. In 1585 there were 115 adults aliens, but for only some individuals do we know their place of origin. Nevele, Deinze and Ghent all point to the County of Flanders.

29 Hardy, "Foreign Refugees at Rye", p. 583. Most of the immigrants came from Dieppe. Some Walloons, Flemings and Hollanders appear in the sources. The only one mentioned with his place of origin is from Wateringen in the County of Holland.

30 As early as 1549, some 230 Walloon weavers came to Glastonbury to revive the economy of the area. This project of Protector Somerset was also an experiment to see how planted communities worked. After the death of Edward VI, they went to Frankfurt: Yungblut, *Strangers Settled Here Amongst Us*, p. 100; Cowell, "French-Walloon Church at Glastonbury".

31 Davies, *Dutch Influences*, p. 5; Bense, *Anglo-Dutch Relations*, pp. 101–3. See also Chapter 1 above, pp. 17–28.

32 Spicer, *French-Speaking Reformed Community*, p. 159.

33 Eßer, *Niederländische Exulanten*.

34 Lucassen and De Vries, "Leiden als Middelpunt".

35 Backhouse, *Flemish and Walloon Communities* (1995)

36 Backhouse, *Flemish and Walloon Communities* (1995), pp. 17–18.

37 Backhouse, Flemish and Walloon Communities (1991), I, pp. 27–8 and 46–8. The most important places in the "Westkwartier" and the "Pays de l'Alleu" for the Dutch-speaking community were: Belle (94), Nieuwkerke (63), Hondschoote (46), Ipres (29), Messines (25), Poperinge (21). Of the small French-speaking community we only have 39 places of origin, again predominately from the "Westkwartier", though Tournai was the most important individual city (9).

38 Backhouse, *Flemish and Walloon Communities* (1995), pp. 19–20.

39 Backhouse, *Flemish and Walloon Communities* (1995), pp. 29–32.

40 For discussion of calculations of the size of the Sandwich community see Chapter 1 above, pp. 20–21.

41 Esser, *Niederländische Exulanten*, pp. 44–5, 49. It could be possible that the number was as high as 6,000 between 1571 and 1582, but thousands of immigrants were killed by plague.

42 Spicer, *French-Speaking Reformed Community*, pp. 2–15, 21, 70.
43 Magen, *Die Wallonengemeinde*, pp. 43–6. Another calculation for the period between 1590 and 1627 gives some 1,000 strangers from 240 different places as brides and grooms in Canterbury: Cross, *History of the Walloon and Huguenot Church*, pp. 24–5. The complete lists can be found in Hovenden, *Registers*.

3

Natural-Born versus Stranger-Born Subjects: Aliens and their Status in Elizabethan London

Lien Luu

"The Laws of England hold Strangers born, in great Suspicion of their fidelitie,
toward the State, and therefore do make provision accordingly."[1]

The refugees arriving in London from the southern Netherlands during the 1560s found many contradictions in the reception they received. While embraced on the one hand by sympathizers and co-religionists as Protestant "brethren" fleeing tyranny, the refugees found that this "brotherly" reception was unmatched by the law. In the eyes of the common law the refugees were treated merely as *strangers* of the realm. As such, they were inferior to native Englishmen and had few legal rights. They had not moved to a freer world, but had merely swapped one kind of discrimination for another. The refugees complained of the humiliation they felt, being treated like any other foreigners in the kingdom, and how they had expected better treatment because of their faith. In a letter to the Queen from the "community of strangers in London" on 29 January 1560, they expressed their surprise at their treatment as well as the futility of having religious liberty without economic freedom:

> Seeing the devotion of your Majesty, [the refugees] cannot believe that you wish those, who, for the sake of the true religion and relying on your piety, have come hither, or may come afterwards, as to a free and safe place, to be precluded from the very first from your dominion. . . . The grant of this temple [Austin Friars for worship by the Dutch] would benefit the strangers little if they had no liberty to reside and to exercise their trade here. Therefore, that no strangers should be forced to return to their native country and endanger their lives, the supplicants pray you to allow all those who . . . join their community and submit to ecclesiastical discipline, to live here freely without any loss of their property and without molestation of those who let houses to them, and to exercise their trades within doors till they have obtained municipal liberty from your Majesty.[2]

This letter alluded to the difference between expectations and legal reality. Though they perceived themselves as "refugees of conscience", they occupied no special place in Elizabethan society. The status of a refugee was an ethical rather than a legal notion.[3] The modern United Nations Geneva Convention for refugees simply did not exist. The reception accorded to them depended very much on the benevolent attitudes of the Queen and her government. In some ways the arrangements surrounding the settlement of refugees in London were highly unsatisfactory. Unlike settlements in provincial towns, there was no legal document clearly defining the economic privileges of refugees in London. The Royal Charter granted to the stranger community in London by Edward VI in 1550 dealt mainly with religious privileges and there was no clause stipulating the economic freedom which they might expect to enjoy. In contrast to the involvement of civic authorities in the arrangements in provincial settlements, the governors of London did not appear to have been involved in discussions of how the arrival of a large wave of Protestant exiles might be fitted into the life of the metropolis. The absence of a royal charter rendered the refugees highly vulnerable in subsequent decades by exposing them to molestation by guilds, and made them dependent on the benevolence of the Queen and her government for protection.

Examination of the legal status of immigrants in Elizabethan England involves two current historical debates. The first concerns the policies of the Elizabethan government. Historians have often claimed that it welcomed the Protestant refugees, and some have gone as far as to suggest that it had also encouraged the immigration of these to bring in valuable skills to develop the backward English economy.[4] If this was indeed true, it raises the fundamental question of why mass naturalization, a policy which was introduced in 1709 to integrate the French Protestants (Huguenots), was not carried out to turn refugees into subjects. Even if governmental policy did not go as far as this, there is also the question as to why efforts were not made to reverse many discriminatory statutes against overseas immigrants. In any case neither option was chosen, and during Elizabeth's reign the legal rights of a stranger were reduced.

The second historical debate concerns the assimilation of aliens. Based on a study of wills, Pettegree has shown how the alien community in London had become settled and prosperous by the 1590s, 30 years after the first mass influx, with extensive contacts with members of the host society.[5] Yet, as the legal position of aliens worsened, there is evidence of increasing restlessness and unease within the alien community, reflected in movements to the Dutch Republic and return emigration to the country of origin.[6] During the 1570s and 1580s discrimination against aliens was extended to the second generation. Though English by birth the second generation struggled to escape the fate assigned to their parents. This chapter examines the legal status of aliens with particular reference to London, the decline of their rights during Elizabeth's reign, the economic and social ramifications of this, and the possible reasons for the absence of a more positive policy.

Nationality Laws: Subjects versus Aliens

Overseas immigrants in England in the sixteenth century faced two types of legal barriers: the common law, and civic laws and customs. Bacon identified four types of persons known to the law of England: alien enemy; alien friend; denizen; and natural-born subject.[7] Allegiance was the key criterion to distinguish a subject from an alien.[8] Those born in England or in countries under the allegiance of the dominion of the king were subjects; those born in territory outside the dominion of the king were aliens.[9] Citizenship, then, had a territorial dimension, as the place of birth and political allegiance were essential in determining status. The concept of a genuine English subject, as opposed to a stranger, may have evolved under the pressure of the movement of population during the Hundred Years War.[10]

Aliens fell into two categories, and these determined their rights and privileges. Alien enemies were those who owed allegiance to a sovereign hostile to the king of England. The Crown possessed absolute rights and powers over alien enemies, including the power to expel. Alien friends had most of the rights of subjects, and were protected by the law, owed temporary allegiance to the king, and were obliged to take the oaths required of subjects.[11] In general, aliens faced several disabilities: inability to own, inherit, or bequeath real property; inability to bring legal action related to real property; being subject to customs duties imposed by king and parliament and by corporate cities; lack of political rights; inability to vote or hold office, or own an English ship.[12] Most economic restrictions placed on aliens were passed during Richard II's reign but were re-introduced in the early sixteenth century. During Henry VIII's reign three statutes were passed – in 1523, 1529, and 1540 – to regulate their activities. With regard to property rights, aliens were prohibited from leasing property, opening or keeping a shop, and purchasing property. With regard to their tax status, they were required to pay double rates of taxation. They were not allowed to engage in retail or "foreign bought and sold", designed to prevent non-freemen from conducting business among themselves.[13] The statutes also specified the rights of aliens' children. They were prohibited from serving an apprenticeship to learn a craft skill. The second generation, too, were effectively precluded from obtaining citizenship.

Alien artisans possessed limited employment rights. They could work and employ up to two alien journeymen but were forbidden from taking on alien apprentices and from working as householders, as they could not have their own shop. Aliens, particularly those born under the allegiance of a political enemy, also faced the possible expulsion in times of war and political conflict. In February 1554, for example, Mary gave all seditious and non-denizen aliens 20 days to depart the realm. In early 1558, when Francophobia spread as a result of war between England and France, a proclamation was issued authorising any citizen to arrest non-denizen Frenchmen.[14]

An alien could become an adopted subject, a denizen, with the acquisition of a letter patent. The power to create such subjects lay with the Crown, the rights they conferred depending upon the wording of the particular letter. The status of denizen cannot therefore be precisely defined. A denizen, it appears, had some but not all of the privileges of a British subject. The status of denizen took effect as from the date of the grant, and not earlier.[15] However, the letter was quite easy to obtain as no conditions needed to be satisfied for the grant of denization. But the letter of denization had a fundamental drawback: denizens could not inherit real property, and the transmission of this status of being a denizen to his descendants depended on the terms of the grant, which might be in the form of a limitation such as to "x and his heirs", to "x and his heirs male", or in some similar form.[16] According to Cottret, the stranger was envisaged essentially in relation to the *law of property* rather than *employment* – there was an obsession with transfer through inheritance.[17]

Aliens could also become naturalized subjects by a special Act of Parliament "with the assent of the whole nation". The key distinction between denizen and a natural- ized subject related to inheritance rights: a naturalized subject could both inherit and pass on his property to his children. Under common law, the natural-born subject was the highest type of subject, next came the naturalized subject, after him the denizen, and the alien occupied the lowest rung.[18] Both the crown and parliament had the power to change the status of an alien, but this method was prohibitively expensive.

Besides the stranger's relationship to the sovereign, there was also his place within a town. Towns had extensive privileges bestowed by ancient charters. The key differ- entiation among townsmen was the *freedom* of the city. As John Evans has explained:

> The all-important dividing line among townsmen was between freemen and non- freemen. Freedom of the city involved both privileges and obligations set down in local ordinances and enforced in the Lord Mayor's Court. The effect of these ordinances was to provide the freemen, or citizenry, with a virtual monopoly over both political and economic affairs. Only freemen could hold civic office and only freemen could vote in municipal and parliamentary elections. Non-freemen and "foreigners" were prohibited from taking on apprentices.[19]

Commonly acquired by serving a seven-year apprenticeship, freedom could also be attained through patrimony (descent) or marriage, or redemption. Freemen of a given city were its citizens with full economic rights, the most important of which was the ability to engage in independent economic activity, such as the freedom to sell and buy goods between them, retail, and open a shop. Non-freemen were known as *foreigners*, a term used to describe a newcomer to the town, and possessed limited rights. As aliens were barred from serving apprenticeship, redemption was the common route to acquire the freedom of the city. However, this method often required "extraordinary means" or "talents", and meant that few could afford the privilege.

The Status of Aliens during Elizabeth's Reign

The most valued aspect of the letter of denization was its grant of permanent residency and protection from expulsion. The letter also gave aliens superior economic rights. Aliens who wished to further their life in London found it expedient to acquire such a letter, and until the 1560s the cost was still reasonable, between 6s 8d and £1 13s 4d, with many paying at the lower end of the scale.[20] However, only a minority of aliens acquired the letter of denization during Elizabeth's reign. The returns of aliens show that in 1568, 13 per cent were denizens, falling to 9 per cent in 1573, and 7 per cent by 1593. Yet the number of householders (those who kept shop) showed a steady increase: nearly 21 per cent were classified as householders in 1571, and 24 per cent in 1593. These figures suggest that many aliens were simply ignoring the various statutes regu- lating their economic activities in London. Aware of this, the City of London in 1571 ordered all free denizens and denizens to show their patent and "what authority they do occupy within the City". They were to pay two pence to the Beadle for "recording their Copy Patent and . . . for warning of them".[21]

There are several reasons why the number of denizens declined. First, the process was cumbersome. To obtain a letter of denization a stranger had to present a petition, which meant hiring a scrivener to write it, and if favourably received a patent would be granted. The length of time taken between the initial entry of the grant and the final registration of the patent varied between a few days and several months.[22] The rising cost of purchasing a letter of denization could also have been a key factor. By 1582 the fee had increased dramatically to approximately £2 12s 4d, an amount simply beyond the means of many aliens, especially recent arrivals.[23] The 1582 subsidy shows that of 1,840 aliens assessed for subsidy in that year, nearly 74 per cent paid just the basic poll tax of 8d, as they neither had goods worth £3 or more, nor land over the value of £1.[24]

Table 3.1   Denizens as a Percentage of Strangers in the City of London, Middlesex and Surrey, 1568–1593

	1568	1573	1593
Denizens (%)	13	9	7
Total Number of Strangers	6,704	7,143	7,113

Sources: *1568 & 1573* Kirk & Kirk, Part 2, p. 156; *1593* Ellesmere MS 2514.

The destitute condition of many aliens, partly due to their failure to transfer resources from abroad, reduced their ability to make appropriate investment. Pettegree found that more than 25 per cent of strangers in London mentioned goods and property abroad in their wills. Besides merchants who had no reason to dispose of lands and goods abroad because they divided their time between London and the continent, it is striking how many who fled as religious refugees did so as well. Many no doubt came to England without the intention of permanent settlement, and if they hoped to return the laborious effort of selling-up was pointless. Perhaps they also kept property abroad as a form of insurance, if a similar order of expulsion like that issued in Mary's reign was ever to re-occur.[25] But an inescapable reason was that some, departing in haste and fearful for their lives, simply did not have time to sell their property. In any case a short-notice property sale would not fetch the full market value.[26] The retention of property abroad and the ability to transfer wealth had two possible consequences. It may have prevented family members from joining them in England. Justinne Ploiart wrote from Tournai to her brother Guillaume le Myeulx, who was living in London in February 1570, explaining how she would love to leave but could not because of the difficulty of finding someone trustworthy to take care of his business, and that she was still waiting for her uncle to give her the money accrued from selling his goods.[27] In addition, material sacrifice and loss of financial resources may have prevented refugees from taking the necessary steps to improve their status and condition in London. Guillame Coppin, once a well-to-do merchant in Valenciennes, had to make drastic revisions to his will in 1572 because "by the trouble that passed in the lowe countries I lost a great deale of my goods which god had lent me." His wife, who previously had been left with 2,700 *livres tournoi*, now had to be satisfied with the remains of his goods. His son, who was to have had 1,400 *livres*, would now get 300, with another 400 "when liberty shall be in the low countries and that profit and sale of my goods which are at Valenciennes may be made."[28] Six years in exile in England, then, had not diminished Coppin's hopes of peace and eventual return to his homeland. If that was his intention, then investment to improve his life in London was dispensable.

For those who could afford it, the letter was not worth the trouble as its funda-mental benefit had disappeared with the passage of an Act of Common Council in 1574, forbidding London citizens to take as apprentice any person whose father was not the son of an Englishman, or born "within the Queens dominion". This meant that children of denizens could no longer serve apprenticeships, and hence one crucial difference between an alien and a denizen had been erased.[29] During the period 1558–1603 there were 1,962 patents granted, and of these 1,669 were secured during the first 20 years of Elizabeth's reign; only 293 were obtained after 1578. During the latter part of the reign it appears that many strangers did not feel the patents were worth the trouble.[30]

In the face of the decreasing value of denizenship, many strangers sought to secure their future by acquiring the freedom of the city. Those who possessed both a letter of denization and the freedom of the City of London were known as *free denizens*. But this was neither cheap nor easy, requiring connections, money, or exceptional skills as the request for admission usually came from the crown or prominent govern-mental members. In 1581, probably at the instigation of Sir Francis Walsingham, nine alien brewers were granted freedom by redemption at a fee of £50 each.[31] In 1609 the king made a special plea on behalf of Robert Thiery that he be admitted into the freedom of the city because of his extraordinary skills and inventions, being the first in England to weave material from the silk of silk worms nourished in England. In this instance it was agreed that he should be admitted to the Weavers' Company on payment of 6s 8d.[32]

From the 1570s the City of London became increasingly reluctant to grant freedom by redemption. Its social problems grew, precipitated partly by the enormous demo-graphic expansion, from 80,000 people in 1550 to 120,000 by the 1580s, before reaching 200,000 in 1600. At the same time, employment opportunities in London, in the cloth trades at least, may have contracted. The same forces that engendered a large influx of refugees to the capital also served to disrupt English foreign trade, especially the embargoes in 1563–4 and 1568–73, as well as the sack of Antwerp in 1576. During 1560–72 an average of 92,600 cloths were exported annually from London, down by one-fifth from the average of 115,200 cloths in the 1550s.[33]

Those working in the cloth-related sectors were the first to feel the impact of this. From the mid-1560s impoverished householders began to complain about unemploy-ment, and called for an end to the export of unfinished cloths in order to provide additional employment in finishing and dressing. By the early 1570s complaints about unemployment in London were heard in other crafts. Petitioners attributed the problem to competition for work from foreigners and strangers, increasing use of apprentices rather than journeymen, and growing numbers of freemen following occu-pations not formally associated with their companies.[34] Faced with these problems, the City's governors became reluctant to comply with the frequent requests from "such honorable persons and good lords and friends" to grant freedom to aliens. Writing to the Earl of Warwick in November 1579, the Lord Mayor explained his predicament:

> It may be that your Lordship is informed that the matter of freedom is of no great impor-tance, howbeit the populousness of this city and specially of the poor and artificers and other is such, and the increase of strangers of that sort so great, and our granting of such freedoms has been so frequent by mean of our readiness to satisfy the requests . . . that our citizens be in very hard case and do much grudge against us.[35]

In response to the Earl's several letters for the admission of John Leonard and Henry Rodes, both strangers, the Lord Mayor felt the need to state his reasons even more bluntly in a separate letter:

> Our number of poor artificers and citizens is so great, and eaten out of their trades and livings by strangers and foreigners, that they doe greatly grudge against us for overready granting of freedoms whereby we are constrained in duty and conscience and for avoiding of great misliking of our governance to stay such grants.[36]

He also explained other reasons for his refusal, including native impoverishment, fears of the burden of poor relief, economic malaise of the country, and the right of natives to find work:

> Her majesty subjects . . . are eaten out by strangers artificers, to their undoing and our burden and the unnatural hardness to our own country, whereas none of her majesties subjects can be suffered (be they never so excellent in any art) in their country to live by their work.

The request by Lady Anne Wraye for the admission of her servant, Thomas Hudd, was also refused. However, the Lord Mayor granted Wilson's request to give Henry Rodes the freedom of the city.[37] In total, only a small percentage of aliens received the freedom: in 1593 70 aliens or one per cent were recorded as free denizens.[38]

The letter of naturalization from parliament offered the most security and rights. Naturalized aliens were able to trade freely, purchase, bequeath and inherit property, and enjoy the same tax status as natural-born subjects. Yet few aliens ever acquired this status as it was simply too expensive. In 1551 it was reported that the letter of naturalization cost only £4, yet other estimates put it at between £65 and £100.[39] During Elizabeth's reign only 12 acts were granted, compared with 71 between 1603 and 1640.[40] This might suggest that the pressure for obtaining a letter of naturalization was even greater in the reigns of James I and Charles I.

Issues of Contention

Despite the passing of various laws and regulations there were repeated offences committed by some aliens over leasing of property, the right to open a shop and to retail, apprenticeship of their children, and the right to trade. These repeated offences suggest that these issues were of some significance to aliens, and that the laws were not rigidly enforced.

The question of whether aliens were allowed to take leases was debated in 1587. It appears that an Italian named Frederico had leased a house in Bear Lane in London, but his right to lease was contested by a man, presumably English, called Jones. The case was brought before the court and the judges had to decide whether a stranger, not a denizen, might take a lease for a number of years. They ruled that a stranger could not, but the ultimate decision lay with the Queen. The Italians therefore went to her to plead their case. While this was being resolved, Francis Walsingham wrote to the Lord Treasurer on 20 May 1587 to instruct him not to allow anyone else to lease the property "until her majesty's pleasure may be knowen".[41] It was not until 1844, and more particularly 1870 (Naturalisation Act, 33 & 34 Vic. c14) that aliens could acquire real property.[42]

During Elizabeth's reign, there were repeated offences concerning opening shops. Aliens were allowed to keep shops, but only "closed" shops, and thus were prohibited from openly displaying their wares. The aim was to prevent passers-by from being tempted to go and place orders, and to alleviate the fear that competition posed by strangers would reduce the market for English goods. The implication of this restriction was that aliens could not sell their goods directly to customers, but were only able to sell their goods by wholesale to English retailers. Without the ability to charge the price for their labour, their right to make a profit was effectively removed.

In 1556 the Chamberlain of the City was instructed to shut discreetly the shop windows opening on the streets and lanes of all strangers born and foreigners, placing lattices before them. In 1566 the Chamberlain was again ordered in "quiet manner" to cause all foreigners and strangers born to shut their shop windows.[43] The trouble persisted, and in 1568 an alien was ordered to "shut up" a cordwainer's shop in Cornhill "in the heart of the city".[44] The persistence of this offence can be explained by the need for natural light to work. This was finally recognized and in 1587 aliens were ordered to have their shop windows and doors "made in such sort as people passing by may not see them at work, and so as their wares and merchandizes remaining and being within the same their shops or places give no open show to any people passing by", and at the same time "leave convenient light for them to work."[45]

This restriction on the freedom to retail had three consequences. First, it encouraged aliens to move to secret or cheaper areas to avoid paying high rent in prized locations. Such a move alarmed the goldsmiths in particular because due to the high intrinsic value of their raw materials it was felt necessary that their members worked in public areas to avoid dishonesty. Yet in March 1574 a Frenchman told the Goldsmiths Company that there were "diverse strangers goldsmiths working some within shoemakers, some within tailors, some within saddlers and others within others."[46] A search undertaken in January 1593 by the Company verified this claim, as a stranger was found working in a "garret in a linen draper's house in St Martins".[47] This raises the question of how many others were working under similar conditions. Second, the move to secret locations indirectly undermined guild regulation of the craft as it was difficult to conduct searches. The Weavers of London claimed that strangers and foreigners lived in "dwellings [which] are in chambers and odd corners, being divers families in one house, do and may live at far smaller expense, and work for lesser gains, and sell for less profit . . . And thereby have almost got all the work and employment of the said Trade of weaving."[48] They also refused to be searched because when the bailiffs and warden of the company came round, they "shut their doors against them".[49] Aliens were also accused of engaging in illegal retailing, and it was claimed that alien weavers and brokers living in the capital sold goods for others from Canterbury, Norwich, and elsewhere in England, and went "from shop to shop, in London and Westminster and other places, furnishing the mercers and haberdashers therewith, and often retailing such silk wares at the houses of the Nobility and Gentry".[50] Third, it was alleged that aliens found a way to circumvent this restriction by trading within the house of a freeman.[51] In other words, they sought to overcome their legal barrier to retail by finding a third party, a freeman, who had the economic freedom to engage in such an activity.

All strangers, including denizens and free denizens, paid taxation at double the rate of English persons, at 5s 4d in the pound on goods above the value of £3, and at 8s in the pound on the land above the value of £1. If the lands and goods fell below these values they had to pay a poll tax of 8d. It was the responsibility of the head of the household to ensure payment of the poll tax. Stranger-born children of stranger parents were subject to the poll tax but the age at which they were first liable varied. In the reign of Henry VIII it was 12 years, during the early years of Elizabeth it became 14 years but after the mid-1570s it was 7 years. English-born children of stranger parents were expected to pay the same rate as English persons.[52] In 1582 a total of £6,585 14s 8d was collected in the City of London, of which £5,734 6s 4d was paid by English persons and City Companies, and £851 8s 4d (13 per cent) paid by 1,840 strangers. Of these, 1,358 strangers had neither land nor goods above the specified values, and so paid the basic poll tax. Of the remaining 482 strangers, 470 paid between £1 and £9, 9 paid between £10 and £20, and only 3 paid above £20, a large sum for that period.[53] Among the highest tax payers were a money lender, Sir Horatio Pallavicino, who paid £35, an Antwerp merchant, Martin de la Falia, who paid £30, and a brewer, Roger James, taxed at £30.[54]

Controversial new acts were also passed during Elizabeth's reign to limit the rights of the children of aliens and denizens born in England. After 1574, as indicated above, children of alien-born parents could no longer be bound apprentice with English masters. In September 1582 Bryan Savell, a clothworker, was ordered to discharge Bryan Marrowe, the son of Peter Marrowe, stranger. As this "was done in ignorance", Bryan Savell was ordered only to pay a fine of 20s. William Tyrone faced a more severe penalty, 40s for taking on William Marrowe, also son of a stranger.[55] Christopher Barker, stationer, was fined even more severely. In addition to a fine of 20s he was ordered to print "at his charges" 200 copies of the Act "for the service of the City". The successful conviction of this case was the work of an informer, as in December the City paid 10s to Gilberte Lylle, merchant tailor, "being half of the sum of 20s received of Xpofer Barker".[56] In addition to fining freemen, the City also instructed Companies to set up a caveat in their halls to remind their members of this new rule.[57]

Free denizens strongly opposed the act and sought to "frustrate and [make it] void", arguing that it was "contrary to all humanitie and reason", and that their children were deprived of the "freedom liberty and benefit of their native country . . . naturally due unto them".[58] Their petition was not successful, as in 1583 John Vere, a Frenchman "being a free denizen", had to request John Hertford to petition the Lord Mayor on behalf of his son, already serving three years of his nine-year apprenticeship with John Yeoman, a merchant tailor, to continue his apprenticeship and receive his freedom at the end of his service.[59]

Even more controversial was the issue of whether children born in England of alien-born parents should be regarded as English. Two reasons against this were put forward. First, it was reported in 1576 that "sundry persons being strangers . . . have of purpose brought over their wives from the parts beyond the seas, to be delivered with child within this city, and in other places within this realm of England, and thereof do take special testimonials thereby to win to those children the liberty that other Englishmen do enjoy."[60] Second, it was argued that a child of alien parents should not be regarded as English because "he cannot be a perfect loyal subject for that he hath no genealogie of native english but all foreign and strangers unto whom (as to his

kindred) nature bindeth him".[61] It was therefore considered unfair to grant such privileges to those children of strangers who "retain an inclination and kind affection to
the countries of their parents".[62] After much debate it was finally decided in 1604 to
"place the children, born within this Realm, of foreign parents as aliens made
denizens".[63]

From the 1570s a vigorous campaign was launched against alien merchants, motivated by resentment of their domination of the lucrative overseas trade and from the
perception of the extensive privileges they enjoyed. English overseas trade was handled
largely by foreign merchants and shipping at the start of the sixteenth century. The
Hansards, the Italians, and a small number of other foreign merchants between them
took more than half of London's exports of cloth and provided more than half of its
imports.[64] The origins of alien merchants in London completely changed with the
influx from the Netherlands, and by the 1570s those from the southern Netherlands
dominated rather than the Germans and Italians.[65] In 1571, there were some 184 aliens
involved in mercantile activities, forming 10.1 per cent of aliens in the capital. The most
significant group of merchants were 36 from Flanders, 19 from Brabant, and 6 from
Valenciennes. Only nine were recorded from Italy (four were stated to come from
"Italy" and five from Venice), and two from Cologne. Despite these numbers, it is
uncertain how many were able to conduct their business, especially as they were
prohibited from trading with the Low Countries after Christmas 1571.[66] Apparently
many were able to travel back and forth to the continent on business, as in 1583 the
French consistory instructed the elders and deacons, who in general were wealthy
merchants and financiers, not to leave the country for business purposes without first
informing their colleagues.[67]

During Elizabeth's reign some English merchants and retailers, supported by the
government who needed them for financial services, sought to reduce the aliens' domination and privileges. In September 1571, the "Citizens of London" sent a petition to
the Queen outlining seven key grievances, six of which were directed at alien
merchants. The first complaint concerned the purchase of property. Contrary to the
requirement that alien merchants had to dwell with their freehosts, Londoners
complained that aliens bought the "fairest houses" in the capital, "divide them up and
take in lodgers". The second grievance was that aliens hold goods and "sell them at
their pleasure" to force up prices, rather than fulfilling the statutory requirement of
selling them within six weeks of landing. The next two grievances centred on the question of retail and "foreign buying". Alien merchants were forbidden to buy and sell
merchandize among themselves but, according to the petitioners, they "do freely
amongst themselves and colourably deal by others procuring some poor freeman to
bear the name", suggesting dishonest business practices. Aliens were also forbidden to
engage in retail but, contrary to this, they were "retailers . . . keep shops inward, and
private chambers, and therein sell by whole sale and retail, send to every mans house,
serve chapmen, send to fairs, and utter their commodities many other ways." The
transport of bullion overseas also annoyed native Londoners. Although "they have
half the trade in import [yet] they employ not a twentieth part thereof, but transport
the money [overseas]." The sixth complaint concerned the separateness of the aliens –
"though they be denized or born here amongst us, yet they keep themselves severed
from us in church, in government, in trade, in language and marriage." The seventh
complaint was directed at artisans. English law stipulated that "no stranger shall use

by handicraft within the city [yet] the strangers use all the several crafts and occupations that any man of this kingdom doth use and theis handicraftsmen serve all things to their own nation wholly". Very few, if any, of them had served the seven-year apprenticeship.[68] Each point is accompanied by a reminder of a number of restrictive laws, dating from the fourteenth century onwards, which had quite clearly been flouted. In 1572 a Bill was discussed concerning the possibility of prohibiting aliens and denizens from retailing goods imported from overseas.[69] The underlying aims were to uphold the privileges of freemen and to reduce competition to native merchants, but also probably to prevent aliens from amassing great fortunes from selling imported goods in London.[70]

To prevent further violations of the laws by merchants, freemen wanted to revive an ancient law of hostage, requiring every alien merchant to reside with an English host, who had to keep an eye on his guest. Five years later, in 1576, an office of "hostager and host" of all foreign merchants in the kingdom was given to William Tipper, a freeman of the City and a grocer by trade, for 21 years. Italian and Hanseatic merchants were exempted. The measure was criticized: Sir Thomas Smith, the great Elizabethan councillor, declared it contrary to the "Magna Carta Angliae" and to humanity; Flemish towns, in particular Antwerp, expressed their worst fears.[71] The regulation did not, however, prove very successful or efficient, and was soon abandoned. In 1582 it was calculated that the Queen would profit some £12,000 in customs by allowing strangers to make cloths "after the manner of the Low Countries".[72] Perhaps in response to this, the Privy Council in May 1587 proposed to grant equal trading rights and liberties to foreigners, strangers, and freemen in the cloth market in London, a proposal rejected by the Lord Mayor. With the recent harassment of strangers in London in 1581 and 1586, the Lord Mayor sent a warning about the "great hazard and disturbance of the common peace and state of this City." He continued:

It is not unknowen to your Honorable what griefs have been conceived and libeled of late against the strangers inhabiting among us . . . The cause whereof is the diminishing and deriving way of commodities which otherwise would grow wholly to the freemen of the City and further how these mutinous intents of Apprentices and other have been whetted and set forward by certain other persons aptly disposed and qualified for spoil and sedition. Now this further liberty granted to Strangers what effect it may work in the minds of these stirring and discontented persons we leave to your Honorable to be considered of . . .[73]

The second means to undermine the domination of aliens was the insistence that they serve a seven-year apprenticeship before allowing to trade. In 1572, native merchants and retailers proposed an Act to prevent strangers who had not served a seven-year apprenticeship from retailing foreign goods in England.[74] This Bill was read twice in June 1572 but was not passed. In 1592, it was again debated in the House of Commons, and members discussed more generally whether a more liberal policy towards aliens should be adopted. Sir John Wolley advocated a liberal policy, which had benefited London as well as Venice and Antwerp, but Sir Walter Raleigh raised strong objections, insisting that the Dutch were self-seeking rather than worthy objects of charity.[75] The Bill was ratified and an Act for the maintenance of English artificers and handicraftsmen was passed, allowing only those, including merchants and retailers, who had completed a seven-year apprenticeship to practise their trade in London; the House of Lords, however, threw the Bill out.[76] It appears that this campaign against alien merchants was not successful, as in May 1593 a survey still enumerated some 126 alien merchants in the capital, forming 11.7 per cent of the alien community, many of whom exported woollen goods made in England.[77]

The Star Chamber Case of 1618–19, when 160 alien merchants were accused of transporting bullion abroad and fined £140,000, seriously damaged their position in London and led to their drastic reduction.[78] In 1621 it was reported that there were some 183 alien merchants in London,[79] yet by 1635 the number had declined to only 94 persons or 2.6 per cent of the total of 3,622 aliens in the capital. Though they were still the third largest occupational group, they were also greatly outnumbered by alien workers involved in cloth-making (713 persons or 20 per cent) and clothes-making (129 persons or 3.6 per cent).[80]

Consequences

Increased infringement of guilds' regulations appears to have led to enhanced guild prosecution, resulting in the aliens' greater need for protection of their communities. This greater dependence can be measured by rising alien church membership. In 1568 the proportion attending English Churches was as high as Dutch and French Church attendance, and there were practical reasons why people went to the English Church in their parish: it was nearby, and the differences between the Calvinist and the Anglican Church may not have seemed so great to them.[81]

Table 3.2   Church Attendance in London, 1568–1593

Church	1568		1571		1593	
	No.	%	No.	%	No.	%
English Church	1,815	27.0	939	20.3	549	14.0
Dutch Church	1,910	28.5	1,450	31.3	1,376	35.0
French Church	1,810	27.0	1,284	27.7	1,344	34.0
Italian	161	2.4	92	1.9	29	0.7
No Church	1,008	15.0	866	18.7	131	3.3
Denizens	–	–	–	–	519	13.0
Total	6,704	100	4,631	100	3,948	100

Sources: Kirk & Kirk, Part 1, p. 439, Part 2, p. 139; Scouloudi, *Returns of Aliens*, p. 90.

By 1593, however, the proportion of aliens attending English Churches had halved, standing at 14 per cent compared to 34–35 per cent attending the Dutch and French Churches. One reason for this change lies undoubtedly in the changing profile of the alien community, containing great numbers of refugees who came for religious reasons. But there are other compelling reasons why membership of a stranger church was highly valued and preferred. Stranger Churches offered the means to worship in their native language and gave them a measure of social identity and representation. They were also a meeting place for strangers uprooted from their homelands needing social and emotional support from fellow countrymen, and a place of information exchange whereby strangers could be kept informed of developments back home. Even more important was the economic benefits provided by the Stranger Churches: they were sources of alms and relief, and their ministers were representatives of the alien communities and mediators between them and the authorities and the host population. They were valuable spokesmen, often petitioning the Queen and the Privy Council on behalf of their members for protection against informers and for securing privileges.[82]

Fear of guild prosecution had an indirect positive effect, by encouraging aliens to move into new trades to circumvent guild control. This is demonstrated in the marked rise in the number of aliens working in the luxury trades, climbing from 14 per cent of all alien households in 1571 to 25.5 per cent in 1593.[83] Expressed as a proportion of artisans this concentration was even more conspicuous: 24 per cent of all alien artisans in 1571 plied a craft in the luxury sector, compared with 37 per cent in 1593. Parallel to this was the decline of aliens in certain occupations, and an overall decline in the total number of trades they practised, which fell from 190 to 136 between 1571 and 1593.[84] The decline of aliens working in traditional trades such as tailoring, botchering (mending old clothes), shoemaking, and shoe repairing was also marked, falling from 23 per cent in 1571 to 15 per cent by 1593. Harassment and prosecution by the two companies involved – the Merchant Tailors and the Cordwainers – was partly responsible.[85] Alien shoemakers were constantly harassed by native craftsmen and the Company of Cordwainers because shoemaking, as one informer claimed, was "well exercised within this Realm, and wherein [there was] no need of any Aliens . . . ".[86] Alien tailors faced even greater harassment. They were first prohibited from working in 1598, and then in 1602 the Merchant Tailors Company, realising the ineffectiveness of the previous measure, sought to solve the alien problem by presenting a bill in Parliament for the expulsion of foreigners.[87] The Bill was, however, rejected as "unreasonable".

Fear of prosecution by guilds affected aliens' residential patterns. In sixteenth-century London there were more than 100 guilds with extensive powers controlling and regulating manufacturing in the capital.[88] Some, such as the Goldsmiths, had clear rules and policies for admitting foreigners and aliens; others, like the Merchant Tailors, did not. To avoid their control, many aliens settled in privileged areas within the city walls and surrounding areas known as the "liberties" or "exempt places", which lay outside guild control. Many of these areas were situated in the surroundings of monasteries, nunneries and other religious houses, and before the Reformation were controlled by ecclesiastical authorities rather than by the city or the Companies. Between 1536 and 1545, 23 religious houses in London were dissolved. Some were converted to aristocratic residences, others provided accommodation for large-scale governmental or industrial enterprises, such as workshops in the former Minoresses' precinct.[89] Some liberties were situated within the walls, such as Blackfriars in the south-west corner of the city and St Martin le Grand just north of St Paul's Cathedral, but most lay outside the walls, including Whitefriars, Charterhouse and Clerkenwell, and St Katherine's next to the Tower.[90] Besides offering accommodation in central, prized districts of the city, these liberties and exempted places also provided extensive immunities, making them the favourite resort for both non-freemen and religious dissidents. In 1580, presumably in a dispute with the city and companies, the residents of "White and Black Friars" reiterated their rights and immunities as follows. First, they claimed that the mayor and his officers had no power to make arrests there; second, guilds had no freedom to conduct searches; third, craftsmen and artificers (even though they were not freemen of the city) were free to exercise their trades and mysteries; and fourth, inhabitants were exempt from taxation, civic duties such as conducting watches of the city, serving on juries, and holding offices. In other words, the inhabitants claimed exemption from all the city's laws and regulations.[91]

The alien population in exempted places rose. Blackfriars saw its alien population grow from 230 to 508 between 1568 and 1593.[92] In St Martin le Grand, where strangers made up half the population in 1550, the number rose from 269 to 286 over the same period.[93] The possibility of working freely in the exempted places precluded the need to acquire a letter of denization, and this may explain why the number of denizens fell.[94] There was a close link between non-denizen status and settlement in exempted places. A survey of the alien population in exempted places in 1583 shows that of the 1,604 aliens settled there, only 316 were denizens (19.7 per cent): non-denizens, in other words, made up 80 per cent of the population.[95]

With the massive influx of aliens and provincial immigrants in the later sixteenth century many London guilds struggled to deal with the increasing flow of unfree labour. However, by the end of the sixteenth century their control over entry to London's crafts and industries had been seriously undermined by the rapid extension of the built-up area around the square mile of the old City, and by the growth of suburban production. By the early seventeenth century, guilds could no longer curb the retail sale of goods by foreigners, or restrict the practice of handicrafts to those who had secured an apprenticeship and were free of a Company.[96]

The lack of economic rights also made aliens unwilling to share their skills for fear of loss of livelihood. Craftsmen in London who had served a seven-year apprenticeship were permitted to practise any trade. This generated fears among aliens that once native citizens had learnt the skills taught by them, they could forbid non-denizen aliens from practising these to reduce competition. These fears were clearly stated in a petition by strangers to Parliament in 1571:

> Those freemen that have been an apprentice by the space of seven years might after the attaining of their freedom, use any other trade or occupation although he had not bin an apprentice to the same by the space of seven years wherein the said poor Denizens and strangers do fear (that obtaining the same) the freemen of the said two cities of London and Norwich would not only intrude in any of their several occupations, whether they have lawful skill there of yea or no But also forbid them to work or use the same themselves for not having bin seven years an apprentice in England thereunto. The like experience is before rehearsed although they well know, that a stranger by the Law may not be an Apprentice in England.[97]

In a period of high occupational mobility among native craftsmen, the retention of new or scarce skills by aliens was regarded as essential to preserve their livelihood and prevent the encroachment upon their crafts.

Since the fifteenth century complaints had been voiced regarding aliens' separatism and favouritism. In 1444 the English goldsmiths complained that alien goldsmiths in Southwark and Westminster took as their servants "aliens born and never of English nation". Between 1449 and 1469, 15 alien goldsmiths took 32 apprentices, nearly all of them boys with Dutch names.[98] The subsidy of 1483 also supports this conclusion. In that year, 445 alien servants (396 male and 49 female) were employed by nearly 400 householders in the City, and a further 285 aliens (269 male and 16 female servants) were employed by Englishmen. It appears that no English servants were employed by aliens. In 1571, alien masters employed 879 male alien servants, but no English servants.[99] This "clannishness" was only reversed from 1573 when, as a precondition for their settlement in London, aliens had to agree to "teach their arts to Englishmen and set no strangers on work but their own children".[100] By 1593 some success had been achieved, when a survey reported that 1,671 English servants and outworkers were employed by alien masters, against 686 alien journeymen, servants, and apprentices.[101]

Conclusion

Overseas immigrants in London, whether refugees or economic migrants, suffered much discrimination. The routes for their social advancement were limited: naturalization was most desirable but too expensive, while denization had limited value. Civic freedom and citizenship were also desirable but the common route of attainment through servitude was blocked because they were not entitled to serve apprenticeship with a freeman, while its purchase was beyond the reach of many. For the large number unable to transcend their status as aliens and strangers life was hard, especially in times of economic depression when law enforcement was tightened. The result was increased reliance upon the Dutch and French Churches to petition the Queen and her government to issue letters of protection.

Their experience appears to have diverged from their counterparts in provincial towns, from those who settled in the Dutch Republic, and from the French Protestants who came in the seventeenth century. In Norwich, for example, the economic "privileges" of aliens and their duties were legally defined, and the boundaries to what they could or could not do were clearly marked. Aliens could trade with other foreigners, sell their clothes at the cloth market from one o'clock to five every day, and were permitted to send cloths to London and other cities. Like their London counterparts, they could not open shops, have premises opening directly onto the street, or engage in retailing. Similarly, privileges were specified in Canterbury: an officer was appointed to affix his seal to woven fabrics, and trading in the foreigners' commodities was limited to one specific hall.[102] Aliens, in other words, were permitted some freedom within the general framework of prohibitions and restrictions. This discrimination stood in stark contrast to the Dutch Republic's policy of positive discrimination to entice technical know-how, capital, and entrepreneurship to harness economic growth. The guiding principle in England was that natural-born subjects should receive preferential treatment, even if aliens were frequently protected by government intervention on the grounds of their economic value to the commonwealth.[103]

The French Protestants (Huguenots) who arrived in the seventeenth century received a different reception because of changes in the economic and social climate. The factors that influenced the demand for general naturalization included the belief that England was under-populated, and that its population was insufficient to maintain or increase England's power. The second factor was religious liberty and religious freedom which, it was felt, would follow as a consequence of an influx of Protestants of varying sects. But the strongest element in the arguments for naturalization, according to Robbins, was the desire to bolster the Protestant interest. There were, however, vehement arguments against general naturalization. The London Corporation and companies were concerned about the possible decline and infringement of their privileges. Freemen who had served apprenticeships, and parents who had paid substantial sums to get their children into livery companies, were also unwilling to see others excused the fees. In addition to the detrimental effects on merchants and guildsmen it was also worried that poor industrious families might be affected by the competition posed by alien-born artisans. But the strongest argument against naturalization was probably simple prejudice. In a speech in 1694, one leading member of government had expressed the fear that "the English breed would be blotted out by increased immigration of other races."[104] The pro- naturalization lobby won the argument and in 1709 the General Naturalization Act was passed.[105]

No debate on naturalization of aliens ever took place in Elizabethan England, partly because it was widely believed that the country was overpopulated. London in particular was overcrowded, facing severe pressure on its resources as a result of massive immigration from other parts of the country and from overseas. Its governors, too, were fearful of a breakdown of law and order, and had not quite recovered from the experience of the Evil May Day in 1517 when, following attacks on aliens and the seeming inability of the city to restore order, royal troops had to be sent in.[106] In addition, it was widely felt that the granting of any privileges to aliens would directly disadvantage English citizens and that these, as natural-born subjects, should receive preferential treatment. The country as a whole was also confronted with too many other pressing priorities such as fears of foreign invasion, religious discord, unemployment, and vagrancy, to bestow excessive generosity upon outsiders. The granting of general naturalization would certainly have given out the wrong signal, perhaps encouraging even more newcomers from overseas, which could have had damaging ramifications, exacerbating political problems as well as upsetting the social fabric of society.

Notes

1   BL Harl 7021, ff. 223 "A Treatise concerning strangers received into a Commonwealth that tis very Prejudicall to a state cause of much Seditions The Laws against Strangers etc".
2   Hessels, Vol. 2, p. 124.
3   Cottret, *Huguenots in England*, p. 53.
4   See, for example, Ward, "Fictitious Shoemakers", p. 83; Grell, "New Home?", pp. 1–2.
5   Pettegree, "'Thirty Years On'".
6   See Chapter 10 below, pp. 196, 201–6.
7   Jones, *British Nationality Law*, p. 31.
8   Allegiance, according to Coke, was the "mutual bond and obligation between the king and his subjects, whereby the subjects are called his liege subjects, because they are bound to obey and serve him, and he is called their liege lord because he should maintain and defend them". Two elements then were involved in the concept of allegiance: protection by the king and obedience by the subject. See Jones, *British Nationality Law*, p. 32.
9   Statt, "Birthright of an Englishman", p. 62.
10 Cottret, *Huguenots in England*, p. 51.

11 Statt, "Birthright of an Englishman", p. 62.
12 Statt, "Birthright of an Englishman", pp. 62–3.
13 See Scouloudi, *Returns of Strangers*, p. 41.
14 Scouloudi, *Returns of Strangers*, p. 6; see also Chapter 6 below, p. 119.
15 Jones, *British Nationality Law*, p. 39.
16 Jones, *British Nationality Law*, p. 39.
17 Cottret, *Huguenots in England*, p.54.
18 Jones, *British Nationality Law*, p. 74.
19 Quoted in Cottret, *Huguenots in England*, pp. 54–5.
20 Scouloudi, *Returns of Strangers*, p. 4.
21 GL, MS 4069/1, f.2.
22 Scouloudi, *Returns of Strangers*, pp. 3–4.
23 BL, Egerton MS 2599, f. 234.
24 Scouloudi, *Returns of Strangers*, pp. 18–23.
25 Pettegree, *Foreign Protestant Communities*, pp. 229–31.
26 Pettegree, *Foreign Protestant Communities*, p. 232.
27 Verheyden, "Correspondance Inédite", Letter 27, pp. 146–8.
28 PRO, PCC 1573 (26 Peter), ff. 195v-196, also discussed in Pettegree, *Foreign Protestant Communities*, pp. 227–8.
29 Hessels, Vol. 3, Part 1, pp. 272–3.
30 Scouloudi, *Returns of Strangers*, p. 5.
31 GL, Brewers MS 5445/6 12 October 1581.
32 Scouloudi, *Returns of Strangers*, p. 11.
33 Rappaport, *Worlds Within Worlds*, p. 98.
34 Rappaport, *Worlds Within Worlds*, pp. 87–122.
35 CLRO, Remembrancia, Vol. 1 [69].
36 CLRO, Remembrancia, Vol. 1, [30–1], [63], [69].
37 CLRO, Remembrancia, Vol. 1 [53], [69].
38 Scouloudi, *Returns of Strangers*, p. 13.
39 *CSP Spanish* 1550–1552, Vol. 10, p. 265; Scouloudi, *Returns of Strangers*, p. 4.
40 Scouloudi, *Returns of Strangers*, p. 5.
41 BL, Harleian 6994/ 37 Secretary Walsingham to Lord Treasurer.
42 Cottret, *Huguenots in England*, p. 51.
43 Scouloudi, *Returns of Strangers*, p. 42.
44 CLRO, Rep 16/f. 385v 29 July 10 Reign.
45 CLRO, Rep 21, f. 430v May 1587.
46 Goldsmiths Company, Court Minutes Book L, Part 2, Vol. 10, f.187.
47 Goldsmiths Company, Court Minutes Book N-O, Part 1, Vol. 12, f.32.
48 GL, MS 4647, fos. 257–8.
49 GL, MS4647 ff. 144–49 (1635).
50 GL, Weavers' Company, Ordinance and Record Book 1577–1641, MS4647/ f. 355.
51 CLRO, Rep 54, ff.147ff, quoted in Scouloudi, *Returns of Strangers*, p. 41.
52 For a discussion of taxation see Scouloudi, *Returns of Strangers*, pp. 17–23.
53 Scouloudi, *Returns of Strangers*, p. 22.
54 Scouloudi, *Returns of Strangers*, p. 23.
55 CLRO, Letter Book Z, 1579–1584, f.241v (1582).
56 CLRO, Letter Book Z, f. 241v, 266, 268.
57 CLRO, Letter Book Z, f.241v.
58 PRO, SP 15/24/67 1580.
59 CLRO, Remembrancia, Vol. 1 [543].
60 CLRO, REP 19, f. 38v.

61 PRO, SP12/157/2.

62 Hessels, Vol. 3, Part 1, pp. 270–2; CLRO JOR 20, Part 1, ff. 176v-177v.

63 *JHC*, Vol. 1 1604 21/4.

64 Clay, *Economic Expansion and Social Change*, Vol. 2, pp. 105–6; Dietz, "Antwerp and London", pp. 192–3.

65 Bratchel, "Regulation and Group-Consciousness", p. 589; Esser, "From the Hansa to the Present", p. 18.

66 Littleton, "Geneva on Threadneedle Street", p. 231.

67 Littleton, "Social Interaction of Aliens", p. 150.

68 PRO, SP 12 /81/29.

69 PRO, SP 12/88/36.

70 BL, Lansdowne MS14/65.

71 Discussed in Cottret, *Huguenots in England*, p. 64.

72 It was assumed that 20,000 pieces of cloths were made annually and this would provide employment for 2,000 wool suppliers: PRO, SP 12/156/11.

73 PRO, SP12/201/31 (17 May 1587).

74 PRO, SP12/88/36.

75 This is discussed at more length in Chapter 6 below, pp. 120–1.

76 The Commons passed the restrictions by a vote of 162 to 82. Yungblut, *Strangers Settled Here Amongst Us*, p. 41.

77 BL Harl 1878/ 75 and 75v. The production of the New Draperies in England by refugees from the southern Netherlands seriously affected production there, as the English product successfully penetrated the Baltic and Mediterranean markets and also began to undersell Low Countries' cloth at home: DuPlessis, "One Theory, Two Draperies", p. 134.

78 See Chapter 10 below, p. 199; Grell, "French and Dutch Congregations", pp. 362–77.

79 PRO, SP 14/88/113 1621.

80 1593 data are based on an analysis the Dugdale return published in Scouloudi, *Returns of Strangers*, pp. 145–237, for 1635 see pp. 101–3. For numbers and significance of alien merchants also Chapter 7 below, pp. 144–7.

81 Evers, "Religionis et Libertatis Ergo", p. 11.

82 See Chapter 10 below, pp. 197–9.

83 These trades included silk-weaving, agate-cutting, diamond cutting, sugar refining, clock-making, and silk dyeing.

84 The number of trades in London trebled from 154 in the 1520s to 490 in the 1690s, reflecting increased specialisation: Keene, "Continuity and Development", p. 7.

85 In 1593, a bill was proposed to bar strangers from practising trades such as shoemaking: Scouloudi, *Returns of Strangers*, p. 65.

86 PRO, SP 46/24/159d, 160.

87 GL, MF 326, Court Minutes, Vol. 3, 1575–1601, f. 440v.

88 Beier, "Engine of Manufacture", p.157. There were 111 trades in London during reign of Henry V 1413–1422: Kahl, *Development of London Livery Companies*, p. 2.

89 Rappaport, *Worlds Within Worlds* pp. 34–5, Keene, "Growth, Modernisation and Control", p. 25.

90 Rappaport, *Worlds Within Worlds*, pp. 34–5.

91 PRO, SP 12/137/74 April 1580.

92 Kirk & Kirk, Part 3, p. 411; Part 2, p. 443.

93 Pettegree, *Foreign Protestant Communities*, p. 18.

94 See table 3.1 above, p. 61.

95 Kirk & Kirk, Part 2, 1583, pp. 376–7.

96 Kellett, "Breakdown of Gild and Corporation Control", pp. 381–2.

97 Hessels, Vol. 3, Part 1, pp. 126–8.

98 Goldsmiths Company, Court Minutes Book A, Vol. 2, ff. 2–3, Reddaway and Walker, *Early History of the Goldsmiths Company*, pp. 128.
99 See Luu, *Immigrants and the Industries of London*, Chapter 4.
100 CLRO, Rep 18, ff. 148v-149v (4 February 1573).
101 Scouloudi, *Returns of Strangers*, p. 90; see also Littleton, "Social Interaction", pp. 152–3.
102 Cottret, *Huguenots in England*, pp. 60–2.
103 See Chapter 6 below, pp. 124–5.
104 This discussion is based on Robbins, "Note on General Naturalization", pp. 170–2.
105 See Statt, *Foreigners and Englishmen*, esp. Chapter 4.
106 See Chapter 6 below, pp. 118–19.

4

"[I]mployment for all handes that will worke": Immigrants, Guilds and the Labour Market in Early Seventeenth-Century London

Joseph P. Ward

In *The Art of Living in London* (1642), Henry Peacham offered advice to those who wished to migrate to the metropolis. The first requirement for the immigrant would be

> to arme himselfe with patience, and to thinke that he is entered into a wood, where there is as many bryers as people, every one as ready to catch hold of your fleece as your self; for we see that sheepe when theypasse through a thorny or a bushie place they leave locks or wooll behind them.

Peacham argued that immigrants must always realize that "a populous Citie could not live nor subsist (like the stomacke) except it have helpe and nourishment from the other parts and members" of the body. After reminding the well-off country gentlemen of business that they must always watch their purses and their servants while in London, Peacham turned his attention to "such as are of the poorest condition and come to the Citie, compelled by necessitie to try their fortunes, to seeke services, or other meanes to live." He asserted that in London may be found "imployment for all handes that will worke," but he also cautioned that those who did not find an occupation would have to "returne home againe before they finde or feele the extremity of want; other-wise they shall finde it farre worse then the Countrey; because if they want, here are more occasions to draw them into ill courses than there." Peacham further observed that those who were unable to find gainful employment would be "constrained to steale, and to shorten their dayes, to seeke death in the errour of their lives, as Salomon saith. Young maids, who never knew ill in their lives, to bee enticed by impudent Bawds, to turne common Whores." He chose to end his pamphlet on a hopeful note, suggesting that if immigrants were able to

> provide themselves, and take honest courses, by the blessing of God they may come to as great preferment as Aldermen and Aldermens wives: For poverty of itself is no vice

but by accident. Whom hath the Citie more advanced then poor mens children? The Citie itself being the most charitable place of the whole, and having done more good deeds then halfe the land beside.[1]

Perhaps the best known example of what Peacham described was Dick Whittington, the famous late-medieval lord mayor of London. According to versions of the legend that were circulating in the early seventeenth century, Whittington was born into a poor provincial family and in his youth went to London in search of work. Once in the metropolis, an overseas merchant discovered him lingering about and offered him menial employment and a room in his garret. The garret was overrun by rats and mice and so Whittington bought a young cat for a penny. That proved a wise investment indeed. Not only did the cat end Whittington's vermin problem, it also became his contribution to the stock of a merchant voyage his master was undertaking. The master's vessel was driven by foul weather upon the farthest coast of Barbary, a place to which no English trader had previously ventured. When the local king heard of the English merchants' arrival, he summoned them to a lavish banquet, but that meal was soon spoiled by the appearance of swarms of rats and mice. The chief English agent announced that they had on their ship an animal that could eliminate the pests, to which the king replied that he would exchange a vast fortune in gold and jewels for it. After a demonstration of feline ferocity and some hard bargaining, Whittington's cat was sold to the Moorish king. Transformed by his new wealth, Whittington attracted the attention of Fitzwarren's daughter. The merchant was delighted to bless their union, and after the wedding he asked his new son-in-law to become his business partner, which he did with great success. His wealth secured, Whittington was soon chosen as a London sheriff and would eventually serve as lord mayor three times.[2]

As Peacham's tract and the Whittington legend suggest, early modern London relied upon immigrants. The metropolitan demographic regime – especially with its periodic outbursts of diseases such as plague – required that large numbers of newcomers from provincial England and abroad move to London in order to maintain its economic and social vitality.[3] Some of those who migrated to London in their youth would subsequently either return to their native towns or villages or else travel even further afield, such as to England's colonies in Ireland and America.[4] Other new arrivals would quickly fall victim to disease.[5] On aggregate, though, London continued to grow rapidly throughout the early modern period because, in addition to being a centre of manufacturing, it was increasingly the focal point of England's international trade as well as the seat of the national government, which gave its economy sufficient vitality to support large-scale immigration.[6]

London's economy was, to a large extent, regulated by livery companies, each of which was chartered by the Crown to oversee a particular trade or craft. Membership in a company had costs and benefits. The costs typically included a full apprenticeship served with a company member as well as regular dues. The benefits included the protection of reputation as well as market, since the company in theory balanced the supply of labour with demand and, in many cases, access to a social safety net of sorts when one's fortunes failed. Many companies had pension funds and almshouses reserved for aged or infirm members and their widows, while the wealthier companies also had funds for dowries and support for sons attending the universities. In early modern London, livery company membership was therefore, to a considerable extent, a class marker because members had access to markets and opportunities formally denied to others. When company members perceived the value of their memberships eroded by the presence of non-citizens in the metropolitan labour market, they were often quick to lodge complaints against the immigrants through whatever legal – and sometimes illegal – means they had at their disposal.[7] Despite their direct or indirect participation in international social networks, Londoners had a well-established reputation for hostility towards immigrants generally, though those from outside England (commonly referred to as 'aliens' or 'strangers') were more likely to receive abuse than those who were natives of the English provinces (known as 'foreigners'). Not surprisingly, this manifested itself, especially in times of general economic distress, in the form of protests against the presence of non-native born workers in the metropolitan labour market. The strangers were especially vulnerable, in large part because those who were newly arrived were often fairly easily distinguished by their accents and their affiliations with stranger churches.[8]

Throughout the late sixteenth and early seventeenth centuries, concerns about the social ills associated with London's growth focused on the ability of immigrants to establish themselves in the metropolis. Queen Elizabeth and King James each issued orders prohibiting the construction of buildings upon new foundations in the metropolis in the vain hope that they would limit the opportunities for immigrants to establish themselves. The orders seem to have done little more than to increase the royal coffers as a result of the fines that builders paid for their defiance.[9] Increasingly, the Crown's attention turned away from housing and towards tighter economic controls in order to attempt to check immigration. Several livery companies responded to the Crown's request for information about the role of aliens in the metropolitan labour market. The officers of the Coopers' Company reported that "if these Aliens were not so employed that then many poor Coopers natural Englishmen which are charged with wives, children, and familes and are not able to maintain them for want of work might be there employed and thereby the better inhabelled to maintain their charge." Similarly, the Clockmakers' officers asserted that members of their company "are interrupted and discredited in the use of their trade by the interposition of manie Strangers invading this Realm, whereby their Arte is not only by the bad workmanship of Strangers disgraced, but they disinhabled to make sale of their commodities at such rates as they may resonably live by."[10] Clearly, according to some London freemen, there was an oversupply of labour in early seventeenth-century London.[11]

A series of petitions submitted to the Privy Council in 1610 attributed London's growth and its swollen labour market to the poor regulation of the metropolitan economy. One of these, expressing a sentiment common to the others, stated that "the necessity of new buildings [is] for that there repair from all parts of the Realm sundry sorts of people and with them many families, which must of necessity have houses wherein to lodge themselves and their household." This petition suggested that there were four types of immigrants. The first were craftsmen who had not served apprenticeships in their trade but who nevertheless moved to London, established shops, and took on apprentices and journeymen in violation of applicable regulations. The second were those who were completely without skills, of which there were two varieties: those who were willing to undertake "honest labors" by working as "porters, hostlers, laborers, broomen and such like", and those who sought instead "to live upon the spoil of other men" through theft and other types of vice. The third type of immigrant also included those who lacked skills but who procured licenses and became alehouse keepers. The fourth were young people sent to London by their families or friends in order to learn a trade, but these were commonly "by evil company drawn away to all manner of lewdness." Such immigrants were encouraged to live in the metropolis by landowners who understood that "profit greatly increases buildings." The petition concluded that the most effective means for reducing the growth of London would be to make it more difficult for immigrants to find employment there, which could be brought about "if all handicraftsmen within ten miles about London were drawn by orderly government into several companies."[12] One of the Crown's most striking attempts at economic reform was the incorporation of London's suburbs in 1636, which superseded the livery companies' claims to economic regulation in suburban London. The new body immediately provoked protests from freemen – especially those in the building trades – who had been in the habit of working throughout the metropolis because it required them to pay an entrance fee, to the Crown, for the right to labour in the suburbs. During its short life, the corporation seems mainly to have served the Crown's financial interest rather than curbing London's growth, and it appears to have fallen into disuse with the outbreak of the Civil War.[13]

Such attempts at reform demonstrated the challenges that any regulatory scheme would face when it came to controlling the economy of a steadily expanding metropolis. In 1606, an Act of Common Council reiterated the exclusive right of citizens to occupy a trade or keep a shop in the City. No "person not being free of the said City," it stated, "may or ought to sell, or put to sale any wares or marchandises within the said City or the Liberties of the same by retaile, or keep any open or inward shop, or other inward place or room for them [sic] sale, or putting to sale, any wares or marchandises, or for use of any Arte, Trade, Occupation, mysterie or handicraft within the same."[14] The City's regulations did not apply to areas of the metropolis that were outside of the lord mayor's jurisdiction, but London's livery companies received their rights through royal charters, which typically empowered them to regulate their trades in the liberties and suburbs within three miles of the City as well as in the City itself.[15] Such policies aside, it was in practice very difficult in the marketplace to tell who was a citizen and who was a stranger. Sara Pennell recently described the chaotic process by which food was sold in London's streets, in which individuals from a variety of professions went after the same customers with little or no regard for any boundaries among trades.[16] In tacit acknowledgment of the difficulty of enforcing such regulations, livery companies often took steps to distinguish their members from those non-citizens who sought to intrude into the market place. The Vintners' Company allowed its members to place a bush outside their shops and ceremonially removed the bush from the shops of those found cheating their customers or otherwise violating company policies. In 1615, members of the Carpenters' Company who were looking for work began to gather at Christ Church so that prospective employers would know where to find them. In 1628, the company's officers regularized the practice by receiving aldermanic approval for a plan to have unemployed freemen carpenters gather every morning during the working week at Cheapside, a similar custom to that observed by unemployed bricklayers and plasterers.[17]

Only the most menial trades were completely open to immigrants to the metropolis, but over time some of these became more restrictive as well. In the early seventeenth century, the City government took a series of steps to ensure that only freemen – that is, members of livery companies – could serve as porters either at the waterside tacklehouses or throughout the streets of the City. The Society of Tacklehouse and Ticket Porters, as the organization came to be known, sought to exclude immigrants of all sorts from one of the most plentiful types of casual employment in London.[18] An order of the Lord Mayor and Court of Aldermen in February 1605 stated that a man would have to have a certificate from the alderman of the ward in which he lived confirming that he was a resident of the City and that he was a freeman before he would be licensed to serve as a porter. The system of licensed porters was a way to offer alternative employment to members of London's livery companies who had lost their businesses or in other ways seen their fortunes, to use the contemporary term, "decay". As a ballad composed to celebrate the creation of the Society of Porters put it:

> As plainly doth appeare,
> by that was lately done,
> for them that burthens beare,
> and doe on businesse runne:
> the Porters of this Cittie,
> some being men of Trade,
> but now the more, the more the pitie
> by crosses are decayed

The Society sought not only to secure work for unemployed freemen but also to provide them with assistance when they had reached the age at which they could no longer labour, which was the sort of social safety net that had long been one of the chief advantages of livery company membership.[19]

Those who were allowed to serve as porters were required to wear tin badges on which their names were engraved that would signify their status to those who would seek to employ them. Porters who failed to wear their badges could be fined for the offence. It soon became clear, however, that some Aldermen showed "compassion towards some foreigners that have been ancient dwellers in and about this City, and many of them charged with wives and children born within the same" by allowing them to continue working as porters despite the order to the contrary. A subsequent order was therefore needed to reaffirm the dangers of allowing non-citizens "to intermeddle as free men, which lenienty and tolleration towards some few has been an occasion of late to invite and draw many other slight and vagrant people from all parts of this Kingdom unto the City, who here (presuming the like favor) become lodgers and inmates." The problem with this hospitality towards immigrants was not only that they took potential employment away from citizens but also that the "multitude of these sorts of people" raised the prices of food and rent for everyone. To make matters worse,

> many of these people under the color and habit of Porters have taken upon them the carriage of trunks and goods of sundry of his majesty's subjects and have gone quite away with them, to the great deceipt and damage of them that set them on work and to the great scandal of the honest poor freemen Porters admitted to use that feat within the City.[20]

Acknowledging its inability to exclude immigrants altogether from the London labour market as well as its desire to give comfort to those who had fled to England from the continent in search of the freedom to follow their Protestant faith, the Weavers' Company created a category of "foreign brethren" to allow immigrants to develop a relationship with the company and, it was surely hoped, submit to the rules of the trade. This system eventually became the centre of controversy within the company as journeymen and apprentices accused company officers of failing to enforce the limitations placed on the strangers.[21] During King James's reign, a group of freemen weavers sent a letter to the elders of the French and Dutch Churches in London in which they complained that aliens were enjoying privileges that should have been allowed only to native-born artisans. They further alleged that many strangers took advantage of English hospitality and defied the regulations of the trade that freemen were expected to obey. The freemen therefore told the elders that they "desire one Lawe, one Punishment upon the Offenders," but they also complained that

> if our maisters and Governors shall allow the Strangers or Alien borne one lesse than the freeborne that hath served seven years to obtain the same favour of the Company, and the strangers not one hour, with four loomes to the stranger and but five to the best of the English, yet will the Stranger in despite of this government . . . set up some of them six, eight, or ten loomes, and not an Englishman his wife and Children any comfort by them.[22]

In the view of the freemen weavers, London's labour market could have accommodated some aliens if they agreed to follow the rules, but the greed of the company's officers was such that they willingly undermined the livelihoods of English weavers by allowing aliens unfettered participation in the metropolitan economy.

Frustrated by their company's officers' willingness to undermine their rights, several freemen weavers began to discuss among themselves new ways to defend their interests. In 1630, the officers of the Weavers' Company complained to the City government that some freemen were holding meetings away from the company's hall in order to plan legal action against the company. In their defence, the freemen alleged that they had been "kept in extreem poverty and wante by reason that the Statute against Intruders upon our trade who never served duely for the same is not duely executed, and also that such orders made by the Lord Mayor and Courte of Aldermen for the well government of the said trade is by the masters of the same government neglected." The weavers therefore began to meet together to plan "some good and laweful course" to defend their economic rights not only against immigrants who illegally intruded into their trade but also against the company officers who allowed the strangers to do so. At these meetings, at least one of which took place at "the Black boye in Cornhill" (presumably a tavern or alehouse), the freemen discussed the possibility of pursuing legal action against their company's officers and took up a voluntary collection of funds to support the effort.[23]

In what appears to be a continuation of that strategy, members of the Weavers' Company sent a list of their grievances against immigrants to the Crown in June 1635. Their argument revealed the sophistication of their understanding of the relationship between the supply and demand for labour in the metropolitan weaving industry. They began by declaring that they had "served their apprenticeships according to the laws of the realm," and yet did suffer because many

> Aliens heretofore (and still) doth come from beyond the seas and worketh in London and the suburbs thereof and other places adjoining . . . few or none of them having served [as apprentices] for the trade of weaving neither have they any certificate of what religion they are or of their learning the said trade or of their good behaviour or of their honest departure out of their own Countreys.

Of particular concern were those aliens who arrived in London in their late teens and found employment with other strangers who had previously established themselves in the metropolis. The result of these successive waves of immigration was "the impoverishing of many hundreds of the native born, their wives and children." Alien master weavers also taught some "youths and Boyes" – "as well Aliens born as English" – how to weave. These, in turn, became journeymen "within a year or two" and began to work "for small wages" whereas native-born youths who followed the Company's regulations normally did not complete their apprenticeships and begin to work for wages before they had reached the age of 24.

The immigrants also imported new techniques and values. Some strangers brought a new type of labour-saving loom – called "Engines" – to England around the year 1610, which utilized up to 24 shuttles per loom, thereby displacing the labour of at least 400 weavers. The petitioners alleged that the advantages the immigrants enjoyed because of their lower wage costs contributed to their growing dominance of the trade in London. The strangers also benefited from their willingness to ignore the rules that citizens were expected to follow when it came to selling their wares. Rather than selling their goods themselves, as required by law, strangers – or at least "the most part of them" – employed brokers, who would take their products "from shop to shop, not leaving any one unsought into from one end of this city to the other, and all other out places." In these ways, the clandestine activities of immigrants as well as their sheer numbers compounded the oversupply of labour in the metropolis, which in turn caused "the raising of rents, enhancing [of] the prices of victuals, the pestering of this City and suburbs thereof with many inmates inhabiting in small rooms to the increasing of contagious infection if God should visit it."[24]

Concerns over the safety of strangers in London increased with the assault on the Spanish ambassador Gondomar on April 5, 1621. According to John Chamberlain, Gondomar was offered "some sleight abuse" as he rode in his litter through the streets of London. Three "young fellowes (or prentises)" were whipped for the offence, although "the punishment was lightly laide on" while "divers affronts and insolencies were don to those that were overseers of the execution."[25] That reaction angered King James. A subsequent royal proclamation asserted that

> there is as just cause at this time to charge their chief magistrates for negligent suffering, as to condemn the inferior and baser sort of people for acting many Insolencies of rude and savage barbarisme, which dayly are committed in the Streets not only towards Ambassadours and publike Ministers of forreigne Princes and States . . . but even towards other Strangers also, to whom all courteous respect and hospitality is due.[26]

The attack on the ambassador also inspired a tract by one "D. N." which claimed to be a letter from an English traveller on the continent to the apprentices of London. The narrator described a dinner that he attended in a French city at which he was joined by an Italian, a Spaniard, and a German, as well as several who were French. The conversation at the dinner began with a discussion of a letter that the Spaniard had received "conteyning the newes of the barbarous misusage of the King of Spayne his Ambassador by the Apprentices of London," and it quickly moved to the topic of the unparalleled incivility of the English towards strangers, with special regard to the apprentices of London. Speaker after speaker related how he personally had been abused and assaulted when visiting London on business, while the narrator admits that he has received nothing but kindness during his many journeys throughout the continent.[27]

The conversation then turned to revenge. The German mentioned that during a visit on business to London he was walking down a street when he "had an old shooe throwne by an Apprentice out of shop ful in his face; which he seeing not to have hapned by mischance, because he saw the Apprentice laugh at his so right hitting his marke; tooke up the shooe, and with no lesse good will to hit right, sent it backe againe towards the head of the Apprentice." Several other apprentices rushed to the scene, so the stranger was forced to retreat "bruized and bloudy-nosed . . . to his lodging, and from thence as soone as he could into a ship, leaving the affaires he came about undone." On his homeward journey the German vowed that he would seek retribution against the London apprentices by retaliating against the first Englishman he would encounter in his native land. Soon thereafter he had occasion to see two Englishmen standing along the bank of the Rhine and so he wasted no time pushing them both into the river. Upon hearing this tale the Italian in the company remarked that it was unfortunate that justice was not served upon the apprentices who had abused the German in London, but that he was surprised that "so few such deserved deeds of revenge do happen" given how poorly the English treated the strangers in their midst. The diners all agreed that the English traveller would do well to counsel London apprentices to stop abusing strangers "at least for such of their own Countrey-mens sakes, as must have occasion to come into these Strangers Countreys, to the end they be not upbraided with it, nor that it not be revenged upon them."[28]

The dinner companions speculated upon the causes of the poor treatment of strangers in London in general and of the Spanish ambassador in particular. The Frenchman suggested that the English were, simply, a quarrelsome people, and that in the absence of strangers they "will fall to justling and shouldring of one another, and rather than faile they will find meanes by hemming at one another to beget quarrells." The Italian considered the possibility that the attack on the Spanish ambassador may have reflected a particular grudge the English held against Spain that dated back to the Armada, though he concluded that such would merely reflect the attitudes "of their more violently affected Preachers, who out of love unto the reformed discipline of Holland, on which the eye of all their hope is fixed, would fayne make the poore weake understanding youths, and the ruder sort of simple people, the subjects of their sedition." After reflecting on this conversation, the English traveller concurred that Puritan preachers were largely to blame for inciting hatred against those of other religions. He therefore encouraged the London apprentices to keep in mind that only God could determine which among the various Christian churches was the most true, and concluded with regard to those of faiths different than his own that "I see no reason of not tolerating their conversation, when they can be content in humane and Civil manner to converse with me."[29]

The antipathy of some London apprentices towards strangers was expressed in a petition directed at Parliament in 1641 that decried, among many other things, the erosion of customary economic rights in the City. Noting that "this City has been renowned in the gazing eye of the world ... Yet the Rights and Liberties thereof being somewhat detracted and abused, as also the Lawes and ancient Customes thereof being extenuated by some malignant and ill-affected persons, it now becomes much deplorable in the sight of all men." One of the chief causes of London's declining fame was, according to the petition's authors, "the abuse of our Apprenticeship: for where we by coercion are necessarily compelled to serve seven or eight years at least before wee can have the immunity and freedome of this City to trade in, Those which are meere Strangers doe snatch this Freedome from us, and pull the Trades out of our owne hands." As a result, when they have completed their legal apprenticeships, they are forced to go to work for the strangers, "who doe thus domineere over us in our owne Trades," which in turn made it difficult for them to establish their own households. "[W]hen we are out of our times [of apprenticeship] and should then begin to trade in the world," they asserted,

> we can get neither House or Shop for our money in regard that these Forraigners and Strangers (as there are many French, Dutch, Walloones, etc.) will give any money to snatch them from us and this is the chiefest cause that houses are so excessive deare in this City and by this meanes many of us loose the losse of years, trade, and time and are compelled to turne Journeymen.

Noting the general concern over the "fearefull dangers, perillous plots, and conspiracies which have, and are still pretended by the papists against us," the apprentices asked Parliament to restore their economic rights so "that the flourishing roote of protestants be not suffered to be fully eradicated to the great discomfort of all men in these Kingdomes."[30]

This petition indicates the passion with which London apprentices may have viewed strangers as threats to their livelihoods. The defence of traditional rights suggests that the apprentices – or, perhaps more accurately, those who sought to insert them into the political process – were, at this stage, somewhat conservative in their aspirations. They saw themselves as participating in an economic system governed by tradition as well as law, but they also sensed that their governors were unable, if not unwilling, to defend them. Their concerns were, therefore, two-fold: that immigrants be required to follow the same rules as citizens, and that their governors defend their economic rights. In this way, the apprentices were undertaking a strategy similar to that of the members of the Weavers' Company who perceived their company's officers to have had greater care for their own economic interests than the did for the interests of freemen generally. It is tempting to think that the weavers gathered at the Black Boye tavern because its name signified their sense that they had no more economic freedom than a slave, but it is also important to note that the purpose of their meeting was to plan a legal – rather than revolutionary – course of action.[31]

Xenophobia also had its limits. Another petition claiming to be from London apprentices to Parliament in 1641 rehearsed the now familiar complaints against immigrants, but it omitted the overt discussion of strangers discussed above and instead railed against "forreiners which keepe their residence within the liberty of this City, which in lower roomes or chambers having friends nigh unto them, take away our Custome."[32] Similarly, what appears to be a draft of a petition from "the apprentices and journeymen" dated July 1647 listed eight issues with which Parliament should be concerned. The first seven of these addressed subjects of national concern, such as implementing the conditions specified in the Solemn League and Covenant, while the eighth and final topic related to London's economy. The authors reported that

> there have been and still are great abuses and insufferable injuries, done to your Petitioners by the sale of freedomes, and Forreigners intruding into the Suburbs and places neer adjacent, to this Citie, whereby your Petitioners are much discouraged in their services, the Freedom of this Citie prejudiced, and the Franchises, and Liberties thereof infringed.

They concluded their text with the request that Parliament take steps "as well for the expulsion of such as have so unduly crept in amongst us, as for the future prevention of the like insufferable Injuries, that may redound to your Petitioners, hereafter."[33] Here, in the midst of the greatest period of instability in seventeenth-century London, apprentices and journeymen could refrain from attacking in a direct way immigrants from abroad (by using the ambiguous term "Forreigners" rather than "aliens" or "strangers") while opposing those who would work in the metropolis without first gaining their freedom.

That does not mean that London apprentices did not, at times, express xenophobia. However, as many of the sources discussed above indicate, in the early seventeenth century many London citizens considered native-born foreigners as much of a threat to their livelihoods as they did strangers. It should also be noted that some Londoners had reasons to view immigrants sympathetically. Many Londoners were not natives of the place. It seems extremely likely that in every household in the City lived at least some members who were born elsewhere or whose parents were born elsewhere. London, as Henry Peacham observed, was like a great stomach that needed constant replenishment. Households required servants and tradesmen required expanding markets. Another source of sympathy towards some aliens was the acknowledgment that those who fled religious persecution on the continent could be welcomed to the metropolis.[34]

The lack of reliable economic data prevents historians from doing more than speculate about the place of immigrants in the labour market of early modern London. The continued growth of the metropolis in the face of early modern urban conditions strongly suggests that immigrants from both provincial England and abroad were able to establish themselves in the metropolis. At the same time, the many complaints of London artisans about the erosion of their customary economic rights as well as the creation of the Society of Tacklehouse and Ticket Porters as a safety net for unemployed freemen suggest that the Henry Peacham and the Dick Whittington legend overestimated the ability of the metropolitan labour market to accommodate immigrants.

Notes

1 Peacham, *Art of Living in London*. For recent research on vagrants, criminals, and servants in early modern London see McRae, "Peripatetic Muse", pp. 24–40; Fumerton, "London's

Vagrant Economy", pp. 206–25; Griffiths, "Overlapping Circles", pp. 115–33; and Meldrum, *Domestic Service and Gender*.

2 This summary of the Whittington legend is based on Heywood, *Famous and Remarkable History* and Manley (ed.), *London in the Age of Shakespeare*, p. 234. For the Whittington legend more generally, see Robertson, "Adventures of Dick Whittington".

3 For discussions of early modern London's population see Finlay, *Population and Metropolis*; Finlay and Shearer, "Population Growth", pp. 37–59; and Harding, "Population of London", pp. 111–28.

4 Wrigley, "A Simple Model", pp. 133–56 and Games, *Migration*. For an examination of the factors that encouraged social stability in London's neighbourhoods see Boulton, *Neighbourhood and Society*.

5 On the sociology of disease in early modern London and its particular characteristics in areas frequented by new arrivals to the metropolis see Slack, *Impact of Plague*, pp. 144–72.

6 The central place of London in the national economy is evident in such general studies of the early modern economy as Grassby, *Merchant Community* and Wrightson, *Earthly Necessities*.

7 Recent discussions of livery company activities may be found in Rappaport, *Worlds Within Worlds*, Archer, *Pursuit of Stability*, Ward, *Metropolitan Communities* and idem, "Livery Companies", pp. 175–78.

8 Recent discussions of antipathy towards aliens in early modern England, and especially in London, include Luu, "'Taking the Bread Out of Our Mouths'" and Goose, "Xenophobia", Chapter 6, below.

9 Barnes, "The Prerogative and Environmental Control", pp. 1332–63; Stone, "Residential Development of the West End", pp. 167–212; Smuts, "The Court and its Neighbourhood", pp. 117–49.

10 PRO, SP14/127/14–15; see also /12 and /21 for similar comments by goldsmiths and leatherdressers.

11 By "labour" in this context is meant available workers in those occupations that required little expertise. Contemporaries (and historians) understood that foreigners and strangers were active in the production of luxury goods. See Peacham, *Coach and Sedan* and Hearn, "Insiders or Outsiders", pp. 117–26.

12 BL, Lansdowne Mss. 160, fols. 95r-96r; see also 160, fol. 97r and 169, fol. 130r-v, 131r-132r.

13 Ward, *Metropolitan Communities*, pp. 20–21.

14 *An Act of Common Councell*.

15 Ward, *Metropolitan Communities*, pp. 27–44.

16 Pennell, "Great Quantities of Gooseberry Pye", pp. 228–49.

17 Ward, *Metropolitan Communities*, pp. 49–50, 55.

18 For the porters generally, see Stern, *Porters of London*, esp. pp. 1–81. For the reliance of indigent freemen on income as porters, see Ward, *Metropolitan Communities*, pp. 59–64.

19 Brewer, *A Newe Ballad*.

20 Guildhall Library [hereafter GL] MS 913, fols. 3r-v, 22r-24r. The relations between London weavers and immigrants in the early seventeenth century had roots extending back to the Elizabethan period. For example, in 1595 members of the Weavers' Company wrote a lengthy letter to the elders of the French Church in London expressing their desire for improved relations between strangers and citizens. The letter is transcribed in F. Consitt, *London's Weavers' Company*, pp. 312–18. Recent discussions of relations between strangers and citizens in the London weaving trade may be found in Ward, *Metropolitan Communities*, pp. 125–43 and Goose, "Xenophobia", Chapter 6 below.

21 Plummer, *London Weavers' Company*, pp. 144–61.

22 GL MS 4647, pp. 144–5.

23 GL MS 4647, pp. 200–2.

24 GL MS 4647, pp. 300–3.
25 McLure (ed.), *Letters of John Chamberlain*, Vol. 2, pp. 360–1.
26 James I. The Proclamation also noted that members of the English nobility and gentry commonly suffered abuse at the hands of apprentices and others while they were in London. For a discussion of the climate of anti-Spanish feeling in the Jacobean period see Cogswell, *Blessed Revolution* and Patterson, *King James VI and I*.
27 D.N., *Londons Looking-Glasse*, pp. 3–11.
28 D. N., *Londons Looking-Glasse*, pp. 11–14.
29 D. N., *Londons Looking-Glasse*, pp. 14–40.
30 Anon., *The Apprentices of Londons Petition*.
31 This would be more consistent with the defence of customary practices that E. P. Thompson observed in eighteenth-century food riots than it would be with the more radical tradition that Norah Carlin has claimed marked protests of artisans in this period. See Thompson, "Moral Economy", pp. 185–258 and Carlin, "Liberty and Fraternities", pp. 223–54. For seventeenth-century plebeian defences of customary rights see Wood, *Politics of Social Conflict*. For early modern English understandings of race, see Hall, *Things of Darkness*.
32 The petition allegedly from London apprentices is appended to Anon., *The Petition of the Weamen of Middlesex*. For the broader context of these petitions see Lindley, *Popular Politics*, pp. 92–197 and Pearl, *London and the Outbreak*, pp. 210–36.
33 Anon, *The Heads of the Petition*.
34 Collinson, "Europe in Britain", pp. 57–67 and Ward, "Fictitious Shoemakers", pp. 80–7. Jean Howard recently suggested that some natives and strangers could have found common cause in their shared misogyny; see Howard, "Women, Foreigners and the Regulation of Urban Space", pp. 150–67.

Part II

Immigrants and their Impact

5

"A Place of refuge and sanctuary of a holy Temple": Exile Communities and the Stranger Churches

ANDREW SPICER

In 1645 Jean Bulteel, minister of the French-speaking congregation in Canterbury, published *A Relation of the Troubles Of the three forraign Churches in Kent*, an account of the dispute between Archbishop Laud and the exile churches about their anomalous and privileged status within the Church of England. Bulteel reproduced a petition to the King which recalled how "these poor flockes . . . hath escaped the fire, the massacres and persecutions" and were "cast by divers stormes and violent tempests on the coasts of this Island, so carefully gathered together by the good Edward the VI and welcomed by him, so favourably maintained and entertained by that vertuous Princesse Queen Elizabeth". England had provided them with the shelter and protection of "a place of refuge and sanctuary of a holy Temple".[1] A further petition to Charles I in 1641 referred to the foundation of the stranger churches in 1550 and went on to record how Edward VI "by the said letters did grant and ordayne, that there should be a Temple or holy housse in the City of London which should be called the Temple of the Lord Jesus where the congregations and assemblies of Germans and other strangers might be made and celebrated".[2]

The petition's allusion was particularly apposite as the temple had come to represent the very heart of the exile community; it was the one place where they gathered together *en masse*. It was the hub of the community's religious life; it is where they met for worship, listened to sermons, and scripture and sang the psalms; baptised their infants; catechized their young and assembled for the sacrament of the Lord's Supper. The temple served as a communal focal point at times of adversity or celebration – often related to the fluctuating fortunes of their co-religionists on the continent – where they met for prayers and fasting, or services of thanksgiving. The consistory, which exercised discipline and watched over the morals of the church members, met in the temple, while at the door was the box for collecting money that was dispensed to the community's poor and needy.

Migration came to be seen in increasingly confessional terms during the sixteenth century, rather than being solely the result of economic or political factors, as it had been before the Reformation. Immigrants arrived in England seeking asylum, escaping religious persecution on the continent, particularly during the later 1560s from the hostile Spanish regime in the Low Countries and from France in the wake of the St Bartholomew's Day Massacre of 1572. In the returns of aliens, these immigrants were recorded as having come for "religions sake". A petition presented to the Queen by one group of exiles recorded that they could not

> endure and abide our consciences to be burdened and in especiall to beare the intolerable clogge of the Spanish Inquisicon: Wee have determined with our selves without regard either of the losse of our goodes or native Contrey to seeke out an other place of habitacon where it may be lawfull for us to live more quietly and Christian like.[3]

Not all of these immigrants were, however, religious refugees: some came for economic reasons but found it convenient to express their motives in confessional terms. Even contemporaries, not least the aliens themselves, were aware that "under their cover and pretence of religion, profane and evil livers should intrude themselves".[4] The situation was more complex than this stark differentiation between religious and economic motives suggests. Undoubtedly for many, it was a combination of reasons as the religious troubles were linked to economic disruption and instability. Nonetheless, the ability to worship freely in the temple meant that the building came to symbolise the reason why many had sought exile.

Early in Elizabeth's reign only half of the city's alien population were recorded as attending either the Dutch, French, Italian or Spanish exile churches, and membership of these congregations was increasingly seen as being synonymous with the immigrant population.[5] The buildings where they worshipped became known as "the French Church", "the Dutch Church" or "the stranger's Church", replacing their original dedications. This was in part the result of government policy which encouraged membership of these churches as a means of controlling the alien population and guarding against foreign sectaries and the churches themselves had, in the early years, aspired to membership of the church replacing letters of denization.[6] The Privy Council even went so far in 1573 as to order that strangers "professing no religion nor frequenting any Divine Service used in this realme . . . shuld be dispatched" out of the capital.[7] Outside London, membership of the exile church even more closely equated with the alien community. There were a series of banishments from Sandwich into the 1580s of those who were not members of the church and an order issued by the Privy Council in 1586 was repeated for the communities at Dover and Maidstone.[8] The Southampton authorities questioned one Frenchman in 1593, with a degree of puzzlement as to why he and his wife "goeth not orderly to the French church as he ought to do".[9] Early in the seventeenth century, the authorities attempted to maintain the distinct identity of the exile congregations as their members became increasingly assimilated and began, partly for financial reasons, to withdraw to the parish churches.[10] In 1621 the Privy Council noted that the Walloon congregation in Norwich "hath beene continued apart from the English by the gracious favour of the late Queen Elizabeth and of the King's most excellent Majestie for the space of five and fiftie yeares or more" and went on to order that its members "although borne within this kingdome shall continue to be of that church and societie soe long as his Majestie shalbe pleased to permitt the same and shalbe subject to such discipline as hath beene by all the time aforesaid most usually practised amongst them". Ten years later, the order was repeated for members of the Dutch Church "without any preju- dice to their priviledges and birthright".[11] In the mind of the authorities at least, attendance at the temple was expected of members of the foreign population, and even of their English-born descendants.

While the temple came to be seen as synonymous with the exile community by the government and the native population, these places of worship have been rela- tively neglected in recent studies of the exile communities during the century between the establishment of the first stranger church and the Restoration. This is surprising as many of the churches and chapels used by the exiles during this period survive; the congregations of the Dutch Church in London and the French Church in Canterbury still meet for worship on the same site as their sixteenth-century pre- decessors. Nonetheless, the vicissitudes of the last 400 years have taken their toll. The Dutch Church in London was restored in the nineteenth century after a fire and then completely destroyed by a direct hit in 1940.[12] The medieval chapel used by the French Church in Southampton was almost demolished, but instead was so heavily restored that little remains of the original building.[13] Even where the fabric of the building has undergone less dramatic change, its subsequent use by other faiths has meant that little survives from the earlier period. The Walloon congregation of Norwich, for example, had worshipped in the church of St Mary the Less since 1637, but the church was later used by the Presbyterians, the Swedenborgians and finally the Catholic Apostles.[14]

In spite of these problems, the churches used by the exile communities deserve to be better known and recognised as distinctive places of worship, equating more closely to the Calvinist churches of Scotland and the continent than the local parish church. This was certainly very clear to contemporaries; Elizabethan Puritans viewed these churches as beacons of the True Religion. A bill placed before Parliament in 1572, attacking the liturgy of the Prayer Book, requested that bishops should be able to permit "such forme of prayer and mynistracion of the woorde and sacraments, and other godlie exercises of religion as the righte godlie reformed Churches now do use in the ffrenche and Douche congregation, within the City of London or elswheare in the Quenes maiesties dominions".[15] The buildings used by these churches were adapted accordingly and in many senses should be viewed as the precursors of the nonconformist meeting houses that developed from the mid-seventeenth century onwards. This essay will therefore consider the significance of these churches and the extent to which they represent a distinctive response to the liturgical demands of the Calvinist worship in late sixteenth- and early seventeenth-century England.

The search for a suitable place for worship lay behind the establishment of the first stranger churches in London. Before the Reformation, alien colonies had worshipped as national groups and frequented particular churches, but they worshipped in the parish churches with the local congregation rather than having their own distinct chapel or meeting place.[16] With the religious changes, the emphasis on the use of the vernacular and the need for the congregation to comprehend (rather than merely follow) the service, French and Dutch aliens in the capital had, by the summer of 1549, started to meet together informally for worship. Bucer and three other Reformers peti- tioned the Privy Council on their behalf in August 1549, seeking official recognition for these gatherings and a further petition the following spring requested a building where they could gather for worship. It was not until 24 July 1550, following the intervention of Jean à Lasco, that a charter was granted to the community, which permitted "the ministers of the Church of the Germans and of other foreigners, an uncorrupt interpretation of the most Holy Gospel and administration of the sacraments, according to the word of God and apostolic observance".[17] In addition to legal recognition and establishing the superintendency of Jean à Lasco, the Privy Council granted the community the church of Austin Friars. Although this was the largest friary church in the country, it was too small to accommodate both the French and Dutch congregations. The French congregation, therefore, rented the chapel of the former hospital of St Anthony from the Dean and Chapter of Windsor, the lease being signed on 16 October 1550. As the Dutch remained in possession of Austin Friars, the rent for the chapel was to be shared by the two communities.[18] The minister Jan Utenhove later commented in a letter to Jean Calvin, that the generosity of the English government, particularly with regard to Austin Friars, had far exceeded the expectations of the exiles.[19] The strangers' use of these churches was, however, short-lived, as upon the accession of Mary and the re-establishment of Catholic worship, Jean à Lasco, the ministers and many of the congregation went into exile.

On Elizabeth's accession, the strangers petitioned for the restoration of their rights and they were promised a place of worship by Sir William Cecil in June 1559. The Dutch congregation initially used a local parish church but after considerable wrangling and appeals, they recovered Austin Friars in February 1560. It had been handed over to the Marquis of Winchester and had served as a government warehouse during Mary's reign. The French also had difficulty in reclaiming the Threadneedle Street church, which they only obtained after the intervention of the minister Pierre Alexander in April 1560.[20] The start of the reign also saw the establishment of two further churches. Casiodoro de Reina wrote to Cecil requesting somewhere for the Spanish immigrants to meet. He argued that it would be less easy for Spanish spies to operate within the congregation and for outlandish claims to be made about their worship, if they were able to meet publicly rather than in private houses. The request was granted and the community was assigned the disused church of St Mary Axe.[21] Although sermons had been delivered in Italian during Edward's reign, it was not until 1565 that the Italian church was formally instituted. Edmund Grindal wrote to the Mercers' Company requesting that one Hieronimus Ferlitus "mighte have liberty to preach the gospell in the companyes chappell". It continued to be used by the Italian congregation in the city into the seventeenth century, and occasionally sermons in Spanish were delivered there after the collapse of da Reina's church, following his flight from the country in 1563.[22]

New communities developed outside the capital during Elizabeth's reign, both refugee settlements and "planted" communities which were formally established, often with letters patent from the crown. The negotiations for setting up these "planted" communities reflected the government's keenness to exploit the economic advantages and skills that these immigrants offered, but they did not lose sight of the religious concerns of the immigrants and provision of a place of worship was an important part of the discussions. In 1567 one group of refugees wrote to the town corporation in Southampton asking "to have one church assigned whether wee may resort to learne to reverence both God and the magistrates within which it may be lawfull to have sermons and other service and sacraments to be used apperteyning to the Christian Religion and administracion as used in the time of the Noble Prince of famous memorie King Edward the Sixth".[23] Similar sentiments were expressed at Canterbury where the opening article of a petition to the Mayor and Corporation began, "Whereas they have left their native land and possessions for the love of religion (which they earnestly desire to maintain with a free conscience) they pray that the free exercise of their religion may be permitted to them within this city, and that as may be convenient, a place of worship may be assigned to them, and a place wherein they may bury their dead".[24] But it was not just the refugees who lobbied for a place of worship: local sponsors also acted on their behalf. The Duke of Norfolk and the Bishop of Norwich both wrote to the Archbishop of Canterbury in December 1565, in support of the Norwich community who wanted "to be admitted to some church within this cittie, where they may resort to heare the word of God according to their former manner in the town of Sandwich".[25]

Although the exiles could be seen as co-religionists by some, the authorities remained concerned about foreign sectaries operating in the kingdom. The exile churches provided one means of ensuring religious orthodoxy amongst the alien population and were seen by the government as a means of combating the threat of Anabaptism.[26] A number of Dutch Anabaptists had been tried and executed by the Henrician regime but, following their establishment, the exile churches themselves took action against heterodox members of the congregation and Anabaptist sympathisers. The surgeon George van Parris was burnt for heresy in April 1551 by the authorities, after having been excommunicated by the Dutch Church for denying the Trinity. The Church also acted swiftly against their minister, Adrian van Haemstede, who had sought a rapprochement with the Anabaptists, and was subsequently excommunicated.[27] Given the strong stance taken by the London stranger churches in ensuring religious orthodoxy, it is perhaps not surprising that they played an active role in setting up the churches in Sandwich, Norwich, Maidstone and Southampton. At Sandwich, the Dutch Church was required to attest that the settlers were men of "honeste and quiet conversacon".[28] Even so, the authorities seemed to have been concerned about the form of worship that would be used. The Archbishop of Canterbury was willing to grant the Norwich exiles the use of a vacant church where they could follow their own form of worship and be subject to their discipline, but he expressed the hope that they would conform as closely as possible to the authorised form of prayers and administration of the sacraments.[29] The Bishop of Winchester seems to have been particularly concerned to isolate the Southampton congregation from the rest of the town. He wrote to Sir William Cecil stating

> that they can not live without great disorders amonge themselves and sects dangerous to the naturall subjectes, oneles by your good meanes also they may have lycence to gather to gether into some one churche and so to lyve undre some godly discipline . . . and there is for that purpose a churche that may well be spared and fytt for them withoute the molestation of any the parishes of Hampton.[30]

Horne's comments did raise further fears about the religious orthodoxy of the community and seem to have held up the negotiations, but it is clear that he was concerned that they should be granted a separate place of worship of their own within the town. It was also ordered that "they will agree in doctrine and rites with the frenshe churche in London and geve a confession of theyr faythe to the bisshop of Winton".[31]

A range of ecclesiastical buildings were assigned to the exiles to serve as their temples. In some cases these were redundant ecclesiastical sites but in other instances the foreign congregations shared a church with the local community. The Walloon congregation in Norwich was granted permission to use the Bishop's chapel for worship while the larger Dutch congregation took possession of the former Blackfriars church. The Southampton exiles used the chapel of St Julien at God's House Hospital in the south-east quarter of the town while at Canterbury they came to use the crypt of the cathedral. However, not all of the exile communities had exclusive use of a particular building. Initially the Canterbury congregation were permitted to use the parish church of St Alphege "in such sorte at suche tyme as the parysheners there be not hyndred or disturbed of theyre commen prayer" by the Dean and Chapter of the cathedral.[32] Similarly the congregation at Sandwich shared the parish church with the local congregation; the exiles received permission to worship at St Clement's church in 1561, but a couple of years later they were granted exclusive use of St Peter's church for holy days and weekdays[33] Even in Southampton the French Church seems to have continued as the chapel for residents of the almshouses of God's House.[34] Where the congregation was relatively small, such as the industrial settlement of glassworkers at Fernfold Wood on the Surrey–Sussex border, such cohabitation is perhaps unsurprising.[35] This was, however, also true of the larger communities which had grown rapidly and without formal approval, with the influx of refugees from the continent, such as at Rye.[36] Although the exile congregations met separately, such arrangements might seem to contradict the governments' concern about the spread of reformed beliefs to the local population and attempts to exclude Englishmen from attending their services.[37]

Initial repairs had to be made to some of these churches to return them to ecclesiastical use. Austin Friars and St Anthony's Hospital in London, and Blackfriars in Norwich, were all part of monastic foundations which had fallen into disuse at the Dissolution. The generosity of the Edwardian regime had extended so far as to undertake the repair of Austin Friars before it was handed over to the strangers. The French and Dutch communities agreed therefore to share the costs of repairing the Threadneedle Street chapel.[38] It was not only the former monastic churches that required attention. The medieval hospital of God's House, Southampton, belonged to Queen's College, Oxford, which undertook repairs and reglazed the chapel in 1567–8.[39] The Walloon congregation in Norwich found the Bishops' chapel to be in a particularly poor condition, later describing it as being "more like a dove-house than a church, full of muck and ordure, the ruffe decayed with age, noe glasse at all in the west windowe, the east windowe in parts and the south side all pittifully broken and shattered, noe desks at all, nor any seates but the Chaire seates in the Quire, and the stone seates in the body of it".[40] The work undertaken by the congregation to refurbish the chapel included reglazing: "nine windowes (of three lights apiece on ye south side of ye said chappel), which formerly were glased with coloured glass in stories and imagerie, are now turned into white glass".[41]

Beyond these repairs to the church fabric, these former Catholic churches also had to be adapted for reformed worship. A tabernacle and image of the Virgin, dating from the early sixteenth century, might have been among the fittings removed during work done at God's House chapel in Southampton.[42] In London the church of Austin Friars was partitioned, as John Stow recorded in his *Survey of London*:

The Friers Church he [Sir William Paulet, Marquis of Winchester] pulled not downe, but the West end therof inclosed from the steeple, and Quier, was in the yeare 1550 graunted to the Dutch Nation in London, to be their preaching place: the other part, namely the steeple, Quier and side Isles to the Quier adioyning, he reserued to housh-olde vses, as for stowage of corne, coale, and other things.[43]

Restrictions on the mendicant orders meant that their churches were primarily intended for preaching rather than the celebration of the Mass, which remained the prerogative of the parish churches. As a result the mendicant churches usually had large aisled naves capable of housing a large audience, generally with a smaller unaisled conventual choir.[44] Austin Friars was therefore ideally suited for the reformed ministry of the Word, and the appropriation of these buildings for Calvinist worship is partic-ularly noticeable on the continent.[45] At Norwich, the fifteenth-century Blackfriars church had been bought by the corporation after the Dissolution with the intention "to make the churche a fayer and large halle" and for a chapel "to pray to Almightye God for the prosperouse preservacyon of your most Royall estate".[46] In contrast to Austin Friars, it was the chancel originally intended for the conventual use of the friars rather than the large preaching nave which was granted to the Dutch congregation in 1564. Although unaisled, the chancel was, however, almost as long as the nave and well lit with five large, tall windows.[47]

Although there are only occasional references to the interior of these temples and their furnishings, they would have reflected the liturgical requirements for reformed worship. The church of God was defined by Jean Calvin as being "where we see the Word of God purely preached and heard, where we see the sacraments administered according to Christ's institution".[48] Preaching lay at the centre of regular weekly worship. In spite of the esteem with which the administration of the Lord's Supper was regarded, it was only held quarterly in the exile churches, although this was later increased to monthly.[49] The layout of reformed temples therefore reflected the impor-tance of the ministry of the Word. The minister was a mouthpiece through which the congregation heard the words of God Himself and therefore they were expected to receive His message soberly and with reverence. It was therefore important for the minister to be both visible and audible to the whole congregation.[50] These needs were reflected in the comments made by the consistory at Austin Friars, when they were looking for a new minister in 1641: "that, besides other qualifications, we want a strong voice, as our church is large".[51]

Where the exile congregation shared the local parish church, such as at Rye and Sandwich, their surroundings must have seemed a somewhat incongruous backdrop for reformed worship. Certainly many of the churches had been purged of the images and furnishings associated with the Catholic ritual of the Mass, but they remained buildings adapted for the use of the 1559 Prayer Book rather than the liturgy used by the stranger churches. In 1571, a "Homily for repairing and keeping clean, and comely adorning the churches" described the essentials for worship after the Elizabethan Settlement: "God's house, the Church, is well adorned with places convenient to sit in, with the Pulpit for the preacher, with the Lord's Table for the ministration of his holy supper, with the font to Christen in." Although the royal injunctions ordered the removal of the rood loft, the screen between the nave and the chancel was to be retained or if necessary replaced. In place of the stone altar, there was to be a "holy table" – not bare but with some suitable covering of cloth or carpet – which was to stand in the place of the altar, except when it was used for communion services when it stood in the body of the choir.[52] Such arrangements meant that the Lord's Supper could not be received by the congregation seated together around a long table in accordance with reformed tradition; the elements were distributed by the minister to the kneeling recipients. It was not until the accession of James VI in 1603 that the English churches began to undergo significant refurbishment and their furnishings came to reflect the increased importance of the sermon within regular worship.[53]

The church could be more appropriately furnished according to the liturgical needs of reformed worship where the exile communities were the sole occupants of the building. The provision of a pulpit and seating were essential pre-requisites for ensuring the delivery of the Word of God and its reverent reception.[54] Shortly after recovering the chapel of St Anthony in Threadneedle Street, the consistory purchased timber from the Dean and Chapter of Windsor in August 1560 to build benches for the church. The deacons accounts of the Walloon congregation at Sandwich record payment of xid for making a bench for the children to sit on when they were catechised.[55] There was also a special bench at the front of the temple in Threadneedle Street for the consistory which, it was critically noted by the minister Everard Evrail, allowed them "to be high and seen of the people".[56] By the early seventeenth century, galleries had been erected in the temple and the leading members of the congregation had their own private pews. In accordance with the reformed tradition, the seating may have been segregated as early in 1632, the men occupying the bench along the wall under the gallery were asked to leave this bench available for women and to take a place in the gallery. At the same date, members with private pews were asked to open them, to provide a place for aged gentlemen of quality to sit during the sermon.[57] In 1632, the interior of Threadneedle Street was refurbished, "the galleries were to be made uniform and the pulpit was to be placed in the middle of the temple".[58] The church, earlier in the year, had accepted an offer from outside the community, from "Monsieur Leviston, Gentilhomme ordinaire de la Chambre du Roy" to meet the expenses for the construction of new galleries in the temple and had appointed two of the elders to work with the carpenter and advise him of the form that these should take.[59] Nonetheless, seating seems to have remained at a premium, with Samuel Pepys recording in 1662 that that he "stood in the Isle all the sermon".[60]

Similar developments seem to have taken place at the Dutch Church of Austin Friars during the early seventeenth century, with leading members of the congregation occupying privileged places within the church. The most prominent seat was occupied by Sir Noel de Caron, the Dutch Agent in London during the 1590s and later the first ambassador of the United Provinces. This was a tradition continued after de Caron's death in 1624 by his successor Sir Albertus Joachimi.[61] It was a stylishly upholstered pew in front of which there was a carpet. Similar seating seems to have been provided in 1652 when the Swedish ambassador was granted his own pew. There were discussions in the early seventeenth century about also providing galleried seating for the male members of the congregation.[62] Such seating was for the elite; less prominent members of the congregation probably brought their own chairs or stools to the service like their counterparts in Norwich.[63]

The pulpit, which was placed against a pillar on the north aisle of the Dutch Church, was the focal point of the church during services. This centralised arrangement was typical of reformed places of worship in Scotland and on the continent, but was at odds with the layout of the English parish churches, which were still arranged on an east–west axis. The ceiling of the church was boarded in, which may also have been an attempt to improve the audibility of the sermon; it was thought, in the sixteenth century, that flat wooden ceilings were better for acoustics than vaulted ones. The interior was plain and whitewashed, although there was a board with the Ten Commandments which has been attributed to Sir Balthazar Gerbier.[64] The church windows gave rise to controversy in the 1640s. A Dutchman complained to the consistory that "in some of the windows we find these idolatrous inscriptions 'The Temple of our Lord Jesus Christ' and in others 'Jesus Temple'".[65]

In spite of the initial foundation charter which had granted Austin Friars to "the Church of the Germans and other foreigners in the City of London", the building became a source of tension between the two exile communities in the capital. The influx of French refugees to London following the Massacre of St Bartholomew's Eve in Paris and other major cities caused the Threadneedle Street church serious problems in accommodating their swollen congregation. In September 1572 they decided to hold two sermons in the morning "because of the large numbers that were coming there and because the temple was too small to house them at just one sermon". The French congregation requested permission from the Dutch Church to use Austin Friars for an additional early morning sermon at seven o'clock, but the church declined on the grounds that they were also considering holding a service at that time. This over-crowding presumably continued to be a problem as the congregation requested permission to use the church again a couple of years later.[66] Nonetheless, in c. 1573 the Dutch Church did grant the French congregation permission to use Austin Friars once a month for the administration of the Lord's Supper, although they were responsible for bringing their own benches and tables for the service.[67] On these Sundays, the Dutch congregation exchanged churches with the French, an arrangement which later irritated Samuel Pepys when he arrived at Threadneedle Street in 1662 to find the sermon in Dutch.[68] In spite of the concession, this was not a harmonious arrangement. In their attempt to obtain permission to use the church in 1573, the French congregation asserted that Austin Friars had been granted by Edward VI to both congregations in 1550. This became an on-going source of tension and dispute between the Dutch and French Churches, the former arguing that the reconstitution of the churches on the accession of Elizabeth denied this right. It was raised at the Coetus in 1579–80 and 1582, and again in 1605, but without any satisfactory resolution.[69] A former elder and prominent figure in the Dutch community wrote in 1605 that permission had only been granted provisionally for the French to use Austin Friars, and also went on to comment "that Wingius [minister of the Dutch Church to 1590] advised us not to lend them the temple for the celebration of the Holy Supper forseeing or fearing that this would afford them a pretext for usurping the whole church".[70] The antagonism over the use of Austin Friars continued into the seventeenth century and even led to changes in the religious practices of the Dutch Church. The French congregation had begun to hold celebrations of the Lord's Supper at Easter in order to please James VI, who was actively pursuing such a policy in Scotland. In 1616, they requested permission to use Austin Friars for their Easter service, which prompted the Dutch to adopt this custom as it provided them with the justification for denying the French the use of the building.[71] The building and its use thereby became the pretext for a change in religious worship for the Dutch congregation and it was a custom which, although adopted in a cavalier manner, was later defended by them against the Puritan attack on holy days.[72]

Members of the exile churches were obliged to contribute to the parish rates, which was defined in the Norwich Book of Orders of 1571 as being "for the discharge of all manner of dewties, growenge to the preste and clarcke of the same parishe".[73] These parish rates were principally related to the ministers' stipend and poor relief, but also encompassed the cost of repair and maintenance for the church fabric.[74] The Dutch congregation in Sandwich initially rented an aisle of St Clements church for 40s *per annum*, but an agreement was made on 25 March 1617 for the congregation to pay a third of all the repair costs of the church.[75] There was an on-going dispute between the congregation and the Dean and Chapter of Canterbury concerning repair to the cathedral crypt. In 1576, the consistory minutes refer to the initial payment of a mark but then further payment of up to £1.[76] The congregation of Austin Friars undertook extensive repairs in 1605 and £1,500 was spent on redecorating and repairing the temple in 1615. The ruinous condition of the spire of Austin Friars led the Lord Mayor of London to write, in 1600, to the Marquis of Winchester to whom it belonged. It was for this reason that the Dutch Church refused an order from the Privy Council to undertake repairs in 1609, although they did offer to contribute. While the discussions continued the spire and remains of the choir were sold to one Henry Robinson; his demolition work in 1613 threatened the east wall of the Dutch Church and had to be halted on the orders of the Council.[77] Furthermore, the building suffered drainage problems, and the light entering the church was blocked by plants because of tenements abutting the church walls.[78] The issue of building repairs was something which was to play an important part in the dispute between the Bishop of Norwich and the Walloon congregation there.

In some senses, the accommodation which served the exile congregations as their place of worship seems ad hoc and makeshift. As there was initially an expectation that the congregations would return to their homelands once conditions had improved, such temporary arrangements are understandable. Furthermore it was a reflection of the different attitude that the reformed churches had towards sanctity and places of worship. In his *Institutes*, Calvin wrote:

> public places have been appointed which we call "temples". These do not by any secret sanctity of their own make prayers more holy, or cause them to be heard by God. But they are intended to receive the congregation of believers more conveniently when they gather to pray, to hear the preaching of the Word, and at the same time to partake of the sacraments. Otherwise (as Paul says) . . . we ourselves are the true temples of God . . . But those who suppose that God's ear has been brought closer to them in a temple, or consider their prayer more consecrated by the holiness of the place, are acting in this way according to the stupidity of the Jews and Gentiles. In physically worshipping God, they go against what has been commanded, that, without any consideration of place, we worship God in spirit and truth.[79]

The temple was not a holy site or a consecrated building, but a convenient place where the congregations could assemble for worship. Like their co-religionists in France, they had no problem in adapting former religious and secular buildings for their use.[80] A sense of this ambivalence and the makeshift character of a reformed place of worship can be seen in the licence granted by Archbishop Abbott to the tapestry weavers at Mortlake. It permitted the Dutch Church in London to appoint a minister "to celebrate divine service, preache the Worde of God, and administer the holy sacraments .. either in the parish church of Mortlack if it may be done conveniently, or in the howse of Sir Francis Crane knight or any other convenient place there".[81] Similarly the workers employed on the drainage and reclamation of Hatfield Chase and the Isle of Axholme during the early seventeenth century had a "place or barne wherin they performe their divine service". Archbishop Neile of York wrote disparagingly about the congregation in a letter to William Laud in June 1636: "A barn of Sir Phillibert Vernatty is the place which they use for their church, whether the whole company have resort on Sondaies, where they baptize in a dishe after their owne manner, and administer the sacrament after their homely fashion of sitting."[82] For the 'Laudian' bishops such as Neile, the use of secular and makeshift accommodation was an affront to their view of the church as the house of God, the place where His presence was felt most strongly. A church was a holy place consecrated for divine worship.[83] Such attitudes help to explain the intense hostility and contempt shown towards the Walloon congregation at Norwich by Bishop Corbet. He attacked the congregation in the following manner: "Your discipline, I know cares not much for a consecrated place, & any other roome in Norwiche that hath but breadth and length may serve your turne as well as a chappell. Wherefore I say unto, without a miracle, *Lazare prodi foras!* Depart, and hire some other place for your irregular meetings".[84]

Corbet's comment was made during the 1630s when the privileged status of the stranger churches was being questioned by the prevailing 'Laudian' religious establishment. While the assault by Archbishop Laud on the foreign churches within his own diocese principally focused on the failure of members of the community who were born in England to attend their parish churches, there does not seem to have been any challenge made to their actual places of worship. In fact the Dean and Chapter of Canterbury, whose predecessors had granted permission for the Walloon congregation to meet in the Cathedral crypt, testified to the good conduct of the congregation and the economic contribution that they made to the city.[85] In Norwich, there was similarly an attempt to make the second-generation exiles attend their parish churches for worship and the example of the Sandtoft community was held up as a model, having initially conformed and accepted a French translation of the liturgy and rites of the Church of England.[86] Furthermore, the Bishops' chapel, which had been used by the Walloon congregation for over 60 years, became the centre of a dispute between the Bishop and the exile community. There had been an attempt made in 1619 to eject the congregation and make them worship in the chapel of New Hall (the former Blackfriars), but they had objected because "the said chappell at the new hall, is too little for their company, and that the sermons of the Dutch & Walloons being at one and the self-same tyme, the voice of the one congregation in singing Psalmes and the like, will hinder and disturb the other".[87] As a result the matter was dropped, but the bishop required the congregation "use no other than their own chayers, which they must remove" when required.[88] During the 1630s, however, under Richard Corbet and his successor Matthew Wren, a concerted effort was made to reclaim the chapel. Wren's attitude was reflected in a letter to Bishop Montague: "As touching the chapel, I reckoned not of it further than thus, That I have it I would [sic] out of the Walloons hand, for the use of my own family; and so I had it at Whitsontide before I removed".[89]

The bishops also pursued the congregation over the cost of repairs for the chapel, but in a detailed petition to Bishop Wren in April 1638, the congregation denied that they had any agreement to maintain the chapel but had paid for repairs as a gesture of good-will for the use of the building. Furthermore they had "been put to the needles charges . . . to repaire and accommodate to their uses a poore and little forlorne Church, graunted them by the Cittyes favour. Which cost might have been spared and bestowed upon the said Chappell in time of neede if they had still continued in it".[90] The church of St Mary the Less – 'nouveau temple' – became the community's place of worship for the remainder of its history.

The first temples built by the foreign Protestant communities were those erected to serve the workers employed in the drainage and land reclamation schemes in the early seventeenth century. In 1622, Joos Croppenburgh contracted with Sir Henry Appleton to embank and reclaim flooded land at Canvey Island. The Dutch community there petitioned Bishop Monteigne of London in 1627 that being

> destitute of those spirituall comforts which they might enioy by the vse of divine service, according to those priviledges which it hath pleased his Maiestie to graunt unto sundry other Strangers within this Realme; And for that purpose they have prouided a house in the sayd Iland sett apart for divine service, and have fitted itt conveniently for the same, vntill they may get a Chappell to be built in the sayd Iland, which they intend by Godes helpe to effect within the space of two or three yeares att the most.

They requested that they be permitted:

> to have among themselves the vse of divine service, together with the preaching of the Word and administering of the holy sacraments in their owne native language either in some parish Church neere the sayd Iland or in the sayd house until they may have a Chappell of their owne.[91]

Nothing seems to have come from this request, as several years later some 200 Netherlanders petitioned the King for permission to establish a small church where they could worship in Dutch. On this occasion the request was granted, a minister was appointed through Austin Friars and a wooden chapel was erected which continued to serve the community into the eighteenth century.[92]

The provision of a suitable place of worship figured prominently in the contracts to drain the Isle of Axholme/Hatfield Chase. In December 1628 Sir Cornelius Vermuyden was permitted "to erecte or build one or more chappell or chappelles for the exercise of religion or devine service to be vsed or reade in the English or Dutch language". Several local landowners were granted permission in 1636 "to erect and build one or more chapel or chapels . . . in the premises most convenient, and at their own expense, to maintain in the same ministers sufficient to celebrate divine service there".[93] Official sanction for a new building was one thing; construction was another. Nonetheless, it was reported in 1636 that "they have burned bricks and are preparing materialls to build a chappele" but the departure of their minister Pierre Bontemps meant that the settlers "resorted to three parish churches in the Isle of Axholme and here have communicated, christened, married and buried". As a result they had started to "sell away the materialls that they had provided for a Chappell which they intended to have built".[94] In spite of this apparent reversal in fortunes, the congregation deliberated further in November 1637, "seeing that these gentlemen take no steps to accommodate this community, we have been compelled to meet two, three or four times to consider how we might obtain a minister and build a church".[95] The participants in the drainage scheme finally entered into a contract with a merchant, Isaac Bedloe, for the construction of a place of worship. Bedloe built and finished the temple and a house for the minister at his own cost, spending £1,159 3s 9d in total on the project. Although some of the money was repaid, Bedloe was forced to go to court in 1640 to recover the remainder, which still remained unpaid in 1661.[96]

Little is known about the appearance of the temple, although a brick tablet inscribed with Biblical references, found during preliminary archaeological excavations in 1989, may have come from the building.[97] The temple itself was at the centre of a dispute between the congregation and John Farmery, Chancellor of the Diocese of Lincoln, which continued the 'Laudian' dispute about the sanctity of a place of worship. Farmery recorded how Etienne Cursol did "administer the sacraments to them in some one of our consecrated churches, Belton or Epworth, and not in the new built wooden house where Bontemps [the previous minister] officiated in his time". Farmery seems to have threatened the community with the forfeiture of their rights if they failed to consecrate their temple. This was in spite of the reformed attitudes about the sanctity of a place of worship. The settlers seem to have been embroiled in a dispute in the ecclesiastical court at Lincoln but in February 1641 petitioned the House of Lords.[98]

The temple was not only at the centre of ecclesiastical disputes, but also became the focus of violence directed against the foreign community as a whole. The building had come to symbolize the foreign community and was subjected to a number of xenophobic assaults by the inhabitants of the Isle of Axholme/Hatfield Chase opposed to the drainage schemes which deprived them of their common rights. In 1645, the minister and representatives of the foreign churches protested to the House of Lords that rioters had thrown down their enclosures, destroyed their crops, as well as breaking ploughs and farming equipment, and "daily threaten to pull down all the Petitioners' houses and their Church". The rioters seem, in part, to have carried through with their threat as the petitioners sought compensation for the damage done, which included "broken and burnt the seats in the church, broken the glass windows, and pulled down the lead from the church and steeple". [99] The most serious outbreaks of violence came in 1650–1 when 84 houses were destroyed, but the temple continued to be the object of attack. The minister was prevented from preaching there in October 1651 and "since that they have made a cowhouse of the church and spoyled it, hewed downe the pulpit, tooke downe the windows, and totally defaced the church, and that hay is layd there ever since".[100] The following petition, made to Cromwell in March 1656, records the repeated attacks on the building and attempts to desecrate and render the building unusable:

> That your petitioners not haueinge the libertye to exercise the Protestant religion in theyr native countryes, did flye into England, and settle their families within the said Levell, and had a church erected for theyr publique seruice of God att Sandtofte, where they had peaceably assembled for almoste twenty yeares.
> That diuers of the inhabitants of the Isle of Axholme, in the County of Lincolne aforesaid, in a moste barbarous and inhumane manner riotously destroyed the corne and rapes, and demolished the habitations and millne of your petitioners, exposeinge them to the extremity of cold and famine.

That the sayd rioters, esteeminge it a little thinge to haue berefte your petitioners of theyr estates and liuelyhood (which they had formerly not accounted deare to them in competition with theyr religion, except they should haue demolished the House of God likewise), did breake doune the windowes, doores, seates, and pulpit of the said Church and did steale away the leade and iron thereof. And findinge that, as your petitioners frequented not theyr Church because it was not conueniently accommodated to God's worshipe, soe neither would they discontinue theyr assembling thear, notwithstanding it was so defaced, made it a slaughterhouse, and a stable and buryed carryon in the same.

That the said rioters findinge all theyr irreligeos practices ineffectual to the keepinge your petitioners from meeetinge att theyr soe noyseome and ruinated place of worship, Mr Danyell Nordell, Sollicitor to the said Isle, with seuerall inhabitants thereof, came to the said Church on the Lord's day, and with armes enforced them thence, sayinge that vnlesse your petitioners were stronger then they, your petitioners should not come there
. . . .

That on the said one and twentieth day of January last, seuerall the inhabitants of the said Isle (with whome the said Mr. Noddell was, att theyr settinge forwards), being armed with guns and diuers other weapons, did come to the said Church, and did beate downe the windowes, dores, seates, and pulpit, haueinge layd them in heaps within the said Church, did sett them on fyer, and threatned to pull downe the stone and tymber thereof, and offered to sell the same.[101]

Although the appeal, made to Cromwell, sought to draw parallels between the Sandtoft community and the persecuted Protestants of Savoy, it does demonstrate how the temple provided a focus for the hostility felt towards the settlers by the local population. The violence of the assault was reminiscent of the attacks made upon Huguenot temples and the Catholic attempt to eradicate the religious threat that their very existence represented.[102]

The experience of the Sandtoft community was unique and was not one shared by the other immigrant churches during the 1640s and 1650s. By the mid-seventeenth century the exile churches had been in existence for 100 years and the anniversary was celebrated in 1650 with a joint service of the French and Dutch congregations in London.[103] Legislation the previous year had led to the abolition of the Dean and Chapter of Windsor and meant that the French congregation took possession of the Threadneedle Street church, which they had rented for a century. In these changed circumstances, in May 1649, the minister Jean de la Marche proposed the rebuilding of the temple; a year later he estimated the cost of the project at between 600 to 700 livres. House-to-house collections began that month and £890 14s 1½d was raised for work on the temple. The extent of this construction work or repair is unclear but it would seem to have fallen short of the complete rebuilding called for by de la Marche. However, it was still a substantial project, for which the mason, Mr Wilson, was paid £208 7s 0d and the carpenter, Mr Tailer, received £195.[104] Whatever work was undertaken was relatively short-lived, for the church was destroyed in the Great Fire of London in 1666.

In spite of the confidence expressed by the reconstruction of the Threadneedle Street temple, the churches of the mid-seventeenth century were very different from those established in 1550 to allow foreign settlers to hear the Word of God in their own tongue. The character of the congregations had changed; the original migrants had either returned to the continent as the political climate there improved, or had settled and, with their descendants, been assimilated into the native population.[105] The situation in London was symptomatic of this changed environment. The Dutch Church had been unable to stem the drift of members to the Independent and Separatist congregations during the 1640s and 1650s, while the French Church was wracked by internal disputes and witnessed the emergence of the rival church of Jean d'Espagne in the capital.[106] While new communities had been established during the early seventeenth century, they were not composed of religious refugees but of foreign artisans involved in the land reclamation schemes of eastern England. Nonetheless, their desire for their own place of worship remained just as important to these new communities as it had in 1550. While the religious refugees of the 1550s and 1560s had been granted temporary accommodation in redundant ecclesiastical buildings or had even shared the local parish church, the later settlers actively lobbied for permission to build a temple.

The temple had a symbolic significance, in some cases representing the last vestiges of the religious persecution that had led many to seek exile in England. The Laudian assault on their privileged position led many to remember the circumstances which had brought these churches into existence and served to revitalise their communities. For external observers, the temple had come to be seen as the physical embodiment of the foreign population. At Sandtoft, it was the focus for the hostility felt by the local inhabitants towards the drainage and land reclamation schemes in which the foreign artisans were involved. The temple also symbolized an alternative religious system to that established by the Elizabethan Religious Settlement. The foreign congregations adapted the religious buildings they were granted and in the seventeenth century built temples from scratch, which reflected the demands of reformed worship. They were more like auditoriums centred on the pulpit, designed for the preaching of the Word of God. They stood in marked contrast to the interiors of the Elizabethan and later Laudian parish churches and had much more in common with the places of worship of their co-religionists in Scotland or on the continent. However, the gradual emergence of 'Puritan' architecture from the end of Elizabeth's reign and, more significantly, the development of the nonconformist meeting house during the later seventeenth century, meant that the appearance of the stranger churches eventually became less unique in England.[107] While the exile churches were viewed covetously by the Elizabethan Puritans as symbolizing a religious ideal, they were regarded as potential "vipers nourished in our bosomes", an affront to religious conformity, by the 'Laudian' bishops.[108] The attack upon these congregations during the 1630s – while ultimately unsuccessful – was largely concerned with their privileges and with limiting access to their services, but at Norwich and Sandtoft the actual temples were part of the dispute between the communities and the ecclesiastical authorities. The temples of the exile churches, although intended exclusively to meet the religious needs of their communities, had become highly visible symbols of the architectural and liturgical response to reformed worship, which until the mid-seventeenth century was at odds with the policies and practices of the established Church in England.

Notes

1   Bulteel, *Relation of the Troubles*, p. 14.
2   Hessels, Vol. 3 Part 2, p. 1876. The wording chosen in the petition echoes that of the original foundation charter of the community: Lindeboom, *Austin Friars*, p. 201.
3   BL, Cottonian MSS Vesp. F.IX, f. 230.

4   Cross, *History of the Walloon & Huguenot Church*, p. 15; Pettegree, *Foreign Protestant Communities*, p. 287.

5   According to the 1568 survey of the capital's foreign population, there were 6,704 aliens of whom 1,815 went to the English Church, while 1,008 didn't attend any church at all. There were 1,910 aliens recorded as attending the Dutch Church, 1,810 the French Church and 161 the Italian Church: Kirk & Kirk, Part 1, p. 393, Part 3, p. 439.

6   Pettegree, *Foreign Protestant Communities*, pp. 142–3.

7   *APC 1571–75*, p. 135.

8   Backhouse, *Flemish and Walloon Communities*, pp. 33–4; *APC 1586–87*, p. 25.

9   Hamilton (ed.), *Books of Examination and Depositions*, p. 97.

10   Spicer, "Poor Relief and the Exile Communities", pp. 252–3.

11   *APC 1621–23*, p. 58; *APC 1630–31*, p. 181.

12   Bradley and Pevsner, *Buildings of England. London*, p. 138.

13   Kaye (ed.), *The Cartulary of God's House*, pp. lxxix–lxxx.

14   Moens, *Walloons and their Church at Norwich*, p. 23; Malster, "Passing of a Norwich Church", pp. 56–59: I am grateful to Dr Esser for this reference.

15   Collinson, "Elizabethan Puritans and the Foreign Reformed Communities", p. 261.

16   Bratchel, "Alien Merchant Colonies", pp. 41–2; Ruddock, *Italian Merchants and Shipping*, pp. 131–3.

17   Pettegree, *Foreign Protestant Communities*, pp. 24–5, 31–2; Lindeboom, *Austin Friars*, p. 201.

18   Pettegree, *Foreign Protestant Communities*, pp. 36–7.

19   Pettegree, *Foreign Protestant Communities*, p. 34.

20   Pettegree, *Foreign Protestant Communities*, pp. 143–4.

21   Kinder, *Casiodoro de Reina*, pp. 21–2.

22   Boersma and Jelsma, *Unity in Multiformity*, pp. 21–4, 40–2, 49–52; Huelin, *Think and Thank God*, pp. 8–11.

23   BL, Cott. MSS Vesp. FIX, f. 230.

24   Cross, *History of the Walloon and Huguenot Church*, p. 15.

25   Moens, *Walloons and their Church at Norwich*, p. 253.

26   Pettegree, *Foreign Protestant Communities*, pp. 44–5; Backhouse, *Flemish and Walloon Communities*, pp. 65–6. See also Duke, "Martyrs with a Difference", pp. 263–81.

27   Pettegree, *Foreign Protestant Communities*, pp. 20, 65–6, 167–72.

28   Backhouse, *Flemish and Walloon Communities*, p. 76; Spicer, *French-Speaking Reformed Community*, p. 29; Pettegree, *Foreign Protestant Communities*, p. 262–4.

29   Moens, *Walloons and their Church at Norwich*, pp. 21, 253.

30   PRO, SP 12/43/16.

31   PRO, SP 15/13/80; Spicer, *French-Speaking Reformed Community*, pp. 33–4.

32   Oakley, "Canterbury Walloon Congregation", p. 59.

33   Backhouse, "Flemish Refugees in Sandwich", pp. 104, 106.

34   *Cartulary of God's House*, 1, p. lxxix. The God's House accounts record regular payments for bread and wine: Queen's College, Oxford, Gods House Accounts Box 4/7–17, 5/18–33.

35   PRO, PCC Probate 11/54 Johannes Carré; Godfrey, *Development of English Glassmaking*, pp. 17–18.

36   Mayhew, *Tudor Rye*, p. 88.

37   Collinson, "Eizabethan Puritans and the Foreign Reformed Communities", pp. 262–5; Pettegree, *Foreign Protestant Communities*, pp. 273–5.

38   Pettegree, *Foreign Protestant Communities*, pp. 36, 37, 38.

39   Queen's College, GHA Box 4/7. Further work seems to have been undertaken in 1575 that included whitewashing the chapel: Box 4/11.

40   PRO, SP 16/387/47.

41 Moens, *Walloons and their Church at Norwich*, p. 278.

42 *Cartulary of God's House*, 1, p. lxxviii.

43 Stow, *Survey of London*, Vol. 1, pp. 176–7.

44 Martin, *Franciscan Architecture in England*, pp. 14–17; Pevsner and Wilson, *Buildings of England*. Norfolk 1, p. 267.

45 See Spicer, "Continental Calvinism and its Churches", p. 303; Spicer, "Iconoclasm and Adaptation".

46 Pevsner and Wilson, *Buildings of England. Norfolk I*, p. 266.

47 Moens, *Walloons and their Church at Norwich*, p. 23; Pevsner and Wilson, *Buildings of England. Norfolk I*, pp. 267–8.

48 Battles (ed.), John Calvin, *Institutes of the Christian Religion*, pp. 62–3.

49 Chanier (ed.), *Les Actes des Colloques des Églises Françaises*, p. 5; Godfray (ed.), *Registre des Baptesmes, Mariages & Morts*, p. 18.

50 Parker, *Calvin's Preaching*, pp. 35–53.

51 Hessels, Vol. 3 Part 2, p. 1869.

52 Addleshaw and Etchells, *Architectural Setting of Anglican Worship*, pp. 30–4.

53 Yule, "James VI and I", pp. 187–92, 197; Stell, "Puritan and Nonconformist Meetinghouses", pp. 52–3. See also Moens, *Walloons and their Church at Norwich*, p. 66.

54 On preaching and the liturgical rearrangement of churches in Scotland, see Spicer, "'Accommodating of Thame Selfis to Heir the Worde'", pp. 405–22.

55 Johnson (ed.), *Actes du Consistoire*, p. 7; Huguenot Library, London, MS J27 Sandwich Deacons accounts, p. 140.

56 Johnson (ed.), *Actes du Consistoire*, pp. xviii, 27. Evrail had offended one elder by sitting in the pew after delivering a sermon and he had subsequently complained to the consistory.

57 FPL, MSS 5, "Actes du Consistoire, 1615–1680", fo. 109. On segregated seating, see Aston, "Segregation in Church"; Spicer, "'Accommodating of Thame Selfis to Heir the Worde'", p. 415.

58 FPL, MSS 5, "Actes du Consistoire", fo. 106

59 FPL, MSS 5, "Actes du Consistoire", fo. 106. "Monsieur Leviston" can tentatively be identified as James Levingston, Groom to the Bedchamber of Charles I. Although further research is needed, it seems that he may have been confused with Sir John Livingston or his son James Livingstone, later first Earl of Newburgh (d. 1670). The former was a Gentleman of the Bedchamber to James VI but died in 1628, and although his son's birth is not recorded, it has been dated to c. 1622. *CSPD 1627–28*, pp. 77, 429, *CSPD 1628–29*, pp. 534, 577, *CSPD 1629–31*, pp. 28, 522, *CSPD 1631–33*, p. 458, *CSPD 1633–36*, pp. 380–1; Foster, *Alumni Oxoniensis*, Vol. 3, p. 905; Venn &Venn, *Alumni Cantabrigiensis*, Vol. 3, p. 79; *DNB*, Vol. 11, p. 1277; Henning (ed.), *History of Parliament*, Vol. 2, pp. 754–5; Mosley, *Burke's Peerage*, pp. 2072–3; Cokayne, *Complete Peerage*, Vol. 9, pp. 511–14.

60 Latham and Mathews (eds), *Diary of Samuel Pepys*, Vol. 3, p. 270.

61 Grell, *Dutch Calvinists*, pp. 48–9.

62 Lindeboom, *Austin Friars*, p. 174.

63 Stools and chairs used during the services at the Dutch Church in Norwich are recorded among the probate inventories of members of the community. Norfolk Record Office, Norwich Consistory Court, Inv. 2A/30/1584, 9/100/1592, 9/303/1592, 17/35/1601, 19/157/1603, 20/47/'603, 21/20/1602, 176/1613. I am very grateful to Mrs Nancy Ives for these references and for sharing this information with me.

64 Lindeboom, *Austin Friars*, pp. 174–5; Grell, "From Persecution to Integration", p. 134; Robertson, "*Il Gran Cardinale*", p. 189.

65 Hessels, Vol. 3, Part 2, p. 1928.

66 Oakley (ed.), *Actes du Consistoire de l'Église Française*, pp. vi, 89, 93; Lindeboom, *Austin Friars*, p. 99.

67 Oakley, "Dispute over Austin Friars Church, 1573", pp. 492–8; Lindeboom, *Austin Friars* p. 99.

68 Lindeboom, *Austin Friars* p. 101; Latham and Mathews (eds), *Diary of Samuel Pepys*, Vol. 3, pp. 276–7.

69 Lindeboom, *Austin Friars* pp. 99–101; Boersma, *Unity in Multiformity*, pp. 67–9, 72–3, 79; *Actes du Consistoire, 1571–77*, pp. 108, 118; FPL, MSS 3, Actes du Consistoire, pp. 55, 123.

70 Hessels, Vol. 3, Part 1, pp. 1166–9.

71 Grell, "French and Dutch Congregations", p. 40; Burnet, *Holy Communion in the Reformed Church*, pp. 67–70.

72 Grell, "From Uniformity to Tolerance", p. 90.

73 Moens, *Walloons and their Church at Norwich*, pp. 255–7.

74 *Journals of the House of Lords*, Vol. 4, p. 165.

75 Moens, *Marriage, Baptismal, and Burial Registers*, p. xx.

76 Cathedral Archives, Canterbury, U47/A1 Actes du Consistoire, 15/11/1576.

77 Moens, *Austin Friars*, p. xxix; Lindeboom, *Austin Friars*, pp. 175–6.

78 Lindeboom, *Austin Friars*, pp. 177–9.

79 *Institutes of the Christian Religion*, p. 73.

80 Mentzer, "Reformed Churches of France and the Visual Arts", pp. 203–4. See also Spicer, "'Qui est de Dieu oit la parole de Dieu'".

81 Hessels, Vol. 3, Part 1, p. 1296.

82 PRO, SP 16/327/47.

83 Lake, "The Laudian Style", p. 165; See Spicer, "Profanation and Consecration" ; Spicer, "Reflections on Post-Reformation Rites of Consecration".

84 PRO, SP 16/400/45.

85 Bulteel, *Relation of the Troubles*, pp. 10–11.

86 Moens, *Walloons and their Church at Norwich*, p. 277.

87 Vane, "Walloon Community in Norwich", pp. 135–6.

88 Moens, *Walloons and their Church at Norwich*, p. 22.

89 PRO, SP 16/400/45.

90 PRO, SP 16/387/47.

91 Hessels, Vol. 3, Part 1, p. 1354.

92 PRO, SP 16/93/2–3; Moens, *Austin Friars*, p. xxxv; Harris, *Vermuyden and the Fens*, p. 39; Wright, *History and Topography*, Vol. 2, p. 589; Cracknell, *Canvey Island*, p. 22.

93 Le Moine and Moens, "Huguenots in the Isle of Axholme", pp. 278–9; Overend, "First Thirty Years", pp. 292–3.

94 PRO, SP 16/327/47, SP 16/331/71, SP 16/345/85.

95 Hessels, Vol. 3, Part 2, pp. 1759–60.

96 HMC, *Seventh Report of the Royal Commission on Historical Manuscripts*, pp. 136, 145.

97 Humberside County Council: Sites and Monuments Record – "Sandtoft Excavations, May 1989", C. Lindsey Archaeological Services. I am grateful to the North Lincolnshire Museum, Scunthorpe, for making this information available to me.

98 PRO, SP 16/310/1; *Journals of the House of Lords*, Vol. 4, pp. 165, 181.

99 *Journals of the House of Lords*, Vol. 7, pp. 706–7; HMC, *Sixth Report of the Royal Commission on Historical Manuscripts*, p. 85.

100 PRO, SP 18/129/144; Overend, "First Thirty Years", pp. 320–1.

101 PRO, SP 18/126/57.

102 Davis, "Rites of Violence", in her *Society and Culture in Early Modern France*, pp. 156–64; Spicer, "'Qui est de Dieu, oit la parole de Dieu'", pp. 175–9, 191–2.

103 FPL, MSS 5, Actes du Consistoire, fo. 354.

104 FPL, MSS 5, Actes du Consistoire, ff. 346, 352; MS62 ff.1–10.

105 See Spicer, "Process of Gradual Assimilation", pp. 186–98.

106 Grell, "From Uniformity to Tolerance", pp. 90–4; Gwynn (ed.), *Calendar of the Letter Books*, pp. 4–18. On the chapel used by d'Espagne's congregation, see Thurley, "Stuart Kings", p. 254.
107 See Stell, "Puritan and Nonconformist Meeting Houses", pp. 50–65. Although the motives are unknown, it may have been the suitability of the "very convenient church" used by the Dutch congregation which led the Independents in Yarmouth to attempt to eject them during the 1640s: Hessels, Vol. 3, Part 2, pp. 1980–2.
108 They were described as such by Archbishop Neile in a letter to William Laud: PRO, SP 16/32747.

6

"Xenophobia" in Elizabethan and Early Stuart England: An Epithet Too Far?

Nigel Goose

Historians disagree fundamentally about English attitudes to foreigners in the early modern period. Some have described the English as quite generally xenophobic, notably Laura Hunt Yungblut, in whose book *Strangers Settled Here Amongst Us* the term "xenophobia" commands an extensive index entry.[1] Although lip service is paid to English support for the concept of asylum and even to an initially warm popular response, the large numbers of aliens, she argues, "brought the legendary English xenophobia to the surface on many occasions".[2] During the reign of Elizabeth I a "rising tide of anti-alien expressions" is detected, rooted in "xenophobic preconceptions and misconceptions", and fuelled by perceived economic competition between aliens and native Englishmen.[3] Nor were these attitudes socially specific, for "distrust of foreigners was not restricted to the lower classes", a statement which is justified by reference to remarks made about French denizens by Sir Nicholas Bacon in 1576.[4]

If Yungblut stands at one end of the spectrum, she is by no means alone in accusing the English of xenophobia. In a recent article on sixteenth-century London Lien Luu also uses the term freely, concluding that "Xenophobia in early modern London took many forms", the most serious of which was not the threat of physical abuse and violence, though this did occur, but parliamentary legislation designed to restrict the economic and political rights of aliens and their children.[5] Luu too argues that the situation grew worse towards the end of the century, with "threats of violence against aliens becoming more endemic and more frequent", until many aliens became disillusioned with life in the English capital, and potential new immigrants from the southern Netherlands were deterred from coming over.[6] Similar conclusions have been drawn by non-specialists in the field, such as Christopher Hibbert, who assures us that in the early eighteenth century the English "were still violently xenophobic", the evidence for which is supplied by a short quotation from César de Saussure's letters to his family, written during a period of residence in London between 1725 and 1729.[7] In a similar vein, if on a narrower canvas, Simon Schama rehearses at some length the

English hostility to the Dutch in the mid-seventeenth century with minimal qualification by reference to "a small and relatively uninfluential group" who desisted from the general condemnation of the Dutch as avaricious, rapacious, untrustworthy, vulgar upstarts, the just proprietors of a reclaimed land so graphically characterized by Andrew Marvell as "This indigested vomit of the sea".[8]

Other authorities are more circumspect, and London historians such as Ian Archer, Stephen Rappaport and Joe Ward have all expressed serious reservations about categorizing Londoners as xenophobic. Archer emphasizes the lack of violence perpetrated against aliens in the sixteenth century, as well as the clear evidence of peaceful co-existence, offering an interpretation of the numerous complaints and libels against aliens in terms of contemporary mechanisms of negotiation between rulers and the ruled. He concludes that English attitudes were "rather more ambiguous and the reception rather less unwelcoming than the regularly recycled comments of foreign visitors would suggest".[9] Rappaport appreciates that tension was often evident between native and alien craftsmen in sixteenth-century London, but argues that this was commonly the result of a perception that aliens were contravening rules to which all artisans were expected to conform, whether alien or native, while he too emphasizes the distinct lack of popular violence in the capital after the serious disturbance of Evil May Day in 1517.[10] And finally Joe Ward has recently also suggested that the term xenophobia is too strong, for both the records of the Weavers Company and the characterization of artisan's attitudes as represented in Thomas Dekker's play *The Shoemaker's Holiday* indicate that, even within an economic group which often found itself in direct competition with the immigrant population, considerably sympathy co-existed with periodic antipathy.[11]

For the provinces historians have been even less inclined to characterize English attitudes and behaviour to aliens in hostile terms. In Colchester there is considerable evidence of economic tension between the Dutch community and the indigenous population in the later sixteenth and early seventeenth centuries, particularly in years of economic difficulty, and there is no doubt that they were often used as scapegoats by "the poorer sort" for more general economic problems. But their privileges were consistently upheld by both Corporation and Privy Council; they were generally treated with an admirable even-handedness; they co-existed peacefully with the indigenous population with very little sign of violence and gradually integrated with the local community.[12] Andrew Spicer reached similar conclusions in his study of Southampton, while Marcel Backhouse placed more emphasis upon conflict in the case of Sandwich.[13]

Why do we find this range of views? There are numerous reasons, but the first is perhaps the most surprising in view of the complexity and emotive nature of this issue, and that is the complete failure to define the terms of reference. One searches in vain for a clear definition in the historical literature of "xenophobia" which, according to nearly all dictionary definitions, should incorporate fear as well as hatred of foreigners, although it is usually employed only to indicate the latter.[14] Interestingly, the *OED* gives a slightly less extreme definition, "a deep antipathy to foreigners", but the examples of usage it offers show that its employment is often lax, that it is too often confused with nationalism and that its misuse can easily trivialize its true meaning.[15] Xenophobia is not racism or racialism, for it pertains to national rather than racial distinctions. But it is more than nationalism, which denotes devotion to one's own nation without *necessarily* implying disrespect, let alone hatred, towards others.[16] If the term is to have any clear meaning at all, then it is more than mere "antipathy", and should indicate at the very least the "*deep* antipathy" of the *OED* definition, if not the "hatred" preferred by most other dictionaries.[17] Furthermore, it is not a *selective* attitude, to be applied to only certain foreigners at certain times, for the mainsprings of such periodic feelings of hostility may well be religious, political or economic rivalry, not a general distaste for or hatred of foreigners in general. Some historians clearly do confuse politico-religious or economic rivalry with xenophobia, and it is clear that it is possible to misrepresent attitudes by selective quotation from the propaganda that periodic conflict could produce.[18] Finally, its attribution to "the English" – as a national characteristic that transcends social class, place and time – needs careful scrutiny, as much for the sixteenth and seventeenth centuries as it does for contemporary England.

A second problem is the manner in which the comments of foreign visitors and diplomats are presented, plundered and repeated without due critical regard. Even some specialists in the field fail to resist the temptation blithely to quote some apparently telling remark, either to set the tone of the discussion which follows, or to provide the punchline at the end, while for non-specialists such evidence can occasionally substitute for any real discussion at all.[19] Ever since William Brenchley Rye published his *England as Seen by Foreigners* in the mid-nineteenth century historians have had to hand a ready source of pithy representations of the English and their attitudes to foreigners that have been repeatedly rehearsed.[20] But the significance of this material is far from straightforward, for the reliability of such sources can be questioned on a number of counts. In many cases the visits of foreign travellers and diplomats were very brief indeed, and such passing acquaintance could hardly be sufficient fully to lay bare the English character. This is particularly true of the Venetian diplomats that are so freely quoted, such as Andrea Trevisano who stayed in London for a few months in 1496–7, describing the English as,

> great lovers of themselves, and of everything belonging to them; they think there are no other men than themselves, and no other world but England; and whenever they see a handsome foreigner, they say that 'he looks like an Englishman', and that 'it is a great pity that he should not be an Englishman . . . ' They have an antipathy to foreigners, and imagine that they never come into their island, but to make themselves masters of it, and to usurp their goods. . . . [21]

Neither the breadth nor depth of Trevisano's familiarity with his host nation is questioned, though he cannot have gained much first-hand knowledge of anywhere but the capital in so short a stay, nor much intimacy with the lower or middling orders of society. Nor is it noticed that he also denies that the English have any solid friendships amongst themselves, that he accuses the English of want of affection for their children or that he claims that they "keep a very jealous guard over their wives", each a highly questionable judgement, the last standing in direct contradiction to the wealth of comment from a variety of sources on the relative freedom enjoyed by English women in the sixteenth century compared to their Italian counterparts.[22] Even such a formiddable traveller as Peter Mundy was well aware that much could be missed, writing in the preface to his *Itinerarium Mundii* that there were times on his journeys when he "took butt a Cursary and superccall Notice as a Passenger, and, To say truth, nott soe punctuall as I ought or Mightt have Don", while "a straunger May live in England Many yeares and perhapps nott know Whither there are any Otters or badgers in the Countrie or noe, because hee hath nott seene Nor enquired affter such, and soe consequently off some Customes, as pressing to Death, etts".[23] Fynes Moryson was particularly concerned about the false impression of the English that only a superficial acquaintance might create:

> I have heard some complaine of England, for the deare rates of diet, and for the peoples inhumanity to strangers, because they had been ill used at Gravesend (where the very English are rudely and ill served), and by some obscure Hosts of London, who use to entertaine and wrong strangers, having otherwise never visited the Citizens of London, the Schollers of the Universities, Gentlemen, or learned men, not having ever gone further then London into the Countrey, which if they had done; they should have found these men, and the very Countrey people not onely courteous, but too much given to admire strangers, so they could make themselves understood, or had with them a guide skilful of the language and fashions.[24]

A third problem with such sources are the related issues of plagiarism, and recourse to precept and proverb. The successive Venetian diplomatic reports (the *relazioni*) were clearly highly formulaic and extremely repetitive. But we should also remember that plagiarism in the early modern period was not the crime that it has become in the modern era and was hence common. Indeed, reliance on respected sources was deemed a virtue, and thus we find that successive agricultural handbooks, county and national descriptions and travel literature, as well as ethnological descriptions, were highly repetitious, usually unapologetically so.[25] An interesting example of this in practice is provided by comparison of the text of a recently discovered unpublished Venetian diplomatic report, probably the work of first secretary to England Girolamo Zuccatto, dated *ca.* 1540, with a work written by a French historian, Guillaume Paradin, published in Paris in 1545. Among the more bizarre statements contained in the Italian report we learn that "The region at any time of the year is most temperate without any bad air, due to which there are few illnesses, and everywhere many men reach the age of 110 and others 120 years" and that sheep "do not drink other than dew . . . ".[26] Paradin appears to have had access to Zucatto's report, for he duly states that in England, "The climate is so healthy that men often live to 120 years, and that labourers never sweat", while "Shepherds never allow their sheep to drink anything but dew".[27] More pertinent to the present argument is the following remark, made in 1598, by Paul Hentzner of Brandenburg who, in a clear echo of Trevisano a century earlier, wrote of the English, "If they see a foreigner very well made or particularly handsome they will say, 'It is a pity he is not an Englishman'".[28] And what of this from Thomas Platter, a Swiss physician, writing in 1599: "Hence, as soon as they see a handsome man, they say he is an Englishman, or if they hold him to be a foreigner, they say: it is a great pity he is not an Englishman".[29] Could Hentzner and Platter have read Trevisano's report, or had this phrase assumed the status of an aphorism during the course of the sixteenth century? The conclusion of Robson-Scott regarding German visitors is that many plagiarized, especially from Vergil and Camden, and Hentzner in particular was almost wholly derivative.[30]

One must also, of course, realize that all western Europeans were prone to national stereotyping, and thus repetition of the supposed untrustworthiness, pride and envy of the English stands on a par with the purported foppishness of the French, the drunkenness of the Germans or the barbarity of the Irish.[31] Moryson devotes several pages of his *Itinerary* to the rehearsal of common proverbs concerning various characteristics of the Europeans nations, the occasional aside to offer qualification or disagreement indicating just how seriously he took them.[32] That there was an enormous common stock of proverbial attributions there can be no doubt, but less generally understood is their intellectual underpinning. In early modern England monogenism was orthodox, and polygenism heretical. To cope with the clear evidence of racial and cultural diversity, therefore, recourse was commonly had to scriptural authority, and hence the two peoplings of the earth described in the Book of Genesis, the migration of nations to their eventual geographical destination, and their subsequent degeneration provided the orthodox and acceptable explanation of diversity.[33] But within this orthodoxy, indeed as a central component of it, stood various degrees of geographical and environmental distinction that took on a determinism of their own. Whether these influences were deemed to stem from post-diluvian migrations, or whether they stemmed, as in the opinion of Jean Bodin, from prior diversities in topography and climate, geographical determinism exerted a powerful and widespread influence upon the thinking of early modern western Europeans.[34] This influence is paramount in the writings of Levinus Lemnius in the mid-sixteenth century, basic to the thinking of Fynes Moryson and Robert Burton in the early seventeenth, evident in the work of Chamberlayne later in that century and still accepted by L'Abbé Le Blanc in the mid-eighteenth.[35] This intellectual pedigree, bolstered by renewed Renaissance reverence for ancient scholarship in general and the Hippocratic Corpus in particular, was the edifice upon which stereotypical images were erected and by which they were justified. They persisted despite the fact that the other face of the Renaissance, which provided the inspiration for closer examination of man and the natural world which he inhabited, could and did produce tension between precept and perception. This tension, evident in the prose writings of Thomas Wright, John Barclay and Francis Bacon – as well as Fynes Moryson – mirrors the development of challenges to national stereotypes, and more favourable perceptions of the foreigner, evident in Jacobean drama.[36]

It is also clear that contemporary writers were not always entirely consistent in their appraisals, and hence it is possible to distort their views by selective quotation. Hibbert, as we have seen, cites César de Saussure's views as evidence for English xenophobia, and it is true that his letters contain several references to English dislike for, and even ill-treatment of, foreigners.[37] But he also describes the English as "generous and grateful", "kind-hearted and compassionate", and towards the end of this four-year stay he wrote,

> So far I have had nothing to complain of, and I have never regretted my visit to London. It is, I find, a most agreeable town to live in, at least for those who speak the language and who appreciate the genius, the good taste, the manner of living and the spirit of the people; who have made pleasant acquaintances, and have their pockets sufficiently well filled with money to be free from debt.[38]

The experiences of Jacques Fontaine as a Huguenot refugee to England, reported in his memoirs, could not have been more diverse. When he arrived at Barnstaple in

December 1685 the residents "sent for all 12 of us, took each of us into their homes, and treated us with incredible kindness and friendship. God provided us fathers and mothers, brothers and sisters, among strangers".[39] A few years later, however, in Taunton he saw another side to the English character, experiencing what he describes as the hatred of the common people as well as resentment of his material success.[40] Another eighteenth-century example is L'Abbé Le Blanc, who in one breath accepts that "a Frenchman is much better received at London, than an Englishman at Paris", and in the next complains that "The bulk of the English nation bear an inveterate hatred to the French . . . ".[41] And finally, moving back two centuries to 1465–7, Leo of Rozmital reported that on his tour of England, "In no place were we held in so great honour as there. For both by the King and by all his subjects, wherever we travelled, we were treated kindly and honourably", but concludes with "I have nothing more to write about the English except that (as it seems to me) they are treacherous and cunning, plotting against the lives of foreigners . . . ".[42]

The typicality of the views offered in the literary sources quoted is a final concern, for they did not all speak with one voice. Here is Levinus Lemnius reporting on his experience of the English in 1561:

> Every gentleman and other worthy person showed unto mee (being a straunger borne and one that never had beene there before) all pointes of most frendly curtesy, and taking mee first by the hand lovingly embraced and bad mee ryghte hartely welcome . . . Therefore, franckely to utter what I thinke of the incredible curtesie and frendlines in speache and affability used in this famous realme, I must needs confesse, it doth surmount and carye away the prick and price of al others.[43]

Pointedly he adds, "they that half suspect and have not had the full triall of the maners and fashions of this countrey, will skarcely be perswaded to beleeve".[44] In 1602 Friedrich Gerschow, tutor to Philipp Julius Duke of Stettin-Pomerania, was also impressed by the friendliness and helpfulness of the English, who he found to be "polite in manners and gestures".[45] It is vital, therefore, to accurately represent the full range and balance of contemporary views, an even-handedness which is not always achieved. Maarten Ultee, for instance, has taken Simon Schama to task for the way in which he uses such sources to paint a consistently hostile picture of English attitudes towards the Dutch in the seventeenth century. Hence Ultee argues that while Schama quotes from pamphlets published in 1652, 1664 and 1672, he makes wholly insufficient reference to the fact that Anglo-Dutch wars were being fought at these dates, which inevitably produced waves of propaganda. He also criticizes Schama for relying upon the pamphlet *The Dutch won't Let us have Dunkirk*, assessed by Douglas Coombs in his book on British opinion during the War of the Spanish Succession as "easily the most violent anti-Dutch piece of Tory propaganda which appeared at this time", and also for citing Owen Feltham without emphasizing his strong royalist leaning. Schama, Ultee concludes, "manages to confirm stereotypes and prejudices by picking them out of the bits and pieces of the seventeenth-century context".[46] Indeed, it is remarkably easy to find contemporary writers expressing a highly favourable, rather than hostile, opinion of the Dutch Republic in the seventeenth century.[47]

This last point is an important one, for it is quite clear that English attitudes were often diverse and ambivalent. It is perhaps not surprising to find considerable admiration for the Dutch Republic: the Low Countries were long-established trading partners, allies against Spain, epitomized the commercial success to which England aspired, and were for the most part Protestant – and one should not underestimate the degree of religious fellow feeling that Calvinism could inspire.[48] It might come as more of a surprise to find that the 'old enemy', France also brought forth praise as well as criticism, evident in the reports of seventeenth-century English travellers. For while they criticized the poverty of its peasantry, its absolutist system of government, its corrupt judicial system and the 'superstitions' with which its religion was imbued, they also admired its populousness, the fertility of its agriculture and the beauty of its countryside, its stately and thriving towns and cities, its literary and intellectual life, its language, civility and conversation.[49] By the early eighteenth century, it has been suggested, "not only were the French the best models of conversation, but the French language itself was held to be the language of politeness *par excellence*".[50] But there was nothing new in respect for the French tongue, which had been particularly remarked upon by Sir John Lauder in the 1660s, while British gentlemen had long sought out those French towns and cities where the language was spoken at its purest.[51] Nor was there anything new in admiration for French fashions, while the adoption of French mannerisms had been a cause for complaint since at least the late sixteenth century. Hence in his *Method for Travell* of 1598 Dallington noted that the "French fashion of dancing is in most request with us", while he also preferred that his traveller "should come home Italianate than Frenchefied".[52] In 1614 Tobias Gentleman noted that "the *French* Men say we are apish, for that we do still imitate them in all needless and fantastical Jags and Fashions; as is most true, indeed . . . ", while three years later Moryson complained that,

> Now the English in their apparrell are become more light than the lightest French, and more sumptuous then the proudest Persians. More light I say then the French, because with singular inconstancy they have in this one age worne out all the fashions of France and all the Nations of Europe . . . [53]

What is more, he had personal experience of the undue influence of French fashions upon one of tender years:

> A familiar friend of mine lately sent his sonne to Paris, who after two yeeres returning home, refused to ask his father blessing after the manner of England, saying, Ce n'est pas le mode de France, It is not the French fashion. Thus whilest (like Apes) they imitate strange fashions, they forget their owne, which is just as if a man should seeke his perdition, to gaine a cloake for ornament.[54]

Such concerns escalate later in the century, the anonymous author of *The Pacquet-Boat Advice* explaining in 1678 how he took a Frenchman into his confidence by "pretending great Kindness to this Nation, a Folly too common, and usually true with the *English*, who are wont, with a Kind of Witchcraft, to dote upon the *French*".[55] At the turn of the century, having complained bitterly against the excessive importation of "toys", "novelties" or "trifles" from France, including "ribands, lace, perfumes, paints and womens dresses", Veryard proceeds to satirize his compatriots' apparently insatiable taste for all things French:

> My lord's perruque fits not well till monsieur has had a hand in't; and my lady relishes not her victuals unless they're served in with a French sauce. The exchange women would

have a poor trade, had they not the knack of Frenchifying their wares; and the courtier could hardly pretend to the quality of Huff and Beau, unless he'd spent some time in a French academy, and entertain'd masters of science of that nation.[56]

By this time, of course, the Grand Tour was well established, for if a period of European travel to complete a gentleman's education became *de jure* in the eighteenth century, it had long been *à la mode*.[57] Its roots can be traced back to the reign of Henry VIII, which inaugurated that rush to book learning and formal education by the aristocracy, supplemented by a period of foreign travel, which was increasingly seen as essential preparation for state service.[58] The emphasis continued during the reign of Elizabeth and into the early seventeenth century, despite the inhibiting influence of the Thirty Years War, growing in popularity in the less volatile conditions that prevailed towards the end of that century.[59] An educational and cultural circuit gradually developed that took in Paris and the French Court, the south of France, the cities of northern Italy, from there to Florence, Rome and Naples, returning to England via Germany and the Low Countries. These young tourists and other travellers found much to admire and, although they constitute a self-selecting sample, both the fact of their journeys and the reports they occasionally produced provide little indication of attitudes that were even remotely xenophobic. Yet at the same time a positive view of what continental Europe had to offer could co-exist with expressions of hostility, hostility towards the French in particular, a paradox that was admirably summed up by L'Abbé Le Blanc in the mid-eighteenth century:

> The frequent wars between the two nations have kindled this reciprocal hatred, which has so long subsisted: their rivalship and jealousy in trade prevent its being extinguished in times of peace. If our neighbours carry this hatred to a greater length than we, 'tis partly the effect of their policy, which is very industrious in fomenting it. They think it their interest to render odious a power that alarms them . . . .They fear and yet despise us: we are the nation that they pay the greatest civilities to, and yet love the least: they condemn, and yet imitate us: they adopt our manners by taste, and blame them through policy.[60]

Le Blanc goes on to suggest that the "national hatreds" of "the mob" are instilled in them for political reasons, and the association between Toryism, disrespect for the French, fear of Popery and overweening national pride is admirably exemplified in Joseph Addison's gentle lampooning of the character of Sir Roger Coverley in *The Spectator* in 1712. On meeting a one-legged waterman, Sir Roger elicits the information that the leg had been lost in battle at La Hogue, in response to which Sir Roger,

> in the triumph of his heart made several reflections on the greatness of the British nation; as, that one Englishman could beat three Frenchmen; that we could never be in danger of Popery so long as we took care of our fleet; that the Thames was the noblest river in Europe; that London Bridge was a greater piece of work, than any of the seven wonders of the world; with many other honest prejudices which naturally cleave to the heart of a true Englishman.[61]

That Addison could indulge in such irony does, of course, indicate that he and his readership could readily share in amusement at the expense of Sir Roger and his ilk, and if it testifies to the existence of such attitudes it also reveals quite clearly that they were anything but universally held. Addison's popularity cannot be doubted, even if Swift went too far in suggesting that if he wished to be king the people could hardly have refused him.[62]

The reference by Le Blanc to manipulation of popular opinion towards foreigners for political ends introduces a further ambivalence or dichotomy, one that cuts across the social spectrum, for the consideration of which we need to turn from what the English *said* to what they *did*. For if we can find evidence of a variety of attitudes towards foreigners and a good deal of ambivalence towards the upper end of the social hierarchy, there can be little doubt that the more violent opposition came from the other end of the social order. Whenever either visiting or resident foreigners either felt or were actually threatened with physical harm, the blame was almost invariably laid squarely upon the shoulders of "the common sort", "the apprentices", "the mob", "the meaner sort of people" or some similar descriptor.[63] Examples of foreign complaint that draw this distinction are numerous, though one must again be aware of the possibility of plagiarism. In 1497 Andreas Franciscus reported that Londoners "Look askance at us by day, and at night they sometimes drive us off with kicks and blows of the truncheon", while Giacomo Soranzo, Venetian ambassador, wrote in August 1554: "The nobility are by nature very courteous, especially to foreigners, who however are treated with very great arrogance and enmity by the people . . . .".[64] A similar distinction was made by Nicander Nucius on his visit to England in 1545–6, and the insolence of "the street boys and apprentices" of London is echoed again by Jacob Rathgeb, private secretary to the Duke of Wirtemberg, in 1592.[65] While he defended his countrymen from the general charge of hostility to foreigners, Fynes Moryson also accepted that in London strangers "are sometyme arronged by the insolency of the baser sorte of Prentisces, serving men Dray men, and like people", but added that "presuming upon theire nombers [they] doe many like insolences to English gentlemen and laydies", a view echoed in a proclamation issued by James I in 1621.[66]

Turning from words to action, or the threat of action, most of the evidence available again comes from London, and the most renowned example – significantly pre-dating the alien influx of the third quarter of the sixteenth century – is "Evil May Day". Evil May Day, which involved an attack upon aliens by a mob of apprentices in 1517, entered into popular mythology as a particularly gruesome and bloody occasion: in the words of an old ballad

> For thousands came with Bilboe blade,
> As with an army they would meet,
> And such a bloody slaughter made
> Of foreign strangers in the street,
> That all the channels ran with blood. . . .
> And hundreds hang'd by martial law,
> On sign posts at their masters' doors . . . [67]

More reliable sources and modern research have shown that the story as presented here is highly exaggerated. The contemporary chronicler Edward Hall offers a more realistic assessment, and reveals that about 1,000 people were involved in the disturbance, an unknown number of aliens' houses were attacked but no life was taken, and just 13 rioters, plus a broker named John Lincoln who had been a prime instigator of the troubles, were convicted of treason and executed.[68] This is not, of course, to deny the clear evidence of anti-alien sentiment that lay behind this disturbance, nor the fact that a riot had indeed taken place. But the concerted response of the city authorities, the charge of high treason rather than riot and the draconian punishment handed down by Lord Edmund Howard of half-hanging, mutilation and live disembowelling may help to explain the lack of future disturbance, for there is no evidence of any further breach of the peace on any scale throughout the remainder of the sixteenth and early seventeenth centuries.[69]

The next serious threat of trouble in the capital came immediately after the mid-century migration, when it was reported that,

> 500 or 600 men waited on the Mayor and Aldermen of London, complaining of the late influx of strangers, and that by reason of the great dearth they cannot live for these strangers, whom they were determined to kill up through the realm, if they found no remedy.[70]

Remedy was, however, found, in the form of a survey of strangers made by the mayor and aldermen, and the institution of precautionary and restrictive orders which appear to have prevented any disturbance.[71] Furthermore, despite the suggestion of the Spanish ambassador that it was the sight of a thousand foreigners gathering at Austin Friars that had instigated the trouble, the prevailing political crisis and severe social distress were more potent causes of discontent, and the readying of the armed bands and private retainers was a response to fears of more general insurrection in both London and its neighbouring counties.[72] In 1563, stirred up by a crown proclamation which authorized the harrying of French subjects at English ports issued in response to a breakdown of the alliance between Elizabeth and the French Huguenots, a number of Frenchmen were imprisoned in London, and it took two further proclamations before the disturbances died down.[73] During the remainder of the Elizabethan era, *threats* of violence have been noted in 1567, 1586–7, 1593 and 1595. Whether or not one regards these as "frequent" is clearly a matter of interpretation, but the fact is that on no occasion did a serious disturbance actually materialize, which indicates both the strength of social and political control in the capital as well as the effectiveness of nego-tiation between rulers and ruled.[74] How serious these threats were is often questionable. In 1567, for instance, the chronicler John Stow tells us that "a great watche" was kept for the week following 17 February, and that "The occasyon of this watche was thrwghe a portar who went about to dyvars prentises, tellynge them that that nyght folowynge wowlde be ye lyke stire agaynst straungers as was at Evyll May Day . . . ". Interestingly, Stow records that some of these apprentices informed their masters, who in turn informed the lord mayor. The porter responsible for the rumour was hanged in Cheapside the Friday following, a survey of the number of strangers was taken and the results distributed to the Livery companies to be read to their members.[75] Periodic resentment by the "poorer sort", therefore, usually in response to short-term economic dislocation, was kept firmly in check by local authorities and the national government who, as discussed at more length below, almost invariably provided both support and protection. On the rare occasions when resentment and distrust was expressed across a broader social spectrum, however – as in 1593 – the security and privileges of the immigrant communities could become more precarious.

The events of 1593 have been described as "the most serious threat" to the foreign communities in London, and there can be little doubt that this was the case.[76] Indeed, their difficulties in this year were widely appreciated, for on 10 August Petrus Plancius wrote from Amsterdam to Assuerus Regenmortell in London, encouraging resettlement from England to Harderwijk, "as it is rumoured here that the ill feeling of the English against the Netherlanders increases more and more . . . ".[77] The most significant component of these events, however, was not the threat of violence, even though the libel published that year read:

> Be it known to all Flemings and Frenchmen, that it is best for them to depart out of this Realm of England, between this and the 9th of July next. If not, then to take that which follows. For that there shall be many a sore Stripe. Apprentices will rise to the Number of 2336. And all the Apprentices and Journeymen will down with the Flemings and Strangers.[78]

A further rhyme set upon the wall of the Dutch Churchyard similarly advised all strangers to "Conceive it well, for Safe-guard of your Lives, Your Goods, your children, and your dearest Wives", but upon this being brought to the attention of the authorities a range of measures were quickly put in place to strengthen their hand, to control the apprentices through their masters and to placate those who felt aggrieved, culminating in the arrest of "several young men", some of whom were put in the stocks, carted and whipped as an example to other would-be trouble-makers.[79] It may well have been the tense popular climate that moved Edmund Tilney to insist that the authors of the play *The Book of Sir Thomas More* which, *inter alia,* dealt with the events of Evil May Day, wholly leave out any depiction of the riot itself, and satisfy themselves with just "a shortt report & nott otherwise att your own perilles".[80]

The real significance of 1593, however, was the congruence of expressions of resentment at various levels in the social hierarchy. Again we have the threat of a rising of the apprentices, but also a series of petitions emanating from the "Artificers Freeman within the City and Suburbs in London", complaining about the trades and occupations practiced by foreigners, as well as remonstrances from the "English shopkeepers" against foreigners keeping shops and selling by retail.[81] But complaint did not end there, for the issue of foreigners selling by retail caused a long and heated debate in the parliament of that year, continuing a discussion that had begun with the introduction of a bill in the previous parliament of 1589.[82] This bill appears to have been brought by the City of London.[83] Among the complaints rehearsed during its debate were the undercutting of English prices and, conversely, the tendency of strangers' retailing activities to raise prices; loss of employment among the English; export of profits overseas; giving to strangers the privilege of retailing not granted to native inhabitants; secretion of wealth to avoid subsidies; the refusal to converse or inter-marry with the English and the refusal also to buy from any but a fellow foreigner; their inordinate wealth and, again conversely, the inordinate number of them living by begging. Strong voices were raised in their defence, among others that of Sir John Wolley who argued that "This Bill should be ill for London, for the Riches and Renown of the City cometh by entertaining of Strangers, and giving liberty unto them".[84] Sir Edward Dymock blamed the problems of English retailers firmly upon the shoulders of "our home Ingrossers", while claiming that it was English, not alien, merchants who were exporting English coin.[85] The religious and moral example of the stranger community was also invoked, as was scriptural precept, but injunctions to charity were balanced by the view that charity should begin at home, for "he that provideth not for his Family is worse than an Infidel".[86] The most significant intervention was that of Sir Walter Raleigh, when the debate took on a new dimension, one firmly rooted in international political and economic rivalry:

> For first, such as fly hither have forsaken their own King; and Religion is no pretext for them, for we have no Dutchmen here, but such as came from those Princes where the Gospel is preached . . . The Dutchman by his Policy hath gotten Trading with all the World into his hands, yea he is now entering into the Trade of Scarborough Fishing, and the Fishing of the New-found-Lands . . . They are the people that maintain the King of Spain in his Greatness. Were it not for them he were never able to make out such Armies and Navies by Sea; it cost her Majesty sixteen thousand pounds a year for the maintaining of these Countries, and yet for all this they Arm her Enemies against her.[87]

The significance of this intervention is underlined by the fact that the popular libel against aliens published in 1593 also takes up such issues:

> Doth not the World see, that you, beastly Brutes, the Belgians, or rather Drunken Drones, and faint-hearted Flemings; and you, fraudulent Father, Frenchmen, by your cowardly Flight, from your own natural Countries, have abandoned the same into the Hands of your proud, cowardly Enemies, and have by a feigned Hypocrisy, and counterfeit shew of Religion, placed yourselves here in a most fertile Soil, under a most gracious and merciful Prince.[88]

Economic grievances were doubtless the basis of the complaint of the artificers and shopkeepers of London, but they were overlaid on this occasion with a political dimension that they also took on board, creating a heady cocktail of grievances that spanned the social spectrum, and which would allow the London populace to claim sanction for their actions from discussions taking place in the House of Commons. Despite a more moderate intervention from Sir Robert Cecil, on 27 March 1593 the bill was carried by 162 voices to 82; it was thrown out by the House of Lords four days later.

Despite the clear evidence of economic grievances against the resident alien population, even encouraged on occasion by parliamentary debate, the fact remains that threats of violence in the capital never materialized. And if this testifies to the strength of London government, its responsiveness and effective policing, it must also call into question both the depth and the breadth of anti-alien hostility, even in the face of severe economic dislocation. For the dates of these threats are also significant, coinciding as they invariably do with economic disruption of one form or another, most commonly caused by dearth, or plague, or both.[89] In the context of the economic difficulties of the period from 1586 to 1597, involving in succession dearth, plague, atrocious weather, prolonged dearth and plague again, it is perhaps unsurprising that there was a certain amount of scapegoating directed at the alien community, but it was these economic conditions that underpinned any increase of resentment that took place, not a "rising tide" *per se*.[90]

The level of anti-alien sentiment in London declined further in the early seventeenth century, partly perhaps because their profile declined as immigration slackened and some of the community returned home, partly because economic dislocation on the scale experienced in the 1590s did not recur, but also because assimilation was taking place: roughly 40 per cent of the Dutch and French congregations of London had been born in England by the early seventeenth century.[91] The situation was similar in Colchester where, as early as 1586, of the 1,291 strangers listed, 504 were "children born in the realm", while a generation later, in 1622, only 15 per cent of the 1,535 immigrants were described as "householders, aliens", and virtually all of the rest were householders, children or servants born in England.[92] As early as 1606 a Dutch minister from Norwich left the town to serve an English parish in Colchester, while in 1621 and again in 1630 it was complained in Norwich that those aliens born in England were now joining the congregations of the English churches.[93] The perception of economic conflict of interest by no means disappeared, and re-emerged with particular force during the economic downturn of 1615–22, while individual foreigners continued periodically to be harassed by informers, and isolated assaults were reported, particularly inspired by the growing Spanish influence at court.[94] But it was the financial demands of James I and subsequently the interference in matters of religion by Archbishop Laud that represented the more serious threats to the foreign communities in the earlier decades of the century, not popular hostility.[95]

How were the stranger communities received in the provinces? The evidence is frequently less rich for provincial towns than for the capital, but there is even less sign of violent opposition. The second largest English community, that in Norwich, begun with just 30 households in 1565, but may have reached 6,000 on the eve of the plague of 1579–80 before falling back to under 3,000 by the end of the century, at its peak accounting for approximately 40 per cent of the town's population.[96] Despite this, or perhaps in part because of it, there is only one occasion when violence threatened – in 1570, when a conspiracy was discovered "to expulse the strangers from the city and the realm", but even then it has been suggested that this had more to do with the rising of the Northern Earls and the disgrace of the Duke of Norfolk than it did with the presence of the strangers.[97] After this, we have to wait until 1683 for further evidence of violent unrest directed towards aliens.[98]

At Sandwich the number of settlers was almost overwhelming, estimated at around 2,400 by 1574 compared to an indigenous population of approximately 2,500.[99] Again we search in vain for evidence of violent opposition, although here quite unusually drastic action was taken to diminish the number of settlers, including forced removal of those not of the Flemish Congregation which, besides voluntary emigration in response to tighter economic restrictions, reduced the community to roughly 1,200 by 1582, whereafter numbers continued to fall.[100] In Canterbury the French Church could boast 1,679 members by 1582, and possibly 4,000 in the first half of the 1590s falling to 2,500 by its end, and this out of a total population of *ca.* 9,000.[101] An attempt was made to limit their number in 1582 by requiring those who had come to escape war rather than for religious reasons to leave, but it was wholly ineffective, and here "generally speaking, relations with the local population were good", with friction confined to little more than trivial annoyances.[102] Rye was another town where the alien population loomed large, although only temporarily in this case, numbering in excess of 1,500 in the early 1580s out of a total population of perhaps 4,000. Many of these were poor refugees, including a considerable number of mariners from Dieppe, given which it is perhaps surprising that there is again so little indication of strife in the town.[103] Although plans were laid for the removal of some of their number in 1586, "divers houses being too much pestered with them" and prices "so excessive dere", the Mayor and Jurats still felt able to accommodate 1,000 of them, to whom they would willingly show "all the courtesy" they were due.[104]

Elsewhere the foreign congregations formed far smaller proportions of the communities they joined, but this does not seem to have had an adverse effect upon their reception or treatment. In Colchester the addition of roughly 1,000 foreign residents in the 1570s to a town that had only housed some 4,000 led the corporation to issue an order in 1580 against further increase, requiring removal of all who were not members of the Dutch congregation or had arrived within the past fortnight. No more were to be admitted without written consent of the aldermen and bailiffs, for "there are a great number of strangers inhabiting within this town presupposed more than the town can well sustain and bear".[105] This was, however, the one and only occasion when expulsion was suggested. In Southampton, where the small French-speaking community consisted of just 297 out of a population of 4,200 by 1596, "there does not seem to be any evidence of serious unrest or hostility towards the exile community", and the same could also be said with regard to the small communities at Maidstone and Yarmouth.[106] Not even on Canvey Island, where conflict arose over religion and land drainage and reclamation in the confined quarters of this marshland community, did serious disturbance occur, and this despite the fact that during the Second Dutch Naval War of 1665–7 Dutch sailors landed on the island, plundered it, damaged barns and took several small boats.[107] Only in the fenlands of the Isle of Ely can we find clear evidence of riotous behaviour inspired by the immigrant presence, for fen drainage was far from universally popular, even if unrest was confined to the Isle of Axholme settlement and did not affect that at Thorney.[108] Anti-alien sentiment clearly paid its part here, in 1630 the fenmen opposing the signing of a contract with Vermuyden, showing "much unwillingness that any contract should be made with an alien born", while in 1606 and again in 1629 the inhabitants of western Cambridgeshire had indignantly rejected the help of "foreign undertakers".[109] Interestingly the Corporation of Lincoln rejected the offer of a Huguenot settlement in 1681 on the grounds that it would "prejudice" the city, while the hopes of Sir John Lowther to encourage the settlement of a few Huguenots in Whitehaven in the mid-1680s also failed due to local suspicion of foreigners.[110]

Notwithstanding the lack of violent opposition, in each of these communities, as in London, there was conflict between the indigenous population and the foreign immigrants, almost invariably over economic and social matters, and the charges levelled against them were legion. They were accused of taking away Englishmen's trade, exporting English coin, employing only their own countrymen, refusing to share their secrets, keeping themselves too much apart, producing inferior goods, using more than one occupation, forcing up the price of food and accommodation, increasing the risk of plague by overcrowded living and even of conspiring against the state. The most frequent complaints were that they traded by retail when they should have restricted their activities to wholesale trading, and that they practised occupations not allowed by the original letters patent that governed their settlement.[111] In many of these communities, too, individual aliens were periodically harassed by informers out to make a profit from any breaches of agreement or regulations, perceived or real.[112]

All of this needs to be kept in perspective, however, for time and again *English* strangers were also targeted by the authorities. Injunctions against incomers – particularly poor incomers – abound in all corporation records, as do injunctions against craftsmen practising without serving apprenticeships or purchasing the freedom, unlicensed trading, forestalling and regrating, and trading outside of the official markets.[113] Among the complaints issued against the Dutch in Colchester in 1631, it was suggested that they bought up bays and says by agreement without bringing them to the public market, and also bought commodities in inns and other private places.[114] But this is a theme that finds an echo in corporation records up and down the country in the late sixteenth and early seventeenth centuries, the vast majority of which had no experience at all of foreign settlements.[115] In Norwich the situation was similar: the corporation was often merely trying to enforce economic and social regulations that applied to all inhabitants, English and foreign alike.[116] It was not that the economic activities of the alien communities were objected to *per se*, though in particularly difficult times, as we have seen, their very presence did represent competition for employment and markets. But most objections, notably those that emanated from the more respectable trades and craftsmen, targeted *abuse* of the privileges granted, rather than those privileges themselves. Hence when on 14 March 1584 seven resident strangers were brought before the mayor and aldermen of Norwich and prohibited from acting as factors for men in London and elsewhere, the corporation also declared itself

> contented that they shall or may use all suche liberties as her majestie hathe graunted unto them using the same accordyng to the trew intent and meaning of her maiesties licence and the letters of the lordes of her honorable privie counsell.[117]

For a similar example from London, when the "yeomen weavers" addressed the French Church there in 1595, their complaint was not about the presence of aliens in itself, "for they are suffered and we are content therewith": what they objected to was their disregard for the rules that governed the activities of English and foreign craftsmen alike. Hence they wrote, "It is not our intents to drive away or expel any distressed strangers out of our land, but to have them live here, that we might be able to live with them and that they should live under government and be obedient to good orders".[118] This is not to suggest that the playing field was to be entirely level, for the ordinances of 1596 allowed bailiffs and wardens of the guild to keep seven looms, those of the livery six looms, freemen not of the livery and denizen foreigners five looms, while non-denizen strangers were restricted to four.[119]

Under all but exceptional circumstances, town corporations acted in harmony with the Crown and Privy Council to uphold the rights and privileges of the foreign communities, while those communities in turn, largely through their churches, sought to regulate their members' behaviour to the satisfaction of their hosts. That the contribution they made to the local economy was appreciated there can be no doubt. In Colchester in 1580 Nicholas Chalyner and Robert Lewis, preachers, along with Robert Searle and Robert Monke, wrote to Walsingham in defence of the Dutch, emphasizing their civility, honesty and godly behaviour, but also the advantages accruing to the town in terms of the employment created.[120] In 1603 a letter written on behalf of the Dutch congregation to Sir Thomas Lucas emphasized the benefits produced by bringing new manufactures to the town.[121] In 1607 the bailiffs wrote to the Earl of Salisbury supporting the Dutch merchants' objection to the proposed imposition of a double subsidy on the new draperies, arguing that this would lead them to leave off their trade, "and many poor people will be very much distressed for want of work, which now they have by reason of that trade".[122] The letters patent to the Dutch community in Colchester issued by James I in 1612 also stressed the economic benefits they brought,[123] and in Norwich too the mayor wrote in 1571 to the Privy Council,

> We find the number very convenient and profitable for this common weal, being a people hitherto (for the most part) well inclined in due obedience to her majesty's laws and well applying themselves in their exercises, whereby both their own people and ours be kept in work ... to the great benefit ... of this city and country adjoining.[124]

At Canterbury in 1623 the Dean and Chapter testified that the Walloon congregation "for many yeeres past, and still doe very religiously, obediently, orderly and civilly demeane and behave themselves towards God and all the Kings Majesties officers, and others in these parts (for any thing we have ever heard to the contrary)", but proceeded also to testify to their industry and diligence and the good example they set.[125] During his dispute with the foreign churches during the 1630s even Laud was prepared to accept that "their Congregations were beneficiall to the English, especially poor", and that the congregations at Colchester, Canterbury and Sandwich "did set a great number of English at work".[126] If the foreign communities of the first refuge in London and provincial England were periodically the object of resentment arising from the populace, therefore, they were almost invariably supported and protected by the "better sort", operating through the mechanisms of both local and national government.

There were many contradictions in attitudes to foreigners in early modern England, and a good deal of ambivalence. There were also clear parameters that defined what was acceptable and what was not, for some foreigners were clearly beyond the pale – in the case of the "wild Irish" both figuratively and literally. The orthodoxy of monogenism did not prevent the emergence of notions of national or even racial inferiority, particularly directed at negroes and the Irish. The fact that Elizabeth I took steps to reduce the number of "blackamoors" in the capital in the late sixteenth century is well known, and finds reflection in Cecil's remark in the Commons in 1593 that it is "a matter of Charity to relieve Strangers, and especially such as do not grieve our Eyes".[127] With regard to the "wild Irish", who continued to resist English incursions, it is hard to find a good word said, for their way of life was widely regarded as synonymous with "barbarism", and steps were also taken to remove a number of Irish immigrants from London in 1594, a move not unconnected with rumours of a possible attempt on the Queen's life.[128] Hierarchical notions, rooted in the Great Chain of Being, indicated both a systematic *and* an evaluative social hierarchy, which were readily transferred to the social, ethnological and ethnographical spheres, and were further reinforced by both religion (Christian *vs* heathen) and contemporary notions of civil society (civilization *vs* barbarism).

The Dutch and French immigrants to England in the sixteenth and seventeenth centuries, however, fell well within the bounds of acceptability. They were settled members of civil societies who conformed themselves to the rule of law, they were white Europeans, they were Christians and – decisively – Protestants who had fled for their consciences' sake. Although toleration was also extended to foreign Catholics, the fact that the Dutch and French refugees were co-religionists was clearly crucial, without which the existence of such large alien populations in England would have been impossible to contemplate.[129] This is not to say that they were given completely free reign, and on occasion the fear of extremist threats to the Anglican *via media* was made extremely clear. Hence in 1573 the Privy Council wrote to the Dutch Church in London warning them to discourage those

> tumultuous and disquiet people, who would bring confusion to what is settled ... Be it far from you, to do any thing whereby you might create any suspision of disturbing the peace of our Common-Welth, and the state of our religion, so well setled ... For by your wisdom you know very well, that the Queen's Majesty would rather drive you out of her Kingdom, than to suffer, that by such guests (who were received on a religious account) by such wicked and unkindely means her state should bee brought in danger.[130]

In response the Dutch promised to "expel from our flock, all such as we find of tumultuous tempers", and it was with such assurances and the quiet practise of their religion that they assuaged any fears of a threat from within.[131] Indeed, the fact that they "doe very religiously, obediently, orderly and civilly demeane and behave themselves towards God and all the Kings Majesties officers", as reported in 1623, was crucial to the maintenance of their privileges.[132] Religion and politics, of course, went hand in hand, and if one of the most distinctive marks of English nationalism was anti-Catholicism, then providing succour to fellow Protestants represented support for both international Protestantism and the national interest.[133] Financial and military support for the Protestant cause on continental Europe came, of course, from native Englishmen as well as from aliens settled in England, as David Trim has so forcefully pointed out.[134] And in the words of another authority who has effectively demonstrated the power of religion to transcend national boundaries, "Protestant nationalism and internationalism were two sides of the same coin".[135]

For much of Elizabeth's reign the Spanish threat was viewed as intimately connected with the power of the Antichrist in Rome, but even when the inevitability of that association began to be questioned in the 1590s, Spanish political ambition could not be divorced from Spain as the champion of Catholicism, as the events at Kinsale in Ireland in 1601 brought so close to home.[136] Thereafter – despite the end of war against Spain under James I – the gunpowder plot, the invasion scares of the 1620s, the proposed Spanish match and the rise of Arminianism all served to ensure that antipopery, and its foreign and particularly Spanish association, retained its currency throughout the earlier seventeenth century.[137] It re-emerged with particular force in the early 1640s, being intimately associated with the political rift between crown and parliament, and was further stimulated by the Irish rebellion and the widespread reports of the massacre of poor Protestants. But while sporadic attacks upon foreigners in London have been identified, the great majority of the violence – as documented for Essex at least – was directed against Englishmen and women suspected of Popish tendencies.[138] Antipopery remained a powerful tradition, however, re-emerging with particular force later in the century.[139] And throughout the period of the first refuge, the immigrants' plight as Protestant refugees from Catholic oppression echoes throughout the statements made on their behalf by national and local governments. When Raleigh turned to attack their privileges in the House of Commons in 1593, it is highly significant that he claimed that those Dutch found in England had migrated from Protestant rather than Catholic areas of the Low Countries and were not, therefore, victims of religious oppression.[140]

As refugees the Dutch and French Protestant immigrants were both a cause for solidarity and suitable objects of charity but – most conveniently – they were also a resource that could be harnessed to English interests. As such they were *invited* to settle in England, by the Crown and Privy Council and by the civic leaders of the towns to which they came, and when resentment periodically flared among the poorer sort, or when they came under attack from Laud, the economic contribution that they made was repeatedly reiterated. In both London and the provinces they co-existed with their English hosts for many decades – often as substantial sections of the communities they joined – living, working and sometimes also worshipping side-by-side in relative harmony, a harmony that is only reflected in the silences in corporation records that sit unremarked between the more tangible complaints. It may be true that a number of strangers chose to return home towards the end of the sixteenth century, responding to the economic difficulties of the 1590s, the peace produced by the Edict of Nantes and Treaty of Vervins of 1598, the economic boom in the United Provinces and their increasing success in their long struggle with Spain.[141] But many chose to stay, as the number of "strangers born within the realm" in the early seventeenth century shows, and – at different speeds in different respects and at different places – they gradually merged with the indigenous population.[142]

It is difficult to accept a general characterization of the English in this period as xenophobic, but they often exhibited considerable arrogance. Here is just one complaint among the many that could be cited, from Giovanni Battista Lionello, Venetian Secretary to England, writing to the Doge and Senate in 1617:

> I have been waiting for some days to discover how best I may raise men in this kingdom to take them to Italy, in accordance with your commands . . . from their conversation and other signs it is clear that the English nation in war and in other things claims to be superior to all other nations . . . [143]

And who other than an Englishman could publish a book in 1618 with the title *The Glory of England, or A True Description of many excellent prerogatives and remarkable blessings, whereby She Triumpheth over all the Nations of the World: With a justifiable comparison betweene the eminent Kingdomes of the Earth and Herselfe; plainely manifesting the defects of them all in regard of her sufficiencie and fulnesse of happinesse.*[144] Even Fynes Moryson, that inveterate traveller and remarkably even-handed commentator, was clearly a lover of his native England. For although he could write that "We betray our ignorance or our selfe love, when wee dispraise forraigne things without true judgement, or preferre our owne Countrey before others, without shewing good reason thereof", he also objected to what he regarded as the pouring of undue praise on things foreign.[145] True to his precepts, when he visited Florence, he wrote of the bridge over the River Arno that it

> is more magnified by strangers then it deserves. It hath little houses upon it, wherewith it is covered, and upon each side are Gold-smithes shops, which make small or no shew at ordinarie times . . . And howsoever some strangers may wonder at it, yet they who compare that bridge with the bridge of London, or those Gold-smiths shops with the daily shew of the Gold-smiths in Cheap-side, shall finde no cause to wonder thereat.[146]

A sense of national identity, even national pride, among Englishmen may have a pedigree that stretches back to the early Middle Ages, and there is certainly extensive evidence of it in the sixteenth and early seventeenth centuries.[147] But national pride could sit side-by-side with tolerance of foreigners, and respect and admiration for their achievements, even if this was frequently muddied by long-standing enmity, religious difference and economic rivalry. Nor were attitudes consistent, even within social classes, and even those who should have known better sometimes had recourse to national stereotypes. In his diary for 1 July 1663 Samuel Pepys reports an entertaining discussion had with William Batten, a barrister of Lincoln's Inn and Sir J. Mennes concerning the debauched behaviour of Sir Charles Sedley, for which he was tried and bound over in the sum of £5,000 for good behaviour. The entry continues, "Upon this discourse, Sir J. Mennes and Mr. Batten both say that buggery is now almost grown as common among our gallants as in Italy, and that the very pages of the town begin to complain of their masters for it".[148] Pepys, of course, moved in cosmopolitan circles, which was not true of all Londoners, whose attitudes were often far from sophisticated. Hence after admiring the spectacle of the procession that accompanied the Russian Ambassador on 27 November 1662, he felt moved to write "But Lord, to see the absurd nature of Englishmen, that cannot forbear laughing and jeering at everything that looks strange".[149] Similar jeering was visited upon the French in 1661 when, in a dispute over precedence in the train of the visiting Swedish ambassador, they had their ears well and truly boxed by the Spanish. Popular disdain for the French might come as no surprise, but the sea-change that could occur over time is shown by the manner in which the Spanish coach proceeded "escorted by a crowd, which came out of all the shops, applauding the event with words and cries, showing great affection for Spain, even ringing bells in some places, and followed the coach to the very embassy . . . ", a spectacle that would have been unthinkable a few decades earlier.[150] Antipopery was undoubtedly alive and well in Restoration England, but this incident suggests that it was no longer intimately associated with all things Spanish.[151]

Change over time is difficult to gauge, and different historians have offered divergent interpretations, while some offer none at all.[152] Definitive statements are inappropriate in the present state of knowledge, further research is clearly needed, and the following are but tentative suggestions. If at all times there was an element of ambivalence, distinction by social class, a range of individual views and differential treatment of both individual migrants and immigrant groups, the combined impact of the Renaissance and the Tudor revolution in government may have marked a watershed between the attitudes prevailing in medieval and early modern England. In 1381, the Peasants' Revolt provided the occasion for concerted violent attacks on both Flemings and Lombards in London, a fact upon which the *Anonimalle Chronicle*, Walsingham, Higden and Froissart are all agreed in their respective accounts of the events of 13–15 June that year.[153] According to the *Anonimalle*,

> At the same time the commons had it proclaimed that whoever could catch any Fleming or other aliens of any nation, might cut off their heads; and so they did accordingly . . . they went to the church of St Martin's in the Vintry, and found therein thirty-five Flemings, whom they dragged outside and beheaded in the street. On that day there were beheaded 140 or 160 persons. Then they took their way to the places of Lombards and other aliens, and broke into their houses, and robbed them of all their goods that they could discover. So it went on for all that day and the night following, with hideous cries and horrible tumult.[154]

It has also been argued that "in the fifteenth century attacks on aliens coincided not simply with trade recessions, as in 1468, but also with wider, national political crises", while "aliens were clearly seen as a group apart and a potential target for attack by those whose real grievances may have lain elsewhere".[155] The same authority urges scepticism regarding Thrupp's claims for integration, and suggests that the attacks on alien property in 1517 "came not as an isolated incident but as the culmination of over a century of fierce anti-alien feeling and direct action".[156] Given that research to date has revealed little evidence of violent attacks on either property or persons in the sixteenth century, Evil May Day may well, therefore, represent the last throw of the medieval dice. At the other end of our period in the later seventeenth century, at the same time as England experienced a further and much larger wave of immigration, the English economy was beginning to throw off its apprenticeship and forge ahead of its European rivals, the rise of party politics stimulated manipulation of the prejudices of the London mob, and the stirrings of a fuller sense of national identity were widely felt which were to eventuate in John Bull's Island.[157] From this perspective, therefore, the England experienced by the immigrants of the first refuge – from the mid-sixteenth to the mid-seventeenth century – may have represented a veritable oasis of tolerance between the more violent prejudice of the medieval period and the arrogant self-confidence that, in some quarters at least, accompanied the rise of English nationalism in the eighteenth century.

Notes

1   Yungblut, *Strangers Settled Here Amongst Us*, esp. pp. 40–60. See my review of this book in *Reviews in History*, http://ihr.sas.ac.uk/ihr/reviews/reviews.mnu.html.
2   Yungblut, *Strangers Settled Here Amongst Us*, p. 115.
3   Yungblut, *Strangers Settled Here Amongst Us*, pp. 40–1, 43, 59–60, 116.
4   Yungblut, *Strangers Settled Here Amongst Us*, pp. 36, 45.
5   Luu, "Xenophobia", pp. 1–22, quote from p. 19; see also Chapter 10 below, pp. 196–207. The term is also freely used in Grell, *Dutch Calvinists*.
6   Luu, "Xenophobia", pp. 2, 18–20.
7   Hibbert, *The English*, p. 337; Van Muyden, *Foreign View of England*.
8   Anon., *Character of Holland*, pp. 575–6; Schama, *Embarrassment of Riches*, pp. 257–88, quotes from pp. 260, 263.
9   Archer, "Responses to Alien Immigrants", pp. 755–74, quote from p. 774; see also Archer, *Pursuit of Stability*, esp. p. 133.
10 Rappaport, *Worlds Within Worlds*, pp. 15–17, 54–60.
11 Ward, "Fictitious Shoemakers", pp. 80–7.
12 Goose, "The 'Dutch' in Colchester", pp. 270–2; Goose, "Dutch in Colchester in the 16th and 17th Centuries", pp. 88–98.
13 Spicer, *French-Speaking Reformed Community*, pp. 140–56; Backhouse, *Flemish and Walloon Communities*, pp. 32–7, 75–100; Backhouse, "Strangers at Work in Sandwich", pp. 70–99.
14 *Collins English Dictionary*, 5th edn (Glasgow, 2000), p. 1763 gives "hatred or fear of foreigners or strangers or of their politics or culture"; *The Chambers Dictionary* (Edinburgh, 1998), p. 1936, "fear or hatred of foreigners and foreign things"; *Chambers 21st Century Dictionary* (Edinburgh, 1999), p. 1643, "intense fear or dislike of foreigners or strangers"; the *Longman Dictionary of Contemporary English*, 3rd edn (Harlow, 1995), p. 1661, "extreme fear or dislike of people from other countries".

15 *Oxford English Dictionary*, 2nd edn (Oxford, 1989), Vol. 20, p. 674: e.g. "a stubborn and unfashionably xenophobic refusal to attempt foreign languages". A recent example of such misuse occurred on BBC Radio 5 on 6 October 2002, when a commentator explained the difference in odds between the Paris Mutuel at Longchamp racetrack and those offered in English turf accountants by the fact that "the French punters at Longchamp tend to get very xenophobic behind their horses".

16 *OED*, Vol. 10, p. 234, Vol. 13, p. 75.

17 Ward, "Fictitious Shoemakers", p. 85.

18 Grabes explicitly equates such rivalry with xenophobia: *Writing the Early Modern English Nation*, p. xiii; for selective quotation see below, p. 115.

19 Hibbert, *The English*, p. 337, as cited above.

20 Rye, *England as Seen by Foreigners*.

21 Sneyd (ed.), *Relation*, pp. 20–1, 23–4. This account is also cited in Luu, "Xenophobia", p. 1.

22 Sneyd (ed.), *Relation*, pp. 24–5.

23 Temple (ed.), *Travels of Peter Mundy*, Vol. 1, pp. 3, 5.

24 Fynes Moryson, *Itinerary*, Part 3, p. 35; and see also Part 3, p. 151.

25 Coleman, *Economy of England*, pp. 112–13; De Beer, "Development of the Guide-Book", p. 35; Towner, "The Grand Tour", pp. 217–18; Hodgen, *Early Anthropology*, pp. 148–54, 162–85; Laurence, "From the Cradle to the Grave", p. 64.

26 Barrington, "Venetian Secretary", pp.176–7.

27 Quoted in Rye, *England as Seen by Foreigners*, p. xlvii. Fynes Moryson also writes that English sheep "seldome drinke, but are moistned by the dewes falling in the night." (*Itinerary*, Part 3, p. 148). The basis of this statement could be the existence of dewponds in some regions, either natural or man-made, while the water requirements of sheep can be minimal at some times of the year, particularly those bred for fleece rather than for meat.

28 Rye, *England as Seen by Foreigners*, p. 111.

29 Robson-Scott, *German Travellers*, p. 75.

30 Robson-Scott, *German Travellers*, pp. 39, 66–7.

31 See esp. Duffy, *The Englishman and the Foreigner*, pp. 13–51.

32 Moryson, *Itinerary*, Part 3, pp. 46–54.

33 Hodgen, *Early Anthropology*, pp. 222–30. Polygenistic thinking only became more common in the eighteenth century, and only seriously threatened the old orthodoxy towards the mid-nineteenth: Augstein, *James Cowles Prichard's Anthropology*, pp. x–xiv, 58–9; Thomas, *Man and the Natural World*, pp. 135–6.

34 Hodgen, *Early Anthropology*, pp. 254–90.

35 Lemnius, *Touchstone of Complexions* (1561), *passim*; Burton, *Anatomy of Melancholy* (1621), Vol. 1, pp. 233–7, Vol. 2, pp. 63–7, Vol. 3, pp. 280–3; Chamberlayne, *Angliae Notitia*, p. 45; L'Abbé Le Blanc, *Letters*, Vol. 1, pp. 5–6.

36 Hoenselaars, *Images of Englishmen and Foreigners*, pp. 21–4, 237–44 and *passim*.

37 Van Muyden, *Foreign View of England*, pp. 111–12, 177–8, 206.

38 Van Muyden, *Foreign View of England*, pp. 181, 190, 346–7. He was also aware that the English were not all the same: p. 195.

39 Ressinger (ed.), *Memoirs*, p. 123.

40 Ressinger (ed.), *Memoirs*, pp. 141–6; Statt, *Foreigners and Englishmen*, pp. 19–20, 166.

41 L'Abbé Le Blanc, *Letters*, Vol. I, pp. 22–3, 25.

42 Letts (ed.), *Travels of Leo of Rozmital*, pp. 54, 61–2.

43 Lemnius, *Touchstone of Complexions*, fols. 47d-48r.

44 Lemnius, *Touchstone of Complexions*, fol. 48r.

45 Robson-Scott, *German Travellers in England*, pp. 61–5.

46 Ultee, "Review Article", pp. 228–30.

47 See, for example, Oppenheim (ed.), *Naval Tracts*, Vol. 5 (1914), pp. 324–6; Overbury, *Observations*, in Rimbault (ed.), *Miscellaneous Works*, pp. 223–30; Fynes Moryson, *Itinerary*, Part 1, p. 23, Part 3, p. 97; Anon., *How to Advance the Trade of the Nation*, p. 367; Burton, *Anatomy of Melancholy*, Vol. I, pp. 74–5; Temple (ed.), *Travels of Peter Mundy*, Vol. 4, pp. 70–5, 81; Peters, *Good Work for a Good Magistrate*, pp. 26–7, 35, 41, 44–9; Anon., *A Late Voyage*, pp. 580–1; C. Hill, *Intellectual Origins*, pp. 280–2; Haley, *English Diplomat*, pp. 299, 304–12; Haley, *British and the Dutch*, pp. 107–23; Davids, "From De la Court to Vreede", p. 245.

48 Ward, *Metropolitan Communities*, p. 127; Ward, "Fictitious Shoemakers", p. 84.

49 Lough, *France Observed, passim*; Lough, "Two More British Travellers"; Crawford (ed.), *Journals of Sir John Lauder*, pp. 21, 25, 30–5, 47.

50 Cohen, "Manliness, Effeminacy and the French", p. 55.

51 Crawford (ed.), *Journal of Sir John Lauder*, p. 82; Letts (ed.), *Francis Mortoft*, pp. 12–13.

52 Rye, *England As Seen By Foreigners*, pp. xxii–xxiii.

53 Gentleman, *Englands Way to Win Wealth* (1614), p. 390; Moryson, *Itinerary*, Part 3, p. 177.

54 Moryson, *Itinerary*, Part 3, p. 3. See also Howes (ed.), *Annales*, p. 869, for the fashion of aping French ruffs.

55 Anon., *Pacquet-Boat Advice*, p. 381.

56 Veryard, *Account of Diverse Choice Remarks*, pp. 108–9. For satire in a similar vein see J. and M. Evelyn, *Mundus Muliebris*, in Mackie (ed.), *Commerce of Everyday Life*, pp. 584–611.

57 For the Grand Tour see especially Stoye, *English Travellers Abroad*; Black, *The British Abroad*; Chaney, *Evolution of the Grand Tour*; Towner, "Grand Tour"; Cohen, "Grand Tour"; Dolan, *Ladies of the Grand Tour*.

58 Hexter, "Education of the Aristocracy"; Simon, *Education and Society*, pp. 150, 272, 346–8; Lehmberg (ed.), *Book Named the Governor*; Guy, *Tudor England*, pp. 19–20.

59 For some quantitative data see Towner, "Grand Tour", table 1, p. 221. For a brief general discussion of the impact of war, particularly the Thirty Years War, on travel in Europe see Stoye, "Grand Tour", pp. 62–7.

60 L'Abbé Le Blanc, *Letters*, Vol. 1, pp. 26–7. See also Horn, *Great Britain and Europe*.

61 *The Spectator*, No. 383, Tuesday May 20, 1712.

62 Myers (ed.), *Coverley Papers*, p. ix [Journal to Stella, October 12, 1710].

63 See, for example, *CSPV 1534–54*, p. 544; Chamberlayne, *Angliae Notitia*, pp. 40–1; Yungblut, *Strangers Settled Here Amongst Us*, pp. 42, 43, 44, 47; Luu, "Xenophobia", pp. 7, 11, 18; Archer, "Responses", pp. 758–9; Brigden, *London and the Reformation*, pp. 130–1; Goose, "The 'Dutch' in Colchester", pp. 270–1; Manning, *English People*, pp. 72, 79. London apprentices have been described as constituting a veritable sub-culture, exhibiting behaviour commonly associated with modern adolescence: Smith, "London Apprentices".

64 Malfatti (transl.), *Two Italian Accounts*, p. 36; *CSPV 1534–54*, p. 544.

65 Cramer (ed.), *Travels of Nicander Nucius*, p. 14; Rye, *England as Seen by Foreigners*, p. 7, and see also pp. 186–7; Letts, *As the Foreigner Saw Us* (London, 1935), p. 15; above, Chapter 4, p. 83.

66 Hughes (ed.), *Shakespeare's Europe*, p. 474; Chapter 4, above, p. 82 and fn. 26.

67 Mackay (ed.), *Collection of Songs and Ballads*, pp. 18–19.

68 Tawney and Power (eds), *Tudor Economic Documents*, Vol. 3, pp. 82–90; Holmes, "Evil May Day", pp. 642–50. The Venetian ambassador gives a figure of 2,000 rioters, confirms the figure of 13 executed, and states that by 5th May there were 5,000 men at arms in the city: *Letters and Papers Foreign and Domestic Henry VIII*, Vol. 2, Part 2, p. 1031. See also Brigden, *London and the Reformation*, pp. 129–33. May Day was the traditional day for

apprentice misrule, and the year 1517 saw a significant rise in the price of flour in the capital: Rappaport, *Worlds Within Worlds*, Appendix A3.1, p. 404.

69 Holmes, "Evil May Day", p. 648. For the sixteenth century, emphasizing the significance of the failure of the chronicler John Stow to notice any unrest, see Rappaport, *Worlds Within Worlds*, pp. 16–17.

70 *CSP Foreign 1547–53*, pp. 119–20.

71 The number given as a result of this survey in the state papers is 40,000 plus women and children, which is absurd. Luu suggests that 40,000 was the number rumoured to be present, and which led to the threat of violence: *CSP Foreign 1547–53*, p. 120: Luu, "Xenophobia", p. 7.

72 *CSP Spanish 1550–52*, pp. 278–80; Pettegree, "Foreign Population of London", p. 145; Brigden, *London and the Reformation*, pp. 467–76. For the extraordinary rise in flour prices in 1551–2 see Rappaport, *Worlds Within Worlds*, Appendix A3.1, p. 405.

73 Pettegree, *Foreign Protestant Communities*, pp. 285–6.

74 Luu, "Xenophobia", p. 2; Archer, *Pursuit of Stability*, pp. 4–8.

75 Gairdner (ed.), *Three Fifteenth-Century Chronicles*, pp. 140–1; Luu, "Xenophobia", p. 7.

76 Luu, "Xenophobia", p. 2.

77 Hessels, Vol. 3, Part 1, p. 957; see also Chapter 10 below, pp. 196–8.

78 Strype, *Annals of the Reformation*, Vol. 4, p. 167.

79 Strype, *Annals of the Reformation*, Vol. 4, p. 168. All those using double trades were to be identified and warned, strangers not belonging to any church were to be "avoided hence", and a public proclamation of these actions was to be made in Guildhall.

80 McLuskie, *Dekker and Heywood*, pp. 26–7.

81 Strype, *Annals of the Reformation*, Vol. 4, p. 167. The historian of the Weavers' Company, however, reports no disharmony in this year, the regulation of aliens laid down in 1590 successfully keeping the peace through to 1595: Consitt, *London Weavers' Company* , pp. 143–4.

82 D'Ewes, *Compleat Journal*, pp. 445–7, 453, 463, 489, 505–10; Strype, *Annals of the Reformation*, Vol. 3, Appendix, pp. 242–5. A bill to this effect was first discussed in the Commons in 1572: PRO SP 12/88/36.

83 A fuller description of the debate, and some of the local background to it, can be found in Scouloudi, *Returns of Strangers*, pp. 57–66.

84 D'Ewes, *Compleat Journal*, p. 506.

85 D'Ewes, *Compleat Journal*, p. 506.

86 D'Ewes, *Compleat Journal*, pp. 507–8.

87 D'Ewes, *Compleat Journal*, pp. 508–9.

88 Strype, *Annals of the Reformation*, Vol. 4, p. 167.

89 Outhwaite, *Dearth*, p. 20; Slack, *Impact of Plague*, pp. 58–62; Grell, *Dutch Calvinists*, p. 16; Ormrod, *Dutch in London*, no pagination; Goose, "Dutch in Colchester in the 16th and 17th Centuries", p. 271; Luu, "Xenophobia", p. 3; Plummer, *Weavers' Company*, p. 147.

90 Quotation from Yungblut, *Strangers Settled Here Amongst Us*, p. 41. For a graphic description of the appalling weather conditions, plague and dearth of 1593–4 see the sermon preached at York by Dr J. King, printed in Strype, *Annals of the Reformation*, Vol. 4, pp. 210–11.

91 Archer, "Responses to Alien Immigrants", p. 758; Grell, "French and Dutch Congregations", p. 363; Littleton, "Social Interactions", pp. 152–8. The economic difficulties experienced in the decade or so after 1615 do not appear to have impacted as sharply as those of the late 16th century.

92 PRO, SPD 12/190/2, 14/129/70.

93 Hessels, Vol. 3, Part 1, pp. 1177, 1490–1.

94 Hessels, Vol. 3, Part 1, pp. 963–4, 980–1, 1037, 1056–8, 1070–1, 1195, 1197–8, 1267–8, 1272,

1325–6; Grell, *Dutch Calvinists*, pp. 19–20, 23–5; Scouloudi, *Returns of Strangers*, pp. 10, 42, 57; and see above Chapter 1, p. 7 and Chapter 4, pp. 82–4.

95 Grell, "French and Dutch Congregations", pp. 369–74. For an excellent first-hand account of dealings with Laud see Bulteel, *Relation of the Troubles*, and for the various petitions and correspondence it elicited see Hessels, Vol. 3 Part 2, pp. 1681–95, 1703–6, 1708–9, 1712–18, 1721, 1728.

96 See Chapter 1 above, p. 18–19.

97 Hudson and Tingey, *Records of the City of Norwich*, Vol. II, p. lxxxi; Vane, "Walloon Community", p. 131; Miller, "Town Governments", p. 579.

98 Vane, "Walloon Community", p. 138; Miller, "Town Governments", pp. 586–9.

99 Backhouse, *Flemish and Walloon Communities*, pp. 22, 27, 34. Figures given here for the native population, 1,600–1,800, are probably an underestimate: see Chapter 1 above, p. 20.

100 Backhouse, *Flemish and Walloon Communities*, pp. 26–7, 33–6.

101 Oakley, "Canterbury Walloon Congregation", pp. 62–3; and see Chapter 1 above, p. 19.

102 Oakley, "Canterbury Walloon Congregation", pp. 62, 67–8.

103 Mayhew, *Tudor Rye*, pp. 23, 82–3.

104 Hardy, "Foreign Refugees at Rye", p. 420.

105 Colchester Record Office, D/B 5 GB1, Assembly Book, 17 October 1580.

106 Spicer, *French-Speaking Reformed Community*, pp. 35–6, 148, 161; Clark and Murfin, *History of Maidstone*, pp. 43–4; Roker, "Dutch Fishing Community ", pp. 306–7.

107 Cracknell, *Canvey Island*, pp. 22–5.

108 Tsushima, "Melting into the Landscape", pp. 107–10. The disturbances in the fens are discussed in more detail in Chapter 5, above, pp. 102–104.

109 Darby, *Draining of the Fens*, pp. 39, 54–5.

110 Gwynn, *Huguenot Heritage*, pp. 47, 150–1.

111 PRO, SPD 12/103/34, 12/240/115, 16/206/58; *CSPD 1611–18*, pp. 474–5; *CSPD 1619–23*, p. 381; *CSPD 1623–5*, p. 164; *CSPD 1629–31*, p. 200; *CSPD 1631–3*, pp. 238–9; *APC 1613–14*, pp. 239–40; *APC 1615–16*, pp. 381–2, 420–3, 590; *APC 1616–17*, pp. 89–90, 303–4; *APC 1623–5*, p. 179; Tawney and Power (eds), *Tudor Economic Documents*, Vol. 1, pp. 301–2, 308–10; Thirsk and Cooper (eds), *17th Century Economic Documents*, pp. 713–14, 716–21, 725–9, 746–7; Backhouse, *Flemish and Walloon Communities*, pp. 74–93; Spicer, *French-Speaking Reformed Community*, pp. 144–6; Miller, "Town Governments", pp. 583–5.

112 Hessels, Vol. 3, Part 1, p. 1238; Scouloudi, "Stranger Community", pp. 50–1; Oakley, "Canterbury Walloon Congregation", p. 69.

113 Goose, "Economic and Social Aspects of Provincial Towns", pp. 366–9; Goose and Cooper, *Tudor and Stuart Colchester*, pp. 93–6, Goose, "Household Size and Structure", pp. 356–8, and sources cited therein.

114 PRO, SPD 16/206/58.

115 Everitt, "Marketing of Agricultural Produce", *passim*.

116 Miller, "Town Governments", pp. 579–80; Hudson and Tingey, *Records of Norwich*, Vol. 2, No. CCCLXVII, pp. 191–2; Consitt, *London Weavers' Company*, pp. 298, 319.

117 Hudson and Tingey, *Records of Norwich*, Vol. 2, No. CCCLXX, pp. 192–3.

118 Quoted in Rappaport, *Worlds Within Worlds*, pp. 57–8. For the full text see Consitt, *London Weavers' Company*, pp. 312–17.

119 Consitt, *London Weavers' Company*, pp. 319–20.

120 PRO, SPD 12/144/18.

121 *APC 1601–4*, p. 506; BL, Addl. MSS no. 11404.

122 PRO, SPD 14/26/4.

123 Cromwell, *History and Description*, Vol. 2, p. 287: see Chapter 7 below, pp. 140–1.

124 Quoted in Miller, "Town Governments", p. 580. For similar testimony from Norwich see also Goose, "The 'Dutch' in Colchester", p. 271.

125 Bulteel, *Relation of the Troubles*, p. 11, cited more fully in Chapter 7 below, pp. 138–9.

126 Bulteel, *Relation of the Troubles*, p. 27.

127 HMC, *Salisbury MSS*, Part 11 (Dublin, 1906), p. 569; *APC 1596–7*, pp. 16–17, 20–1; D'Ewes, *Compleat Journal*, p. 509. See also Walvin, *Black and White*, esp. pp. 1–15; Shyllon, *Black People in Britain*; Hall, *Things of Darkness*.

128 Quinn, *Elizabethans and the Irish*, pp. 157–9 and *passim*; Moryson, *Itinerary*, Part 3, pp. 74, 160–4, 180–1; Temple, *Irish Rebellion*, pp. v, 2–13; Laurence, "From the Cradle to the Grave", pp. 63–84; Noonan, "'The Cruell Pressure'", pp. 151–77.

129 For the foundation of the Spanish and Italian churches see Chapter 5 above, p 94.

130 Strype, *Annals of the Reformation*, Vol. 2, Appendix, pp. 58–9. For the execution of Anabaptists, see Chapter 5 above, p. 95.

131 Strype, *Annals of the Reformation*, Vol. 2, Appendix, pp. 59–60.

132 "Certificate and good testimony of the Dean and Chapter of Canterbury", quoted in Bulteel, *Relation of the Troubles*, p. 10. For a similar appreciation by James I on taking the crown, see Strype, *Annals of the Reformation*, Vol. 4, pp. 386–7.

133 For anti-Catholicism see, for instance, Clifton, "Fear of Popery". Clifton argues (p. 156) that "It was this detestation of popery which led to repeated assaults by Londoners on Catholics leaving the foreign embassy chapels throughout the century", but apart from events in the early 1640s these assaults are neither specified nor referenced.

134 See Chapter 11 below, pp. 211–22.

135 Collinson, "Europe in Britain", p. 64. The association did not, however, inevitably lead to advocacy of a bellicose policy: see Lowe, "Religious Wars".

136 See esp. Maltby, *Black Legend*; and for changing perceptions of the relationship between Spain and Rome, Lock, "'How Many Tercios Has the Pope?'".

137 Lake, "Anti-Popery", esp. p. 80; Cogswell, "England and the Spanish Match", pp. 107–33.

138 Hunt, *Puritan Moment*, Chapter 11; Manning, *English People*, pp. 72–83; J. Miller, *Popery and Politics*, p. 83.

139 Miller, *Popery and Politics*, *passim*; and see Chapter 1 above, p. 7.

140 D'Ewes, *Compleat Journal*, p. 508; and see above, pp. 7–8.

141 Luu, "Xenophobia", pp. 18–19; Littleton, "Social Interactions", pp. 157–8; Parker, *Dutch Revolt*, 225–66.

142 For a discussion of the multi-layered nature of integration see Goose, "Dutch in Colchester in the 16th and 17th centuries", *passim*.

143 *CSPV 1615–1617*, pp. 431–2.

144 Gainsford, *Glory of England*.

145 Moryson, *Itinerary*, Part 3, p. 35.

146 Moryson, *Itinerary*, Part 1, p. 148.

147 For an excellent historiographical discussion see Clark, "Protestantism, Nationalism and National Identity". For a re-statement of the role of reformed religion in the development of a sense of nationhood, and the particular role played by pamphlet literature and the writing of national histories, see Grabes (ed.), *Writing the Early Modern English Nation*.

148 Latham and Matthews, *Diary of Samuel Pepys*, Vol. 4, 1663, pp. 209–10.

149 Latham and Matthews, *Diary of Samuel Pepys*, Vol. 3, 1662, p. 268.

150 *CSPV 1661–1664*, pp. 54–5.

151 Sharp, "Popular Political Opinion", pp. 13–29; Miller, *Popery and Politics*, esp. Chapter 4; Kidd, "Protestantism, Constitutionalism and British Identity"; Robertson, "Re-Writing the English Conquest", pp. 837–8.

152 Compare, for instance, Lipson, *Economic History*, Vol. 3, pp. 56–61, and Langford, *Englishness Identified*, pp. 219–25.
153 Dobson (ed.), *Peasants' Revolt*, pp. 161–2, 175, 188–9, 201.
154 Dobson (ed.), *Peasants' Revolt*, pp. 161–2.
155 Bolton (ed.), *Alien Population*, p. 39.
156 Bolton (ed.), *Alien Population*, p. 40. See also Thrupp, "Aliens in and Around London", pp. 251–70; Palliser, "Role of Minorities", p. 183.
157 See esp. Newman, *Rise of English Nationalism;* Colley, *Britons;* Harding, "Controlling a Complex Metropolis", pp. 32–3.

7

Immigrants and English Economic Development in the Sixteenth and Early Seventeenth Centuries

Nigel Goose

It was argued in chapter one that recent historiography places more emphasis on the economic progress achieved in this period than it does upon the obstacles to growth that loomed large in the writings of a previous generation of economic historians. Quite clearly a period of demographic growth in general, the years between *ca.* 1570 and 1640 were also a period of significant urban expansion, most notably in London but in the provinces too, whilst profit inflation in the agrarian sector, the spread of industry, product innovation, commercial re-orientation and a distinct quickening of internal trade all marked this period out as one of economic expansion and commercial intensification.[1] What part, if any, did foreign immigrants play in this process? With occasional exceptions, historians both old and new have been quick to recognize their contribution, from the classic study produced by Cunningham over 100 years ago to the appraisals offered in a range of publications over the last quarter-century.[2] Few authors of recent general texts have, however, fully appreciated the breadth of this contribution, and so it has fallen to specialists in the field to remedy this situation, although to date most emphasis has been upon the impact of the 'second wave' of Huguenot immigration that followed the Revocation of the Edict of Nantes in 1685 rather than upon the contribution of earlier settlers.[3] This chapter will begin to redress the balance by outlining the various aspects of industry, commerce, finance and agriculture that benefited from foreign immigration and influence in the sixteenth and early seventeenth centuries, and will attempt also to assess the importance of that influence as a component of overall economic development.

In his augmentation of Stow's *Annals* published in 1615, Edmund Howes offered an extensive list of innovations that could be attributed to foreign influences, direct and indirect. After noting that printing and gunpowder were invented in mid-fifteenth century Germany, he explains how in 1560 one Mistress Montagne introduced silk stockings to Elizabeth I who, from henceforth, swore never to wear any but silk. In 1564 one Guylliam Boonen, a Dutchman, introduced coaches to England, the appeal of which produced "within twenty yeeres . . . a great trade of Coachmaking", while

Boonen's wife became first starcher to the queen, her skill in starching allowing ruffs to be made of lawn and cambric, cloths which were soon to enter into common use. She was quickly followed, in 1564, by one Mistress Dinghen from Flanders, who charged a fee to teach English women how to starch, and how to make starch. The introduction of embroidered and trimmed gloves, girdles and other garments, suitably perfumed, was attributed to a visit to Italy by Edward de Vere, Earl of Oxford, while worsted stockings were first made after an English apprentice in 1564 'borrowed' a pair from the lodgings of an Italian merchant and copied them, "and so in short space they waxed common". Howes, like other contemporaries, noted the aping of French fashions, which included the making of a ruff "a full quarter of a yearde deepe and 12 Lengths in one Ruffe", called in London "the French Fashion", but in Paris "the English Monster". The making of Spanish felts was the work of both Spanish and Dutch immigrants near the start of the reign of Henry VIII, inaugurating the development of a trade that was to culminate in the establishment of a strong, independent Company of Feltmakers in the capital under the grant of James I in 1605. The introduction of the distaff during the reign of Henry VII is attributed by Howes to an Italian named Anthony Bonvise, which stimulated the production of Devonshire kersies, while "About the fift yeere of Queene Elizabeth, beganne the making of Bayes in England by Dutchmen".[4] Howes's list does not end there, for under "Observations not altogether unworthy remembrance" he also mentions the introduction of various fruits, fish, fowl and flowers, tobacco, women's masks, busks, muffs, fans and periwigs, furnaces for earthenware, Spanish needles (taught by a German) and licorice, and in a rehearsal of the well-known rhyme that is often quoted in abbreviated form, he reports that,

> Turkeys, Carpes, Hops: Piccarels and beere,
> Came into England: all in one yeere.[5]

There are a number of significant points to be drawn from this list, the first of which is the simple fact that contemporary writers such as Howes were in no doubt that England had benefited considerably from the emulation of continental nations – German, Spanish, Italian and particularly Dutch – while the direct influence of migrants from these countries that had settled in England was appreciated too. Howes makes particular note of the impact of immigrants from the Netherlands, especially after 1563, and in stark contrast to some of the more resentful remarks that can be found argues that,

> whereas before their coming, fayre houses in London were plentious, and very easy to be had at low, and small rents . . . and not any man desirous to take them at any rate, were all very sudainely inhabited, and stored with Inmates, to the great admiration of the English nation, and advantage of Landlords, and Leasemongers . . . [6]

He goes further, noting the additional benefits that accrued from the subsequent influx of refugees from the civil wars in France, chiefly into London, arguing that,

> all which together with the encrease of our owne Nation, who from that time, have infinitely conjoyned in marriage with straungers, and the greate freedome of Traffique and commerce into France, Spaine, Italy and Turky, etc. that then, and for many yeares after, this land enjoyed, was and is the maine cause of our encrease of wealth, and great shippes,

the undecernable and new building of Goodly howses, shoppes, shedes, and lodgings within the city . . . [London] being at this day one of the best governed, most richest, and flourishing Citties in Europe, plentiously abounding in free trade and Commerce with all nations . . . [7]

Howes's account has been given lengthy consideration because of the awareness it shows of the variety of ways in which England benefited from continental influences: through emulation of techniques and fashions learned abroad, through the direct influence of immigrant settlements in England, the stimulus to urban economies (particularly the housing market) that those settlements could engender, and in the development of international commerce which a policy of openness produced – the very life-blood of the economy of the English capital.

Howes was by no means alone in this appreciation, for a very similar line of argument was adopted by Sir John Wolley, MP, when speaking on behalf of the London immigrant communities in the parliamentary debate of 1593 on the bill to prevent aliens from selling foreign wares by retail. There he argued that "This Bill should be ill for London, for the Riches and Renown of the City cometh by entertaining of Strangers, and giving liberty unto them", citing Antwerp and Venice as examples of the success produced by similarly hospitable policies.[8] Indeed, we can hardly forget that successive English monarchs had invited immigrants to settle in England, even before the religious troubles of the mid-sixteenth century, precisely to learn the superior skills they possessed, while similar invitations from both Privy Council and local corporations from 1550 forwards were anything but disinterested expressions of Protestant solidarity. In Norwich the Book of Dutch and Walloon strangers in 1564 rehearsed the fact that "the comodities of worsted makynge is greatlye decayed", claiming that the town was impoverished in consequence, while Elizabeth's letters patent of 1565 emphasized that the introduction of "certeyne Douchemen of the Lowe Countryes of Flaunders being verye skillfull" was designed to achieve the "helpe, repayre and amendmente of our Citye of Norwiche . . . ".[9] They were not to be disappointed, for just a few years later it was reported that the Dutch had

> Brought a great commoditie thether, viz., the making of bayes, moccados, grograynes, all sort of tuftes, etc., which wer not made there before, wherby they do not onely set on worke their owne people but do also set on worke our owne people within the citie as also a grete nomber nere 20 myles aboute the citie, to the grete relief of the porer sorte there.[10]

Indeed, time and again the privileges of immigrant communities were upheld and ratified by both local and national governments, and repeatedly it was the economic benefits they brought to the communities where they settled that was highlighted. Hence in Colchester James I's Letters Patent of 1612 emphasized

> how beneficiall the strangers of the Dutch Congregation there have bene and are unto the said towne, as well in replenishing and beautifying of it, as for their Trades which they daily use there, setting on work many of our poor people and subjects both within the said town and in other places thereabouts . . . [11]

In Canterbury, similarly, a certificate issued by the Dean and Chapter of the town in 1623 stressed how the Walloon Congregation most painfully and industriously labour in their severall vocations, so as none of them are chargeable or any wayes burdensome to the English, but rather very helpful to the poorer sort, by setting them to spinning and other workes, whereby they are much relieved and kept from idlenesse . . . And we are verily perswaded that the example of their painfull industry and diligent labours, doth move and stirre up the honest poore of our nation to set themselves to worke.[12]

Even Laud, no friend of the foreign churches, was persuaded to accept

that their Congregations were beneficiall to the English, especially poor; that their Congregation of the Dutch in Colchester who were 700 Communicants in number, did imploy 17000 English at work in and about Colchester and that they of Canterbury and Sandwich did set a great number of English at work.[13]

The point needs labouring no further: the economic benefits perceived to accrue to the English economy echo throughout the extant local and national documentation and – notwithstanding periodic complaints about the competition they gave to the indigenous inhabitants – this is the overwhelming view of informed English opinion throughout and beyond the period which encompasses the first refuge.

What was their particular contribution? Notwithstanding Howes's emphasis upon starched ruffs, perfumed gloves and silk stockings, it was not in the realm of luxury clothing that foreign settlers made their most important contribution but in the wider and more mundane realm of cloth production. The context that renders this so important is the difficulties the traditional English cloth industry laboured under towards the mid-sixteenth century for, following a period of considerable expansion of cloth exports, depression struck in 1550, and the consequences were long term. A combination of factors was responsible: overproduction, currency manipulation, reduced spending power due to plague and harvest failure and the political turmoil in Europe which eventually led to the closure of the Antwerp entrepôt to English merchants, severing the umbilical cord between Antwerp and London that had for so long underpinned English commerce.[14] The 1550s and 1560s were years of great instability in the cloth trade, and when the level of exports settled down again in the 1570s they stood some 20 per cent lower than the early 1550s peak.[15] Expansion of cloth production in the early sixteenth century had been dangerously reliant upon increasing demand for thick, heavy English broadcloth, and exports dependent to a large degree upon the continued viability of the London–Antwerp axis. The lesson of the mid-century crisis was that demand for this expensive product was relatively inelastic. In the long-run, changes in fashion, in incomes and the rise of new types of cloth conspired against the traditional product, and it quickly became clear that the future lay with those cheaper, lighter, more colourful cloths known collectively as the "new draperies".[16]

This context explains importance of the Dutch contribution, for it was they who brought with them expertise in the manufacture of these new cloths. Worsted cloth not dissimilar to the new draperies had, it is true, been made in England before they arrived, but it had belonged to a peasant economy which produced cloth of inferior quality for local consumption, and worsted exports were insignificant. Full commercialization of worsted production had proceeded farthest and earliest in Flanders, and before the mid-sixteenth century new drapery production had already started to spread outside of the southern Netherlands – to Holland, France and Germany – but there was little sign of a similar evolution in England before the immigrants arrived. When they did arrive, the English textile industry in the areas where they settled, notably East Anglia, was transformed within a generation. A key feature of many of the new draperies – the variety of which defies description – was that they often combined elements of traditional woollen cloth production with worsted-making techniques: hence, for example, many bays were fulled (a process of cleaning, shrinking and felting the cloth by heat, pressure and moisture), which traditional worsteds never were, while calimancoes were glazed to resemble satin. There was no particular *invention* associated with these cloths – indeed, the new draperies were more labour intensive than the old – but they incorporated a range of *innovations* that produced a great variety of colours and designs and, in the major centres of production at least, were produced under strict regimes of quality control that further enhanced their marketability.[17]

How do we measure the importance of these developments? Despite the paucity of commercial data and the almost complete absence of industrial data, both global and local evidence can be brought to bear. At the global level there are export figures for London and the provincial ports which, although vitiated by smuggling and complicated by the different manner in which customs were levied on the old and the new draperies, give an approximate indication of the relative importance of the two types of cloth in the foreign market. By the early seventeenth century, the new draperies already accounted for 23 per cent of the customs paid on cloth, indicating considerable export growth since the later sixteenth century, providing compensation for the stagnation of traditional cloth exports from London of which historians have made so much. By 1640 the new draperies accounted for 42 per cent of the total, and hence were beginning to challenge woollen cloth for supremacy in the export trade.[18] They had also helped stimulate a diversification of the geographical horizons of English commerce, for by the 1630s and 1640s about two-thirds of these cloths were sent to Spain, Africa and the Mediterranean, breaking the over-reliance upon northern and central European markets.[19] It is also likely, given their variety and affordability, that they were even more successful in the home market, although contemporary estimates suggest great variation in eventual market by type of cloth, with possibly two-thirds of all says, serges and perpetuannas exported in 1688 but only one quarter of Norwich stuffs. Whatever the scale, however, there can be little doubt that they found ready sale at home as well as abroad.[20]

At the local level the impact of the new draperies can be demonstrated through a case study of Colchester in Essex.[21] The economy of Colchester towards the mid-sixteenth century was in the process of readjustment. Cloth production had long been central to its economic vitality, employing 30 per cent of the occupied male population in the early sixteenth century, but by mid-century this had fallen to just 18 per cent and lack of employment found expression in a threatened uprising in 1566.[22] Some compensation may have come from expanding eastern coastal trade in the early sixteenth century, while more intensive regulation of internal trade in the 1550s and 1560s suggests growth here too. The 1550s also witnessed a substantial increase in the number of burgesses purchasing the freedom, though interestingly only 16 per cent of those admitted between 1550 and 1570 were textile workers.[23] Perhaps like Norwich, as its textile industry waned, the town was re-orienting towards greater reliance on its trading role.[24] Notwithstanding these compensations, decline of the labour intensive cloth industry was bound to exacerbate unemployment and poverty, concern over which was expressed through the introduction of compulsory rating for poor relief in 1557, the institution of additional voluntary collections at sermons in 1561 and in the erection of a new hospital in the early 1570s.[25] In this context the town's corporation had little doubt that the introduction of Dutch immigrants would bring economic benefits.[26]

The first settlers arrived in Colchester in 1565, numbering 55 persons in 11 households. Their numbers grew slowly at first, reaching 185 by 1571 and 431 by 1573, followed by more rapid growth to produce a total of 1,291 by 1586. The influx slowed thereafter, and the community peaked at roughly 1,500 in the second quarter of the seventeenth century, by when they formed some 14 per cent of the town's population.[27] The letters patent of James I of 1612 testifying to their beneficial impact is but one of many similar examples.[28] In 1580 Nicholas Chalyner and Robert Lewis, preachers, along with Robert Searle and Robert Monke, wrote to Walsingham in defence of the Dutch, emphasizing their civility, honesty and godly behaviour, but also the advantages to the town in terms of the employment created.[29] A letter written to Sir Thomas Lucas in 1603 on their behalf also stressed the benefits produced by their bringing new manufactures to the town.[30] In 1607 the town bailiffs wrote to the Earl of Salisbury in support of a petition from the Dutch merchants objecting to the proposed imposition of a double subsidy on the new draperies, arguing this would lead them to leave off their trade, "and many poor people will be very much distressed for want of work, which now they have by reason of that trade".[31] But we need not rely on such testimonies alone, for a range of quantitative evidence can also be brought to bear. On the back of the new draperies, employment in the Colchester cloth industry experienced a remarkable revival, until by the early seventeenth century the textile industry accounted for as much as 37 per cent of the occupied male population (the leading occupation was that of baymaker).[32] Evidence from fines paid to the Dutch Bay Hall for faulty workmanship ("rawboots") show continued growth in the seventeenth century, peaking in the 1680s.[33] Overseas trade also expanded, based largely upon growth of new drapery exports to the Low Countries, while imports grew and diversified.[34] Direct export of cloth from Colchester was, however, dwarfed by the quantity shipped coastwise for export from London, while further cloths were sent to the capital by road.[35] There is no doubt that, despite short-term setbacks, Colchester's economy prospered in the later sixteenth and seventeenth centuries, permitting substantial growth in the population from *ca.* 4,600 in the 1570s to *ca.* 11,000 by the 1620s, a total that was sustained through to the 1670s.[36] This is why the Dutch were granted substantial economic privileges and authority in the town and why, in the face of all complaints, they were given fair hearing and were protected, their privileges repeatedly upheld.

Norwich provides a similar, well-documented example of a town experiencing economic difficulties around the mid-sixteenth century, whose economy revived and indeed flourished following the introduction of new drapery production by the immigrant community.[37] Textile production expanded rapidly after 1565: between 1567 and 1586 the number of cloths produced by aliens rose from 1,200 to 38,700, an increase of 3,225 per cent in 20 years.[38] Renowned worldwide, the Norwich "stuffs" were characterized by several distinct features, the first being their extraordinary variety. Before

1565 textile production focused on six products (worsteds, russels, lace, dornicks, linen and carded woollens), but by 1611 the Walloons were manufacturing 40 different types of cloths (including bays, says, ollyet, damasks, valures, carrells, grograins, and fustians).[39] The second distinguishing feature was their use of linen, silk, and cotton, which increased choice as a greater variety could be made with more exotic qualities. But an equally important feature of Norwich stuffs was their affordability. The success of Norwich lay precisely in this ability to provide a variety of cloths at different prices, "cheap enough for the broad base of the population to buy, while other cloths were more upmarket, and could appeal to the more affluent of society."[40] The revival of cloth production underpinned the town's economic and demographic vitality, for it expanded in the seventeenth century from an estimated population of 12,000–13,000 to 30,000, and the continued growth of its new drapery trade was essential to that process, notwithstanding the diminishing role the stranger community itself played.[41]

New drapery production was, however, anything but a purely urban affair, rapidly spreading into the East Anglian countryside, and if the main centres for weaving remained towns like Norwich, Colchester, Braintree, Bocking, Coggeshall, Sudbury and Halstead, the spinning of wool for the trade became an important source of rural employment.[42] Contemporary testimony to this has already been cited for the hinterland of Norwich and Colchester, Laud suggesting a figure of 17,000 English so employed "in and about Colchester" in 1635, which explains the acute distress experienced across this region during the trade slumps of 1620–4 and 1629–31, as lack of vent for cloth put pressure on employment and wages.[43] A century later, with the Colchester industry now in decline, Defoe could still write that "The town may be said chiefly to subsist by the trade of making bays ... though the whole county, large as it is, may be said to be employed, and in part maintained, by the spinning of wool for the bay trade of Colchester, and its adjacent towns", while in Norfolk he noted that "the vast manufactures carried on (in chief) by the Norwich weavers, employs all the country round in spinning yarn for them; besides many thousand packs of yarn which they receive from other countries, even as far as Yorkshire, and Westmoreland ...".[44] The success of new drapery production across Essex, Norfolk and Suffolk may help explain why by the later seventeenth century East Anglia was one of the more advanced economic regions in the country, possessing a large numbers of urban centres that exhibited both occupational diversity and economic specialization.[45] Nor was new drapery production confined to East Anglia, but was also introduced by the immigrant communities to Canterbury, Sandwich, Rochester, Hastings and Maidstone in Kent, to Southampton in Hampshire, while in London their skills in dyeing were particularly important.[46] It spread also, of course, to many towns that failed to establish or maintain a foreign community, for as noted in 1607 "the Englishmen which dwell at Coxsall Braintree Hastinges and other places that make Bayes nowe in great aboundance did learne the same of the straungers by reason whereof many thousandes aswell of verie poore people as others gitt their lyvinge therby".[47] Even in the case of smaller towns, such as Sandwich, the industry's influence also spread into the countryside, for it was again claimed in 1607 that "great nombers of the English nation in East Kent and other places ... gitt their lyvinge with Spinninge, Cardinge, weavinge of Jarsey and fatt wooll and such like labors ... ".[48]

If new drapery production was the most important immigrant innovation, it was far from their only contribution to English industrial life. Other innovations in textiles include the establishment of thread-making at Maidstone for, although the Dutch here first specialized in cloth production, by 1605 the corporation could claim the trade had now been "learned and taken from them by the Kinges borne subjects inhabitinge within the said towne".[49] By the 1620s thread-twisting was the principal means of livelihood for the Dutch, and by 1640 overshadowed the cloth trade, having been readily taken up by the indigenous population and providing a stimulus to flax-growing in the mid-Kent area.[50] Other industries allied to the new draperies were also developed, including lace making, ribbon making and stocking knitting at Norwich. The importance of stocking knitting, interestingly one of those trades attributed by Howes to French and Italian influences, has probably been underestimated, for in 1615 it was calculated that fully one-third of the combed wool used in England went into stocking knitting, two-thirds into the new draperies.[51] Like the new draperies, it may also have had a rural handicraft background, but its growth and development again coincided with the foreign settlements of the 1560s. By the start of the seventeenth century it was established in Wales, Gloucestershire, Cornwall, Devon, Nottinghamshire, Yorkshire, Northumberland, Cumberland, Westmorland and Durham, as well as Norwich, and by the 1690s it has been estimated that as many as 15.3 per cent of labouring and pauper families could have supplemented their incomes by knitting as a by-employment.[52] If the early innovations are attributable to foreign immigration, however, the absence of significant foreign settlement in many of these areas testifies also to indigenous development, and the removal of William Lee from England to France in order to exploit his stocking knitting frame, which was refused a patent in England, also indicates that even by the end of the sixteenth century the exchange of ideas was already becoming a two-way process.[53]

Some stockings, of course, were made of silk, and their adoption by Elizabeth I was noted above, but silk weaving extended beyond the realm of legwear, and this was another industry to benefit considerably from foreign immigration. The development of the industry in London from the 1560s has been attributed to the influx of Dutch and French immigrants, particularly Walloons, many of whom took the trade up upon arrival, probably assisted by the small number of foreign silk weavers already established in the capital. There were 183 alien silk workers recorded as householders in London in 1571, and their number had more than doubled by 1593, some of whom weaved mixed fabrics as well as pure silk.[54] In 1594 the London Dutch Congregation, appealing to the Lord Keeper of the Great Seal against molestation, claimed also to have introduced the art of silk twisting, and that 16 or 18 households of them set on work at least 1,000 English poor, while by their dyeing skills they had also replaced previously imported thread.[55] The silk industry continued to develop in Spitalfields in the early seventeenth century, providing a firm foundation for the larger Huguenot settlement that followed the Revocation of the Edict of Nantes in 1685.[56] In Canterbury too the industry came to assume considerable significance, overtaking the new draperies in importance in the early seventeenth century and again providing a solid foundation for reinforcement after the Revocation of 1685.[57]

A range of other industries, perhaps less vital to the English economy and certainly far less important in international trade, were also stimulated by the foreign influx. Among these we can list the various leather trades, brewing, glassmaking, pottery, furniture making, hatmaking, starching, soap making, alum and copperas making, cutlery making, tapestry making, pin making, watch- and clockmaking, gold- and silversmithing, vinegar making, and the distilling of aqua vita and other "strong waters".[58] It was in the capital that such industries usually assumed particular importance, and by the end of the sixteenth century the Dutch dominated the London brewing industry, having been involved in beer-brewing, both here and in Colchester and Canterbury, since at least the early sixteenth century.[59] Nor does this short catalogue begin to do justice to the range of occupations they followed in the capital. In May 1593 a breakdown of the 7,113 strangers then residing in the Liberties of the City of London and adjoining parishes also gives a list of trades practised by the "masters of Severall famelies; And some fewe Jorneymen", both within the wards of London and in the out-parishes of Surrey and Middlesex.[60] They numbered 1,862 individuals in 143 trades, led by silkworkers (355), merchants (163), tailors (118), brewers (85), shoemakers (66), goldsmiths (61), cutlers (42), joiners (40), "gentlemen and women" (35), thread twisters and dyers (33), sempstresses (31), hemp dressers (27) and hatmakers (27).[61] Another incomplete list, probably drawn up in July 1611, gives a total of 686 dwelling within the liberties spread across 89 occupations, while a further return, probably from October 1616, gives 1,343 strangers in 121 trades, with weavers (presumably mainly silkweavers) easily the most numerous (349), followed by merchants (183), tailors (148), shoemakers (43), dyers (39), brewers (37), jewellers (35), cutlers (22), joiners (20) and goldsmiths (20).[62] By 1635 the distribution of occupations among 1,322 alien tradesmen was similar, though by now there was greater concentration on cloth-making, no doubt as the silk industry grew further, while all other leading trades exhibited smaller numbers than 20 years earlier. Indeed, by now cloth-making accounted for 54 per cent of all tradesmen listed, its nearest rival, tailoring, with 104 representatives, accounting for just 8 per cent.[63]

Provincial immigrants settlements exhibited a less extensive range of occupations. Starch making, first developed by the Dutch in London, soon spread to a number of provincial towns, including Norwich, King's Lynn and Yarmouth. Despite controversy over its reliance upon wheat, which might otherwise have fed the poor, the industry flourished in the early seventeenth century and, if it is impossible to estimate the numbers involved, it has been described as far more than a "paltry industry".[64] In Colchester a list of 55 "old strangers" and 130 "new" for 1571 shows that cordwainers were particularly prominent among the established immigrants, and while baymaking was dominant among the recent incomers they also included at least one of the following: preacher, gardener, parchment maker, needle maker, hop planter, merchant, surgeon, cardmaker, labourer, potmaker, turner and a "stereman".[65] Extant Colchester wills from the late sixteenth century indicate the continued predominance of new drapery production within the Dutch community, but also identify merchants and mariners, gardeners, cordwainers, beer-brewers, a tapestryworker, papermaker, currier, baker, chairmaker and a grocer.[66] Evidence from other provincial towns confirms that immigrants were far from confined to the textile sector, but were active in a range of trades, at least some involving specialist skills they had introduced.[67]

Considerable numbers were also active as merchants in London and in the provinces, but they have attracted far less historical interest than their counterparts in industry.[68] The London list of 1593 identifies 163, or 9 per cent of the total enumerated, while by 1616 there were 183 constituting 14 per cent of all strangers listed, and at both dates they stood second only to silk workers. By 1635 their number had fallen to 81, just over 6 per cent of the total, by when they stood in third place behind cloth workers and tailors.[69] Bare numbers, of course, give only an approximate idea of the changing importance of particular trades, though it is unlikely that the 81 merchants identified in 1635 were more wealthy and driving a greater trade than the 183 found in 1616. Nor is their number an accurate measure of their relative importance, for there is no doubt that the collective wealth of the stranger merchants at each of these dates would have exceeded that of the tailors, and quite possibly also that of the far more numerous silk workers. This is one point upon which all historians agree: the merchants were generally the wealthier members of their communities, and often held positions of authority within their churches.[70] With respect to the Dutch in London, most of the £33,000 in charitable funds collected between 1627 and 1642 came from merchants in the congregation, virtually all of whom resided in the City rather than the suburbs, and they also contributed approximately two-thirds of every church collection.[71] A further indication of merchant wealth is the fact that James I was able to extract a loan of £14,500 from the "merchant strangers" in London in 1607, and a further £20,000 from the Dutch merchants in 1617, the latter amounting to fully one-sixth of the total loan levied. Just two years later, following accusations of illegal export of bullion, 18 merchants strangers were fined a total of £140,000, three of whom (two French and one Dutch) were asked to pay £20,000 each. The fines were never paid, but their size gives at least an impression of their wealth.[72] There was also a smaller group of very wealthy financial operators: Philip Burlamachi, Sir William Courten, John de Moncy, Pieter van Loor, Robert de la Barre, Gillis van der Put and Philip Jacobson all acted as bankers to the English crown.[73] Burlamachi's ability to raise funds on bills of exchange in all of the major European financial centres made him crucial to government finance in the 1620s when he frequently acted as paymaster for English forces on the continent and, in the sphere of government borrowing, the 1620s has been described as "the era of Burlamachi", his bankruptcy in 1633 largely due to the government defaulting on its obligations. Even lesser figures, however, raised substantial sums, Courteen making loans to James I and Charles I of £18,500 and £16,500 respectively.[74]

Merchants were prominent too in provincial towns: among alien Colchester will-makers their number was exceeded only by textile workers.[75] Here, however, they were not necessarily the wealthiest in their communities, for bay and saymakers also left impressive bequests, even if their wealth could rarely compete with some of the merchant strangers of London.[76] Nevertheless, early in the seventeenth century Daniel Beake, merchant, of St Mary's in Colchester, was wealthy enough for his will to be proved in the PCC, as was Michael Butterdryer of St Peter's, while another Dutch merchant, Francis Pollard, left cash bequests totalling over £500 in 1630, besides two houses in Colchester and farms at Kelvedon and Fordham.[77] Later in the century merchants such as John Rebow and Andrew Fromanteel, who both had relatives in London, left even larger cash sums, the latter also devising a number of houses in Colchester, besides lands at Frating, Great or Little Bentley and Stanway in Essex, at Aldham, Hadleigh and Stratford in Suffolk and at Bennington and Boston in Lincolnshire.[78] In the early seventeenth century Dutch merchants, not necessarily residents, figured quite prominently in Colchester trade. In 1616 the town complained of the "great concourse of strangers" shipping to and from the town, and in both 1616 and 1619 it was reported that the town's shipping was much decayed.[79] Port Book evidence suggests that while in 1621–2 vessels from Colchester and Wivenhoe dominated trade with Rotterdam, Calais and the Azores, on other trade routes, particularly that to Camp Vere, roughly 40 per cent of exports were in the hands of strangers.[80] By the end of the century, however, Colchester vessels and Colchester merchants dominated the town's export trade, imported Dutch and German linens and a vast array of other products from Rotterdam, and also wood, iron and pitch from Norway.[81]

In Southampton in the second half of the sixteenth century refugee merchants made a substantial contribution to overseas trade. They were particularly involved in new drapery exports, accounting for about 70 per cent of the says exported for the period 1573–80, unlike in Colchester where new drapery exports were dominated by merchants from London. This contribution continued into the later part of the century, despite their loss of dominance and gradual integration.[82] At Sandwich a small number of Flemish and Walloon residents operated as merchants, and may well have played a part in the Elizabethan revival in the town's trading fortunes, but it is impossible to say more than this without detailed examination of the town's port books.[83] The French Protestants who temporarily settled in Rye in the 1570s and 1580s also included a handful of merchants, between 10 and 13 being identified in 1573, 1578 and 1581, and their activities continued into the early 1590s, while the influx of mariners from Dieppe also stimulated the town's trade.[84] At Yarmouth more than half the alien householders listed in 1571 were either fishermen or in some other way connected with the sea, and although by 1633 the Dutch Church there had dwindled to 50 persons, there is no doubt that they served to stimulate the town's staple herring-fishing industry, while even in the late seventeenth century Dutch fishing fleets regularly visited the town, providing custom for local suppliers of foodstuffs and beer.[85] In Dover, which possessed a small foreign community with a somewhat chequered history, 9 of the 64 male strangers listed in 1571 were merchants, as were 8 of the 62 male strangers, old and new, listed in 1622, when a further 14 were described as mariners.[86]

The contribution to English economic development made by immigrant merchants is difficult to assess, and the involvement of Dutch and French merchants settled in London from the second half of the sixteenth century complicates an otherwise clear trend towards declining foreign involvement in English overseas trade. In the first half of the century a large proportion of English trade had been in foreign hands, their share of cloth exports rising to over half during the mid-1540s when customs duties were temporarily equalized between native and foreign merchants. The German Hanse were the dominant force, followed closely by the Italians, with an unknown proportion in the hands of traders from the Netherlands. Thereafter, the English government increasingly pursued a policy of economic nationalism, imposing higher duties on foreign merchants, tightening regulations, revoking foreigners' privileges and assisting native merchants that, allied to the difficulties which the demise of the Antwerp entrepôt caused the Italians, effectively transformed English overseas trade, until by the end of the century neither the Italians nor the Germans were significant players.[87] The immigrant influx from the Low Countries and France failed to transform this picture. Most appear to have concentrated upon the import rather than the export trade, using their contacts in the Low Countries and northern Europe rather than branching out into new markets, features which are particularly underlined by a detailed study of those active in the import of damask and diaper linens.[88] The sketchy figures available for London's export trade in the early seventeenth century suggest that the share of alien merchants was in decline, even from the comparatively low level it had already reached. For the six years between 1598 and 1603 English merchants shipped on average 99,454 shortcloths per annum, while alien merchants shipped on average 4,494. By 1636 alien merchants were shipping only 1,256, and the number for 1640 was just 503, in which year English merchants exported 86,924. In terms of other exports, which were dominated by the new draperies, their trade held up better. For the three years for which data are available, the value of these other alien exports amounted to £81,072 in 1612, £65,745 in 1636 and £85,136 in 1640. As a proportion of the total, however, even here their contribution was in decline, for while in 1612 native merchants exported £275,140 by value of goods other than woollen cloth, by 1640 this had grown to £609,722.[89] Even in the linen import trade, where they had such an obvious advantage over their English counterparts, they were important rather than predominant.[90]

In comparison with native merchants the number of alien traders was small. Estimates of the total number of merchants in London in the later seventeenth century vary widely, from 600–1,000 full-time merchants to 2,000, but both of these figures are difficult to square with the 2,000 "eminent" and 8,000 "lesser" merchants estimated for the nation as a whole by Gregory King in 1688, the majority of whom must surely have been Londoners given the continued dominance of the capital in overseas trade, a view confirmed by Grassby's estimate of the size of the London and provincial 'business community' in the late seventeenth century.[91] King's figure accords well with Grassby's estimate of a London business community comprising ca. 8,000 individuals with personal wealth in excess of £500 in 1688, but both King and Grassby appear to have extended their remit beyond those who were strictly merchants, and these figures undoubtedly err on the generous side.[92] Calculations from burial data show that merchants accounted for 11 per cent of London's adult male occupations for the period 1601–40, and as the population stood at 200,000 in 1600 and 375,000 in 1650, a rough calculation (taking the average of these totals and allowing five to a household) would suggest a merchant population in excess of 5,000, besides which figure the 81 foreign merchants remaining in London in 1635 looks of minor significance.[93] The evidence from the provinces is at present too sketchy for any definitive assessment, but it would appear that foreign merchants may have played a more prominent part, in relative terms, in the much more circumscribed commercial activities of some provincial ports, with indigenous merchants increasingly coming to dominate as the seventeenth century progressed.

Finally we can turn to agriculture, where there are stark differences of opinion with regard to the immigrant contribution, and where measurement of their contribution is most difficult. Fussell has emphasized the superiority of the agriculture of Flanders from late medieval times, and has identified three routes of communication between Flanders and England: through the settlement of refugees, the Dutch and German influence upon the new agricultural literature that flowered from the mid-sixteenth century and the visits of Englishmen to the Low Countries for the purposes of trade, war or education.[94] In terms of the introduction of new root crops and grasses, the development of new rotations, the growth of market gardening and the adoption of convertible husbandry, he concluded that,

> The influence of the Low Countries' example on the development of arable farming in Great Britain is sufficiently remarkable, and there is at least some kind of a measure of

it. Besides this there is a persistent rumour in contemporary and subsequently secondary sources of the importation of living animals.[95]

In contrast, in attempting to make a case for an early "agricultural revolution" in the sixteenth and seventeenth centuries, Kerridge argues it would be wrong to exaggerate foreign influences. Many of the newly popular grasses and virtually all of the new root crops, he suggests, were indigenous; the floating of water meadows was an English invention; the only livestock introduced from overseas were some Flemish horses and a few Friesian cows; and the convertible husbandry adopted in the plain countries was uninfluenced by foreign ideas. Consequently, "England seems to have borrowed precious little".[96]

What are we to make of this? Both lines of argument are open to criticism, for although there is no doubting the general superiority of Dutch agriculture,[97] Fussell appears too ready to assume that foreign techniques were adopted and popularized on the basis of flimsy evidence, while Kerridge chooses to deny any foreign influence whenever the smallest indication of pre-existing practice or presence in England can be found. There can be little doubt that some popular agricultural writers were inspired by foreign example, such as Barnaby Googe, whose *Four Bookes of Husbandry*, published in 1577, was a translation of a German text.[98] More famous still is the work of Richard Weston, published by the indefatigable Samuel Hartlib in 1650 as *A Discours of Husbandrie Used in Brabant and Flanders*.[99] Although written by Weston in 1645 as a legacy for his sons, Hartlib took the opportunity to publicize the valuable lessons Weston had learned first-hand when visiting the Low Countries for the improvement of "barren and heathie" land through rotation of flax, turnips, oats and clover-grass, together with the costings that testified to the greater profitability of such practices, and the potential for linen manufacture also entailed.[100] But this remarkable document is also revealing in other ways, for it testifies to the efforts farmers such as Weston were *already* making without foreign example, having 30 years experience of husbandry before travelling to the continent when he improved his land "as much as any man in the kingdom".[101] He also notes that in some respects English practice was actually *ahead* of the farmers of Flanders, for "We have not onely dung to enrich our Land, but also Lime and Marl, of which they know not the use . . . ".[102] As if in direct response to the arguments of Kerridge, Weston also accepts that "Flax, Turnips, and Clover-grass alreadie grow in England . . . ", but proceeds to explain that "there is as much difference between what groweth there, and here, as is between the same thing, which groweth in a Garden, and that which groweth wilde in the Fields."[103] The failure of the indirect influence suggested by Fussell is also indicated when Weston wonders at "the ignorance and sloathfulness of Our Countrie which beeing near to Flanders, and many Merchants and Gentlemen travelling thither daily, none should understand, or at least put in practice these Husbandries, there being so much Barrren and Heathie land in England of very little value . . . ".[104] And finally he shows that some at least of his contemporaries may have already started to experiment with Flanders' rather than indigenous species, or were at least able to do so, for "If any desire to have the great Clover of Flanders, or the best sort of Hemp or Flax seeds of those parts; Let them enquire at Mr James Long's shop at the Barge on Billings-gate, and they shall upon timely notice have them procured new, and very good, from Flanders at reasonable rates".[105]

This exegesis of Weston's pamphlet suggests a farming community in 1645 where there was at least a vanguard of gentleman farmers actively attuned to change; a regime that was far from lagging behind the continent in every respect; where a variety of crops were already grown; but one where there was great scope to learn how to grow those crops better and where the lessons of best continental practice remained to be diffused on a widespread scale. Such an interpretation sits easily with the conventional orthodoxy about the limited progress made by English agriculture before the mid-seventeenth century, at least compared to the century which followed.[106] This is why agricultural prices continued to rise into the second quarter of the seventeenth century, despite the extension of the area of cultivation through the release of church and crown lands, disparking, encroachment, conversion to arable land from pasture and land reclamation.[107] But it also reveals the potential for future change and the role that continental example could play, at least where the soil and topography was appropriate, for neither wet clays nor hill lands were generally well-suited to turnip cultivation, and counties such as Herefordshire fared better by concentrating upon their natural strengths.[108]

Continental example was, however, already beginning to bear fruit in two more specialized areas. The first of these was in market gardening, and its development was the direct result of the arrival of Dutch refugees. We have already seen that Edmund Howes, albeit as a subsidiary consideration, noted the recent introduction to England of a range of horticultural items, explaining that "Aprycoks, Mellycatons, Muske-Millions and Tobacco, came into England about the twentieth yeere of Queene Elizabeth, and since that sundry strange fruites, and flowers", while the planting of licorice was attributed to "about the first yeare of Queene Elizabeth".[109] Writing at a similar date, a Venetian report records how the "filth" of the city of London provided excellent manure for land in the environs of the capital, by which means were raised "a great quantity of vegetables", particularly praising "their most beautiful and fine flavoured artichokes . . . the size of their cabbages, which sometimes weigh 35lbs the pair . . . extreme white and very large potatoes, cauliflowers, parsnips, carrots, turnips etc . . . ". As for fruit, "The apples are really very good and cheap . . . The pears are scarcely eatable and the other fruits are most abominable . . . ". They were widely eaten nonetheless, for "between meals one sees men, women and children always munching through the streets, like so many goats . . . ".[110]

Vegetable and fruit growing were not new to the later sixteenth century – Colchester already had an established vegetable market in 1529 when it was ordered that "the pease and root market, with the onions, garlick, and cucumbers, and other garden stuff and wares" should be held hard by St Nicholas' church and nowhere else, an order that was renewed in 1620.[111] But the early markets sold surplus produce from kitchen gardens, and dedicated commercial market gardening probably dates from the mid-century.[112] This coincides with the refugee influx and their influence, in London and the provinces, was crucial.[113] In London, market gardening was rapidly taken up and expanded by the indigenous population, spreading in Westminster, Lambeth, Battersea, Fulham, Putney, Brentford, Whitechapel, Stepney, Hackney and Greenwich, growing so rapidly that the Gardeners' Company received its first charter in 1605.[114] By the time the 1593 list of strangers was compiled there were only eight alien gardeners in the metropolis, in 1616 a mere four, and by 1635 just one.[115] By 1635 market gardening had spread further to Kensington and Chelsea, these two parishes together with Fulham sending 20,000 loads of roots per year to the markets of London and Westminster.[116] And if roots were not new to England, and many varieties were indigenous, it was the Dutch that first grew them on a commercial scale, first to feed the poor and later the rich as well.[117]

In the provinces the arrival of the Dutch may have marked the beginning of commercial market gardening. In Colchester there are no gardeners listed among the established strangers in 1571, but among those who had recently arrived there were six hop-planters and one gardener, all from Flanders.[118] A general muster for the town dated 1590 lists "Dewchmen in the North Ward, generally baymakers and gardeners", while in the parish of All Saints a further seven Dutch gardeners are identified.[119] Occupational analysis from wills reveals no gardeners for the period 1500–79, but five feature in 1580–1619.[120] Unfortunately burgess admissions give occupations only erratically, but the first gardener recorded as admitted to the freedom was Robert Surra in 1606, followed by John Webb in 1616, John Turner in 1620 and Lucas Fairfield in 1627; in 1614 John Crosse, gardener, took an apprentice, as did John Turner in 1620.[121] Gardeners increase in number later in century in the testamentary evidence, with Dutchmen such as Jacob Stickalorum and John de Clark still involved.[122] The town retained its reputation for market gardening into the nineteenth century, when it was described by Cromwell as "not perhaps exceeded by that of any other place in the kingdom, London excepted", the rich, black, sandy soil being highly favourable to the cultivation of fruit and vegetables.[123]

Market gardens were also established under foreign influence in the later sixteenth century at Norwich, Canterbury, Maidstone and Sandwich.[124] The growing of horticultural produce was far from confined to these towns, however, for as early as 1607 Norden could write as follows:

> For the first, namely, your low and spongy grounds trenched is good for hops, as Suffolk, Essex, and Surrey, and other places do find to their profit. The hot and sandy, (omitting grain) is good for carrot roots, a beneficial fruit, as Orford, Ipswich, and many sea towns in Suffolk: as also inland towns, Bury, Framlingham, and others in some measure, in the same shire, Norwich, and many places in Norfolk, Colchester in Essex, Fulham and other places near London. And it begins to increase in all places of this realm, where discretion and industry sway the minds of the inhabitants.[125]

It is odd that Norden fails to mention Kent, the veritable home of hops, from whence Reynold Scot wrote his *Perfite Platforme of a Hoppe Garden* in 1574, having gained personal experience from a visit to Poppering in Flanders in 1560, while Peter de Woolfe had been invited to teach hop-growing in the county as early as 1550. For religious refugees from France and the Low Countries, Kent was often one of the first destinations, and it is likely that regular intercourse helped disseminate foreign agricultural ideas here as much as anywhere. It was, however, apparently an Irishman, Richard Harris, who first undertook commercial fruit-growing in the country, at the behest of Henry VIII in 1533.[126]

Market gardening continued to spread throughout the seventeenth century until by 1695 Gregory King could estimate the value of home-produced fruit and vegetables at £1,200,000, representing employment for possibly 20,000 men.[127] The increased availability of fruit and vegetables, and their increasing acceptance by even the landed classes as the seventeenth century wore on, partly due to their tendency to ape the

French,[128] must have increasingly assisted in the development of an agricultural surplus, which allowed the export of grain in all but exceptional years while keeping the price of bread low and hence stimulating home demand for non-food items. But market gardening was also important because of the lessons it offered to field agriculture, and they were not ignored.[129] The use of root crops, spade-digging, sowing in rows with standard spacing (and hence drilling) and hoeing – these were all market garden techniques that were eventually applied to arable cultivation, albeit after much-needed experimentation and resistance from labourers had delayed their introduction on any scale until the eighteenth century.

A final aspect of English agriculture to which the Dutch made an important contribution was fen drainage. Again Kerridge is determined to diminish their role, arguing that while many Dutch drainage engineers were employed here, this was more due to their financial than their engineering ability, that English engineers had more experience and expertise in fen drainage, and where the Dutch did excel, in the reclamation of saltings, they played only a minor part.[130] This is, of course, to turn conventional wisdom on its head and, while providing a valuable corrective to the view that the drainage of fen and coastal land was entirely a Dutch achievement carried out almost single-handedly by Cornelius Vermuyden, it is again unsustainable. Although it is true that land drainage was by no means new to the later sixteenth century, and had long been practised upon various English coastlines, it is also true that the pace of reclamation increased as population pressure grew in the sixteenth century, and that the drainage of the East Anglian Fens in the seventeenth century was an undertaking on a wholly new scale, in the words of Darby "one of the mighty themes in the story of Britain".[131]

That drainage projects could call upon both native and Dutch expertise, not without a degree of competition or even antagonism, is amply demonstrated by the case of the reconstruction of Dover harbour in the late sixteenth century, an undertaking eventually overseen by the Englishman Thomas Digges, but at one stage also involving a contribution from the Brabanter Humphrey Bradley.[132] It was Bradley who, in 1589, drew up one of the earliest comprehensive plans for the drainage of the Fens, working closely with the English surveyor Ralph Agas, but his efforts foundered upon the rocks of vested interest, political manoevring and the ineptitude of the Commissions of Sewers. This is perhaps just as well, for although he was involved in small-scale Fen drainage projects, his grand scheme was technically inadequate.[133] Other Dutch engineers were invited as consultants on smaller projects from the 1590s, such as works on the Thames estuary and Canvey Island, and it is quite clear that whatever expertise existed at home it was to the more experienced Dutch that English landowners continually deferred, familiarity with their work often the result of periods of military service in the Low Countries.[134] Despite these early efforts, with their various domestic and foreign contributions, it was the grand plan of Cornelius Vermuyden, drawn up in 1642, that was eventually put into operation in 1650 when he was appointed Director of the Works, and it is to the expertise of Vermuyden, aided by the enterprise and financial ability of English landowners such as the Earl of Bedford, that credit for the drainage of the Fens must go.[135] The result, taking into account work in the East Riding of Yorkshire, Lincolnshire, Cambridgeshire and Huntingdonshire, was the addition of at least 500,000 acres of land fit for arable cultivation, some 400,000 acres of which represented a permanent accession.[136]

The economic ascendency of the Dutch in the early seventeenth century has been fully acknowledged by Charles Wilson, who writes that by the early seventeenth century, "In all the arts of commerce, and many of industry, the Dutch were indisputably ahead".[137] In the first edition of his *England's Apprenticeship 1603–1763* he added the following rapturous appreciation of the importance of Dutch influence to English economic development:

> From the time of Alva's persecution until late in the seventeenth century English industry was able to draw on the special skills of entrepreneurs and craftsmen from the Netherlands. There is hardly a branch of manufacture where we cannot identify technological innovations, often individual innovators, from across the North Sea. Agricultural innovators drew on the same source.[138]

In the second edition of this book, published some 20 years later, this effusive appreciation is missing. Now it is duly acknowledged that immigration, both the first and the second refuge, did indeed produce benefits: "On both occasions new knowledge and skills became available, new and flourishing trades and manufactures sprung up and prospered." But now it is also recognized that "'improvement' [did not] depend on the immigrants alone", while the propensity of the English to learn from foreign technical gadgetry or economic ideas is given due credit.[139] This change of emphasis is appropriate, reflecting as it does increased appreciation of the role played by Englishmen themselves, the appetite with which they embraced new ideas and methods, and the importance of the high degree of tolerance the nation displayed, particularly compared to countries such as Spain.[140] But it may not go far enough, for far from every economic innovation of the early modern period was foreign in origin. Even within the cloth industry, although Dutch influence upon new drapery production was clearly crucial in East Anglia and South East, in the west of England the old draperies gradually gave way to the so-called Spanish Cloths, which were an adaptation of a traditional, indigenous product. The quality of this cloth may well have been improved by settlement of small numbers of Dutch craftsmen skilled in the finishing processes in the later seventeenth century, but it did not originate with them.[141] In Devonshire serge-making developed in the seventeenth century without a significant influx of foreign craftsmen, the lighter, narrower cloths previously manufactured here perhaps making the transition easier than in the old broadcloth regions.[142] By the later seventeenth century the West Riding of Yorkshire had also turned to the production of new draperies, again without the direct aid of foreign immigrants, while fustian manufacture flourished in East Lancashire, far away from the main areas of immigrant settlement.[143] Even in Norwich, where immigrant skills had clearly proved so crucial, during the 1550s the "Fellowship and Companye of Merchantes and Russells Making" were excluding aliens from apprenticeships, allowing them only as journeymen, claiming that "the fyrst practising of ye making of ye said russells etc, within ye same citie was first invented by ye said merchauntes . . . ".[144] It was the Englishman William Lee who developed the stocking knitting frame in the 1590s, and although he moved to work in France instead when refused a patent, on his death his workmen returned to England and established a thriving trade in the capital, while hosiers in the Midlands continued to concentrate upon hand-knitted stockings.[145]

In other industries too there are many examples of native enterprise to set alongside foreign contributions. In the area of non-ferrous metal mining and smelting, the old orthodoxy of substantial inputs from German miners and entrepreneurs has been stridently refuted by Burt, who finds "no evidence that German experts introduced any new technique, machine or method that had a significant and sustained impact on the industry during this period".[146] Much production, in tin for example, remained small in scale throughout the seventeenth century, and due recognition must be given to continued processes of improvement, modification and development by native miners and smelters in response to local conditions which leave little trace in the historical record.[147] In the iron industry there is more evidence of foreign involvement, the influx of over 500 workers of Walloon descent from Normandy between the 1490s and 1540s serving to establish the two-stage process of furnace and forge in pig iron production, even if Wealden ironmasters remained predominantly Englishmen in 1574.[148] The entrepreneurs in the Yorkshire industry were English too, but there is evidence of migration of forgemen from the Weald to Yorkshire helping to spread the two-stage process, among whom were craftsmen who were anglicized immigrants.[149] The importation of foreign craftsmen did not necessarily lead to success. When James Blount, 6th Earl of Mountjoy, began his alum and copperas mining operations on his manors of Canford and Puddletown in Dorset in 1562, with a 25-year monopoly from the crown granted in 1566, he brought in experienced workmen from Italy. But the venture proved financially disastrous for Mountjoy and his successor Henry Hastings, 3rd Earl of Huntingdon, for while the mines yielded a considerable amount of copperas, little of the more valuable alum was found.[150] Howes too, while fully appreciative of foreign influences, was also aware of native innovations, ranging from the "bandora" (bandore), a lute-like instrument devised by John Rose in the fourth year of the reign of Elizabeth, to the fine knives made by Richard Matthew at Fleet Bridge, to the earthen furnaces made by Richard Dyer at "London without Moregate", having learned the art in Spain, to Lee and his knitting frame.[151] Gough's *Rise of the Entrepreneur* identifies numerous examples of native enterprise while, despite the strictures still being offered by Fynes Moryson in 1617, by the early seventeenth century both the English aristocracy and the gentry were becoming much more actively involved in commercial enterprise.[152]

It may also be true that, on occasion, both historians and contemporaries are prone to exaggerate foreign influence. Thirsk is, of course, to be thanked for demonstrating that there was far more to English industry than textiles, leather and tin, but may overstate foreign influence upon salt production, where English efforts must surely have outweighed foreign influence, or in pin making, where contemporary listings reveal so few foreign pin makers and where the degree of debt owed to foreign innovation is far from clear.[153] The origins of the pillow lace industry in the east Midlands was once attributed to the immigration of workers from Flanders, a story apparently developed by one T. Wright in *The Romance of the Lace Pillow* published in 1919, but modern research has found absolutely no documentary support for this theory.[154] The importance of foreign immigrants, notably one John Kemp, to the establishment of cloth production in the fourteenth century is a frequently reiterated theme; but the story, while not entirely apocryphal, is wildly exaggerated, for cloth-makers had long been present in numbers in the English countryside, and the expansion of the industry at this time owed more to the low price of wool and availability of labour than it did to foreign innovation.[155] Defoe attributed the rise of the English industry to the foresight of Henry VII in inviting Flemish cloth-makers to settle, by which time it was already very well established, a view also expressed by Aubrey regarding the industry in Wiltshire, again with precious little hard evidence.[156] The same exaggeration can also be found regarding some branches of horticulture.[157]

Such mythologies find a parallel in the stereotypical view of the English as followers of others rather than inventors or innovators, a view which echoes across the centuries. As early as 1577 an English writer remarked that we should favour those strangers who had produced such benefits through the introduction of bays and other cloths, "because we are not so good devisers as followers of others".[158] In the later editions of his *Angliae Notitia* Chamberlayne noted that the English were

> generally of a warm and elevated genius, of brisk and solid parts, apprehensive and subtle; successful in finding out new discoveries; but most of all in improving of old, especially . . . mechanicks; there being few curiosities of art brought over from beyond seas, but are here improved to a greater height.[159]

The view is echoed once again by Mandeville in 1720, who described the British as "excellent artificers in most handicrafts, but more noted for improvements than invention".[160] Defoe expressed it well when writing that,

> *It is a kind of proverb* [my emphasis] attending the character of English men, that they are better to improve than to invent, better to advance on the designs and plans which other people have laid down, than to form schemes and designs of their own . . .

Although he was writing as late as 1728, he still thought this proverb "to be really true in fact, and the observation very just, whether this reproach is raised upon the suggestions of foreign observers, or whether it be our own upon our selves, is not worth while to examine . . . ".[161] It was certainly the view of at least one foreigner contemporary with Defoe, for in 1727 Saussure wrote that, "English workmen are everywhere renowned, and that justly. They work to perfection, and though not inventive, are capable of improving and finishing most admirably what the French and Germans have invented".[162]

By the second quarter of the eighteenth century these views were unsustainable, and their proverbial nature must also cast doubt on their accuracy even for earlier periods. Writing at the end of the seventeenth century, having rehearsed the orthodoxy cited above, Chamberlayne goes on to describe some recent English achievements:

> Here are the best clocks, watches, locks, barometers, thermometers & c . . . curious telescopes, microscopes, perspectives, mirrors, spheres, globes, charts, maps and all sorts of mathematical instruments, dials, balances, sea-compasses & c . . . the late improvements in making glass; of polishing the insides of great iron guns; in weighing up ships that are sunk . . . and many other noble inventions and improvements; as weaving silk-stockings, mill of all sorts, mortlack tapestry, earthen ware of Fulham, speaking trumpets, air pumps, spinning of glass, cutting of tobacco, printing stuffs, linnen, paper; making damask, linnen, watering silks; the way of separating gold from silver; boulting mills; langthorns of divers sorts, cane chairs, making horn ware & c . . . [163]

If the balance in terms of technological leadership for much of the early modern period had favoured the continent in general and the Dutch in particular, by the early eighteenth century that balance had swung decisively in favour of the English. Indeed, in the later seventeenth century, France, Germany, Austria, Sweden and Russia were all engaging in industrial espionage in England, surely an important indicator of techno-logical leadership. In 1696 the export of stocking frames from England was prohibited, while by 1719 the situation was serious enough to produce legislation prohibiting the enticement overseas of any "artificer or manufacturer" on pain of £100 fine and three months' imprisonment.[164] Furthermore, if the rise of England to economy hegemony was a gradual, drawn-out process, and if England had benefited in some respects from foreign example in achieving an "advanced organic economy" by the later seventeenth century, the leap that was crucial to the divergence of England was the transition from a purely organic economy to one increasingly founded on mineral sources of power.[165] In the development of coal for use in an increasing range of industrial processes, England had already begun its divergence from the continent of Europe in the late sixteenth century, and by the start of the eighteenth had a very considerable advantage indeed.[166] As industrial leadership moved increasingly to the Midlands and the North from the later seventeenth century, the overall influence of foreign immigrants and ideas in the South and in East Anglia diminished in importance. In agriculture too it is clear that there were indigenous developments occurring alongside the borrowing of ideas from best overseas practice, both of which owed much to the willingness of at least a section of the landed classes to embrace innovation and the prior existence of an appropriate rural economic and social structure, features which in conjunction allowed the diffusion of improvement across the varied English landscape and the spread of best practice from the later seventeenth century forwards. In overseas trade the influence of foreign immigrants was of relatively minor importance, and that importance diminished as the seventeenth century wore on. Nor had the general commercialization of English society, emphasized so heavily by Wrightson, depended upon foreign input, for while the English may well have admired aspects of the Dutch economy in the seventeenth century, they aspired to emulate its achievement rather than its structures and forms. In this they more than succeeded, with a political and social structure and factor endowments that were fundamentally different to those of their economic rivals, and if receptivity to foreign ideas formed part of that process, it was by no means the whole story, nor even the major element of it. If in some respects England had indeed served an "apprenticeship" during the sixteenth and early seven-teenth centuries, the relationship had been one of interaction as well as tutelage, and the new master that was emergent by 1700 was endowed with a power and potentiality that far surpassed the capacities of the old, for England now stood at the forefront of the European economy, and on the threshold of industrial revolution.

Notes

1   See above, Chapter 1, pp. 9–12.
2   Cunningham, *Alien Immigrants, passim*; Coleman, *Economy of England*, pp. 80–1, 86–7, 155–6, 164; Wilson, *England's Apprenticeship 1603–1763*, pp. 73, 75–6, 195–8, 381; Clay, *Economic Expansion and Social Change*, Vol. 2, pp. 80–2, 214–15. One of the surprising features of the stimulating interpretation offered in Wrightson's book is the paucity of references to the impact of foreign settlers.
3   Most recently Gwynn, *Huguenot Heritage*, pp. 74–117; see also Scoville, *Persecution of Huguenots*, Chapter 10, pp. 321–64.
4   Howes (ed.), *Annales*, pp. 866–70.

5   Howes (ed.), *Annales*, p. 948.
6   Howes (ed.), *Annales*, p. 868.
7   Howes (ed.), *Annales*, p. 868.
8   D'Ewes, *Compleat Journal*, p. 506.
9   Hudson and Tingey, *Records of Norwich*, Vol. 2, pp. 332–3; Hessels, Vol. 3, Part 1, pp. 41–3.
10 Tawney and Power (eds), *Tudor Economic Documents*, Vol. 1, p. 315.
11 Hessels, Vol. 3, Part 1, p. 1240.
12 Bulteel, *Relation of the Troubles*, pp. 10–11.
13 Bulteel, *Relation of the Troubles*, p. 27.
14 Fisher, "Commercial Trends", pp. 159–60; Stone, "State Control", p. 106; Ramsay, *English Overseas Trade*, p. 22; Gould, *The Great Debasement*, pp. 140–1; Dietz, "Antwerp and London". A good summary is in Coleman, *Economy of England*, pp. 79–80. See also Chapter 2 above, pp. 48–51.
15 Coleman, *Economy of England*, Fig. 5, p. 63.
16 Coleman, "Innovation and its Diffusion", pp. 423–5; Coleman, *Economy of England*, pp 64–5.
17 Coleman, "Innovation and its Diffusion", *passim*.
18 Calculated from Gould, "Cloth Exports", table 1, p. 251. By the end of the seventeenth century the export value of the new draperies comfortably exceeded that of the old: Clay, *Economic Expansion and Social Change*, Vol. 2, table XV, p. 146.
19 Coleman, *Economy of England*, p. 64.
20 Kerridge, *Textile Manufacture*, p. 220; Wrightson, *Earthly Necessities*, p. 166.
21 See Goose, "The 'Dutch' in Colchester".
22 Occupational analysis from examination of all Archdeaconry, Consistory and Prerogative Court wills: Goose, "Economic and Social Aspects", pp. 159–70; Cockburn (ed.), *Calendar of Assize Records*, p. 51.
23 CRO, D/B 5, Court Rolls, 3 & 4 EdwVI – 1 & 2 Eliz I.
24 Pound, "Social and Trade Structure", p. 138.
25 CRO, Liber Ordinacionum, fo. 94, 24 Nov. 5 Eliz; Goose, "The 'Dutch' in Colchester", p. 265 and refs. therein.
26 For a fuller discussion of the town's economy, see Goose and Cooper, *Tudor and Stuart Colchester*, pp. 78–81.
27 Goose, "The Dutch in Colchester in the 16th and 17th Centuries", pp. 88–9.
28 See above, pp. 138–9 .
29 PRO, SPD 12/144/18.
30 *APC 1601–4*, p. 506; BL, Addl. MSS no. 11404.
31 PRO, SPD 14/26/4.
32 Goose and Cooper, *Tudor and Stuart Colchester*, table I, p. 77 and pp. 81–2.
33 Goose and Cooper, *Tudor and Stuart Colchester*, table III, p. 83.
34 Goose and Cooper, *Tudor and Stuart Colchester*, pp. 84–7.
35 Burley, "Economic Development of Essex", p. 149.
36 Goose, "The 'Dutch' in Colchester", p. 264 and refs. therein.
37 Pound, "Social and Trade Structure"; Pound, *Tudor and Stuart Norwich*, Chapter 5, pp. 46–67.
38 Martin, "Rise of the New Draperies", p. 253. These figures are based on cloths sealed in the Norwich Bay Hall, the Camiant Hall and the Say Hall. The Camiant Hall series only starts in 1570–1, however, and this possibly understates production in the later 1560s, hence exaggerating the percentage increase. Already by 1570–1, however, the combined output of the Bay Hall (Dutch) and the Camiant Hall (Walloon) was 13,584 cloths, and the average for the five years 1583–8 was 36,397: Williams, "Two Documents", pp. 356–7.
39 Martin, "Rise of the New Draperies", pp. 247, 254

40 Martin, "Rise of the New Draperies", pp. 248, 251,267.
41 Corfield, "Provincial Capital", *passim*. The Norwich industry relied very heavily on the home market by the late seventeenth century, having shifted away from overseas markets around mid-century: *ibid.*, pp. 279–80; Martin, "Rise of the New Draperies", p. 255.
42 Pilgrim, "Rise of the 'New Draperies'".
43 See above, p. 139; Thirsk and Cooper, *17th Century Economic Documents*, pp. 210–16, 224–32; Supple, *Commercial Crisis and Change*, pp. 52–72, 102–12.
44 Defoe, *Tour*, pp. 58, 84.
45 Patten, *English Towns*, pp. 282–96; Corfield, "East Anglia", pp. 34–6; Defoe, *Tour*, p. 85.
46 PRO, E101/347/19; Backhouse, *Flemish and Walloon Community*, pp. 74–82, 96–108; Clark and Murfin, *History of Maidstone*, pp. 47–8; Clark, *English Provincial Society*, pp. 139, 301, 356; Spicer, *French-Speaking Reformed Community*, pp. 71–91; Ormrod, *Dutch in London*, unpaginated. Early settlers at Dover were also mainly cloth-makers, but the community here had a chequered history, and their impact on the town's economy is uncertain: Overend, "Strangers at Dover", p. 111, and see above, Chapter 1, pp. 26–7.
47 Hessels, Vol. 3, Part 1, p. 1198.
48 Hessels, Vol. 3, Part 1, pp. 1198–9.
49 Morant, "Settlement of Protestant Refugees", pp. 212–13.
50 Chalklin, *Seventeenth-Century Kent*, pp. 124, 128; Clark, *English Provincial Society*, pp. 301, 356; Clark and Murfin, *History of Maidstone*, pp. 47–8, 81–2; Thirsk, *Economic Policy and Projects*, pp. 47–8.
51 Thirsk, *Economic Policy and Projects*, pp. 44–5; Thirsk and Cooper (eds), *17th Century Economic Documents*, p. 204; and see below, pp. 000.
52 Thirsk, *Economic Policy and Projects*, pp. 45, 167–8.
53 Howes (ed.), *Annales*, p. 869; Thirsk, "Fantastical Folly", pp. 254–5.
54 Luu, "London Silk Industry", *passim*.
55 Hessels, Vol. 3, Part 1, pp. 963–4. A return of 1593 lists 20 silk twisters (18 within the wards of London and 2 in the out-parishes) and 11 silk dyers: Huntingdon Library, San Marino: Ellesmere MS 2514.
56 Ormrod, *Dutch in London*.
57 Clark, *English Provincial Society*, p. 301; Oakley, "Canterbury Walloon Congregation", p. 66; Gwynn, *Huguenot Heritage*, p. 83. New cloths which were silk mixes were also introduced in early 17th century Norwich: *ibid.*, p. 79.
58 Ormrod, *Dutch in London*; Thirsk, *Economic Policy and Projects*, pp. 53–5, 78–97: Gwynn, *Huguenot Heritage*, pp. 90–100. Glassmaking provides one of the best examples of continued influence of foreign craftsmen and methods, for despite indigenous improvements in the 18th century French plate glass retained its superiority: Harris, "Origins of the St Helens Glass Industry", pp. 195–6, and Harris, "Saint-Gobin and Ravenhead", pp. 34–5. See also Godfrey, *Development of English Glassmaking*. For goldsmiths see Luu, "Aliens and their Impact", Mitchell, "Innovation and the Transfer of Skill", and Chapter 8 below, pp. 169–71.
59 PRO E179/108/147; E179/108/162; E179/108/169; Luu, "Dutch and their Beer Brewing", pp. 101–33; Ormrod, *Dutch in London*; Mathias, *Brewing Industry*, pp. 3–4.
60 Huntingdon Library, San Marino: Ellesmere MS 2514.
61 Huntingdon Library, San Marino: Ellesmere MS 2514. 19 "factors for merchants" are excluded from the total for merchants.
62 Kirk & Kirk, Part 3, pp. 138–40. Again, 13 "factors" are excluded from the merchant total.
63 Calculated from Scouloudi, *Returns of Strangers*, Appendix VI, pp. 133–4. Only 12 silk weavers are specifically identified, alongside 609 simply designated as "weaver". See also Scouloudi, "Stranger Community", pp. 47–9.
64 Thirsk, *Economic Policy and Projects*, pp. 83–93.

65 PRO, SP 12/78/9(1).

66 Based upon all extant PCC, Consistory and Archdeaconry wills held at the PRO and Essex CRO.

67 For example, Backhouse, *Flemish and Walloon Communities*, pp. 123, 126–9.

68 The lack of research in this area is reflected in the sparse attention afforded them in Gwynn's otherwise admirable survey: see *Huguenot Heritage*, p. 112.

69 Calculated from Scouloudi, *Returns of Strangers*, Appendix VI, pp. 133–4.

70 Grell, *Dutch Calvinists*, p. 46; Mitchell, "Merchant Strangers", pp. 122–4, 130–1.

71 Grell, *Dutch Calvinists*, pp. 45–6, 97.

72 Ashton, *Crown and the Money Market*, p. 22; Grell, "French and Dutch Congregations", pp. 369–72.

73 Ashton, *Crown and the Money Market*, pp. 21–2; Grell, *Dutch Calvinists*, p. 46.

74 Ashton, *Crown and the Money Market*, pp. 20–22, 165, 169.

75 Above, pp. 140–1; and see fn. 69. The apparently increasing number of merchants in London may be an illusion if a substantial number of the 35 "gentlemen and women" listed were merchants, for no such title was used in 1616, but whatever the case they would still have increased as a proportion of the total.

76 Goose, "The 'Dutch' in Colchester", p. 271.

77 PRO, PROB 11, Dale f.68 (1621); PROB 11, Byrde f. 18 (1624); Essex CRO, D/A CW 11/188.

78 PRO, PROB 11, Foot f.125 (1687); Pett f. 80 (1699).

79 *CSPD 1616–17*, pp. 59–60; PRO, SP 14/105/114.

80 PRO, E190/602/1.

81 PRO, E190/606/5; E190/610/3; E190610/11; E190/619/12; E190/620/4. For a fuller discussion of Colchester trade see Goose and Cooper, *Tudor and Stuart Colchester*, pp. 84–7, and Goose, "Economic and Social Aspects", pp. 177–87.

82 Spicer, *French-Speaking Reformed Community*, pp. 37–70, 164.

83 Backhouse, *Flemish and Walloon Communities*, pp. 93–5, 112, 128–9.

84 Mayhew, *Tudor Rye*, pp. 83–7.

85 Roker, "Dutch Fishing Community", pp. 306–8.

86 Overend, "Strangers at Dover", pp. 111, 165–6.

87 Davis, *English Overseas Trade*, pp. 42–3; Clay, *Economic Expansion and Social Change*, Vol. 2, pp. 182–4; Coleman, *Economy of England*, pp. 54–5, 58–60; Dietz, "Overseas Trade", pp. 120–1, 126–7.

88 Grell, *Dutch Calvinists*, p. 173; Mitchell, "Merchant Strangers", pp. 128–33.

89 Figures calculated from Fisher, "London's Export Trade", table 1, p. 153.

90 Mitchell, "Merchant Strangers", p. 128.

91 Earle, *Making of the English Middle Class*, pp. 34–5: Earle suggests a similar number of part-time merchants; Jones, "London Merchants", p. 350 fn. 30; Laslett, *World We Have Lost*, table 1, pp. 32–3; Grassby, *Business community*, pp. 54–9, 247–51.

92 Grassby, *Business Community*, pp. 54–7, 59.

93 Data from Beier, "Engine of Manufacture", table 13, p. 148; Finlay and Shearer, "Population Growth", table 1, p. 39.

94 Fussell, "Low Countries Influence", pp. 612–13. For the new agricultural literature, Thirsk (ed.) *Agrarian History*, Vol. 5, Pt. 2, pp. 534–7.

95 Fussell, "Low Countries Influence", pp. 613–19.

96 Kerridge, *Agricultural Revolution*, pp. 325–7.

97 de Vries and van der Woude, *First Modern Economy*, pp. 198–210.

98 Thirsk (ed.), *Agrarian History*, Vol. 5, Pt. 2, p. 535.

99 It is the expanded 2nd edn of 1652 that has been consulted here: Hartlib, *Discours of Husbandrie*.

100 Hartlib, *Discours of Husbandrie*, pp. 2–7, 24.
101 Hartlib, *Discours of Husbandrie*, p. 5.
102 Hartlib, *Discours of Husbandrie*, p. 4.
103 Hartlib, *Discours of Husbandrie*, p. 26.
104 Hartlib, *Discours of Husbandrie*, pp. 7–8.
105 Hartlib, *Discours of Husbandrie*, p. 30.
106 Thirsk (ed.), *Agrarian History*, Vol. IV, pp. 161–99; Thirsk (ed.), *Agrarian History*, Vol. 5, Pt. 2, pp. 533–42, 552–3; Clay, *Economic Expansion and Social Change*, Vol. I, pp. 112–37.
107 Thirsk (ed.), *Agrarian History*, Vol. 4, Tables VI–VIII, pp. 846–58.
108 Jones, "Agricultural Conditions and Changes".
109 Howes (ed.), *Annales*, p. 948.
110 *CSPV 1617–19*, pp. 318–19.
111 Cromwell, *History and Description*, Vol. 2, p. 299.
112 Thirsk (ed.), *Agrarian History*, Vol. 5, Pt. 2, p. 503.
113 Thirsk (ed.), *Agrarian History*, Vol. 5, Pt. 2, pp. 505–6.
114 Thirsk (ed.), *Agrarian History*, Vol. 4, pp. 196–7.
115 Scouloudi, *Returns of Strangers*, Appendix V, p. 132, Appendix VI, p. 134; Kirk & Kirk, Part 3, p. 140.
116 Thirsk (ed.), *Agrarian History*, Vol. 5, Pt. 2, p. 505.
117 Thirsk (ed.), *Agrarian History*, Vol. 5, Pt. 2, pp. 505–6.
118 PRO, SPD 12/78/9.
119 Essex CRO, D/Y 2/2 fos. 182, 189–90. Part of the muster is printed in Moens (ed.), *Register of Baptisms*, pp. 105–6.
120 Goose, "Economic and Social Aspects", table 3.21, p. 218.
121 Burgess and apprenticeship data was extracted from a wide range of borough documentation, mainly Court Rolls and Books, too numerous to list.
122 Goose, "Economic and Social Aspects", table 3.21, p. 218; ERO, D/A CR 8/119; D/A CW 17/163.
123 Cromwell, *History and Description*, Vol. 2, p. 296.
124 Thirsk (ed.), *Agrarian History*, Vol. 5, Pt. 2, p. 506; Backhouse, *Flemish and Walloon Communities*, pp. 81, 98; Moens (ed.), *Walloon Church at Norwich*, p. 262.
125 Thirsk and Cooper, *17th Century Economic Documents*, p. 109.
126 Thirsk, "Agriculture in Kent", pp. 83–4, 101–3.
127 Thirsk (ed.), *Agrarian History*, Vol. 5, Pt. 2, pp. 506–30; Thirsk, *Economic Policy and Projects*, p. 163.
128 Thirsk (ed.), *Agrarian History*, Vol. 5, Pt. 2, pp. 508–9
129 Thirsk (ed.), *Agrarian History*, Vol. 5, Pt. 2, pp. 581–7.
130 Kerridge, *Agricultural Revolution*, pp. 317–18.
131 Darby, *Draining of the Fens*, p. 28.
132 For an extended discussion of this see Harris, *Two Netherlanders*, pp. 11–35.
133 Harris, *Two Netherlanders*, pp. 46–78. Bradley's plan is reproduced in Darby, *Draining of the Fens*, Appendix I, pp. 263–9.
134 Harris, *Two Netherlanders*, pp. 80–6; Cracknell, *Canvey Island*, pp. 18–22.
135 Darby, *Drainage of the Fens*, pp. 70–82; Clay, *Economic Expansion and Social Change*, Vol. 1, p. 110.
136 Darby, *Drainage of the Fens*, pp. 86–116, 153–5; Clay, *Economic Expansion and Social Change*, Vol. 1, p. 110.
137 Wilson, *England's Apprenticeship*, 1st edn (1965), p. 41 and 2nd edn (1984), p. 41.
138 Wilson, *England's Apprenticeship*, 1st edn (1965), p. 361.
139 Wilson, *England's Apprenticeship*, 2nd edn (1984), p. 381.
140 For appreciation of the importance of cultural factors in economic development, and

recognition of the role that immigrants could play, see David Landes' *tour de force*, *Wealth and Poverty of Nations*, *passim* and esp. pp. 516ff.

141 De L. Mann, *Cloth Industry*, pp. 11–14, 286; Coleman, "Innovation and its Diffusion", p. 428; Wilson, *England's Apprenticeship*, 2nd edn, p. 78.

142 Coleman, "Innovation and its Diffusion", p. 428; Clay, *Economic Expansion and Social Change*, Vol. 2, pp. 17–18.

143 Clay, *Economic Expansion and Social Change*, Vol. 2, pp. 19, 38.

144 Hudson and Tingey, *Records of Norwich*, Vol. 2, pp. 408–11.

145 Chapman, "Genesis of British Hosiery", pp. 7–13; Thirsk, *Economic Policy and Projects*, p. 99.

146 Burt, "International Diffusion", p. 251.

147 Burt, "International Diffusion", pp. 251–4.

148 Goring, "Wealden Ironmasters", pp. 204, 210–11; Awty, "Continental Origins", *passim*; Evans, "Skilled Workforce", pp. 144–5.

149 Collinson, "Enterprise and Experiment", *passim*; Evans, "Skilled Workforce", pp. 145–6.

150 Bettey, "Fruitless Quest for Wealth", pp. 1–9.

151 Howes (ed.), *Annales*, pp. 869, 948.

152 Gough, *Rise of the Entrepreneur*, *passim*; Moryson, *Itinerary*, Part 3, pp. 133, 149, 222; Rabb, *Enterprise and Empire*, *passim*.

153 Thirsk, *Economic Policy and Projects*, pp. 55–6, 78–83; Scouloudi, *Returns of Strangers*, pp. 131–4; Kirk & Kirk, Part 3, pp. 138–40.

154 Spenceley, "Origins of the English Pillow Lace Industry", p. 89.

155 Howes (ed.), *Annales*, p. 870; Burn, *History*, p. 5 (citing Fuller's *Church History*); Postan, *Medieval Economy and Society*, pp. 193, 196; Miller and Hatcher, *Medieval England*, pp. 247–51.

156 Defoe, *Plan of English Commerce*, pp. 96–7, 225; Powell, *John Aubrey*, p. 117.

157 R. Duthie, "Introduction of Plants", *passim*. For similar thoughts re their influence in Kent see Edwards, "Interpretations", pp. 286–8.

158 Quoted in Kamen, *Iron Century*, p. 96.

159 Chamberlayne, *Angliae Notitia* (19th edition), p. 48.

160 Mandeville, *Free Thoughts*, p. 331.

161 Defoe, *Plan of English Commerce*, p. 224.

162 Van Muyden, *Foreign View of England*, p. 218. See also MacLeod, *Inventing the Industrial Revolution*, p. 208.

163 Chamberlayne, *Angliae Notitia* (19th edition), p. 48.

164 Harris, "Industrial Espionage", pp. 165–6, 172–3.

165 Wrigley, "Divergence of England", pp. 138–9. See also his *Continuity, Chance and Change*, Chapters 2 and 3.

166 Harris, "Industrial Espionage", p. 173.

8

Immigrant Cultures in Tudor and Stuart England

Raingard Esser

Migration studies have traditionally been the domain of social historians.[1] Social science theories of push- and pull-factors, statistical analyses of age, social status, family structure and gender of migrants, have dominated the research agenda. These studies were influenced by the availability of mass data collected and analysed by computers, which have become an important tool in migration research since the 1970s: "who, when and why" were the key questions usually asked by migration historians. Patterns of integration were assessed through an analysis of the degree of intermarriage, the nomination of members of the host society as testators in wills and testaments and as godparents for the children of the migrant community. Only recently have migration historians responded to the challenges of the New Cultural History, which has opened new perspectives on historical research over the last 15 years. This interest has, so far, been rather one-dimensional. Historians of the New Cultural History have not discovered migratory movements as a new and important section of cultural analysis. Moreover, patterns of cultural change have, so far, been most successfully studied by anthropologists, who offer important approaches and methods for historians.[2] Researchers in anthropology were and are interested, for instance, in minorities' contributions to popular festivals and processions in the host society and in questions as to how a migrant culture could and did influence the popular culture they encountered in their new surroundings (and vice versa).[3]

The project of an "Encyclopaedia of Migration, Integration and Minorities in Europe since the 17th Century", currently being undertaken by the Institute for Migration Studies at the University of Osnabrück is, perhaps, the first major historical enterprise that addresses these issues. Here, norms and concepts taken from "traditional" migration studies such as acculturation and assimilation are applied to the complex of cultural change in a migrant community. Representation and identity expressed through cultural practices are key areas of research into the culture of immigrant societies and their changes as proposed by the editors of the "Encyclopaedia", migration historians Klaus Bade and Jochen Oltmer, and their Dutch partners Pieter Emmer and Leo Lucassen.[4] Their concept is based on the underlying assumption of an "imagined community" (Benedict Anderson) of immigrants, who share a common cultural heritage and common cultural practices, that were expressed in a specific form sanctioned by the expectations and prejudices of the host society and by the needs of a community in exile. Clearly, given the diversity even among the Dutch and Walloon refugee communities in Tudor and early Stuart England with members from different parts of the Low Countries such as Brabant, Flanders, Friesland and even some Germans, to cite just a small cross-section of exiles in the Norwich Dutch refugee community, a certain standardization in cultural practices and norms (and, in some instances, language) was required to ensure a successful and quiet community life among the dominant English population.[5] The approach of Bade and his team is convincing and promises exciting new insights into immigrants' lives. What is missing in the "Encyclopaedia's" concept, however, is a discussion of the impact that the immigrants could and did make on their host society. Transfer of culture as a key element of integration is, so far, only studied in the light of the adaptations and adjustments of the migrant society; their influence on the cultural practices and norms of their hosts is not included in this concept.

Immigrant culture, its changes and the impact the refugees made on the culture that they encountered has, so far, only been addressed indirectly in the case studies written on the various exile communities in Tudor and early Stuart England. Culture includes the role and position of religion and religious practices in a community. All studies of immigrant societies in early modern England focus on the religious organization of the refugee communities, the structure of the churches and the contacts of church elders and ministers with English members of the clergy and, sometimes, men and women on the fringes of the Anglican establishment.[6] Clearly, the Dutch and Walloon example of a godly community was widely discussed, particularly by members of the English clergy during the reign of Edward VI when new doctrines as well as new forms of church service and ritual were debated and tested.[7] The following study tries to shed some light on aspects of the cultural impact that immigrants made on their English host society which are not, or at least not directly, related to religion. It addresses issues of material culture both among the elite and the less prosperous men and women in Tudor and Stuart England. It also discusses forms of representation and identity in the immigrant communities and their changes over time. The concept of "cultural impact" will be understood in a wider sense, thus not merely signifying the transfer of culture and cultural change from one community to another. It will also be used to analyse the co-existence of two cultures within urban society as expressed, for instance, in the inclusion of the Dutch and Walloons as distinct representatives of the cultural diversity of a city during town festivals and public processions. The analysis has to remain rather impressionistic. One of the reasons why historians have so far not studied aspects of immigrant culture in greater depth is the distinct lack of information available on this aspect of immigrant life. Very little is known, for instance, about the curriculum of the refugee schools or any form of cultural activity which went beyond the daily prayers and religious exercises. This lack of information is even more surprising in the light of the cultural life and its diversity that the migrants, most of whom had been town dwellers in the Netherlands, had left behind in their native country. Examples that are chosen to highlight a few areas of immigrant culture and their interaction with the host society are taken mainly from the two largest communities in Tudor and Stuart England, London and Norwich. The period under investigation will extend to the Restoration, thus including the beginnings of the consumer revolution, which inaugurated the introduction of new consumer goods and items of material culture that became closely associated with immigrants and their crafts in England.

Book production, book ownership and reading patterns have been a key area of interest for the New Cultural History. The studies of French historians, such as Rogier Chartier, have inspired research into the print and book markets in exile towns such as Emden and the distribution of the more than 300 works produced by the exile press from the second half of the sixteenth century among the Dutch exile communities in England, Germany and the Churches under the Cross in the Netherlands.[8] London quickly emerged as the centre of intellectual life among the exile communities in England. It was here that the merchant-historian Emmanuel van Meteren wrote his *Belgische Ofte Nederlantsche Historie van onsen tijden*.[9] Van Meteren had close connections to the leading Dutch artists and intellectuals of the time. He lived next door to Marcus Gheerhaerts the Elder and his son of the same name, painters at the royal court. Lime Street in the parish of St Dionis Backchurch, where both van Meteren and the Gheeraerts family lived, quickly rose to become a centre of learning and a meeting place for international scholars and scientists.[10] James Cole, alias Jacob Coels, the son of a wealthy silk merchant with a keen interest in the natural sciences, arranged meetings between his uncle, the renowned cartographer Abraham Ortelius, and leading members of the Dutch intellectual elite in London. Ortelius and van Meteren were particularly close, since the orphaned Ortelius had been raised in van Meteren's household. Contacts were also established between Ortelius, who frequently visited his relatives and friends in London, and the English historian William Camden. Scholars working on Camden's *Britannia* emphasize Ortelius's influence on the production of the work and thus the introduction of chorographical studies into England, which were based on archaeology, history, numismatics and geography.[11] From the 1570s onwards Lime Street became one of the centres of the European Republic of Letters: Ortelius himself left a rich correspondence with his nephew James Cole, in which they discussed new books, recent research into botany, numismatics and other sciences and their own academic plans and publications.[12] The Cole family kept close links with the famous botanist artist George, alias Joeris, Hoefnagel, who lived in London for a time in the 1570s before he joined the court of Emperor Rudolf in Vienna, and with Francis Raphelengius, one of the heirs to the famous Plantijn printing press in Antwerp.

The production of the Emden press cannot be matched by the publications of refugees in England, but the establishment of a printing press in Norwich, the second biggest refugee centre for Dutch and Walloon exiles in England, is an exceptional and unique indicator of an immigrant culture, which was interested in the written word and its distribution among a community with a comparatively high degree of literacy.[13] Norwich hosted the only refugee printing press in England. It was established in the early years of the refugee settlement and survived only until 1572. A list of Dutch immigrants collected by the Norwich city authorities in 1568 includes a "Anthonius de la Solemme typographicus cum uxore et duobus pueris ex Brabantia".[14] Solemme, alias de Solempne, had been a spice trader in Antwerp before he left his native country for England in 1567. Whether he was also working in the printing business in the Low Countries is not known. De Solempne was a prosperous man. Two years after his arrival in Norwich he purchased the freedom of the city for the sum of 40 shillings.

163

The entry in the Norwich Assembly Book registering his freedom identifies him as a "prynter not apprenticed" and restricts his economic activities in the town to "his arte of prynting and selling of Rhenyshewine".[15] At this stage de Solempne and his family lived in the parish of St Andrews, close to Norwich's city centre. Two years later, he moved into a house called "The Dove" in the parish of St John Maddermarket, situated in the immediate vicinity of the guildhall and Norwich's main market square. He is registered in the lay subsidy roll for 1581 where he is ranked among the most prosperous strangers resident in the parish.[16] De Solempne was not registered at the influential London Stationers' Company, which monopolised the printing business in England at that time.[17] He was also unacknowledged by the two academic printing presses in Oxford and Cambridge. Despite this apparent lack of professional affiliation, de Solempne was commissioned to work for the town authorities and printed some of their decrees and orders.[18]

To assess his influence as an alien printer on the English book market and among his countrymen and countrywomen in exile, a closer look at his book production is necessary. William K. Sessions and David Stoker have tried to reconstruct de Solempne's output.[19] They have identified eight books as products of de Solempne's printing press. The majority of these works are of a religious nature. The oldest book attributed to de Solempne is "De C. L. Psalmen Dauids.1568" which contains 150 psalms and a catechism, both in a French translation by Peter Dathenus. This version of the psalms and the catechism was first printed in Flanders in 1556, and became the standard edition for use in the exile churches.[20] Other works such as the "Belijdenisse ende eenvoudige wtlegghinge des wearachtigen gheloofs ende der algemeynen articulen van de suyvere Christelicke religie.." ("Confession and simple lecture on the true faith and the common articles of the reformed Christian religion" – a popular edition of the so-called "Helvetische Confession") responded to the religious needs of the refugee communities in England. Besides these works, de Solempne printed for an English readership. In 1570 he published an English polemic against Thomas Brooke, a Norfolk gentleman who had severely attacked the presence of the strangers in Norwich.[21] Two years later he published another English work, a morning prayer, which was apparently commissioned by English church officials in the city. Somewhat unusual in his oeuvre is the publication of a perpetual calendar in 1570.[22] This calendar clearly addressed a Dutch readership. It listed the sunrise and the tides in the major continental harbours and the dates of the most important fairs in Europe. Important events in recent Dutch and English history are included: the trial of the Duke of Somerset, the death of Edward VI, the coronation of Queen Elizabeth, the arrival of the Duke of Alva in the Netherlands and the establishment of the Dutch Church in Norwich. It is interesting to note that its religious agenda had some Catholic resonances: Catholic feast days such as Candlemass, All Saints and the Annunciation are remembered; Catholic saints from the diocese of Utrecht feature prominently; St Amandus, Bishop of Utrecht, has an entry on 11 May; St Celidonius, a regional Utrecht saint, is remembered on 3 March. These references to the religious traditions of the diocese of Utrecht are even more surprising in the light of the absence of refugees from the area in Norwich. The list of 1568 only counted one family from Utrecht as members of the exile community in the city.[23] It is not known who commissioned the work itself. Thus, further investigation into this particular publication is difficult. No copies of de Solempne's works could be traced among the possessions of the Norwich refugees listed in inventories and mentioned in testaments of community members and little is known about the book market in Norwich itself.[24] Although at least three early members of the refugee community identified themselves as booksellers and book-binders, their economic activities in the city are not recorded.[25]

Unlike London, Norwich did not host an intellectual circle of merchants and scholars who met regularly to discuss matters of religion, politics and the sciences. However, most refugees tried to provide their sons with a solid education that matched the requirements necessary for a successful career both in England and in the Low Countries. Information about a refugee school in Norwich is patchy. An entry in the city's Mayors Court Book on 7 September 1590 penalised a Dutch schoolmaster called Ffraunces van Water for holding school during time of plague, when larger gatherings of people were officially forbidden in order to keep the infection at bay.[26] Some years earlier, in 1577, another refugee called Jan Ruijttinck wrote a letter to the London Dutch Church, in which he politely declined a fellowship at Leiden University on the grounds that he was the only French teacher in Norwich who could teach both the Dutch and the English children of the city.[27] This lack of information, possibly reflecting lack of initiative by the strangers to set up their own schools, is not restricted to Norwich. Attempts to employ their own teachers were rather half-heartedly made and eventually aborted in London. Of the Dutch congregations only Sandwich employed its own schoolmaster, probably because the town itself lacked sufficient facilities.[28] More prosperous strangers in Norwich sent their children to the city's grammar school and later to Gonville and Caius College and Corpus Christi College in Cambridge, which both had special relations with the city of Norwich. Moreover, the city magistrates offered an annual fellowship for a bright young man whose studies at Corpus Christi would be financed by the city. In 1618 the son of the Walloon minister, Nathanaell de Lawne, was nominated for this fellowship, thus clearly indicating the good relations between the leaders of the refugee community and the city authorities.[29] Many refugee students left Cambridge for the new Dutch university at Leiden, where they completed their studies and often met fellow exiles from the other refugee communities in England. They either returned as ministers to the Dutch and Walloon communities in England or continued their fathers' businesses in international trade.[30]

Although little is known about the literary world in Norwich, book ownership was relatively widespread among the city's refugees.[31] Of the 60 surviving inventories of strangers' possessions in Norwich covering the years between 1565 and 1639, books are mentioned in 34.[32] Book possession was recorded for the prosperous, but also for less well-off members of the community and ranged between one and ten volumes per household.[33] Not surprisingly, by far the greatest number of books were Bibles followed by separate Old and New Testaments and Calvin's *Institutions*. Besides these religious books the refugees treasured works written by Dutch historians. Benjamin Bernard, for instance, left "a book written by Immanuel van Meteren called *The Low Countries and their Neighbours actions* to his father-in-law".[34] Maps of the Low Countries were also often included in the inventories. These reminders of the old home might have been used to decorate the refugees' houses.[35] Two inventories also list English books: One English Bible is recorded in the inventory of Eli Philippo and John Foxe's *Book of Martyrs* was found in the possession of George van Sabele, thus indicating an interest in English literary works with a strong Protestant message, which certainly appealed to a readership that sometimes presented themselves as martyrs for religion in their own way.[36] The first works of a Dutch exile from Norwich to achieve national acclaim were the military manuals of Jan Cruso, a refugee from Hondschoote, who was a prominent member of the community and served as Captain in the Norwich Dutch Militia until 1647. His English publications were highly praised in English military circles.[37]

This overview of the literary interests of the Dutch and Walloon community in Norwich, which is probably more representative of the refugee communities in England than the London community with its comparatively high percentage of intellectuals, demonstrates the solid interest of the exiles in books and education. Not surprisingly, religious exhortations and Bible studies ranked high among the strangers, which is reflected in the high percentage of religious works in the possession of refugees. Other interests were clearly related to the home of the refugees as indicated by the possession of Dutch historical works or maps outlining the 17 provinces or other parts of the Low Countries. Interest in English publications remained limited. Reading longer English texts might have been challenging for most refugees. Where possible the strangers tried to provide their children with an education that would support their careers in England, which were often based on international trade or a position in the exile church. Contacts were established with English and Dutch fellow students which might later turn into successful business relations and trading links. Little interest was shown in other career opportunities for university-trained young men: no barristers, school teachers, doctors or academics could be found among the second-generation refugees in the city.[38]

More visible forms of cultural representation of immigrants in Tudor and early Stuart England can be found in the festivals and processions of the time. The strangers clearly contributed to the pageants, triumphal arches and public speeches delivered, for instance, to celebrate the visit of a monarch or the coronation of a new king. These occasions gave the refugee communities the opportunity to emphasize their contribution to the prosperity and cultural diversity of their places of refuge. Since most of the refugee communities were established with royal protection, it seemed particularly important to ensure the visiting monarch knew of the success of the settlement and the strangers' contributions to the economic and social life of their refuges. These demonstrations also served as a reminder for the resident population of the achievements of the refugees in their midst. Both town authorities, the leaders of the refugee communities and the royal authorities were well aware of the symbolic power of such a contribution, which could also provide the refugees with an opportunity to display their own wealth and their own cultural identity expressed through particular forms of music, architecture, poetry, drama or simply by the amount of money invested in the event.

Both in London and in Norwich strangers played an important part in the cities' festivals organized to honour the monarch. In summer 1578 Queen Elizabeth and her large entourage visited Norwich. She was greeted by the city with a set of pageants positioned at the main streets of Norwich. The living images symbolized key aspects of Norwich's urban life. The Dutch and Walloon refugees had secured a space at St Stephen's Street for their display. The street, leading into the city centre through St Stephen's Gate, was an extension of the road to and from London, thus being the first port of entry for the Queen's party, which arrived at the gate on 16 August. The strangers, therefore, were the first to greet the monarch on her arrival within the city walls.[39] The strangers' pageant must have been very impressive. It was twelve metres long and three metres wide. Under the confident motto "Good Nurture Changeth Qualities", which was displayed on the top of the presentation, the refugees reminded the onlookers of their contribution to Norwich's textile industry. In a *tableau vivant* a group of young girls were shown working in the traditional areas of strangers' expertise: they represented weavers and knitters. Further details of the pageant, such as the dresses of the girls (which might have been a display of traditional Dutch fashion, an allusion to classical style or an adaptation of local costumes), or the background of the pageant (which might have been decorated with scenes of Dutch history or with Protestant iconography), are not preserved. Three days later, the strangers had another opportunity to shine: Herman Modet, then minister of the Norwich Dutch Church, was invited to give a speech to the Queen, in which he thanked her for her generosity and hospitality. Along with the encomium, which he delivered in Latin, Modet presented the Queen with a silver beaker made by a Dutch silversmith and worth approximately £50. Blomefield records that the Queen was pleased with the speech and the present and donated £30 to the refugee churches. Unfortunately, no other events of a similar symbolic quality are recorded for the strangers in Norwich. However, the episode highlights the importance of the refugee community within the city, which was acknowledged by the town officials who planned the celebrations, and by the Queen, who responded positively to the exiles' contributions.

More detailed information is available for the Dutch and Walloon contributions to the coronation celebrations in London. Here, the coronation of James I in 1604, Charles I in 1625 and Charles II in 1661 provided the refugee community with occasions to signpost their presence and their role in the city.[40] The triumphal arch financed and erected by the Dutch refugee community in 1604 turned out to be a remarkable success in advertising the strangers' presence in London. It was one of only seven arches commissioned by the city to celebrate the new monarch and it turned out to be one of the biggest and finest on display. It was conveniently and rather symbolically positioned at Cornhill Street near the Royal Exchange. Another apparently considerably smaller and less ornate arch was commissioned by the Italian community in the city; the remaining five were sponsored by the Mayor and the Livery Companies of London. The idea to greet the new monarch with a triumphal arch was in itself an adaptation of a practice that was widespread in the Low Countries and remained an integral part of the royal entries in the Southern Netherlands.[41] The Dutch community collected the considerable sum of £1,000, and commissioned renowned artists, architects and workmen from the Netherlands, who then finished the construction, which was 87 feet high, 37 feet broad and 22 feet long, in the remarkably short time of four weeks. The iconographic programme of reliefs, paintings and sculptures displayed a clear Calvinistic message, a homage to the new king, and a representation of Anglo-Dutch friendship. This programme was displayed on the two sides of the arch, with the front dedicated to the praise of the new monarch and his relations to the Dutch exile community and the back to the story of the Dutch achievements in England and in London in particular. In line with his own royal iconography James was represented as the new British Salomon. A picture of the king in the centre was flanked by Pietas on the right and Religio on the left with the inscription: "who has got these guards lives in safety and protection".[42] Immediately below the picture on the main gallery twelve trumpeters, four drummers and four flautists commissioned by the Dutch community provided the music for the spectacle. Seventeen young women representing the 17 provinces of the Low Countries were positioned at a stage in front of the main gallery. They were dressed in elegant traditional costumes of the Netherlands and in the colour of the province they represented, each holding the coat of arms of her province. Clearly, at this stage the refugees did not accept the separation of their native country into the Northern United Provinces and the Southern Spanish Low Countries, but saw themselves as members of a larger, older alliance. It might even be argued, as with Ole Peter Grell, that the repertoire of Old Testament kings and prophets shown on the front of the arch contained a critique of James's policy *vis-à-vis* Spain and the peace treaty that was just signed between the two states. Representations of David, Josiah, Isaiah and Amos might have been included as a message to the king, that peace had been achieved for the sacrifice of religious honesty and integrity.[43] On the back side of the arch pictures, sculptures and inscriptions emphasized the economic character of the Anglo-Dutch friendship. Maritime trade was presented in different media underlining the character of the Dutch economic activities and their role as international merchants. Paintings show Dutch men and women involved in all kinds of textile work, thus symbolizing the second strand of the exiles' activities in England. The message of the arch was unmistakable: it symbolized the cultural identity of the Dutch community as clearly embedded in the Calvinistic faith and in the traditions of the 17 provinces of the Low Countries. According to contemporary report the Dutch arch was a major success and a highlight of James's procession through the city.[44] When the king arrived at the Royal Exchange, he was greeted at the arch by a delegation of more than 50 leading members of the Dutch community. A young Dutch scholar called Samuel Beerens delivered a Latin speech in verse explaining the iconographic programme of the construction. The king listened, apparently admiring the architecture, then continued his procession. The arch was illuminated the following night and for another couple of days. Here again, the Dutch organizers particularly highlighted their Dutch heritage: the brightest spotlight lit the 17 coats of arms left on stage after the 17 women were gone.

This robust, confident programme completely disappeared at the coronation arch prepared for Charles I and his wife Henrietta Maria. The procession of the king and his queen through the streets of London never took place. It was cancelled due to an outbreak of plague in late spring 1625 and the couple eventually entered the city by boat on 24 June. However, details of the planned Dutch arch for this occasion are preserved in the contemporary account of the Dutch minister Cesar Calandrini.[45] From his description, a remarkable change in the iconographic programme of the arch can be detected. The emphasis on Dutch traditions and virtues had completely disappeared. There are no references to the economic achievements and contributions of the Dutch in London. At this stage, the Anglo-Dutch friendship had started to turn sour. Rivalries between the Dutch and the English East Indian Companies had claimed their first victims a few years earlier in the so-called massacre of Amboyna, where English traders and sailors were allegedly killed by their Dutch rivals. In this climate it seemed inadvisable to emphasize the achievements of the Low Countries and their people in London, even though the majority of the refugees originated from the Southern Netherlands still under Habsburg rule and not from the Northern United Provinces. Likewise, the Protestant agenda was considerably toned down, thus paying tribute to the Catholic queen and Charles's dislike of strict Calvinism. Old Testament kings and prophets were replaced by allegorical figures taken from classical iconography such as Mercurius, who represented trade and industry without a distinct national affiliation. At the same time, the ties of the Dutch community members to their places of origin might have been significantly loosened. The majority of the members of the Dutch Church was already born in England and would, perhaps, no longer have wanted to be represented by symbols of the 17 provinces of the Low Countries. Despite these programmatic changes, however, the Dutch could secure their place in the planned festival. In cooperation with the Walloon and the Italian community they would erect one of the five arches planned for the royal visit. It had been considerably more difficult for the community leaders to finance the enterprise, which ended in failure, but the community was apparently still confident in their particular status within London society and their distinct contribution to the economic and social welfare of the city and the country.

By 1661, however, the strangers' contribution to the coronation celebration of Charles II was reduced to a subsidy of £400 to the city's scheme. They no longer stood out with their own, distinct display. At this date Anglo-Dutch relations were again overshadowed by trade rivalries which culminated three years later in the second Anglo-Dutch war. A visible representation of Dutch economic enterprise and success, even for the benefit of the city of London, was clearly not appropriate at such a juncture. However, the Dutch contributed indirectly: most of the triumphal arches commissioned by the city for the occasion were designed by the Dutch architect, painter and military engineer Sir Balthasar Gerbier, who had come to London in the entourage of the Dutch ambassador Sir Noel de Caron in 1616 and married into the Dutch community. His style was clearly informed by the grandiose entry of Ferdinand of Austria to the Spanish Netherlands in 1635, thus copying the distinct style of Spanish Habsburg's architecture and painting for the London occasion.

The strangers' strong and highly visible participation in national events and festivals provides insights into an immigrant culture which, at least in the first 30 years of its residence in England, publicly emphasized their distinct Dutch identity and culture, which was closely related to the Calvinist faith and the reference to the traditional 17 provinces of the Low Countries. The refugees highlighted their contributions to England's economy and the traditionally good relations with the monarchy. Even at times when the climate in England had become more distinctly anti-Dutch, the immigrant communities claimed their special place in the coronation processions planned in the capital. The iconographic "language" of their contributions had been adapted to the political requirements of the day. The emphasis on Calvinism and the Dutch traditions were also gradually declining in the refugee community. A programme orientated towards "classical" virtues and achievements might have been more appealing to an immigrant group that had become increasingly anglicized and might fear xenophobic reactions from their host society in case of a strong display of Dutch achievements and international economic power.

Other expressions of a distinct immigrant identity based on Dutch culture and traditions and their changes over time are difficult to trace. Little is known about the assimilation in costumes and fashion, for instance. Excavations in Norwich have unearthed Dutch jewellery items, which were used as fashion accessories in the Netherlands in the late sixteenth and early seventeenth centuries. However, the two so-called "voorhoofdsnaalden", specific hair pins made in the Netherlands and now discovered in Botolph Street and St George Street in a quarter inhabited by Dutch refugees, remain isolated finds. They were probably worn by more prosperous Dutch women and did not serve as fashionable trendsetters for the English neighbourhood.[46]

More is known about the introduction of so-called Delftware, a kind of pottery with a characteristic white tin-glaze, which was probably first introduced by the strangers in Norwich and then made in refugee workshops in London. Excavations by the staff of the Norwich Castle Museum and the Norwich Archaeological Unit have unearthed rich findings in pottery made in the Netherlands. Some of them can be further identified as originating from the province of Holland. Similar objects found at the same sites were clearly made in England, but copied the distinct Dutch style. Tin-glazed earthenware had a distinctive white glaze, made by the addition of tin oxide to a lead glaze. Archaeologists and specialists in ceramic research agree that these find-ings are clear indications of the influx of new ideas and new styles in ceramic design from the Netherlands to England, and that refugee potters as well as ordinary men and women of the refugee communities who took their household goods from their places of origin to England transferred these new tastes in pottery to their new homes.[47] The archaeological evidence is supported by archival sources, which identify the Antwerp exiles Jasper, Joris and Lucas Andries and Jacob Jansen as potters and tile makers working in Norwich, Colchester and London between 1567 and 1593.[48] In 1570 Jacob Jansen and Jasper Andries wrote a petition to Queen Elizabeth asking for a 20-year patent for tin-glazed earthenware and the sole right of manufacture in England. They based their claim on the fact that they were the first to use tin-glazing in England.[49] Their petition was rejected, but the two potters set up a highly successful business in the liberties of London in Aldgate. In the following 40 years the workshop attracted 13 specialized potters of Flemish origin who worked in an establishment called "the Rose" in an area known as Duke's Place, in walking distance of the Dutch Church of Austin Friars.[50] The workshop specialized in tin-glazed earthenware and also in tin-glazed paving tiles and probably some wall tiles. The potters working in the Aldgate workshop apparently kept their expertise within the confined circles of men trained in the Low Countries and preferably in Antwerp. They did not apprentice English boys or employ native potters. Thus, the workshop went out of production after the death of the last Flemish specialist, probably in 1617. Delftware production was revived a little later by another refugee, Christian Wilhelm of the Palatinate, who prob-ably picked up the art through connections with Dutch artisans whom he met through his Dutch wife. He set up a workshop in Southwark and further specialized the production by the addition of the characteristic blue pigment derived from cobalt. At this stage, Chinese designs started to become fashionable, and gradually overtook the traditional Dutch style in popularity. Christian Wilhelm quickly responded to this new fashion and specialized in Ming-style patterns. Interests in Delfware were also met by increased import of tiles, pots and vases from the Netherlands.

On the level of fine art and luxury goods, the impact of refugees from the Continent on changing tastes and styles has long been the subject of investigation. Alien gold- and silversmiths had been working in London since the fourteenth century. With the arrival of Dutch and Walloon refugees in England in the reign of Elizabeth their number rose. Lien Luu estimates the number of specialist alien goldsmiths active in London at more than 500.[51] The transfer of skills and the diffusion of fashion and style, however, is difficult to assess. Contact was clearly curtailed by the London Goldsmith's company, which regulated the number of workers and apprentices in the craft. The most skilled and experienced alien goldsmiths worked outside the professional networks of the Company. They were officially prohibited from keeping an open shop and therewith could not participate in the lucrative retail trade of the city. These restrictions were often circumvented by the choice of residence and workshop outside the city's – and therefore the Company's – jurisdiction. Aliens preferred to stay in Blackfriars, Westminster and in the parish of St Martins in the Field. They worked independently and had little contact with the native workforce. Less experienced artisans such as journeymen could sometimes be found in English workshops. Whether they were expected to share their foreign expertise or to support English standards and style is difficult to assess.

The Huguenots who fled to England in the later decades of the seventeenth century have been regarded as trendsetters and transmitters of what was seen as a more refined taste in decorative objects and luxury items, such as silver and gold dishes, plates and candlesticks. They were praised as the agents of a French culture which was regarded as highly sophisticated, and the new bourgeoisie and the urban elite of Restoration London in particular expressed a keen interest in the "New" or "French Fashion". It fed into a new pattern of consumerism which favoured the ostentatious display of dressing plates and other silverware in the salons of sophisticated metropolitans.[52] The introduction of colonial products such as tea, coffee and cocoa, exotic fruit and spices facilitated product innovations such as services for tea, coffee and chocolate, whose novelty was matched by new designs. The foreign masters in London worked largely outside the established professional networks provided by the London Goldsmith's Company. Like their Dutch and Walloon predecessors they often lived and worked outside the City's jurisdiction in the west of London, especially in St Martins in the Fields and Westminster under royal and aristocratic patronage. David Mitchell has pointed up the difficulties in assessing the stranger gold and silversmith's relations to their native competitors.[53] The strangers certainly provided the prototypes of the new style, which were then copied by English masters. Sometimes English retailers employed both English and stranger craftsmen, but not necessarily for the same production. Lastly, there is evidence of English boys who were apprenticed to stranger silversmiths, while stranger journeyman also worked illegally for English masters.[54]

This rather impressionistic overview of the strangers' cultural impact upon Tudor and Stuart England has addressed some key research areas of the New Cultural History. Case studies of the intellectual networks of the strangers and their contribution to the European Republic of Letters, and the culture of popular festivals and processions, have produced an image of a robust Dutch and Walloon community which celebrated its distinct identity and its prominent place within the host society. Economic achievements and a strong Calvinist faith ranked high among the virtues highlighted by the strangers in England. This emphasis on trade and industry was matched on the level of material culture by the production and popularization of household goods and luxury wares such as Delftware pottery and tiles and, at a later stage – largely related to the Huguenot immigration into Restoration London – "French style" silverware. These products were specifically associated with a Dutch and French culture, and were regarded as sophisticated, tasteful and of high quality. The refugees secured their specific niche in the English market by emphasizing their special expertise and high training which they were reluctant to share with the host community. These observations fit well into the concept of Klaus Bade and his team, which aimed to provide a new and innovative approach to migration studies and cultural history: the cultural identity of the refugees was expressed in a specific form which was sanctioned by the expectations and prejudices of the host society and the requirements and expertise of the immigrant community. Overall, the Dutch and Walloon exiles in Tudor and Stuart England and the Huguenots of a later generation were able to meet these parameters, which facilitated a largely peaceful co-existence between refugee community and host society, and ensured the survival and gradual change of an immigrant culture largely on their own terms.

Notes

This study has profited greatly from discussion with students in my seminars on Migration and Minorities in Early Modern Europe. In particular, I would like to thank Barry Skene for his comments and suggestions.

1 For a discussion of migration history as social history see Brettel and Hollifield (eds), *Migration Theory*, pp. 1–26; Tilly, "Neuere angloamerikanische Sozialgeschichte", pp. 38–52.

2 For a general discussion on anthropology and migration theory see Brettel, "Theorizing Migration".

3 See, for instance, Mutsaerts, *Rockin' Ramona*; Oliver, *Music in Britain*; Werbner, "Shaping the Earth in the Name of Allah".

4 Bade *et al.*, "Migration and Integration".

5 For a discussion of the composition of the Norwich exile community and its regional diversity see Eßer, *Niederländische Exulanten*, pp. 43–51.

6 See, for instance, Grell, "Friendship Turned Sour".

7 See particularly Pettegree, *Foreign Protestant Communities*.

8 Chartier (ed.), *Les Usages de l'Imprimé*; ibid., *L'Ordre des livres*; Pettegree, *Emden and the Dutch Revolt*.

9 The book was first published in Dutch in Delft in 1599, but went to numerous editions over the following 20 years. For Emmanuel van Meteren's contribution to Dutch historiography see Janssen, "A 'Trias Historica'".

10 See Harkness, "Maps, Spiders and Tulips".

11 See, for instance, Rockett, "Structural Plan of Camden's Britannia".

12 The Cole-Ortelius correspondence was published as the first volume of Hessels. It was later reprinted as Hessels (ed.), *Abrahami Ortelii*.

13 For a discussion of literary interests and education in the Norwich refugee communities see Eßer, *Niederländische Exulanten*, pp. 117–36.

14 Quoted in Moens, *Walloons and their Church at Norwich*, p. 214.

15 Norfolk Record Office (hereafter NRO), Norwich Assembly Minute Books, 1568–1585, fol. 180.

16 Lay Subsidy roll 1581, quoted in Moens, *Walloons and their Church at Norwich*, p. 166.

17 The London Stationers' Company received a royal patent in 1557 stating that only members of the company were allowed to work as printers in England.

18 See, for instance, NRO 18d Norwich Clavor's Book No. 2, 1556–1646, fol. 20: "Payed to Anthony de Solempne Prynter for Pryntyng the Lawes for Passages Boates for Redid howses and for scavyngers XVs".

19 Sessions and Stoker, *First Printers in Norwich*. See also Woods, "Publications connected with the Dutch Church", pp. 29–36.

20 Sessions and Stoker traced five original copies of this work: two are kept at Trinity College, Dublin, one is preserved at the Bodleian Library, Oxford, the Ryland's Library in Manchester and the Meermanno-Westrenianum Library in The Hague.

21 "Certayne versis writtene b Thomas Brooke Getleman in the tyme of his imprisonment the daye before his deathe who sufferyd at Norwich the 30. of August 1570, Imprynted at Norwich on the Paryshe of Sayncte Andrews by Anthony de Solemne.1570". The only surviving copy is preserved at the Bodleian Library, Oxford.

22 "Eenen Calendier historiael/eeuwelick ghedurenden. 1570". A copy is kept in the Bodleian Library.

23 Moens, *Walloons and their Church at Norwich*, p. 214.

24 Most of the books listed in the inventories were described rather generally, which makes a closer identification impossible: NRO, Probate Inventories of the Norwich Consistory Court (hereafter NCC).

25 Johannes Paetz was registered in Norwich in 1567. He returned to his native Leiden in 1572. Anthonius Rabat was also registered as a bookbinder and bookseller in Norwich in 1567. In the same year two other members of the trade, Cornelius van Hille and Petrus Jass alias Jason, became members of the Dutch refugee community: see Moens, *Walloons and their Church at Norwich*, p. 214.

26 NRO, Mayor's Court Book, No.12, fol. 473.

27 Hessels, Vol. 2, No. 161.

28 For schooling and higher education in London see Pettegree, *Foreign Protestant Communities*, pp. 106–48, for Sandwich see Backhouse, *Flemish and Walloon Communities*, pp. 66–70.

29 NRO, Mayor's Court Book, No.15, fol. 186, fol.187v.

30 See Tammel, *The Pilgrims*. See also Grell, "The Attraction of Leiden University", pp. 221–40.

31 Book ownership among the English inhabitants of Norwich was also surprisingly widespread among different strata of society: Pound, *Social and Trade Structure*, pp. 246ff.

32 NRO, Probate Inventories of the NCC.

33 Some entries remain vague and just record books without giving the specific number of items found in one household. For a detailed discussion see Eßer, *Niederländische Exulanten*, pp. 133–6.

34 Norwich Archdeaconry Court Wills, 1618, Barker 26, Benjamin Bernard.

35 NRO, Probate Inventories of the NCC, 18.261 Michael de Baere; 16,8, Susan Backowe. See also the testament of John Decocke, NRO, NCC Wills, 1603 Norfforthe, 143.

36 NRO, Probate Inventories of the NCC,43, 184, Eli Philippo; 9,303, George van Sabele.

37 Cruso, *Militaire Instructions for the Cavallrie; ibid., A Short Method*. Much less is known about Cruso's religious writings, which feature prominently in his oeuvre: see, for instance, *ibid., Uytbreydinge overn den Achsten Psalm Davids*.

38 Some students, such as Abraham Langebilck, preferred to stay in Leiden after they had finished their studies in the city: see Tammel, *The Pilgrims*, p.168.

39 A detailed account of the royal visit is provided by Francis Blomefield. See Miller (ed.), *Francis Blomefield*, pp. 317–37. The discussions among the aldermen and the refugees on their role and position in the festival are not preserved.

40 For further details see Grell, "Tribute and Triumph", pp. 163–90.

41 For a detailed discussion on entry processions in the Habsburg Netherlands with particular reference to the Joyous Entries of Archdukes Ferdinand and Isabella see Thøfner, "Domina & Princeps Proprietaria".

42 Contemporary descriptions of the arch are provided: Jansen, *Beschyvinghe vande Herlycke Arcus Triumphal*.

43 See Grell, "Tribute and Triumph", pp. 172–3.

RAINGARD ESSER

44 See Grell, "Tribute and Triumph", esp. pp. 173–4.
45 Provided in van Toorenenbergen (ed.), *Geschiedenissen ende Handlingen*, pp. 480–2.
46 Norwich Castle Museum Ascalton; Seagar 50.989; 15v/500 and communication with Dr Sue Margeson, Norwich Survey, December 1989.
47 *East Anglian Archaeology*, 26, Excavations in Norwich, 1971–1978, Part 2, Norwich 1985; see also Hume, *Early English Delftware*; Britton, *London Delftware*.
48 Hume, *Early English Delftware*, Appendix II, pp. 107–14.
49 BL, Burghley Papers, Lansdowne MSS, Vol. 12, pp. 288–97. The petition is fully cited in Britton, *London Delftware*, p. 20.
50 Hume, *Early English Delftware*, Appendix II, pp 107–14. Artefacts from excavations in London's Aldgate Ward have shown a remarkable similarity to the findings in Norwich, allowing the conclusion that the same potters and/or their apprentices were at work here.
51 Luu, "Aliens and their Impact", p. 45.
52 For the new consumerism in late seventeenth and eighteenth century England see, for instance, Brewer and Porter (eds), *Consumption and the World of Goods*; Bermingham and Brewer (eds), *Consumption of Culture*. For the popularity of French fashions see also Chapter 6 above, p. 116.
53 Mitchell, "Innovation and the Transfer of Skill", pp. 5–22.
54 Mitchell, "Innovation and the Transfer of Skill", p. 21.

Part III

Immigrants and the
International Community

9

The Strangers, their Churches and the Continent: Continuing and Changing Connexions

Charles G. D. Littleton

Throughout the late sixteenth century the composition of the stranger community in England and the timing of their immigrations was conditioned largely by events across the Channel. The majority of the strangers who arrived in England during the reign of Elizabeth I came from the Netherlands, and especially the southern and maritime provinces of that region – Artois, Flanders, Walloon Flanders, Tournai, Hainaut, Brabant, Zeeland and Holland. Protestantism, and especially Calvinism, was increasingly popular in these regions from the 1550s, often promoted in the Francophone southern provinces by Huguenots from neighbouring France and in the more northern provinces by exile communities in Emden and Wesel. The continuous persecution of the new religion from 1558 forced many Protestants to look to England, now ruled by the Protestant Queen Elizabeth, as a safe refuge. In particular, the violence and eventual failure of the first Dutch Revolt in 1566–7 and the Duke of Alva's harsh imposition of military rule from August 1567 led to the flight of a large number of people from the Low Countries, and especially from the southern cities which had been at the heart of the troubles of 1566–7, such as Valenciennes, Tournai and Antwerp. War was renewed in 1572 and from that time the provinces of Holland and Zeeland remained a safe place for Calvinists to practise their faith. The southern provinces remained in the balance during the following years, but as of 1579 the Francophone provinces of Artois, Hainaut and Walloon Flanders allied themselves with Catholic Spain in the Treaty of Arras, while Flanders, Tournai and Brabant were steadily reconquered by the Duke of Parma throughout the 1580s. Thus another major wave of immigrants came from these provinces throughout the 1580s. This latter campaign culminated, after about 1585, in the proscription of Protestantism in Flanders, Brabant, Artois, Tournai, and Hainaut, now firmly in the control of Catholic Habsburg power. Repression in France also caused the flight of large numbers of Huguenots from that kingdom, especially after the St Bartholomew's Day Massacre and its provincial imitators in 1572. As in the Netherlands, another major wave arrived in England from around 1585, when the Catholic League was on the ascendant and

France was plunged in the long years of the 'War of the Three Henries' and the subsequent conflict with Spain. After 1598, however, those Huguenots exiled in England could return to France and enjoy a measure of religious toleration under the terms of the Edict of Nantes. This was not possible for those refugees who had adhered to the Protestant faith in the southern provinces of the Habsburg Netherlands, whose faith was banned in their original homelands after the mid-1580s, and who thus formed the bulk of the stranger population in England throughout the late sixteenth and early seventeenth centuries.

Despite the impetus for flight that such war and religious persecution could provide, it becomes clear from the censuses of aliens taken by the English government (the "returns of aliens") and the minutes of the consistories of the stranger churches established to minister to these refugees (the Dutch Church, French Church and much smaller Italian Church, whose names indicate the language used in their services) that the primary cause driving a large number of these immigrants to settle in London was, as Jehan du Rasieu put it to the consistory of the French Church of London in 1596, "to earn a living" (*pour gagner sa vye*).[1] According to the government return of July 1568 only 259, slightly over half of the 470 aliens who had arrived in the City of London since March 1568, claimed that they had come for the sake of the Protestant religion.[2] Yet that impression changes when we confine our view to those who claimed membership of one of the stranger churches. Out of the 425 members of the French Church of London recorded in a return of November–December 1571 as having arrived in England in the past five years, 269 (63 per cent) claimed that they had come over "for religion's sake" or to avoid the "troubles" in their homelands, while only 20 claimed that they had come to seek work or to join relatives already living in England.[3] There was always a large body of immigrants in England who had come over for the traditional reason, to make a better life for themselves, but as of 1558, and particularly after 1567, there was a substantial number who had been forced over by religious persecution and events beyond their control, and who had good reason to maintain their connexions with their suffering homelands. Most of these also joined one of the stranger churches which practised the faith for which they had fled.

In this chapter I will show that, despite their exile for religion's sake, most strangers in England maintained connexions with their families and friends at home through frequent correspondence and visits, even during periods when France and the Netherlands were dangerous places for a Protestant to be found. It was the cause that drove so many of the strangers to England's shores – the desire to practise their Calvinist religion freely in their own churches – which also provided them with the strongest reason for maintaining their continental associations. The stranger churches were greatly concerned with the state of Protestantism throughout Europe, not just in their former homes, and both the churches as institutions and the individuals who constituted their congregations, showed themselves intent to assist their Protestant brethren on the continent in a number of ways. The stranger churches' official correspondence and papers, fullest for the Dutch Church of London during this period, reveal the extent and nature of the churches' connexions, as institutions, with their colleagues and fellow ecclesiastical bodies overseas. Much about the individual strangers' active and vibrant involvement in all affairs in their homelands can be further gleaned from the various disciplinary matters involving congregation members that came before the churches' consistories, which are most complete, and provide more circumstantial details, in the records of the French Church of London.[4] Using these two sources, and others, I will show both the continuing involvement of the strangers with the affairs of the continent, and the slow changes those relations underwent as the stranger community of London entered the seventeenth century.

First, though, an examination of the consistory records of the French Church puts to rest any reassuring image we may have of masses of defenceless Protestant refugees finding safety and permanence in the secure bosom of the stranger churches in London. For many of the exiles England was more of a staging ground for continued excursions to the continent and it was at best a temporary and transient "refuge". This has been noted in most histories of the Revolt of the Netherlands, which place a good deal of emphasis on the role of the exiles, and their return, in fomenting the unrest of 1566–7 and furthering and consolidating the initial successes in Holland and Zeeland in 1572.[5] Jacques Taffin, for example, who had been one of the leading members of the Protestant community in Tournai during the revolt of 1566, was in London by 1569, where he officially served as the elder of the French Church for the Cripplegate section of the city in 1571–2.[6] That responsibility and office did not prevent him from remaining active in continental affairs, for at the time of the November 1571 return he is noted as "at this presente in Fraunce", although the rest of his household was still residing in London.[7] By September 1572 he was in Flushing in Zeeland, recently captured by the Sea Beggars, and to where the consistory of the French Church addressed a letter to him inquiring if he intended to return to continue his duties in his London *quartier*; by November the consistory had determined that Taffin was "beyond hope of returning to his duties".[8] He remained active in the Revolt of the Netherlands until his death in 1583.[9]

The constant migrations of the strangers in England, however, continued well after the mid-1580s, when conditions in both the southern Netherlands and France were becoming increasingly dangerous to Protestants. Roughly a quarter to a fifth of the cases heard by the consistory of the French Church in the period 1583–1603 involve members' journeys and sojourns on the continent. Jehanne Petit and her husband Nicolas Bride left the Walloon community in Canterbury sometime in the mid-1580s, impelled by want ("*a cause de la necessité*"), and settled in Amiens. Jehanne and Nicolas were forced to attend Catholic Mass at Amiens in 1588, but eventually they got away to Valenciennes, where Jehanne still played it safe by giving her newborn infant a Catholic baptism, although she herself tried to stay away from such "idolatrous" services. She appeared again in London in January 1592, where the consistory of the French Church insisted that she reconcile with the French Church in Canterbury, as that was from where she had started her long travels.[10] As the above example attests, these highly mobile people could stay overseas for several years before appearing before the consistory again to be readmitted to the church. Ezechias Cohier and his wife were admonished by the consistory in 1592 for marrying in a Catholic service on the continent, where they had both lived for about seven or eight years before returning to London. What made their offence even worse was that Cohier's wife had made her confession of faith in the French Church of London many years previously at age 17, having then already been in London for about four years.[11] The minutes of the French Church for the 1580s and 1590s are filled with cases of long-time members of the church having to account for their apostasy, usually forced, while abroad. Louis Darembourg, who had faithfully been "*de la religion*" for 34 years, had, sometime previous to his appearance before the consistory in March 1592, been made a prisoner in Antwerp and had been compelled to go to mass about four times. In 1595, Jan Cauneux explained to the consistory that his child had been taken from him "*par violence*" and baptized in a Catholic church while he and his wife had been overseas; he still had to do repentance.[12] A few members appear to have gone to the arch-enemy Catholic Spain as early as 1605, only shortly after James I had made peace with that country, and subsequently had to repent for their pragmatic concessions to the prevailing Catholic culture there upon their return to the church in London.[13]

Many of these travellers went abroad for personal needs, such as to see old friends and relations.[14] Antoine de Sailly and Pierre Noel were just two of many young people who had to make the potentially dangerous journey home to receive their parents' permission to marry, as the consistories of the stranger churches insisted that they could not proceed with any marriages before such approval was granted. De Sailly's mother in Tournai refused to grant her permission, but the consistory allowed him to go through with his marriage plans in any case, as he had at least done his duty in consulting her (he even brought along to the consistory witnesses to attest that he had made a sufficient effort). Noel's mother in Geneva also withheld her approval, but he took a course opposite to de Sailly and stayed in Geneva, refusing to return despite the insistence of the French Church to the Company of Pastors of Geneva that he be forced to honour his marriage promises. In 1591 Eloy du Rieu told the consistory, backed up by witnesses who were also there, that he had recently been in Leiden to attend his wife on her deathbed.[15]

It was principally the wars in their homelands that drew members of the stranger churches back to the continent – the same wars that had driven many of them to England in the first place. Their involvement in these wars, and the disruptions in morals and family life it caused to their fellows in England, appears clearly in the consistory minutes of the stranger churches. A number of the congregation appear to have been members of the Sea Beggars, the motley group of Flemish and Walloon privateers based in the south-eastern ports of England who unexpectedly captured The Brill in Zeeland on 1 April 1572 and thus revived hopes of a new assault against Spanish power in the Netherlands. On 5 December 1571, Anthoine Agace was reprimanded by the French Church consistory for having the affrontery to present himself at communion, "having returned from the ships" (*retourné des beateaus*), without having first checked in with his elder. Jean Druast had been a member of the church for about a year before he too left "to go on the ships", where he had served for two years before returning at Easter 1571. Summoned to the consistory in January 1572 for his absence from services, he explained that he had been too ashamed to come due to his dissolute life on the ships, where he "took and looted all that he could, and led a very disorderly life". The consistory was insistent on knowing of the behaviour and morals of the many soldiers and sailors passing through London. In September 1572 the consistory decided, after seriously reprimanding Jehan Bandart for returning from Flushing without a "passport" from the officials there attesting to his good behaviour, not to receive anybody serving in the Dutch wars who did not bring sufficient evidence of their last posting and their reason for coming to England. They further decided to write to the elder Jacques Taffin in Flushing to ask him, if he was unwilling to return to his post in London, to desist from "lightly" issuing passports to soldiers wishing to cross the Channel.[16]

Despite the loss of Artois, Hainaut and Walloon Flanders to Catholic rule in the 1580s, many members of the French Church continued to fight on into the last decades of the sixteenth century, directing their energies to the battlefronts in the northern Netherlands or France. These soldiers moving back and forth between home and battlefield left a host of moral and marital problems in their wake. In May 1592 Jehan Wery admitted to the consistory that he had been campaigning for the past 13 months in Flushing to get away from his wife and her "bad behaviour" (*mauvaise gouvernment*). Clement Fontaines was also denied communion in February 1594 because he had similarly deserted his wife in London when he went off to fight in the wars. Later in the decade Baudouin le Poing confessed that although he had made his confession of faith in the French Church ten years previously he had since debauched himself during the wars, even going so far as to roam the countryside using the name of another man.[17] Often such soldiers, when in London, were called upon by the consistory to account for what they had seen or heard of a comrade's death in battle, so that his widow could legally enter into a new marriage in England.[18]

Many strangers also travelled back and forth across the Channel to continue or improve their economic situation, just as so many arrived for the same reason. Stranger craftsmen and merchants had ample reason to travel to markets overseas to purchase supplies and raw materials or sell their goods or labour. Pierre Heuzeck confessed to Habsburg officials in 1563–4 that many of the fellow exiles he had known in London crossed over frequently to purchase cloth and other supplies at the market at Hazebrouck.[19] In 1583 the consistory added to the church's discipline the provision that elders and deacons, the officers of the church, were not to leave the country for business purposes without first informing their colleagues.[20] An extraordinary cache of 79 letters written by people in the Netherlands in January and February 1570 to their friends and families in England reveals the continuing close personal and business contacts between those separated by exile, even during the worst days of Alva's persecution, and the maintenance of networks of trade and exchange during this troubled time.[21] Of these largely personal and familial letters, about a third also discuss continuing business transactions and economic connexions between the writer in the Netherlands and the addressee in England; most of these involve the exchange of money and goods or the making and marketing of textiles. Pierre Taiart, for example, after sending greetings and family news to Arnould de le Rue in London, castigates him for failing to pay the money due "for the merchandise which I sold you and delivered to you and my brother" and for other cloths made for de le Rue by Taiart's brother and sister. In another letter, Martin Desquint provides his brother Michel with the family's news and adds that he is sending him a collection of tools (*verges*) to help him in his work. A father, unnamed, provides his son in London with detailed news of the family cloth trade, and provides him with advice and instructions for his side of the business in England.[22]

These correspondents were obviously writing their letters on the assumption that there was a secure, reliable and frequent courier service which would deliver their missives. And the exchange of letters between the homeland and the immigrants in England does appear to have been constant, if occasionally haphazard. These 79 letters show that correspondents were writing to each other frequently, partly because they could not always be sure that their letters were reaching their destination. In his letter to Arnould de le Rue, Pierre Taiart claims that he is "surprised that I have no news from you, for I have sent you many letters for the past four months".[23] Indeed, 15 of these writers acknowledge receipt of a letter or letters sent to them from England, suggesting both that communication was frequent and that it was haphazard enough that correspondents had continuously to assure each other that their letters were getting through.[24] Justinne Ploiart was able to tell her brother, Guillaume le Mieulx, in her letter dated 3 February, that she had received his letter of 30 January, although she also remarks that she is surprised that he has not received her previous five letters.[25] That delivery rate of four days is exceptional; on average about a month elapsed between the date of the letter received from across the Channel and the date on which their family member or friend had cause to respond. A month is also the average delivery time for a letter from one of the Dutch Church's correspondents in the Netherlands in 1571–4 (the most common being the Reformed communities in Antwerp, Emden, Dordrecht, Flushing, Schiedam and Enkhuizen). On three occasions in 1573 only five days elapsed between a letter's composition in Dordrecht and its receipt in London, while letters sent in 1571 from Antwerp and Emden could take over two months to arrive.[26]

The letters of February 1570 provide us with further indication as to the methods of transmitting this correspondence: it depended on the chance arrival in town of a person known to be a courier to England. Jacques Jappin starts his letter to his aunt by writing, "learning that somebody was going to you, I wanted to write you this news".[27] Indeed, 32 per cent of these letters were written "in haste", or so the authors stated, in order to catch the messenger to England before he left town; one was even written at five o'clock in the morning.[28] Justinne Ploiart notes in her letter to her brother that she had to write her letter quickly, "the messenger was in a hurry", and further begs him to send back his news "by the bearer of this letter".[29] Perhaps Justinne Ploiart's case was like that of Marie Lengilon of Armentières, who informed her husband Guy Joire that "I received your letter by the bearer (*porteur*) of this one [to you]".[30] That this was an enterprise run by a group of "*porteurs*" dedicated largely to the task of criss-crossing the Channel bearing letters is further corroborated by those letters which make mention of the need to pay the *porteur* for his services.[31]

These letters, collected over the course of a month from cities and towns in Hainaut, Walloon Flanders and Flanders, were found hidden in the false bottom of a basket otherwise filled with food on the person of Henri Fléel, who was travelling on his way from St Omer to Calais. Fléel admitted under torture, though, that the basket had been given to him by Michel du Buis in a place near Hondschoote in Flanders, who had asked (and promised to pay) Fléel to hand it over to Donnèque Olay who would be expecting him in the tavern "des Trois Rois" at Calais. Fléel was furthermore accompanied in his clandestine journey by the ten-year-old Jean Desmadry, son of a refugee in England, who was also to make the passage from Calais with Olay so he could rejoin his family in England. Apparently, then, there existed a sophisticated network of couriers, drop-off points and smuggling apparatus by which to transport these letters.

Jean du Quief may have been another one of these *porteurs,* or perhaps even a sixteenth-century equivalent of a modern-day people smuggler, aware of all the safe inns and best routes by which to get to England. In December 1571 the consistory of the French Church reprimanded du Quief for committing adultery with Jeanne du Bois because "he is a public person in whom one trusts, placing all that one has overseas in his hands ... and he having regard neither of God nor of men committed adultery with the wife of his neighbour who was entrusted to him and given to his charge with the highest recommendation possible."[32] From this pronouncement and the evidence provided in the case it appears that du Quief was an agent for the stranger churches and the strangers settled in England, entrusted with bringing new or returning arrivals and their goods safely across the Channel. Cateline Midy, the wife of Robert Bloquet, deposed before the consistory that a party of six set out from Arras on St Christopher's day, 25 July 1571, and travelled for ten days to London. On the first night out from Arras they all slept in the same room in an inn, but du Quief himself, apparently acting as sentry, did "not dare to sleep because someone had told the sergeant of the place that they were going to England". The second night they were at Hesdin, where the behaviour of du Quief and Jeanne du Bois aroused the suspicion and anger of the inn's hostess. From there they reached Boulogne, when Jeanne was able to go into du Quief's room "as legitimately as a husband would with his wife" and where both Cateline and her husband were able to hear the bed in du Quief's room "cracking" (*fort craquer*). After that scandalous night, the party took sail at Boulogne and made landfall in England at Sandwich, travelling on from there to London.[33]

Such frequent escapes of exiles and potential rebels obviously worried the Habsburg government and they tried to take measures to stem the flow. The port of Nieuport appears to have been particularly troublesome. As early as 1561 it had been indicated as a major point of entry and exit for the exiles, and its usefulness to the refugees is suggested by the case of Jean Berthelot, sentenced in May 1568 to be confined to the city for three years after being found trying to take ship while in possession of 40 letters destined for recipients in England.[34] The government was so concerned about people escaping via this and other Flemish ports that in July 1567 it issued an order to the magistrates of Nieuport, Dunkerque, Gravelines, Middelburg, Flushing and Arnemuiden ordering them to take special notice of those who were sailing to England with their goods to determine whether they were going there legitimately to trade or in order to settle there with their wealth.[35] The futility in trying to stop this flow of men, money and goods is shown by a letter from a government official to Alva from January 1568 informing him that although the officials in those Flemish ports were trying their best to fulfill their orders, the rebels in England, who were planning to launch an invasion in 1568, had decided to bypass those entry points altogether by landing at Boulogne and entering the Netherlands through Artois.[36] There were just too many Channel ports for the transit to be halted and continental Protestants, so many of whom were merchants themselves, were able to make use of the existing and frequently-used trade routes between the continent and England to transport not just their trade goods, but letters, money, household items, and even people (often themselves) to the refuge of England.

The letters confiscated from Henri Fléel in February 1570 provide us with only the smallest glimpse of what must have been a voluminous correspondence between the strangers in England and their friends and families on the continent, but few other personal letters have survived. The formal institutional correspondence of the Dutch Church of London has survived, though, preserved by the officials of the consistory for future reference. Through these letters and the other surviving records of the churches we can see how the stranger churches maintained contact with other reformed churches and their officials throughout Europe, and how they co-ordinated their actions to further the Protestant cause both in the countries of Europe and in the minds of their own congregation members.

From the early days of the refuge there were attempts to make the connexions between the stranger churches and the developing reformed churches on the continent formal, especially by incorporating the exile churches within the developing system of presbyterian-synodal government of the national churches. The European reformed churches put a great deal of emphasis on forming a hierarchical system of consultative and deliberative bodies – regional *classes* and colloquies, provincial and national synods – to which individual congregations sent delegates to discuss and decide general matters of church government and specific matters of concern to individual congregations. In 1571 the French and Dutch stranger churches in England were invited to attend the forthcoming synod of the Netherlandish church communities to be held in Emden, but they declined to attend (although they did get as far as choosing representatives).[37] The stranger churches were well aware that the English government and Church, on whose continued protection they relied, was highly unlikely to approve of a church within its own kingdom, and nominally under the supervision of the Bishop of London, submitting itself to the authority of a foreign ecclesiastical body. The synod of Emden, though, made matters more uncomfortable for the churches in London by "admonishing" them in one of the resolutions to organize themselves into local *classes*, groups of churches of a common locality, whose ministers and elders would then convene together for regular administrative meetings. Presumably the *classes* in England would then be considered one of the constituent *classes* of the Dutch Reformed Church, also established at Emden.[38] The French and Dutch Churches throughout England held a meeting in London on 10 March 1572 in which they determined to write to the organizers of the synod to inform them that they could not attend any synods or like gatherings overseas and they could not consider them subject to the synod's decisions, as they were unlikely to receive permission to do so from their English ecclesiastical superiors. Three months later they wrote again to inform Emden that the English authorities also prohibited the division of their churches into *classes* and to have such deliberative gatherings.[39]

Despite these arguments, successive synods of the reformed churches in the Netherlands continued to push for the same measures – that the stranger churches send delegates to their assemblies, and that they divide themselves up into *classes*. The provincial synods of Holland and Zeeland of June 1574, which met at Dordrecht, insisted on these points in its correspondence with the Dutch churches in England, assuring them that their delegates could attend without being considered bound by the decisions of the synod.[40] By this time, though, the Dutch churches of England were feeling bolder and in March 1575 their representatives met together in London for their first "colloquy", thereby fulfilling the request to group themselves in *classes*. They did not, however, use this word, perhaps aware of its connotations for the English authorities then attacking the English Puritans for their "classical" meetings. Surprisingly, the English government took no action to stop this gathering, and the Dutch churches continued to have similar colloquies almost annually throughout the remainder of the century. At the request of the Walloon churches of the Netherlands to divide themselves up into *classes*, the French and Walloon churches in England met together for their first colloquy in May 1581, and they too were able to meet regularly thereafter.[41]

By establishing colloquies, the stranger churches were able to state their membership and integration in the continental reformed church. The Dutch Churches looked to the synods of the Dutch Reformed Church, while the French Churches were more divided, having allegiances to both the Walloon churches within the Dutch Reformed Church and to the French Reformed Church. But the stranger churches' connexion was limited to "fraternal union" with the continental churches, and they certainly never risked becoming subject to these overseas institutions. The first resolution of the first colloquy of the Dutch churches in England was that they would continue to have such colloquial meetings and that they would send representatives to the next synod in the Netherlands, "nevertheless without any prejudice to the freedom which our churches in this kingdom have thus long enjoyed and still enjoy".[42] The French churches followed suit in their first colloquy, where the first article determined that the churches would send a delegate to the forthcoming national synod at Middleburg, "as witness of the union which the churches of the French language, refuged in England, wish to have with their brothers who will be assembled as the said synod; and not in order to subject ourselves to that which will be decreed among them". [43]

Despite their insistence, aimed primarily at the English governors, that they were not subject to the authority of the foreign synods, the stranger churches made it clear through the acts of their colloquies that they considered themselves members of the overseas churches and took their directions from them. At the first Colloquy of the Dutch Church, it was explained that their brethren in the Walloon churches in England had not been invited to the gathering because the synod of Dordrecht, whose communications had prompted the colloquy, had not specified the Walloon churches by name in their letters.[44] In terms of doctrine and church government, the Dutch churches followed the lead of the continental church of which they felt themselves members. In 1576, at the second colloquy, it was resolved that any new minister in one of the Dutch churches should subscribe his name to the French and Dutch Confessions of Faith (the Belgic Confession) before taking up his post; this condition for ministers had been laid down as the second article in the synod of Emden.[45] In 1609, to the question whether there should be a written discipline and church order for the Dutch churches in England, it was answered that the church would base it on the church order of the "overseas communities" (overseesche Ghemeenten) as much as is possible.[46]

The career of the leading minister of the French Church for the period 1574–1611, Robert le Macon, sieur de la Fontaine (usually referred to merely as La Fontaine), reveals the close, but often ambiguous, relationships the stranger churches in England had with the national reformed churches on the continent. For most of his pastorate in London the Reformed Church of France, in the name of the congregation at Orléans which La Fontaine had served until his flight to England in 1572, continued to claim that he was merely "on loan" to the London church, and could be called back to Orléans at any time by the synod. Finally, at the synod of Saumur in 1596, the Reformed Church of France decided to grant him permanently as pastor to the London congregation.[47] Even after that decision the synod looked on him, and used him, as the Huguenots' and their Church's main point of contact and liaison in England. In the synods of 1598 (Montpellier) and 1601 (Gergeau) it was resolved that La Fontaine would be asked to inform the synod of the polemical writings against the reformed church order produced in England by Adrian Saravia and Matthew Sutcliffe and to try to effect a "right understanding" between all the parties.[48] Although he did not officially attend the synod of Gergeau (1601), La Fontaine was in France at the time and took the opportunity to have informal communications with leading Huguenots, to whom he conveyed his plans, approved of by the Archbishop of Canterbury and several English bishops, for a union of the Church of England and the French Reformed Church.[49] La Fontaine also was often called upon to act as the local spokesman of the Huguenots in England, as he did in 1603 when he tried to defend – before James I himself – the bellicosely anti-Catholic articles recently passed at the Synod of Gap, articles of which La Fontaine did not personally approve.[50]

Many of the matters discussed in these colloquial or synodal meetings reveal the reformed churches' strong impulse to coordinate their pastoral endeavours across congregations and to maintain the discipline over a far-flung and mobile flock. In 1584 and again in 1603, the French churches in England, meeting in colloquy, decided that La Fontaine would write letters to the continental reformed churches (both the Dutch and French synods) requesting them not to accept into their congregations fleeing members of the English stranger churches who did not have with them proper *tesmoignages* from their consistories.[51] As a rule any person coming from abroad and wishing to join the communion of one of the stranger churches had to appear before the consistory bearing a *tesmoignage* from the consistory of their most recently attended church, a testimonial that would attest to his or her good behaviour and sincerity of faith. Failure to produce such a *tesmoignage* would lead to a strong censure by the consistory, which was then likely to address a letter to the church of origin asking for further information. Often in addition one church had to call upon another to execute the measures of the ecclesiastical discipline it was unable to apply to a distant congregation member. In 1589 the French Church consistory was able to extract from Robert Elloy the promise that he would perform a public repentance before his home church in the *"pays de Caux"* if and when that church was ever re-established, and the following year it received the same assurance from Francoise Michu, who had apostasized from her home church in Tournai (under Spanish rule by that time). That same year the French Church urged the Dieppe community "for the interest of our consistory" to censure Jacob de Bers for his insults against the London church elder Mr de St Leger at the Royal Exchange in London.[52] Correspondence concerning *tesmoignages* and other disciplinary issues between churches crop up repeatedly in the consistory minutes of both the French and Dutch Churches, attesting to the constant and collegial contact the stranger churches had with their brethren across the sea, away from the formal gatherings of colloquies and synods.

The stranger churches could provide material assistance to their "brethren" churches abroad, a less bellicose complement to the substantial contributions in money and men they also made to the Protestant war effort.[53] The stranger churches took it upon themselves to train and supply the churches on the continent with ministers, and the records of the Dutch Church in particular are filled with churches in newly liberated areas requesting more pastors or news of the progress of the church's students for the ministry ("proponents"); the French Church could receive such requests as well.[54] The churches in England showed themselves charitable with money to their brethren in need in their homelands. The consistory of the Dutch Church of London sometimes called on the richer merchants of the congregation, the "notables", to provide an extraordinary collection for a suffering community, as it did in December 1582 when 92 such "notables" raised £104 for the relief of the church at Brussels.[55] At other times, a larger section of the congregation appears to have contributed, such as with the aid offered the communities in Ghent and Ostend in February 1584, for which the church raised the large sum of £303.[56] In a different arena of war, the church at Montpellier called upon the assistance of its brethren in London in May 1580, and the French Church consistory duly decided to hold a collection for the oppressed church.[57]

The churches were able to look beyond the communities of their own homelands and could show their concern for the universal church, for the Protestant cause, in generous ways. Geneva was seen as the founding city of the Calvinist Reformation, and its frequent calls for aid against the incessant attacks of the Duke of Savoy always succeeded in raising funds among concerned Protestants throughout Europe. The city, though, had a special meaning for the French Church of London, for while the congregation of the church may have been made up primarily of Walloons, its ministers were almost to a man Huguenots trained in Geneva. The first minister of the re-established church, Nicolas des Gallars (1560–3), was dispatched from Geneva to serve in London by John Calvin himself, and all of des Gallars's successors in the ministry in the sixteenth century – Jean Cousin (1563–74), Pierre l'Oiseleur de Villiers (1574–9), Robert le Macon de la Fontaine (1574–1611), Jean Castol (1582–1601) and Aaron Cappel (1591–1619) – were natives of France or Geneva (except the English-born Cappel) and trained at Geneva. The leader of the Calvinist movement in Geneva, Théodore Beza, clearly relied on La Fontaine in particular as an important contact in England, especially when he sought his help in furthering in England the collections for Geneva's relief. In October 1582 Beza entrusted his envoy sent to England to raise money for the relief of Geneva entirely to the guidance of La Fontaine, whom Beza was sure would be able to direct Geneva's representative to the best sources of donations and advise how to approach them.[58] For their part, in 1583 the Dutch churches throughout England, who had fewer direct ties to Geneva, were still able to contribute £92 for its relief, just part of the large sums raised throughout England for this cause.[59] La Fontaine and his assistant pastor Jean Castol also helped to direct Geneva's fundraising efforts when the city turned to England again for support in 1589 and 1603. For the drive in 1603 the Dutch Church gave the very large sum of £303.[60]

La Fontaine and Jean Castol served Geneva and the wider Calvinist movement in other ways, as when they acted as a direct link between Geneva and those Scottish Presbyterian ministers who settled in London and solicited Geneva for its support after the Black Acts of 1584 had proscribed Presbyterianism in their country.[61] Théodore Beza himself corresponded frequently as an individual with both La Fontaine and with his colleague Jean Castol, a native of Geneva. Those few letters between La Fontaine and Beza that do survive suggest that their correspondence was frequent and that Beza saw La Fontaine as a good friend and respected colleague, judging by the chatty personal news he includes and the theological advice and opinions he solicits.[62] Castol's letters to Beza reveal a detailed knowledge of all aspects and crises in the contemporary Calvinist world and a deep pessimism for the course of the Reformation in both England and the continent. "Considerable for his correspondences in foreign parts", Castol also frequently provided the Earl of Essex's secretary Anthony Bacon with detailed military and political intelligence from the continent in the 1590s. The variety of interests shown in these letters, and Castol's surprising knowledge of the details of Henry IV's campaigns in France, show that he was well-informed and actively engaged in all events that affected the European Calvinist world.[63]

La Fontaine also conducted a frequent and wide-ranging exchange of letters with the acknowledged leader of the Huguenots, Philippe Duplessis-Mornay. Their initial meeting in 1577, when Duplessis-Mornay was on a diplomatic mission to England, began a long friendship and a friendly exchange of letters between these two men which was to continue until La Fontaine's death.[64] In December 1591, when Mornay was in London again to enlist English aid for Henry IV's struggle against the League and Spain, he even offered La Fontaine a professorship at the Academy of Saumur which he had just founded. La Fontaine turned the post down as he thought that his "presence here is perhaps not useless to all of our stranger churches and possibly even to our affairs in France".[65]

His presence in London was, indeed, far from useless, for during the last years of the sixteenth century La Fontaine, perhaps under the guidance of Duplessis-Mornay, acted as the unofficial representative of Henry IV to the English Court during the French King's war against Spain and the Catholic League. During this time he was in direct communication with the monarchs of both England and France, and with influential royal councillors and courtiers, such as Villeroy and the Duc de Bouillon in France and Cecil and the Earl of Essex in England.[66] He even helped draft the Treaty of Greenwich, which formed a formal military alliance between France and England, being entrusted with these sensitive negotiations because, as the chief French negotiator of the treaty, de Sancy, wrote to him, "we did not think that we could employ for this task anyone more trustworthy than you, nor one who was more acceptable to them [the English negotiators]".[67] After the war was ended and peace made with the Huguenots in 1598, La Fontaine resigned his commission but continued to serve the Huguenot movement in France as its unofficial representative in England, keeping in touch with events in France and the Huguenot churches through his continuing correspondence with Duplessis-Mornay. In his final years La Fontaine remained active in Anglo-French affairs, translating into French *Triplex nodo, triplex cuneus*, James I's defence of the oath of loyalty, and sending it off in 1608 to be published by Duplessis-Mornay at his press in Saumur.[68] La Fontaine died three years later in 1611, having officially been a "stranger" in England for 39 years, over half of his life, while yet maintaining an active interest and involvement in all aspects of the Calvinist movement, both in his homeland of France and throughout Britain and Europe.

This chapter has focused on the first four decades or so of the "first refuge" – effectively the reign of Elizabeth I. It was during this period when the situation for Protestants in the Netherlands and France was most in flux, and the participation of the exiles based in England of most importance in determining the outcome of their conflicts. For the majority of these exiles, the continent was never off-limits and the members of the stranger churches in particular were able to remain actively involved in events on the continent. They frequently criss-crossed back and forth across the Channel in order to do business, to see their families and friends, to look for work, and to fight in the wars that may have caused them to leave their homes in the first place.

After about 1610, religious peace, often uneasy and certainly transient, had been achieved in the battlegrounds of the Netherlands and France. The Protestants there and their churches were no longer so immediately threatened and could concentrate on consolidating and strengthening their position. During the seventeenth century the immigrants in England, and the increasing number of their children and grand-children born in that country, became a more settled and inward-looking community, but by no means did they ignore or slight their ancestral homelands and the Protestant cause which brought their ancestors to England. They continued, for instance, to donate generous funds for the relief of continental Calvinists. During the Thirty Years War the Dutch Church of London provided a great deal of monetary and administrative assistance to the refugee Calvinists from the Palatinate settled in Hanau (Lower Palatinate) and Nuremberg (Upper Palatinate). The extraordinary lengths the Dutch Church took to assist the exiles, the large funds raised (over £11,000 between 1628 and 1639), and the impressive organization deployed (which reveals that the Dutch community could still rely on sophisticated networks of mercantile communication with the continent well into the seventeenth century) has been set out in impressive detail by Ole Grell.[69] Significantly, though, the Dutch Church was entrusted by the English government itself – in two Royal Briefs, issued in 1628 and 1631 – with collecting and disbursing the funds raised throughout England for the Palatine refugees, from English donors as much as from the stranger churches. These Royal briefs made the Dutch Church of London the final destination for the funds amassed in England, and then provided that the church's elders, many of them prominent merchants with extensive continental contacts, were to ensure that the money made it safely to the exiles in Hanau or Nuremberg. The case of the persecuted Protestant Palatines was a rallying cry for all Calvinists, and especially the English "brethren", whose princess Elizabeth had married the unfortunate Elector Palatinate whose lands had been overrun by Catholic forces. The English gave generously, despite the reluctance of William Laud (then Bishop of London) and Charles I to support fully these collections for the English Calvinists' "fellow travellers". The fund-raising campaign was not a case of the members of the Dutch Church looking out only for their own people in the Netherlands, for it involved the entire Protestant world, the "Protestant Cause", both in England and on the continent. The members of the stranger churches had certainly always had a loyalty first and foremost to their places of origins, but over and above that was a commitment to the Protestant cause throughout Europe wherever it needed succour, in Geneva and Nuremberg as much as in Flanders, Brabant or Artois.

The fact that the strangers in England were settled and integrated but still maintained an active interest in international Protestantism boded well for the Huguenot refugees, and perhaps even the Dutch followers of William of Orange, in the late seventeenth century. When the Huguenots arrived in England *en masse*, fleeing the persecution of Louis XIV, they found already in the French Church of London an established, wealthy and well-integrated institution that could receive them generously and provide them with aid and security. The influx of the Huguenots of the late seventeenth century dominates popular perceptions of pre-modern immigration to England, but it is important to recognize that the "second refuge" would not have been as resounding a success story if it had not been for the continuing interest and involvement in the continental Calvinist movement of the immigrants of the "first refuge" and their English-born descendants, and the many networks of communication, aid and support with that movement they had spent so many years establishing.

Notes

1 FPC 4, fol. 249.
2 Kirk & Kirk, Part 3, pp. 440–1.

3   Kirk & Kirk, Part 2, pp. 1–154. No data is given for this category of question for the remaining 136 members.

4   The Dutch Church of London's correspondence is in Hessels, Vols 2 and 3. The French Church of London has a complete run of consistory minutes from 1571 to 1615 in Oakley, *Actes du Consistoire* and FPC 3 and 4. There is a gap in the existing consistory records of the Dutch Church from 1585 to 1609. For another treatment of this subject, see Pettegree, *Foreign Protestant Communities*, pp. 215–61, which concentrates on the earlier period of the refuge.

5   See Crew, *Calvinist Preaching*; Pettegree, *Emden*; Pettegree, *Foreign Protestant Communities*; Parker, *Dutch Revolt*, pp. 72, 108–10, 118–20.

6   Moreau, *Histoire du protestantisme à Tournai*, pp. 149–50, 345–6; Kirk & Kirk, Part 1, p. 396; Oakley, *Actes du Consistoire*, pp. 10, 56–7, 65.

7   Kirk & Kirk, Part 2, p. 38.

8   Oakley, *Actes du Consistoire*, pp. 90, 94.

9   See the biographical notice and further documents on Taffin in Coussemaker, *Troubles Religieux*, Vol. 2, pp. 47–50, 56–60, 121, 186.

10   FPC 4, pp. 121, 123, 126.

11   *Ibid.*, p. 159.

12   *Ibid.*, pp. 125, 239.

13   FPC 4, ff. 435r (Suplie Gedeon), 442v (Noel Renault), 440r, 442r, 445v (Pierre Ballinchcon).

14   Coussemaker, *Troubles Religieux*, Vol. 2, p. 235 (daughters often visiting mother in Armentières).

15   FPC 4, pp. 95, 97, 132–4, 160; *Registres de la Compagnie des Pasteurs*, Vol. 6, pp. 291–2.

16   Oakley, *Actes du Consistoire*, pp. 39, 53, 56, 58, 89–90.

17   FPC 4, pp. 111, 130, 191, 291.

18   *Ibid.*, pp. 108, 142, 176, 181.

19   Coussemaker, *Troubles Religieux*, Vol. 1, pp. 349–52.

20   FPC 3, p. 162.

21   Verheyden, "Correspondance Inédite".

22   *Ibid.*, nos 2, 24, 40. Other letters regarding the textile trade are nos. 15, 18, 30, 33, 45, 47, 55, 57, 65 and 71.

23   *Ibid.*, no. 2.

24   *Ibid.*, nos 3, 5, 12, 16, 19, 20, 21, 25, 26, 27, 34, 36, 37, 45, 54.

25   *Ibid.*, no. 27.

26   Hessels, Vol. 3, Part 1, pp. 148–52, 219–20, 239–40 (nos. 175–7, 242, 265–6).

27   Verheyden, "Correspondance Inédite", no. 17.

28   *Ibid.*, letters no. 2, 7, 14, 15, 17, 25, 27, 29, 32, 33, 36, 37, 41, 42, 49, 50, 53, 56, 58, 61, 62, 78; no. 11 was written early in the morning.

29   *Ibid.*, no. 27.

30   *Ibid.*, no. 45.

31   *Ibid.*, nos. 18, 27, 35.

32   Oakley, *Actes du Consistoire*, p. 46

33   *Ibid.*, pp. 45–6.

34   Coussemaker, *Troubles Religieux*, Vol. 1, p. 87, 350; Verheyden, "Protestantisme à Nieuport".

35   Coussemaker, *Troubles Religieux*, Vol. 4, p. 352.

36   *Ibid.*, Vol. 1, p. 183.

37   Hessels, Vol. 2, pp. 365–9, 378–87 (nos. 105, 108); Oakley, *Actes du Consistoire*, pp. 17, 19, 20.

38   Rutger, *Acta van de Nederlandsche Synoden*, p. 61

39 Oakely, *Actes du Consistoire*, pp. 51, 54, 56, 60–2, 67–9; Hessels, Vol. 3, Part 1, pp. 150–52 (no. 177); Vol. 2, pp. 391–3 (no. 110), 410–11 (no. 117).

40 Hessels, Vol. 3, Part 1, pp. 265–6 (no. 300); Vol. 2, pp. 504–16 (nos. 135–8).

41 Boersma, *Vluchtig Voorebeeld*, pp. 209–11.

42 Toorenenbergen, *Acten van de Colloquia*, p. 6.

43 Chamier, *Actes des Colloques*, pp. 1, 3–4.

44 Toorenenbergen, *Acten van de Colloquia*, p. 4.

45 *Ibid.*, p. 19; Rutger, *Acta van de Nederlandsche Synoden*, p. 56.

46 Toorenenbergen, *Acten van de Colloquia*, p. 104.

47 Quick, *Synodicon in Gallia Reformata*, pp. 124–5, 185; FPC 4, fol. 234.

48 Quick, *Synodicon in Gallia Reformata*, , pp. 203, 218.

49 FPC 4, ff. 362, 368–9; Duplessis-Mornay, *Mémoires et Correspondance*, Vol. 9, pp. 418–19.

50 BL, Additional MSS 39779, ff. 62–4, printed in Littleton, "Unpublished Letter".

51 Chamier, *Actes des Colloques*, pp. 7–8, 43–44.

52 FPC 4, pp. 15, 47, 48, 51.

53 Trim, "Protestant Refugees".

54 Hessels, Vol. 3, Part 1, pp. 173–81, 191–6, 208–9, 217–18, 222–3, 228–9, 233–6, 276–7 (nos. 205–7, 210, 211, 220–22, 233, 240, 245, 253, 259, 310), etc.; Boersma and Jelsma, *Acta van het Consistorie*, pp. 486, 509, 510, 514, 517; FPC 4, p. 80; Boersma, *Vluchtig Voorbeeld*, pp. 212–19.

55 Hessels, Vol. 3, Part 1, pp. 688–92 (nos. 823–4); Boersma and Jelsma, *Acta van het Consistorie*, pp. 641, 790–93.

56 Boersma and Jelsma, *Acta van het Consistorie*, pp. 794–8.

57 FPC 3, p. 48.

58 Hessels, Vol. 2, pp. 729–33, 764–5 (nos. 198, 208); Schickler, *Les Eglises du Refuge*, Vol. 1, pp. 241–3; Vol. 3, p. 102.

59 Boermsa and Jelsma, *Acta van het Consistorie*, pp. 668–9; Collinson, "Europe in Britain", p. 64.

60 Hessels, Vol. 2, pp. 839–43 (nos. 242–3); Vol. 3, Part 1, p. 1088 (no. 1540); Schickler, *Les Eglises du Refuge*, Vol. 3, p. 144; FPC 4, p. 45; *Registres de la Compagnie des Pasteurs*, Vol. 8, pp. 440–1, 460; Ruytinck, *Gheschiedenissen*, pp. 166–71.

61 *Registres de la Compagnie des Pasteurs*, Vol. 5, pp. 52–3, 276–7, 283–5; Schickler, *Les Eglises du Refuge,* Vol. 3, pp. 139–41.

62 Hessels, Vol. 2, pp. 657–8, 771–3, 787–9, 869–72 (nos. 180, 211, 217, 251); Schickler, *Les Eglises du Refuge*, Vol. 1, pp. 232, 235–6 ff.

63 For a sample of Castol's letters to Beza, see Schickler, *Les Eglises du Refuge*, Vol. 3, 138–51. For correspondence with Anthony Bacon, see Birch, *Memoirs*.

64 This correspondence is scattered throughout Duplessis-Mornay, *Mémoires et Correspondance*, Vols 4–10. See also Hessels, Vol. 2, pp. 907–8, 936–40 (nos. 267, 276–8).

65 Duplessis-Mornay, *Mémoires et Correspondance*, Vol. 4, pp. 343–4.

66 Much on La Fontaine's diplomatic activities can be found in Kermaingant, *L'Ambassade de France*. Summaries of his correspondence can be found in *CSP Foreign*, while his letters to the Earl of Essex are transcribed in Birch, *Memoirs*. For La Fontaine's career in general, see Littleton, "La Fontaine".

67 Kermaingant, *L'Ambassade de France*, pp. 46–7.

68 Hessels, Vol. 2, pp. 936–40 (nos. 276–8).

69 Grell, *Dutch Calvinists*, pp. 176–223.

10

Alien Communities in Transition, 1570–1640

Lien Luu

Letters written home to friends and families in the 1560s and 1570s testify to the initial euphoria and optimism felt by refugees about their new life in England. Writing from Norwich on 21 August 1567 Clais van Wervekin described life in the city to his wife in glowing terms: "You would never believe how friendly the people are together, and the English are the same and quite loving to our nation. If you come here with half our property, you would never think of going to live in Flanders. Send my money and the three children. Come at once and do not be anxious".[1] Janssz Beverloo, having fled to Emden in December 1571, wrote to his wife of his intention to go from there to England where business was "good". Such ebullient optimism soon dissipated, and by the mid-1570s some disillusioned refugees were re-migrating to the Dutch Republic.

Freemen registers of Dutch towns such as Leiden show that emigration began as early as 1576 and escalated from the 1590s. Between 1576 and 1640 some 127 Flemish and Walloon families emigrated from London to Leiden, while the number from provincial towns far exceeded this: 245 families from Colchester, 419 from Sandwich and 597 from Norwich.[2] The higher rates of emigration from provincial towns might reflect both stronger pressures to emigrate from there than those in London, as well as their greater suitability for the Dutch labour market. With some members of the alien community once again on the move it is evident that by the 1590s, some 30 years after the major influx, the alien communities in London and elsewhere were far from completely settled, stable and assimilated. What push factors prompted aliens to uproot themselves from England? What was the attraction of the Dutch Republic? What kinds of aliens re-migrated?

In the early decades of Elizabeth I's reign, there was a sizeable alien population in England. The existence of a survey of the alien population in several English towns and cities in the 1570s makes it possible to ascertain that there were at least 16,000 continental immigrants living in six south-eastern English towns and cities – Canterbury, Colchester, London, Norwich, Sandwich and Southampton.[3] This figure underestimates the actual number of aliens in the country: London probably had some 10,000 members in 1571; Norwich had several thousand members, reaching 4,600 members in 1582; Sandwich had 2,400 members in 1574; Canterbury had 1,679 members in 1582; and Southampton, 200 members. In total, there may have been some 20,000 aliens in England in the 1570s.[4]

Many of these aliens, as explained elsewhere in this volume, had come as part of the large exodus from the southern Netherlands in the late 1560s. In summer 1567, the news spread of the imminent arrival of Spanish troops headed by the Duke of Alva to suppress the 'troubles' and to bring to justice those who had involved in the iconoclastic movement that had occurred the previous summer. In response to this, some 30,000–50,000 may have left the Netherlands, half of whom are believed to have gone to Germany and the other half to England. The wars of religion in France, especially after the St Bartholomew's Day Massacre in 1572, also brought significant number of French refugees to England, particularly to London. But these political and religious troubles alone do not explain why such a high number of refugees came to England. The number of destinations open to the refugees could also influence the volume to each destination. In the 1570s, Protestants from the southern Netherlands and France had three main places of refuge: Germany, England or Geneva. For those from the western part of the Netherlands and France, the nearest destination was England, while for those in the eastern part it was easier to reach Germany or England via Antwerp. Protestants in the south-eastern part of France may have preferred to travel to Geneva.

For many aliens life in England was far from settled, and involved regular travelling back and forth to the continent. Some went to the continent to conduct business, some were forced back to find work, while others travelled for personal reasons – such as to seek permission to marry or because of a death in a family.[5] For those who had been banished with no possibility of travelling back and forth, life in exile was particularly hard as many had left families behind and were under constant pressure to return. The extant letters written to the refugees from their relatives in the Low Countries provide a unique insight into the anxieties, agonies and suffering facing many broken families, as well as the difficulties in reuniting.[6] Writing to her husband, Isabeau Parent expressed the conflicting advice she had been receiving: "You ask me to come – wise people advise me not to go yet".[7] Letters from wives or parents often expressed the hope that the exiles would return. In a letter written in February 1570, the wife of Martin Plennart (banished from Valenciennes in 1568) confirmed that although the goods of those banished had been confiscated, his had not, and she told him not to worry. She also reported that people were daily returning home and wished that he could come back, as she could not go to England with the children because the roads were not safe for her to travel. She also told him how his daughters were asking when he would return, and that one of them said that he could not as his feet hurt too much.[8] Parents also urged their children to return from England because business was getting better (although local wool had to be used because of a shortage of English and Spanish wool), and that the police were no longer looking for people. It was advised that the safest way to return was to come back via Calais and join the people at the market there on Saturdays. A father reassured his son that if he returned he would be as safe as he was in England.[9] Other letters demonstrate the many agonies facing wives left behind with children. Jacqueline Leurent, writing to her husband, explained how she had been writing to him in vain for two years. She asked him for advice as to what she should do about their properties, how to find money to feed the children and what was the best way to get to him.[10]

The alien community in England may have begun to experience some decline from the 1570s. As early as 1572 there was some return migration to Holland and Zeeland when an edict was issued ordering refugees from Holland to return home or face punishment. Following the publication of the edict on 7 March 1574, around 3,000 returned from Emden, and presumably some also went back from London.[11] In 1576, the decline of the baize-making industry and the tensions with the native inhabitants prompted many Sandwich aliens to head to the Dutch Republic. Leiden, with its thriving textile industry, inevitably attracted the biggest number, where 281 families settled between 1576 and 1625, and a handful in other towns.[12] If this and Tammel's figure of 419 families who emigrated between 1576 and 1640 are both correct, it means that 138 families moved after 1625. In Norwich, the alien population began to decline in the 1580s. By 1624 it has been suggested that there were less than 1,000 Dutch and other aliens in Norwich, the number dropping further to 678 by 1634, although alternative estimates suggest less drastic contraction.[13] In Southampton, there were 186 communicants in 1584 and by 1596 there were 296 aliens in the city.[14] The immigrant population in Southampton rapidly declined after 1604 as a result of assimilation, the devastating effects of plague epidemic and the return of some exiles to the continent. By 1635 the community had only some 36 members.[15] In Canterbury in 1582 there were 1,679 aliens, in 1591 there were 2,760, and in 1593 they numbered 3,013, while the Colchester community grew from 431 in 1573 to 1,297 by 1586 and remained at a similar in size by 1616.[16] Thus, the Canterbury and Colchester alien populations grew steadily in size during the 1580s and 1590s, in periods when other communities experienced rapid decline, and some of the smaller ones disappeared altogether.[17]

In London, the returns of aliens suggest that their number had declined by the early 1580s. In 1581, a return recorded only 4,047 aliens in the City and Middlesex, or roughly a 40 per cent fall since 1571. It is possible that the Pacification of Ghent in 1578 and the brief period of peace in France may have caused the scale of immigration from the Low Countries and France to tail off at the end of the 1570s and early 1580s. In addition, these events may have encouraged some refugees in London to return to their homeland.[18] But available evidence suggests that there was continuous immigration into London during this period. Littleton's study of the French Church in London also confirms this. In 1593, the length of residence of 330 French-speaking households was recorded; in the period between 1567 and 1573, 27 per cent had arrived; 17.5 per cent between 1574 and 1582; and 37 per cent between 1583 and 1589.[19]

During the time of the Armada the influx of foreigners was restricted. As reported by the Spanish Ambassador to the King in September 1588, "The Queen did not care to admit other foreigners into her country, except those who came from Holland. Amongst them there were a number of musketeers, and some Englishmen from the Dutch garrisons". It was further reported that "during the time that the Armada was in the Channel all foreigners in London were forbidden to leave their houses, and the shops were to remain closed."[20] The number had certainly stabilized by this time, and a survey in 1593 certified 7,113 aliens in the metropolis, a third of whom had been born in England. In the early seventeenth century, however, the alien population appears to have fallen considerably. In 1619 the Dutch Church reported that there were only 1,613 foreigners left in the capital, among whom were 77 denizens and 882 persons born in England of Dutch parents, but there are considerable discrepancies between different surveys.[21] A further survey of 1621 claimed that there were as many as 10,000 strangers in the City of London alone, carrying out 121 different trades.[22] The increase in the

1620s was due to the arrival of new refugees from France, primarily from Normandy in 1621, who were forced into exile by the beginning of the second phase of the religious wars.[23] By the mid-1630s, however, there had been a drastic decline in the number of aliens in the capital. During the period, John Bulteel calculated that the Dutch Church had 840 communicants and the French Church 1,400, making a total of 2,240. Grell has suggested that the figure for the Dutch Church only included men and women, married couples or single heads of households, but no servants or children, and thus underestimates the total number of Dutch in London, which probably stood at around 980–1,120 people (10–20 per cent less than the French Church). In other words, there were probably a minimum of 2,500 aliens in London in the mid-1630s, while the estimates offered in chapter one above suggest that the number could have been considerably higher.[24] Although a survey in 1635 enumerated a higher population of 3,622 aliens,[25] there is evidence to indicate that London, in comparison with some other provincial communities, lacked vitality. In 1645, for example, the leaders of Sandwich asked the London community to assist the 100 refugees who had fled Flanders due to the devastation caused by warfare. The London community suggested that these refugees should be sent to other Dutch communities, where their skills would be in demand, adding that: "Agriculture flourishes at Maidstone; weavers of wool have now a very good trade at Colchester, and they want workmen. Those who work in stuffs find employment at Norwich and also at Canterbury if they understand French".[26]

By the 1640s, the membership of London's Dutch and French Churches had experienced a considerable change, for they were no longer composed of first-generation immigrants. Around 40 per cent had been born in England, being either children or grandchildren of the original refugees. Being brought up in England, many inevitably had a poor command of the Dutch language. During the 1650s an increasing number of members requested the consistory of Austin Friars to provide them with an attestation in English since they did not understand the language. Likewise, a growing number of ministers' and elders' children had to be examined in English in the main tenets of the reformed faith before they could be confirmed as members of the church.[27] Moreover, the French Church had for the first time since its establishment in 1550 outnumbered the Dutch Church. Within the French Church there was also a change in composition. From its establishment until the St Bartholomew's Day Massacre in 1572 (which brought the first significant number of French refugees to London), the French community had consisted almost entirely of Walloons from the southern Netherlands. With a steady inflow of new French refugees in London in the 1620s, the French began to outnumber the Walloon members of the Threadneedle Street congregation.[28]

In the 1630s, the alien community in London was possibly half the size of that of 1593, although we should bear in mind both the margins of error involved in these calculations and the possibility that the 1635 return is not entirely complete.[29] Austin Friars had seen a gradual decline in membership, from a peak of around 2,000 at the end of 1580s, to below 1,000 in the second half of the seventeenth century.[30] What factors caused this decline? According to Grell, there were two: the cumulative effect of anglicization and integration, and the lack of renewed waves of immigration to mitigate these trends.[31] In addition, there was also mortality. Devastating diseases such as plague were a frequent occurrence in London, in 1563, 1593, 1603, 1625, 1636 and 1665 inflicting a heavy toll on the metropolis's crowded populations. Although the plague in 1593 is thought to have been less severe than that of 1563 (when nearly a quarter of London's population died), it is unclear how many aliens died. The plague that occurred ten years later took a severe toll among the Dutch community. Grell believes that the mortality rate among the Dutch was at least as high as among the English, which would mean the death of around one-fifth of the community. Simon Ruytinck, who served Austin Friars as minister from 1601 to 1621, wrote that 370 Dutch households were affected by the plague and that some 670 people died.[32] Mortality from the plague, however, does not wholly explain the reduction in the size of alien community.

Table 10.1 Citizens from England and Scotland in Amsterdam, 1531–1606

1531–9	1540–9	1550–9	1560–9	1570–9	1580–9	1590–9	1600–6	Total
2	1	1	2	2	5	26	25	64

Source: J.G. van Dillen, Bronnen tot de Geschiedenis van het Bedrijfsleven en het Gildewezen van Amsterdam (Rijks Geschiedkundige Publicatië, 69, 1929), p. xxxiii.

Emigration to the Dutch Republic also precipitated a decline in the alien population. Already in January 1593 ministers of the Dutch Church had reported to the Privy Council that "many members of the said church do daily depart".[33] Although there are limitations to the use of freemen registers to measure the scale of emigration – it was not only immigrants who became freemen – it is possible to infer two significant points from the freemen registers of Amsterdam. First, the "stresses" in England were not as strong as those of other European countries because emigration from England and Scotland (64 persons) in the sixteenth and early seventeenth centuries was lower than all other nations. The number from France was higher (109), but the scale from other parts of the Netherlands (4,485), Belgium (1,491), and Germany (1,046) was unmatchable.[34] Second, they confirm that the periods of stress date from the 1580s, accentuated in the last decades of Elizabeth's reign. Table 10.1 shows that emigration from England increased in the 1580s, but the outflow intensified in the 1590s and 1600s.

An examination of the economic and social climate in England makes it easy to comprehend why some immigrants decided to move to the Dutch Republic from the late 1580s. England experienced hard times from the 1580s, and some historians have described this period, particularly the 1590s, as a decade of "crisis", characterized by high prices, failed harvests from 1594 to 1597, food shortages, increasing poverty and vagrancy and war commitments in Ireland and against Spain.[35] There was also severe inflation in the 1590s, caused by harvest failure and the enormous costs of warfare. The poor harvests in 1585–6 led to a rise in prices, such as flour, which rose by 65 per cent. The harvests of 1594 and 1595 were also well below average, and England suffered successive dearths in 1596 and 1597. The effects of these dearths were much worse than those of 1555–6 because these occurred at a time when supplies of grain had already been reduced by the poor harvests of 1594 and 1595.[36] Living standards fell as real wages reached their lowest point in 1597. All in all, the last decade and a half of the century was a time of hardship for Londoners and English people in general.

It should be remembered, however, that these difficulties were a European phenomenon, with England faring better than many other countries. Furthermore, some historians believe that the depth of the "crisis" may have been exaggerated. Michael Power has argued that "Londoners seemed to be able to live through the period with comparative ease".[37] Food shortage was remedied by imports of corn from the English counties and the Baltic; the Privy Council encouraged prosperous residents of the city to give charity to the less fortunate; vagrants were kept under control by increased watches and by efforts to provide employment at Bridewell.[38] The metropolitan economy also showed considerable resilience. The greater diversification of craft production in London, and reduced dependence on key staples like cloth, may have rendered it less vulnerable to depression, while London's rising role as a social centre for the gentry may have fuelled demand for luxury goods and services. Freemen may have enjoyed the benefits of this, but how did aliens and foreigners cope in this period?

Economic hardship in the decade of "crisis" appears to have precipitated rising anti-alien feelings in London, as reflected in a string of incidents. In September 1586, the Plasterers' apprentices conspired against the strangers, levelling their hostility "especially against the French".[39] Apprentices waited outside the French Church on Sundays and abused Frenchmen as the latter were leaving their church.[40] To alleviate this situation, Francis Walsingham advised the stranger churches to establish a French community in Scotland.[41] In 1587, apprentices and servants of linen cloth workers and small silk wares retailers were suspected of having been responsible for the libels against strangers living in St Martin-le-Grand.[42] Several libels were dispersed in the city, and there was a growing fear that these might "grow dangerous to the quiet estate and peaceable government of this City".[43] In the early 1590s, the Dutch-speaking community became the target of popular hostility. In April 1593, the London apprentices threatened to kill the Flemings in London if they did not leave within three months: "apprentices will rise to the number of 2336. And all the apprentices and journeymen will down with the Flemings and strangers".[44] On 4 May 1593 a slanderous rhyme was written on the wall of the Dutch Church threatening violence.[45] These threats produced much fear and anxiety, and may have provoked Peter Coale, an immigrant "painter-drawer" who lived in Aldersgate Street, to threaten to set the city on fire.[46]

Even more troublesome for many alien residents in London was the constant harassment and "molestation" by informers. They were easy prey for the informers because of their status as *aliens* and *strangers*, or non-denizens. Without a letter of denization from the Crown giving them a legal right to practise a trade in the capital, aliens were working illegally and liable to prosecution by the relevant guilds. Successful prosecution could result in a punitive fine as well as the forfeiture of goods. Informers had a material incentive in the prosecution of aliens because they would receive half the value of the fine. The numerous petitions from Dutch and French members to their churches to elicit help and protection from the Queen from the late 1590s and early 1600s indicate the extent of the problem they faced. In 1594, ministers of the Dutch Church wrote to the Lord Keeper of the Great Seal about the molestation by informers suffered by "certain poor members" of their congregation whose principal offence was that they were not free denizens of this realm. The ministers stressed the economic benefits brought by these aliens, their responsibilities to their wives and children, their poverty, the absence of an economic threat as aliens did not pose competition and the cultural needs of the community for their services. They focused on five occupational groups and explained the reasons why they should be permitted "quietly to use their several trades and occupations to maintain themselves and their families". First, silk twisting was not an occupation practised by Englishmen and 16 or 18 silk-twisters employed at least 1,000 English poor people. Second, thread was being dyed and twisted here and this was beneficial because otherwise it had to be imported from abroad, which was expensive. Moreover, the thread-dyers and twisters provided valuable employment for the old and impotent women, setting them to spin. Third, there were few alien bakers in London and they did not compete with English bakers because they baked brown bread, not white, to serve the "poorer sort of their nation". The better off either baked bread themselves or "else buy white bread of Englishmen". Fourth, the candle-maker should be allowed to follow his craft because he was now "being trodden" as a result of the loss of sight which forced him to make candles to support his poor wife and children. He also sold them "not outwards to the street, but backwards in his house". Fifth, the tailors should also be left in peace because they were poor, "charged with wife and children". Moreover, they did not compete with Englishmen because they "work to none but Strangers" who only wore "apparel after the Dutch fashion".[47] Economic segregation of the alien community in the capital, then, was regarded as non-threatening and desirable.

The difficult economic conditions up to 1597 led to intensified harassment by informers. In March 1598, 16 candle-makers successfully petitioned the Privy Council for protection against an informer named John Symes.[48] However, the Privy Council's instruction to the Lord Mayor of London to stop any suit against the Dutch candle-makers did not end the activities of the informers. In April 1599, the Dutch and French Churches joined forces and presented a petition from a "great number of poor Strangers" to the Queen. To elicit her protection, the strangers stated seven reasons. While appealing to her humanitarianism, they also stressed their godly character, their sacrifices, as well as the malicious character of informers. They argued that, first, the Queen had in an "ancient proclamation" given the freedom to those strangers from the United Provinces to ply their trades. Second, all those daily "molested and so grievously vexed by informers, are of good religion, quiet and good conversation, and of the Dutch and French Congregations". Third, there were not any of them that go begging, but they paid all duties, as subsidies, fifteenths, setting forth of soldiers, and all other taxes. This suggests that the community was self-reliant and that some members were doing quite well. The aliens also contributed to the maintenance of hospitals and the poor of their parishes as well as those of their own congregation. Fourth, they were strangers who came from enemy areas, and fled for their conscience, and many of them "being of great substance, lands and livings have abandoned and left all together with their native countries, and betaken themselves to handy labours according to Gods word". Fifth, the petitioners asked,

> what profitable husbands for her Majesty or her commonwealth these kind of informers be [who only thought of their] own private gain, live by the sweat of the poor strangers brows, And when they vex them to make of some, 10 shillings, of some 12 shillings, 14 shillings, and of some 20 shillings more or less, as some of them have done in secret manner, and the poor strangers for fear of them, glad to be quiet so.

Sixth, some strangers who were molested were free denizens and naturalized subjects. Seventh, her majesty had recently promised her "princely care and inclination towards these strangers".[49] Whatever letter was issued in response to the petition, it did not deter informers. On 22 January 1600 the French and Dutch Churches listed 17 people who were molested. Many were afraid "to go out their door, even to Church", while merchants, accused of avoiding exporting goods without paying customs, were afraid of travelling abroad. Some free denizens were troubled because their wives "sell pins and such trifles". On 26 January 1600 another 19 people who were harassed were listed.[50] Harassment continued and, failing to realize their aims, the Dutch and French Churches had to present a petition to the House of Commons in 1606.[51]

Worse was yet to come. Instead of taking action against informers, in April 1606 the city of London passed an Act of Common Council forbidding aliens from using any trades in the capital. The stated aim was to "avoid damage and prejudice to freemen and citizens" and to "provide for their common profit and good".[52] This was immediately followed by a petition three days later (on Thursday 17 April 1606) from the strangers of the Dutch and French congregations to the Lord Mayor to "dispense with the Act of Common Council". The petition stressed their need for a sanctuary to practise their religion, the ancient grant for their settlement, their small number and their inability to acquire civic freedom due to poverty and the "extraordinary favour and means" required. Finally, it also underlined how their trades were profitable to the Commonwealth with many poor English and alien families being set on work.[53] It is unclear what the City's response was, presumably allowing aliens to continue to work as long as they abided by certain conditions set. However, the harassment did not stop, as in 1626 the Dutch and French Churches reported that between 1592 and 1618 members of the government and the Lord Mayor of London had to issue an instruction on nine occasions to stop the "Informations against aliens".[54]

Difficult economic and social conditions returned between 1615 and 1625. The country was inflicted with two consecutive bad harvests between 1621 and 1622, which caused food prices to soar. When the economy recovered, the country was faced with an outbreak of plague in 1625. In these conditions xenophobia was rife, especially in London. James I took advantage of the negative attitude to the strangers in the City by initiating the Star Chamber case against the merchant strangers for the illegal export of bullion (of the exorbitant sum of £7 million) in December 1618.[55] Initially, 160 merchant strangers were accused of such an offence, but by December 1619 only 18 merchants were prosecuted. They were fined £140,000 in the Star Chamber, but the Dutch ambassador, Sir Noel de Caron, negotiated to have the fine reduced to £60,000. This case traumatized the foreign churches, as ten of those convicted were members of the Dutch Church and four of the French Church, while it also illustrated the vulnerability of the alien community without the protection of the Crown.[56]

In the mid-1630s the alien communities faced another crisis with the campaign for religious uniformity championed by Archbishop Laud. Seeing the alien churches as the "nurseries of ill-minded persons to the Church of England", he sought to dissolve them. On 7 April 1634, eight months after his promotion to the archbishopric of Canterbury, Laud summoned the French and Dutch congregations in Canterbury, Sandwich and Maidstone to Canterbury. When the representatives arrived they were asked to report three issues: (1) Whether they used the Anglican liturgy in Dutch and French, and if not, what other liturgy they used? (2) How many of their members were born in England? and (3) Whether those born in England would conform to the Anglican ritual? After consulting with the mother churches in London, the three congregations avoided answering these questions. They were then summoned in December 1634 to be presented with Laud's injunctions: all their members who were born in England should from 1 March 1635 attend their English parish churches, and the remaining members were to use the Anglican liturgy translated into French and Dutch. The churches objected, pointing out that their congregations maintained their own poor, and even if their members did attend English parish churches who would look after them? Negotiations eventually led to a compromise whereby the "natives of the first descent" were to remain within the stranger churches, and those that attended parish churches would still be required to pay their fees to the alien churches for the maintenance of the poor.[57]

Years of particular economic depression also witnessed tensions between strangers and natives. In May 1635, for example, the shop-keepers in London complained that there were an infinite number of "foreign" tradesmen in the City and suburbs. Another petition also stressed the vast number of strangers as well as "foreigners" who had served no apprenticeship and did not contribute to the church nor to the poor of the parish, and "pester and inmate themselves in garrets . . . and back courts falsifying trade to the undoing of the [natives]". Due to these "pitiful petitions from tradesmen and shopkeepers that their livelihood had been taken away by strangers and foreigners", the Privy Council ordered a survey in September 1635 to investigate the truth of the complaints. The survey certified only 2,663 (another source put the number at 2,545) aliens in London. On behalf of the foreign churches, Bulteel stated that the total membership of all the stranger churches throughout the country only came to 5,213 persons, nearly half of whom (2,240) lived in London.[58]

In this climate of religious intolerance and economic depression, both Englishmen and aliens may have gone abroad in search of better opportunities. In 1634–5, for example, the port registers of London recorded 7,507 people leaving the country – some on short business and personal visits, others never to return. Excluding the 1,595 soldiers, the majority (4,878 persons or 65 per cent) boarded ships for the American colonies, and a smaller number (1,034 persons or 14 per cent) for the continent. Their reasons for travelling included "to return to residence abroad" (30 per cent), "on affairs or business" (23 per cent), "with masters or parents" (11 per cent), "to join family" (or visit relatives and friends) (9 per cent), "unknown" (10 per cent), and "to fetch ship" (8 per cent).[59] A few aliens were among the passengers destined for the continent. Some, it appears, left England in search of a better future for their children. Jane Deboyes, a Frenchwoman, may have decided to return to her home town in Valenciennes in Hainaut as she boarded a ship to Calais in April 1635 with her four children, while her husband, Peter Deboyes, a weaver, stayed behind as he was listed in a survey in London in October of that year. Two Dutch boys were also taken to Haarlem in May 1635: 12-year old Francis Anthony, son of William Anthony, and 6-month old Anthony Terreame, son of Anthony Terreame.[60] Orphans of deceased alien parents were also sent back: Samuell (aged eight) and Elizabeth (aged five) Vanderpost were two recent orphans of Dutch parents who were sent to live with "friends" in Middelburg, "their parents being deceased".[61] Some travelled to the continent to collect debts or inherited money. The 21-year old Elizabeth Vandigom from Southwark, for example, left on 14 January 1634 for Brussels because her Dutch parents had died, leaving her some land and she was travelling there to receive "money upon lands fallen to her" and return.[62]

Of those who headed to the continent whose destinations were known, more than half went to the Dutch Republic, and the destinations included Rotterdam, Amsterdam, Middelburg, Flushing, the Hague and Leiden, leading cities renowned for trade, economic prosperity and nonconformity. Seeking work was an important motive for leaving. Among those who travelled to Amsterdam to work "on their occupations" were 25-year old Mathew Read, a bit-maker, 27-year old John Mumfield, a tobacco-pipe maker, 40-year old Thomas James, 20-year old Edward Deane and 33-year old Peter Greene, shoemakers, and 28-year old James Hall, a weaver.[63] Their names suggest that they were Englishmen who left in search of better economic opportunities abroad.

The Dutch Republic and the Recruitment of Emigrants

The adoption of an active policy of recruitment by the Dutch Republic helped encourage emigration there. In August 1593, a time of increased hostility against aliens and scarcity of food in London, the Amsterdam preacher, Peter Plancius, spread the news that several towns in Holland "desire to encourage persons from England who wish to settle" there. Plancius assured them that these areas were far from their enemies, living was cheap there and the Church enjoyed peace. He also enclosed a resolution of the town of Harderwijk, a small town in Holland, which guaranteed full rights to those who came over. Those who had craft skills or worked in the new drapery were particularly encouraged and were promised "immunities . . . over and above those of the ordinary citizens".[64] Admissions into citizenship of Harderwijk, although they do not necessarily reflect the actual number settling in the town, suggest that few took up the offer as this small fishing town of less than 3,000 inhabitants on the Zuider Zee in Gelderland offered few opportunities for aspiring artisans. For the period between 1581 and 1600 only one person from Scotland became a citizen, and between 1636 and 1655 just one person from England.[65] Larger towns such as Amsterdam and Leiden were more successful in their recruitment. Indeed, immigrants formed a significant proportion of their populations.

What was so attractive about Dutch towns? Many city authorities pursued an active policy to attract skilled artisans and merchants by offering specific advantages, such as tax privileges, free housing and free burghership (citizenship), and even working capital bearing no rent. Often, the new settlers were allowed to practise their trade outside the guilds. At times, premiums were paid: for example, in 1577 the city of Haarlem contracted Jan Hendrixsz from Brabant, who promised to work for six years in return for 72 guilders. In 1598, a number of immigrants (34) obtained sums ranging from £300 to £700 for operating a loom in Haarlem. Gouda converted six disused monasteries into workshops for weaving and dyeing premises, manned by Flemish refugees.[66]

Rising wages in the Dutch Republic, an indicator of the robustness of the economy, at times of falling wages in London, were the second attraction for prospective emigrants. Wages for masters and journeymen in the west Netherlands grew consistently from 1575. Wages for masters doubled between 1575 and 1595, from 9.57

stuivers to 18.59 stuivers per day (summer wages). Over the same period, wages for journeymen also doubled, from 8 to 16.70 stuivers per day. Wages for the unskilled increased less, from 5.75 to 11.75 stuivers.[67] In other words, those with skills received healthy financial rewards. Religious freedom and the ease of upward mobility also proved enticing. In an age when many communities suppressed religious nonconformity and discriminated against aliens, Amsterdam welcomed people from all religions and nationalities. There was also no obstruction to upward mobility as the status of *poorter* (citizen) could be acquired at a small cost (f.8 until 1622 and f.14 thereafter). The city of Amsterdam also assisted newcomers, finding housing for them and offering inducements to masters deemed capable of starting new industries or improving techniques in those already established.[68]

Table 10.2 Immigrants in Dutch Towns, 1622

Town	Population	Number of Immigrants	% of Immigrants
Alkmaar	12,417	1,800	14.5
Amsterdam	104,932	35,000	33.4
Delft	22,769	4,000	17.6
Dordrecht	18,270	6,000	32.8
Gouda	14,627	5,500	37.6
Haarlem	39,455	20,000	51.0
Leiden	44,745	30,000	67.0
Middelburg	40,000 (?)	25,000	62.5
Rotterdam	19,780	8,000	40.1

Source: J. Briels, *Zuid-Nederlandse Immigratie 1572–1630* (Haarlem, 1978), p. 21.

Besides economic benefits, there were added advantages for some southern Netherlanders to move to the Dutch Republic – fewer linguistic barriers and the assertion of their superiority. Southern Netherlanders felt superior to their northern relatives in many ways. Their jokes about the Dutch were numerous, portraying these northern neighbours as "dull and stupid".[69] They, especially those from Brabant, also felt superior in taste and manners to the Hollanders.[70]

Occupational Backgrounds of Emigrants

What kinds of craftsmen from England were most likely to move to the Dutch Republic? The occupational backgrounds of those who emigrated to Amsterdam between 1531 and 1606 offer a clue. As table 10.3 demonstrates, the largest groups, in descending order, were those involved in clothing, taverns and public houses, trade and transport (merchants) and metal working. Those involved in the clothing trade were most likely to emigrate from England because of declining demand and prosecution by the guild. In 1571 the return of aliens enumerated 121 tailors and 52 botchers (menders of old clothes) in London. The number of tailors remained constant, and in 1593 a return listed more than 202 aliens working in the clothes-making sector, among whom were 118 tailors.[71]

Table 10.3   Occupations of Citizens from England in Amsterdam, 1531–1606

Trades	1531–1574	1575–1606
Primary products (Oerproductie)	—	—
Clothing firms (Kleedingsbedrijven)	1	20
Building trades (Bouwvakken)	—	2
Wood/bone/sugarcane workers (Bewerking van hout, been en riet)	—	1
Leather working and rope-making (Leerbewerking en touwslagerij)	—	—
Metal working (Metaalbewerking)	—	6
Textiles (Textielindustrie)	—	1
Food & drink (Voedings- en genotmiddelen)	—	1
Makers of earthenware, glassmaking, diamond-cutting (Aardewerk, glas- en diamantbewerking)	—	—
Oil-mills, soap boilers (Olieslagerij, zeepziederij enz)	—	2
Book printers & sellers (Boekdrukkerij, boekhandel)	—	—
Trade and transport (Handel en verkeer)	3	8
Shipping (Scheepvaart)	1	1
Taverns and public houses (Herbergen en tapperijen)	—	10
Other occupations (Overige beroepen)	—	2
No recognized occupation (Zonder bekend beroep)	2	3
Total	7	57

Source: J. G. van Dillen, *Bronnen tot de Geschiedenis van het Bedrijfsleven en het Gildewezen van Amsterdam* (Rijks Geschiedkundige Publicatië, 69, 1929), pp. xxxviii, xxxix, xliii.

Yet work was irregular and seasonal. The seasonality of demand became marked under Elizabeth I, when it was claimed that the trade "consists principally in the Spring and the Four terms in the year funerals & some weddings".[72] Thus, when its members were under pressure to employ English servants in 1608 the Dutch Church told the Merchant Tailors' Company that their members could not fulfil this condition because,

> sometimes they keep servants and sometimes none because often times they have no work at all for them selves, and there houses being very little they never keep any apprentices at all, neither are the most part of them of ability to keep servants or prentices idle when they have no work to doe.[73]

The tailoring trade was particularly hard hit by the deterioration in economic and social conditions in the 1590s. The dispensable nature of clothing meant that when levels of incomes fell, demand – particularly from low income groups – contracted. The fall in demand for clothing in London in the 1590s intensified competition for work between native and alien tailors. Native tailors accused aliens of expropriating work from them. In 1591, the Merchant Tailors' Company was pressed to take tougher action against aliens by the "poorest sort of the bretheren . . . [who] take discontentment and find themselves aggrieved that foreigners and strangers which work inwardly, and take the work . . . out of freemen's hands".[74] The greater competitiveness of aliens was attributed by native tailors to the evasion of costs, or as the Company pointed out in 1598, they were not free of the city nor members of their company, and therefore not "subject to the laws customs and government [of the Company] nor chargeable to the duties of the Company and other charges and services" of the city.[75]

In the face of stiff competition, native craftsmen exerted strong pressure on the Company to clamp down on aliens. Already as early as 1576, the Company had taken an ameliorative measure by forbidding its members to employ "any foreign stranger or foreign denizen a work".[76] However, this proved inadequate for it merely forced aliens to continue working in secret locations rather than stop altogether. The demand for clothing probably fell to its lowest point in 1597, as real wages reached a trough.[77] In March 1598 the poorer members demanded further "aid and assistance of [the] Company for the repressing and putting down of foreign Tailors".[78] The Master and Wardens took up the matter with the Lord Mayor, who in turn appointed a committee to investigate the complaints by the tailors. The ensuing investigation apparently found 410 foreigner and stranger householders in the city, keeping 910 servants, making a total of 1,320.[79] Following this report, the city prohibited foreigners and aliens from working in London to alleviate pressure on the tailors.[80]

Poorer members of the Merchant Tailors' Company, however, pressed for the expulsion of foreigners and aliens. This was opposed by the Company, the city and Privy Council on humanitarian and political grounds.[81] The Lord Mayor, for example, opposed such a plan because he feared that "to expel them all away might breed a mutiny or inconvenience. And that diverse of them having long lived in the City and seated themselves here and taken their houses and married wives and have many children and therefore desire to be admitted into the freedom for some reasonable fine". Queen Elizabeth was concerned about the situation and instructed members of the Privy Council to write to the Lord Mayor to urge him to "forbear proceeding against aliens and strangers".[82]

It was not until 1601 that the rulers of the Merchant Tailors' Company endorsed the expulsion of aliens. The greater recognition of the livery and yeomanry governors of their responsibilities towards "handy trade men" during a period of economic difficulties may explain this change.[83] After a meeting in May 1601 when the master, wardens and assistants of the Company were again reminded by their members of the "great wrong and Injury that is offered to the poor freedom of this company by the intrusion of aliens and foreigners", they considered "the suppressing expelling or avoiding of the said aliens and foreigners".[84] The Company adopted two measures to expel strangers and foreigners. First, it called upon the services of informers to harass foreigners and aliens. In September 1602, the Company was told that, as a result of vigorous prosecution, 207 alien and foreign tailors had "gone", 68 were made free and only 206 were "now remaining".[85] Second, the Company presented a bill in Parliament for the expulsion of foreigners, but this was rejected because it was regarded as "unreasonable".[86] The Company therefore, having already spent over £100 on legal costs,[87] had to consider whether it was worthwhile to present another bill in parliament. After much discussion and debate, it decided "not to proceed any further in parliament, but thoroughly to examine the authority granted us by charter, which we find to be very large and liberal".[88]

The stranger churches and the Ambassador for the States of the Low Countries, Sir Noel de Caron, sought to prevent the expulsion of strangers by their direct and personal petitions to the King, Privy Council and the Company.[89] In October 1608, the French and Dutch Churches appealed to the Company on humanitarian grounds to allow Dutch and French tailors to remain in London, for they "have been ancient dwellers within this city and came over in time of persecution for freedom and liberty of conscience, and for none other",[90] and promised that their members would be obedient. In 1608, therefore, the Company sent a list of conditions to the stranger churches, which among other things, instructed alien tailors to work only for stranger customers, employ English servants and allow the wardens to search their premises. They were also requested to provide a bond of £20 each to the Lord Mayor. This new working arrangement sought to bring aliens under greater control of the Company and prevent them from being serious competitors. However, the strangers, in their reply, stated their inability to employ English servants because of lack of work, or to pay a large bond because "they are very unable and some of them not worth so much as is required at their hands".[91]

Merchants were also likely to emigrate because of increasing restrictions on their ability to trade. Alien merchants had since the mid-sixteenth century long been the target of natives' resentment. In 1571 an anonymous "Complaint of the Citizens of London against the great number of strangers in and about this city" was sent to the Queen. As six of the seven grievances were directed at alien merchants, it is possible to infer that native merchants were probably responsible.[92] In the following year, native merchants and retailers proposed an Act in Parliament to prevent strangers who had not served a seven-year apprenticeship from retailing foreign goods in England.[93] In 1593 Parliament debated a bill introduced to prohibit aliens from involving in the retailing trade and passed the restrictions with a vote of 162 to 82.[94] In addition, alien merchants were vulnerable to various financial exactions, as demonstrated in the Star Chamber case of 1619, while in September 1588 the Queen had asked the foreign merchants in London for a loan of 70,000 crowns.[95]

There were 189 alien metalworkers in London in 1593, more than a third of which were goldsmiths and silversmiths.[96] Without patronage, these faced limited opportunities for advancement, as the goldsmiths' trade relied on an aristocratic and elite market, and a successful goldsmith had to be far more than a good craftsman; he also had to have a good address, a reputation as a man of integrity and discretion, the right family network and marital opportunity and access to consumers.[97] To be successful, they also had to have the right to open a shop and to retail, both of which were denied as long as they remained aliens. For example, as non-freemen, aliens were not entitled to have their work assayed at the Goldsmiths' Hall and touched with the Company's mark. Unmarked silver could not be sold within the precincts of the city. This had several implications. To gain a livelihood, an immigrant goldsmith had to work as a journeyman in the workshop of a native English goldsmith, or induce a freeman of the Company to take in their work with his own to the Hall for assay and touch, or sell their goods to English goldsmiths.[98] Both denied them the right to operate independently. Even more serious was the lack of prospects for their children, who could not expect a better future than their fathers because they could not serve apprenticeships, and were in effect denied the right to acquire the city's freedom and citizenship. In theory, aliens could teach their sons the skills of a goldsmith, but without the freedom their children could not work as independent masters and build their name and reputation, as their goods had to be marked with the names of freemen who sold them.

The lack of opportunities for upward mobility may have rendered London an unattractive place of permanent residence, and many continental goldsmiths returned to their place of origin. Of the 45 goldsmiths from Antwerp who are known to have worked in Elizabethan London, at least 17, or nearly 40 per cent, returned there. Many of these had come for their *wanderjahre* training, and stayed for a period of anything between a few months and 12 years. Peter van Doncke was recorded working in London in 1571. Later that year he returned to Antwerp but by 1587 was recorded as a master goldsmith in Frankfurt, presumably having emigrated there after the fall of Antwerp in 1585.[99] Peter Noblet, who came to London for religious reasons in 1568, returned to Antwerp by 1578.[100] In 1578 Noblet became a free master of Antwerp and, presumably due to the Sack of Antwerp in that year, he moved to Frankfurt where he became a *poorter* in 1581.[101] Marten van de Sande, a jeweller from Bruges, is known to have been in London in 1568. Later, he went back to Antwerp, and after 1585 moved to the Dutch Republic.[102] Many alien goldsmiths, then, returned to their hometown but later re-emigrated to the northern Netherlands and German towns when conditions in the south deteriorated.

In the early seventeenth century the goldsmiths' trade suffered a major blow with the general onset of an economic depression in Europe in the 1620s, and particularly the outbreak of civil war in England in the early 1640s, bringing the production of plate to a halt.[103] Large quantities of plate were also destroyed as corporations, the clergy and the landed gentry gave up their holdings of plate to pay for heavy taxation levied upon them to finance the huge military expenditure.[104] Moreover, during the middle of the seventeenth century the demand for goldsmiths' skills was low and the plate produced was relatively simple, due to the unwillingness of consumers to invest heavily in "fashioning" – the price paid for the goldsmith's work as opposed to the investment in the material itself – when it was likely that the work would soon have to be melted down in response to new tax demands.[105] On 18 January 1643 the beadle of the Goldsmiths' Company complained to the Court of Assistants that he was unable to collect quarterage from the members of the company. He said the economic crisis had taken away the goldsmiths' trade and, as a result, many shops were shut. In the last quarter, he claimed, he had made up the payments out of his own pocket.[106] In contrast, the economic prospects in Amsterdam were good, and foreign silversmiths enjoyed greater freedom. Those who could prove their skill were admitted without much difficulty to the guilds.[107] On 20 January 1634, 23-year old William Best left London for Amsterdam to "work on his occupation" as a gold-wirer and drawer.[108]

Conclusion

The alien communities in England experienced an overall decline in the early seventeenth century as a result of assimilation, mortality from the plague, lack of renewed immigration and emigration. Some aliens left London for the Dutch Republic as a result of increasing hardship in their life in the metropolis. Economic and social difficulties since the 1580s fed growing xenophobia and hostility in the capital, culminating in harassment by informers and prosecution by guilds, threats of violence, increasing curtailments of aliens' economic activities and financial exactions.[109] From the freemen registers of Amsterdam, it appears that the tailors, merchants and metal-workers were groups most prone to emigrate. The common reason for their emigration was probably their relative inability to integrate into their respective crafts. The alien tailors were excluded and prosecuted by the Merchant Tailors' Company, the merchants were restricted in their ability to trade and were vulnerable to financial exactions, and the metalworkers, although licensed to work by the Goldsmiths' Company, faced limited opportunities for social advancement. The textile workers were the exception. Although textile workers were the fourth largest occupational group among the immigrants in Amsterdam, it is noticeable that only one of the 57 who left London between 1576 and 1640 fell into this category. The textile workers were the largest group in London (a survey in 1593 listed 502 aliens)[110] but were fewest among the citizens from England. This perhaps reflects their greater success in integration. The clear and open admissions policy of the Weavers' Company in the seventeenth century enabled aliens to work freely. To obtain admission, aliens were required to show proof of church membership (French and Dutch Church), proper qualification acquired in England or abroad and pay a fee (11s 10d for journeymen and £4 or £5 for masters).[111] Between 1610 and 1642 at least 32 aliens sought admission into the Weavers' Company.[112] Those with exceptional skills were admitted gratis.[113] Their origins also explained their disinclination to emigrate. Many textile workers, especially silk-weavers, were Walloons from the southern Netherlands for whom emigration to the Dutch Republic probably did not alleviate cultural barriers such as language. Many stayed put in London, and with the influx of the refugees from France as a result of the Revocation of Edict of Nantes in 1685 French-speaking immigrants in London outnumbered their Dutch counterparts. These changes in the patterns of immigration to London steadily weakened the domination of the Netherlands as a cultural and economic model.

Notes

1 Printed in Moens, *Walloons and their Church at Norwich*, p. 220.
2 Tammel, *Pilgrims and other People*, pp. 320–35.
3 Williams suggested there were only 12,000 in the 1570s: "The Crown and the Provincial Immigrant Communities", p. 118.
4 See also Chapter 1 above, pp. 17–18, where a figure of 23–24,000 is suggested for the 1590s.
5 Littleton, "Social Interactions", p. 150.
6 Verheyden, "Correspondance Inédite", letters 12, 26, 27, 28, 29. I am extremely grateful to Guillaume Delanoy (Lausanne, Switzerland) for his assistance with the translation of these letters, which are currently being prepared for publication.
7 Verheyden, "Correspondance Inédite", Letter 28, pp. 148–9.
8 Verheyden, "Correspondance Inédite", Letter 12, p. 128–9.
9 Verheyden, "Correspondance Inédite", Letter 40, p. 166.
10 Verheyden, "Correspondance Inédite", Letter 31, pp. 152–3.
11 I am grateful to Dr Alastair Duke for this information.
12 Backhouse, "Strangers at Work", p. 92.
13 Martin, "New Draperies in Norwich", p. 255. But compare Bulteel, *Relation of the Troubles*, p. 22, who gives 759 communicants in Norwich in 1634: see Chapter 1, pp. 18–19.
14 Spicer, *French-speaking Reformed Community*, p. 161.
15 Spicer, *French-speaking Reformed Community*, p. 164.
16 Spicer, *French-speaking Reformed Community*, p. 161; Goose. "The Dutch in Colchester in the 16th and 17th Centuries", p. 88.
17 See also Chapter 1 above, pp. 17–28

18 The high mobility of the alien population also accounts for the fluctuation in their numbers. For a discussion of this see Littleton, "Social Interactions", pp. 149–51.

19 Littleton, "Social Interactions", p. 149.

20 *CSP Spanish*, Vol. 4 Elizabeth, 1587–1603, pp. 415, 480.

21 Lindeboom, *Austin Friars*, p. 122.

22 Of 1,343 whose occupations were specified, the largest groups were 349 weavers, 183 merchants, 148 tailors, 35 jewellers, 25 diamond-cutters, 20 goldsmiths and 15 clockmakers. See Smiles, *The Huguenots*, p. 91.

23 Grell, "French and Dutch Congregations", p. 363.

24 Grell, "French and Dutch Congregations", p. 363; Chapter 1, p. 16.

25 Scouloudi, *Returns of Strangers*, p. 100; and see Chapter 1 above, p 16.

26 Grell, "From Persecution to Integration", pp. 101–2.

27 Grell, "From Persecution to Integration", p. 100.

28 Grell, "French and Dutch Congregations", pp. 362–3.

29 Scouloudi, *Returns of Strangers*, p. 100.

30 Grell, "From Persecution to Integration", p. 100.

31 Grell, "From Persecution to Integration," p. 109.

32 On Dutch fatalities see Grell, "Plague in Elizabethan and Stuart London", p. 428. The 1603 plague claimed the lives of roughly 31,000 people in London, over one-fifth of the city's population: Rappaport, *Worlds Within Worlds*, p. 72.

33 Washington, Folger Library, MS V.b.142, fo.87.

34 Van Dillen, *Bronnen tot de Geschiedenis van het Bedrijfsleven en het Gildewezen van Amsterdam*, p. xxxiii. The other parts of the Netherlands included north and south Holland, Utrecht, Gelderland, Overijsel, Friesland, Groningen, Drente, Zeeland, north Brabant and Limburg.

35 See Clark, "A Crisis Contained?".

36 See Rappaport, *Worlds Within Worlds*, esp. Chapter 5.

37 Power, "London and the Control of the 'Crisis' of the 1590s", p. 385.

38 Power, "A 'Crisis' Reconsidered", p. 134; and also Archer, *Pursuit of Stability*, esp. pp. 1–17, for an alternative explanation of how stability was maintained in London.

39 Wright, *Queen Elizabeth*, Vol. 2, p. 308.

40 CLRO, Rep. 21, f. 330v (September 1586).

41 Hessels, Vol. 2 [no. 220], p. 794.

42 CLRO, JOR 22, f. 97 (29 March 1587).

43 CLRO, JOR 22, f. 97 (25 March 1587).

44 Strype, *Annals of the Reformation*, Vol. 4, pp. 234–5.

45 See also Chapter 6 above, p. 120.

46 Manning, *Village Revolts*, p. 204.

47 Hessels, Vol. 3, Part 1, pp. 963–4.

48 Hessels, Vol. 3, Part 1, pp. 1034–6.

49 Hessels, Vol. 3, Part 1, pp. 1037–8.

50 Hessels, Vol. 3, Part 1, pp. 1056–8.

51 Hessels, Vol. 3, Part 2, p. 2898.

52 Hessels, Vol. 3, Part 1, pp. 1182–5.

53 Hessels, Vol. 3, Part 1, p. 1185.

54 Hessels, Vol. 3, Part 1, p. 1323.

55 Grell, "French and Dutch Congregations", p. 369.

56 Grell, "French and Dutch Congregations", p. 371.

57 Grell, "French and Dutch Congregations", pp. 372–4.

58 Scouloudi, *Returns of Strangers*, pp. 96–7; Bulteel, *Relation of the Troubles*, p. 22.

59 Games, *Migration*, pp. 21, 31–2.

60 PRO E157/20 f. 77v.
61 Games, *Migration*, p. 33.
62 PRO E157/20 Licences for travel December 1634–35. This volume begins with passengers bound for America, the reverse side lists those bound for the continent.
63 PRO E157/20 [printed number], f. 71, 72, 73v, 75.
64 Lindeboom, *Austin Friars*, p. 120; Hessels, Vol. 3, Part 1, pp. 956–8; Hessels, Vol. 2, p. 867.
65 I would like to thank Dr Clé Lesger, University of Amsterdam, for this information.
66 Hart, "Freedom and Restrictions", p. 118.
67 de Vries, "Labour Market", p. 73.
68 Barbour, *Capitalism in Amsterdam*, p. 16.
69 Jokes about the Dutch were common: see Verberckmoes, "Seventeenth-Century Low Countries Jests", p. 294.
70 The Brabanters were particularly conscious of their own smartness, as too were other foreign observers like Fynes Moryson, who also noted how the Flemish and Brabant women were not only better clothed than the Dutch but were also prettier. The northerners, for their part, resented southern Netherlanders' arrogance. See van Deursen, *Plain Lives*, pp. 41, 43.
71 Scouloudi, *Returns of Strangers*, p. 131.
72 Sleigh-Johnson, "Merchant Taylors Company", p. 362.
73 Hessels, Vol. 3, Part 1, pp. 1207–8.
74 GL, MF 326, Court Minutes, Vol. 3, 1575–1601, f. 241v.
75 CLRO, Rep 24 (23 March 1598), ff. 382v-384 ("The order towching forren Taylers").
76 GL, MF 310 Ancient Manuscript Books, Vol. 2, ff. 54–54v ("Thordynnce for foreyns straungers and forreyn denizens", 1576).
77 In 1597 Rappaport's index of real wages stood at 59 (base 100 in 1457–71): *Worlds Within Worlds*, p. 407.
78 GL, MF 326, Court Minutes, Vol. 3, 1575–1601, f. 367.
79 CLRO, JOR 24 (23 March 1598), ff. 382v-384.
80 CLRO, JOR 24, ff.382v-384 (23 March 1598).
81 GL, MF 326, Court Minutes, Vol. 3, 1575–1601, f. 388v.
82 GL, MF 326, Court Minutes, Vol. 3, 1575–1601, f. 392v-393.
83 The governors of the Merchant Tailors' Company were largely wealthy merchants rather than craftsmen. Of the liverymen admitted during the period 1580–1645 only 7 per cent were handicraftsmen. See Sleigh-Johnson, "Merchant Taylors Company", pp. 138, 339.
84 GL, MF 326, Court Minutes, Vol. 3, 1575–1601, f. 431v.
85 Merchant Tailors' Hall, Ancient Manuscript Books, Vol. 54 T3, ff. 113.
86 GL, MF 326, Court Minutes, Vol. 3, 1575–1601, f. 440v.
87 Sleigh-Johnson, "Merchant Taylors Company", p. 338.
88 GL, MF 327, Court Minutes, Vol. 5, 1601–11, ff.1-4.
89 In June 1608 the Company agreed to meet to consider the letter written by de Caron "in favour and for tolleration of diverse Dutch men inhabitinge in London and using the handicraft of Taillory". The Company agreed to hold a conference with the representatives of the strangers to consider "whether any or howe many and what persons are to be tollerated, and to what orders and government they are to be subject". GL, MF 327, Court Minutes, Vol. 5, 1601–11, ff. 310, 330, 347.
90 GL, MF 327, Court Minutes, Vol. 5 1601–1611, f. 330, "An agreement concerning French and Dutch taylors".
91 Hessels, Vol. 3, Part 1, pp. 1207–8.
92 According to this complaint, alien merchants committed six offences: 1) took lodgings and houses within the city; 2) kept their merchandizes as long as they liked; 3) sold their merchandize by retail; 4) did not keep their money within England; 5) sold merchandize

one to another; 6) and formed a commonwealth within themselves. The last complaint was directed at alien craftsmen. PRO SP 12/81/29. This complaint is discussed in detail by Littleton, "Geneva on Threadneedle Street", pp. 171–4.

93 PRO, SP 12/88/36.

94 Yungblut, *Strangers Settled Here Amongst Us*, p. 41.

95 *CSP Spanish*, Vol. 4 Elizabeth, 1587–1603, p. 415.

96 Scouloudi, *Returns of Strangers*, p. 131. There were 61 goldsmiths and 3 silversmiths; cutlers and knife makers formed the second largest group (42 persons or 22 per cent).

97 Glanville, "Introduction" in Mitchell (ed.), *Goldsmiths, Silversmiths and Bankers*, p. 3.

98 Hayward, *Huguenot Silver in England*, pp. 19–20.

99 Kirk & Kirk, Part 2, p. 11, Briels, "Zuidnederlandse Goud- en Zilversmeden in Noordnederland Omstreeks" (southern Netherlands gold- and silversmiths in northern Netherlands), p. 137.

100 See Antwerp Stadsarchief, A4487, f. 100v, 159, Schlugheit, "Alphabetische Naamlijst op de Goud en Zilversmeden te Antwerpen voor 1600" (Alphabetical list of gold- and silversmiths in Antwerp before 1600) p. 22.

101 Mrs G. van Hemeldonck is currently preparing *De Antwerpse Goud- en Zilversmden 1550–1600*, (Antwerp's gold- and silversmiths 1550–1600) (a two-volume study of Antwerp goldsmiths due to be published and I am extremely grateful to her for giving me access to this material), entry 1135.

102 Briels, "Zuidnederlandse Goud- en Zilversmeden in Noordnederland Omstreeks", p. 102.

103 For background to the economic climate see Sharpe, *Early Modern England*, pp. 16, 21; Mitchell, "Innovation and the Transfer of Skill", p. 11.

104 Turner, *Introduction to English Silver*, pp. 5–6.

105 Turner, *Introduction to English Silver*, p. 6.

106 Prideaux, *Memorials of the Goldsmiths Company*, Vol. 1, p. 209.

107 See de Vries, "Labour Market", pp. 63–73 for a discussion of wages, den Blaauwen, *Dutch Silver*, p. xxiv.

108 PRO E157/20.

109 Cf. the rather different interpretation offered in Chapter 6, above.

110 Scouloudi, *Returns of Strangers*, p. 131.

111 Waller, *Extracts*, pp. xvii–xviii.

112 Ten were admitted as masters, one as brother, thirteen as journeymen, but six were ordered to bring in the necessary evidence and two were ordered to leave: see Luu, *Immigrants and the Industries of London*, Chapter 6.

113 The Company also sought to encourage production of new types of silk, offering free admission to a producer of alamode silk in 1684 on condition that he would employ some English persons in making alamode and lustring silks for one year: GL, MS4655/9/ fos. 37–8.

11

Immigrants, the Indigenous Community and International Calvinism

David Trim

This chapter explores the ways in which different communities in Elizabethan and early Stuart England supported militant Protestants in France and the Netherlands in the wars fought by the Huguenots and Dutch rebels against the Catholic Valois kings and the Spanish monarchy. These wars, especially those in the Netherlands, were fought not only over religion, but were regarded as essentially confessional by many English people of the time and especially those who were most prominent in assisting continental co-religionists.[1] This essay stresses that the stranger churches of Elizabethan "foreign Protestant communities" in England who have been so illuminated by recent scholarship,[2] played an active military role in the wars of religion in their homelands, but also emphasises that they generally did so jointly, together with native Englishmen. Aid to the continent from Elizabethan England is often portrayed as coming either from stranger churches, or from sympathetic English nobles, such as the Earl of Leicester. In fact, while the indigenous population generally took the leading role in helping continental co-religionists, 'stranger' Protestant refugees were an integral part of 'English' efforts to resist papistical tyranny in Europe. This essay also argues that the co-operative nature of this support given to French and Dutch Protestants, undertaken by Calvinists to help fellow Calvinists, helped to integrate the immigrant and indigenous communities; in "transcending traditional xenophobia" in England "religious solidarity" was a factor of great importance,[3] but it owed as much to shared endeavour as to shared doctrine.

Combined action was the order of the day from the very beginning. The relatively large force of English 'volunteers' who went to Normandy in the first War of Religion (1562) under the leadership of the zealous Calvinist Henry Killigrew, co-operated closely with Huguenot exiles as well as with the local Protestant forces.[4] During the Third Civil War in France (1568–70) the Protestants received much assistance from England – assistance that was the fruit of co-ordinated action between the English and the French. The emphasis at this time was not on supplying troops: a few exiles did return home to fight, but as individuals; the only *units* were entirely English. However, considerable quantities of arms and other *matériel* were supplied thanks to the efforts of many people on both sides of the Channel. Two exiles, Odet de Coligny, *quondam* Cardinal de Châtillon, and the Vidame de Chartres were of particular importance because they were crucial links between, on the one hand, Condé, Navarre and the other Huguenot leaders in France and, on the other, their English sympathisers in the city of London, in the country and at court – men such as Nicholas and Richard Culverwell, successful merchants from a godly London family; or Sir Arthur Champernowne, the Vice-Admiral of Devon, whose nephew Henry was a trusted lieutenant of the Prince of Condé and whose son Gawain married a daughter of the Comte de Montgommery, a leading Huguenot commander.[5] Montgommery had emigrated to England in 1559 and though he returned to France, his family stayed as refugees in England from 1563 until after the Comte was captured and executed in 1574. They were admitted to communion at the French Church in Southampton in 1575, and in many ways became integrated into English society, though the children eventually returned to live in France.[6]

During the 1566 rebellion in the Netherlands, in which returned exiles are known to have played an important role, the involvement of Englishmen is often overlooked.[7] Two English merchants participated in the Calvinist movement at Bergen-op-Zoom, one of them even serving as a member of the consistory. In Antwerp, Englishmen as well as émigrés were among the iconoclasts who 'cleansed' the city's churches in August 1566, one of them being executed at the order of the Prince of Orange for theft and sacrilege whilst another, the ardently anti-Catholic Thomas Churchyard, was chosen by the mob as one of their captains due to his military experience.[8] From 1567, a number of Englishmen fought with the *bosgeuzen* (or Wood Beggars), whose guerrilla war in the *Westkwartier* of Flanders was co-ordinated by the Dutch Churches in Sandwich, Norwich and London and seems to have been funded jointly by those churches and by sympathetic English merchants.[9] Between 1568 and 1572 the Dutch *watergeuzen* (or Sea Beggars) and the Huguenot corsairs of La Rochelle recruited not only from Dutch and French exiles in England, but from native Englishmen, with whom they also co-operated intimately in equipping their enterprises.[10] The commander of the King of Navarre's fleet, Jean de Sores, was a member of the French Church of Southampton and, in the words of G. D. Ramsay, this "international camaraderie … made possible … the setting-forth of ships, whether as privateers or pirates, with crews of mixed nationalities".[11]

It was, however, from 1572 that co-operative military activity became truly extensive, stimulated by the beginning of the *opstand* in the Netherlands and the horrific St Bartholomew's Day Massacre in France. The Comte de Montgommery led an expeditionary force of English (and Welshmen) as well as Huguenot refugees to La Rochelle, helping it to survive the great royal siege of 1573. After peace was concluded, this multi-national force went, under the command of Montgommery's son, to the Netherlands to aid William of Orange in the desperate fighting around Haarlem.[12] Later in 1573, the count raised more troops in the exile communities of Dover, Rye and Sandwich, which went as reinforcements to the garrison of Flushing and to Montgommery's son in Holland. These troops were partly French followers of Montgommery, Walloon émigrés and indigenous English.[13] At the beginning of the Fifth War of Religion in early 1574, Montgommery himself led another expedition (which would be his last), this time to Normandy. His force was made up of his followers from France, English soldiers and probably of men from both the French and Dutch exile communities in England, and it was funded partly by English supporters and partly by the French congregation in Southampton.[14]

Meanwhile, in the Netherlands in 1572, the year of the *opstand*, it is well known that, from the storming of Den Brielle by Lumey de La Marck on 1 April, the rebellious Dutch towns bombarded England, particularly the stranger churches, with appeals for military assistance.[15] These appeals met with a positive response: soldiers and supplies crossed the North Sea in April and May. In the fullness of time, Thomas Morgan and Sir Humphrey Gilbert led a large number of Anglo-Welsh 'volunteers' to Flushing in June and July: because of its size and the complicity of the Elizabethan regime in its dispatch, their force has overshadowed all other English succour to the rebels. The standard historical accounts of these events, though essentially accurate, are nevertheless somewhat misleading. First, they portray the early assistance sent from England as being supplied solely by the stranger churches; second, they indicate that the only significant English intervention in the Netherlands at this time was that led by Morgan and Gilbert; and third, they depict the support of the refugee communities as distinct from that of English captains and grandees.[16]

Let us take these points in order. The immigrant communities undoubtedly made an important contribution to the war effort across the narrow seas. They did so as conscious members of an international Calvinist community, for émigrés' actions to aid the war effort on the Continent were taken collectively and organised through the consistories of the stranger churches. The strangers undoubtedly made an important contribution to the war effort. By the end of April, the French Church of London had raised £300, the Austin Friars congregation £200 and the two churches had jointly bought enough arms for 1,700 men; while Lumey in Den Brielle had received volunteers from London and Sandwich.[17] In May the fund-raising efforts continued in London, where the French Church recruited 200 men who were sent to Flushing, while the Norwich church raised 125 soldiers at the behest of an agent of the Prince of Orange, who led the men to Ter Veere.[18] Just half a dozen Dutch families in Ipswich sent six of their men to Den Brielle, having equipped three of them and raised an extra £15, whilst the Dutch Church in Colchester raised and shipped over to Flushing nearly 40 soldiers.[19] The support of the exile congregations was not restricted to April and May. In June, although more than 25 of the members of the Dutch Church in Norwich who had gone to Flushing in May had already been slain, over 100 more Dutch and French exiles, raised at a cost of £160 to the Dutch Church, crossed the North Sea.[20] By the end of June, the number of men raised and sent to Brill and Flushing by the stranger churches of London, Sandwich, Norwich, Ipswich, Colchester and Yarmouth totalled at least 450 and maybe as many as 750 men.[21] Yet the support of the exile congregations did not end then. By the end of 1572 Austin Friars had raised £1,400 and sent to Flushing 200 fully equipped soldiers, while wealthier members of the church, acting as individuals, had sent another 50 men to Holland and Zeeland. Even the small community at Maidstone had raised £13.[22]

However, it is not clear that those 250 men raised by the members of the Dutch Church of London, for example, nor any of the other troops raised by the various refugee communities, were recruited only from immigrants. Thus we come to the second point. Native English military assistance to the Dutch rebels was not restricted to Morgan and Gilbert's force – it was, indeed, more common and widespread. Reports

from Spanish diplomatic agents in London, the correspondence of émigré congregations and the records of officers of the English companies in Zeeland, all indicate that
many Englishmen, including discrete units, were among the ranks of those 450–750
men raised by the stranger churches.[23] English soldiers had already played as significant a role as had returned refugees during the fighting in April and May. Englishmen
(as well as Huguenot exiles) served in de La Marck's own company at the storming of
Den Brielle and his force also included at least one distinct English foot-band.[24] The
appeal of the magistrates and captains of Flushing to all the Dutch Churches in
England on 26 April 1572 for men and money is well known;[25] it is less well known
that some 300 English soldiers had already disembarked at Flushing two days earlier.[26]
De La Marck received three more foot-bands, raised in England from the indigenous
population, as reinforcements in May.[27] When Louis of Nassau captured Mons in that
same month there were a number of English volunteers in his force, including some in
his own guard; they served in the campaign in Hainaut throughout the summer and
remained with him until the bitter end in the autumn.[28] Nor were the men of
Humphrey Gilbert's well-known force the only English troops to arrive in the Low
Countries after summer had come. Edward Chester, son of Sir William Chester (one-
time Lord Mayor of London and a notable patron of godly ministers), led to Ter Veere
a force raised probably partly independently of Gilbert, though Chester later linked
up with the main English body.[29] At around the same time that Gilbert's brigade left
England for Flushing, a unique battalion arrived in Den Brielle. Commanded by a
Dutchman and possible refugee, Jan van Tryer, it was of special interest to students of
the integration of immigrant communities, because of the make-up of its rank and file.
Generally, Englishmen served in Dutch units only as isolated individuals, while the
nominally English bands were made up almost entirely of English and Welshmen,
rather than Continentals. However, van Tryer's unit comprised 163 Dutch and
Walloons, all evidently recruited from the immigrant communities (mostly those in
East Anglia), plus 179 English and Welsh volunteers, all fighting together under the
same captain.[30]

This last example leads us to the third point: the co-operative nature of the military
and financial aid delivered to the Dutch rebels from Elizabeth's realm. Just as the
soldiers supplied by foreign congregations were not necessarily refugees, not all the
money and supplies collected by the stranger churches came from exiles. The ships
which left Southampton in early June and late August 1572, probably for Zeeland,
were carrying money, victuals, arms and munitions, probably gathered by the French
Church of Southampton, but men were also transported – some English and some
émigré. As this was the diocese of the strongly Calvinist and internationally minded
Bishop of Winchester, it is quite possible that some of the *matériel* had been gathered
by members of the indigenous as well as immigrant community.[31] As Professor
Collinson has shown, the stranger churches included Englishmen in their membership, while other native members of the population regularly co-operated with the
churches' leadership or contributed to the strangers' fund-raising enterprises.[32] How
was the cash raised in Threadneedle Street and Austin Friars, the Cinque Ports and
East Anglia actually delivered to Flushing, Den Brielle and Enkhuizen? Much of it was
transferred as bills of exchange by the English merchant Ferdinand Poyntz, who also
arranged the transportation of the bulk of the arms and munitions. Later, in the autumn
of 1572, Poyntz raised jointly with a merchant from Flushing the extraordinary sum

of £20,000 to buy and transport to Holland munitions, powder, beer, biscuit, salt meat and corn.[33] In early 1573 he was a member of a consortium of English and Dutch merchants who arranged the sale in England of goods captured by Zeeland privateers, with the profits used to provide "victuals . . . stores" and "payment" to the English companies still in Flushing.[34]

This is not to denigrate the efforts of the émigrés; but it needs to be understood that the supply of men, money or arms and armour was generally the action not of *either* English or exiles, but of both, frequently acting together. The uprising in Holland and Zeeland in spring and summer 1572 was only the beginning of joint action between the stranger churches and a variety of English mercenaries and merchants. The revolt was soon confined to those two rebellious provinces and the English government tried to distance itself from what appeared to be a lost cause, "preferring an uncertain peace to uncertain wars".[35] As a result, the stranger churches took on a new importance. William of Orange and his supporters bombarded all the stranger churches with appeals for help from the end of 1572 throughout 1573. Several times he had cause to reproach them for their lack of zeal in assisting their brothers in the Netherlands, but though they were not always able to provide what the Prince asked (or as much as he asked), they were still, in relative terms, quite supportive, furnishing money (in particular) and men (albeit to a lesser degree) for the forces already in the Netherlands.[36] They served as a valuable source of information for the Dutch rebels about developments in England,[37] and they must also have been an invaluable line of communication to the English sympathisers whose support, as Philip II of Spain recognised, was crucial to the rebel cause.[38]

Their support was partly necessary to ensure supplies from the stranger churches would not be impeded by agents of the English crown.[39] But they also took an active role in co-operation with co-religionist friends in the immigrant community. In addition to Poyntz, other English merchants also played an important role in supplying the rebels, shipping lead and gunpowder to de La Marck in Brielle in 1572–3, for example.[40] In the mid-1570s, another London merchant, Thomas Pullison (who lived in the London parish of St Antholin's, then a hotbed of Puritanism), took over half the States of Holland's debts to Colonel Edward Chester, in order that his men should be paid and fed and so keep fighting.[41] Two fellow parishioners at another radical parish, St Mary Aldermanbury in Cripplegate, were Elizabeth's famous Puritan Secretary of State, Sir Francis Walsingham, who also worshipped at the French Church at Threadneedle Street, and an affluent 'godly' merchant, Thomas Myddelton, who was, additionally, a member of the Dutch Church at Austin Friars, whose minister he helped pay for. Myddelton began his career as an apprentice to Ferdinand Poyntz, for whom he was a factor at Flushing in 1578. By 1582, he was in business for himself at Antwerp; his brother William fought as a mercenary under the celebrated Sir John Norreys and Thomas Morgan (who returned to the Netherlands in 1578) and it is therefore not surprising that Myddelton advanced cash to Morgan and to Henry Norreys (Sir John's younger brother) for their personal mercenary bands.[42]

In 1583, the 4,000 Anglo-Welsh troops then in the Low Countries still relied to a great extent on the initiatives of English merchants, due to the financial situation of the States-General; but some supplies of "beer, bread and other victuals, besides much merchandise, as shoes and such other", probably came from the stranger churches of

Sandwich and Dover.⁴³ In sum, the craftsmen and merchants of the Dutch and French communities in south-east England did make a major contribution to the Calvinist war effort on the continent, but as part of a much wider network of merchants, English and émigré alike, who took on considerable financial commitments, with a poor chance of profits.

Even when the war was taken over by the English crown in 1585 the immigrant communities continued to contribute to the war effort, now under the royal banner. The Dutch in London raised the money to pay several companies of mercenaries led by Sir John Norreys, which was the force the Elizabethan regime initially planned to send. The government soon changed its plans and decided to wage open war on Spain and these troops were quickly subsumed within the crown's expeditionary force, but the Dutch Church still collected more money for the reinforcements raised by the Earl of Leicester in late 1585. All in all, the Austin Friars' congregation reckoned its members had raised £1,072 in 1585.⁴⁴ Furthermore, exiles continued to serve alongside English and Welshmen, including those raised through the efforts of private sympathisers.

The numbers of troops in Leicester's army were equalled by volunteers in the pay of the States-General. Although these companies were mostly native English, one company was under "a Wallowne Captayne" and was made up of men of the stranger communities of Norwich, Colchester and elsewhere in East Anglia.⁴⁵ Francis Castilion, one of Leicester's officers in the Netherlands in 1586, was a member of the Italian immigrant community, the son of Gian Batista Castiglione, Elizabeth's Italian tutor.⁴⁶ In 1588, the stranger churches raised 500 men to reinforce the queen's garrison in Bergen-op-Zoom.⁴⁷ Christopher Levens, a Huguenot captain who had emigrated to England after the First War of Religion and then served the Dutch rebels from 1572 onwards, was in the English expedition to Lisbon in 1589 and settled back in England, in one of the garrisons on the Isle of Wight thereafter.⁴⁸ Later, in the 1590s, the four sons of the Dutch statesman, Adolf van Meetkerke (whose support for the Earl of Leicester had resulted in his family being exiled to England in the late 1580s) all led companies or regiments of the English army. In 1602 the Dutch congregations of London, Norwich, Sandwich, Rye, Winchelsea, Maidstone and Dover were targeted by the recruiting parties of Sir Francis Vere, raising troops to succour the garrison of besieged Ostend.⁴⁹

Under the circumstances it is unsurprising that, though some natives were worried about the economic consequences of immigration,⁵⁰ many Englishmen were welcoming to strangers – at least those with the right confessional credentials. Certainly Englishmen could distinguish between different types of foreign immigrants, but it was the Calvinist religion that helped bind the native English and the émigré communities together, and it was the stranger churches that provided the link between immigrants and their indigenous supporters.

Sir Thomas Bodley (Elizabeth's ambassador in the Netherlands 1589–95) was a friend of a number of members of the exile communities in London, and occasional attender at the French Church of London, as his father had been before him. He and Sir Henry Killigrew (who, after his exploits with the Huguenots in 1562, turned diplomatist, including several missions to the Netherlands) had helped the consistory of the Threadneedle Street church deal with complaints from the London mercantile community in June 1572.⁵¹ John Stubbs, who in 1579 published a virulent pamphlet against the proposed marriage of Elizabeth to the Duke of Anjou, was nevertheless on excellent terms with the minister of the French Church of London, Monsieur de la Fontaine le Masson. Their relationship probably predated Stubbs's experience as a staff officer in the English army in Normandy in 1589, but his master, Lord Willoughby, had served in the Netherlands from 1586–8.[52] Those who had participated in Europe's Wars of Religion and their kin and clients, tended to be positive about those with whom they (or their lords, followers or friends) had fought shoulder to shoulder – literally as well as metaphorically.

It is notable that the muster-master of Norwich allowed Dutch strangers to serve in its trained bands.[53] This was probably due at least partly to their knowledge of gunpowder technology, but it still indicates that soldiers were accepting of 'strangers'. Among the intimate friends of Robert Devereux, 2nd Earl of Essex, was Gabriel de Montgommery, younger son of the Comte de Montgommery, who spent his youth in exile in England after his father's death in 1574 and who may have had an Englishwoman as his first wife.[54] Baldwin van Meetkerke, second son of Adolf van Meetkerke, was a client of the Earl's, by whom he was knighted at Cadiz in 1596, and at this time several of the other, indigenous, soldiers and diplomats in Essex's circle were friends of the well-known Dutch historian Emmanuel van Meteren, who spent much of his life in London.[55]

So greatly was English soldiers' xenophobia diminished that trans-ethnic marriages became relatively common. In 1591, Sir Thomas Bodley, the friend of a number of members of the exile communities in London, as his father had been before him, wrote to Lord Burghley that about 40 English soldiers had married Dutch wives; and the municipal archive of Leiden, an English garrison town, preserves records of many marriages between English soldiers and townswomen in the 1590s and early seventeenth century.[56] Lust is, of course, a more obvious motivation for ordinary soldiers stationed abroad to marry local females than pluralist acceptance of foreigners, but it was also the officers and gentlemen in the English units who contracted such alliances. Some were probably motivated by money, but others are known to have married for love. In 1588, Sir William Browne, lieutenant-governor of Flushing, married a Huguenot exile.[57] Le Strange Mordant, later a captain in Ireland and a baronet, married the daughter of a former citizen of Antwerp (his family themselves exiles in the Dutch Republic) around 1600.[58] From 1590 into the early 1600s, four colonels (Sir Callisthenics Brooke, Sir Edward Conway, Sir Thomas Knollys and Sir John Ogle), a lieutenant-colonel (Thomas Holles) and at least two captains (Thomas Poyntz – a cousin of Ferdinand Poyntz – and Captain Randolf) all married Dutch women. Conway even named a daughter after Den Brielle in Holland, where she was born while her father was governor. Ogle went further, naming three daughters after the cities in the Netherlands where they were born and, though his wife and children settled in England, they were never naturalized. Thomas Poyntz's family settled permanently in the Netherlands; and Holles's son grew up to speak "French and Dutch ... better than English".[59]

John McGurk, in examining the marriages of Irish soldiers settled in the Spanish Netherlands to local women, rightly warns of the danger that "highly selective evidence" will "lead to ... exaggerated conclusion[s] about assimilation".[60] However, the marriages just cited arguably represented more than simply the normal adjustment to local conditions that takes place whenever soldiers are garrisoned in a foreign country. A number of marriages that took place across national and linguistic borders were not to locals, but to women from Dutch immigrant families in England. For example, a Mr Nicholas, probably an Englishman who worshipped at the French Church in Threadneedle Street, married a woman from Mons, in the southern Netherlands, in 1572.[61] In 1607 Lieutenant John Braddedge married a Flemish woman who emigrated to England and settled in Lambeth with her husband. Sir Edward Conway's foreign wife, similarly, came from a Ghentish family that had fled to London, where her first marriage had been to John West, a grocer.[62] At least one member of the aristocratic Cromwell family, many of whom fought in the Netherlands, married an émigré Dutch woman.[63] Similar marriages also occurred in the rank and file. For example, at Leiden in 1603, Thomas Smith wed Jannetgen Swyetijn of Colchester. Also at Leiden in 1603, William Segar married Sara Meeuwels of Sandwich; when Segar died in 1607, Sara remarried another English soldier, Giles Hall, and in the same year Oliver Augustine of Gloucester married Cathelijne Douwes of Sandwich, also at Leiden.[64]

The inculturation of English soldiers by foreign service can also be seen in the experience of Sir Thomas Morgan – the same man who fought at Flushing in 1572 and received financial aid from Thomas Myddelton. In 1589, Morgan eloped with a daughter of Jan van Merode, the Marquis of Bergen. The Marquis, and particularly his wife, were not happy at having as a son-in-law a grizzled Welsh veteran closer to their age than their daughter's. In the end, it was Morgan's Dutch friends, including some on the Council of State, who intervened to mend fences between Morgan and his mother-in-law. Later, the son born to this union (named in honour of Maurice of Nassau) also married a Dutch noble woman.[65] Thomas himself, when writing to a Continental confidant, used English, French and Dutch – all in the one letter.[66]

This is indicative of how mutual participation in confessional conflicts on the Continent could integrate indigenes and immigrants. Whatever their language, they were all fighting for the reformed faith, for the Holy Scriptures, which taught them "There is neither Jew nor Greek, neither slave nor free . . . for you are all one in Christ Jesus."[67] Sir Arthur Champernowne reflected this in the year of crisis, 1572, writing to the queen:

> Of one side your highnes may see Flushing, the Flemmyngs, and germans in good labor, on the other side, Rochell and the persequted frenchemen, at hard point, . . . we be made up with them in one band together . . . with them to stande in strength. . . .[68]

This sense of being part of a common cause – 'la cause commun' – was not felt by all English people, but was felt especially strongly by those who were committed to the Protestant cause and they applied it not only to Protestants in foreign countries but also to foreign Protestants who had emigrated to England. In the words of one English military writer at the end of the century, "this noble and most mighty nation of Englishmen . . . are always most loving . . . & ready to cherish & protect strangers".[69] A few years later, William Bradshaw took such sentiments to their logical conclusion in an oft-quoted passage: members of the stranger churches, "being all the same household of faith that we are . . . are not aptly called forreyne . . . [A]ll members of the Church, in what country so ever they be, are not . . . accounted Forreyners one to another, because they are all Citizens of heaven".[70]

One last example will conclusively demonstrate how confessional conflict helped to integrate refugees into English society. Adolf van Meetkerke's four eldest sons were all born in the Netherlands, but each served in English units during the war against Spain, fighting in the Low Countries, in Portugal and in Spain itself; two lost their lives in the queen's service. Were they Dutch? Were they 'strangers'? In virtually all contemporary English narratives they are clearly regarded as English. Sharing the burden of confessional conflict helped to engender a sense of unity; that shared burden and the shared experiences which resulted made English and refugee alike better appreciate each others' qualities and helped to break down barriers. Common effort in the cause of the Calvinist faith that transcended national borders played an important role in integrating immigrants into the wider early modern English community.

Notes

This chapter is a development of my essay, "Protestant refugees in Elizabethan England and confessional conflict in France and the Netherlands, 1562–c.1610", originally published in Vigne and Littleton (eds), *From Strangers to Citizens*, pp. 68–79.

1   Trim, "Fighting 'Jacob's Wars' ", pp. 34–6, 303–8.
2   Pettegree, *Foreign Protestant Communities*, pp. 252–3; Grell, *Dutch Calvinists*.
3   Collinson, *Birthpangs of Protestant England*, p. 16.
4   See Trim, "The 'Foundation-Stone of the British Army'?", pp. 71–87; Miller, *Sir Henry Killigrew*, pp. 75–78, 84–85; *CSP Foreign . . . Elizabeth I*, Vol. 5, no. 130, p. 66.
5   Trim, "The 'Secret War' of Elizabeth I", esp. pp. 190–3 and the sources cited at 198–9. See *DNB*, Vol. V, p. 288; Collinson, "Elizabethan Puritans", pp. 554–5; Usher, "Silent Community", pp. 287–302; Emery, *Dartington Hall*, pp. 73–80.
6   Spicer, *French-Speaking Reformed Community*, p. 133; C[okayne] *et al.*, *Complete Peerage*, Vol. 9, p. 138; BN, Fonds Clairambault MS 1907, fols. 132r–133r.
7   Pettegree, "Exile Churches", pp. 82, 84.
8   Rand al Starkey and George Kyghtley to William Cecil, June 1568, KL, no. 1690, Vol. 5, p.108; Ramsay, *Queen's Merchants*, p. 48; Churchyard, *Lamentable and Pitifull Description* pp. 22–34; *idem*, *Pleasant Discourse of Court and Wars*, sig. A2v.
9   Backhouse (ed.), "Dokumenten Betreffende de Godsdiensttroebelen", pp. 138, 191, 268, 293–7, 335–6, 344; *idem*, "Guerrilla War and Banditry", pp. 234–40, 247–9; Pettegree, *Foreign Protestant Communities*, pp. 252–3; *idem*, "Exile Churches", pp. 84–5, 95–6.
10 Richard Clough to Thomas Gresham, 28 Sept. 1567, KL, no. 1622, V, p. 15; Guzmán de Silva (Spanish Ambassador in London until Sept. 1568) to Elizabeth I, 14 July 1568, BL, Galba MS C iii, fol. 233; Guerau de Spes (Spanish Ambassador in London from Sept. 1568), Memorandum, Mar. 1569, KL, no. 1860, Vol. 5, p. 320; Louis of Nassau to Earl of Leicester, 17 Oct. 1569, BL, Galba MS C iii, fol. 306; de Spes to Duke of Alba, 23 Jun. 1570 and to Cecil, 27 July 1570, KL, nos. 2078, 2088, Vol. 5, pp. 669, 681; de Meij, *De Watergeuzen en de Nederlanden*, pp. 37–42, 169, 313–16; Molhuysen *et al.*, *Niuew Nederlandsch Biografisch Woordenboek*, Vol. 8, cols. 71, 365, 977, 1254; French, "Privateering", pp. 171–80 (I am grateful to Alastair Duke for this reference); Delafosse, "Les Corsaires Protestantes", pp. 191, 215; Spicer, *French-Speaking Reformed Community*, pp. 131–7.
11 Jean de Pablo, "L'Armée de Mer Huguenote", pp. 65–6, 74–6; Spicer, *French-Speaking Reformed Community*, pp. 133–4; Ramsay, *Queen's Merchants*, p. 86.
12 BN, MS Français 20787, fols 52r, 17v; Williams, *Actions of the Lowe Countries*, pp. 138 and 241n.; Sigismond di Cavalli (Venetian ambassador to France) to the Signory, 27 May and 12 July 1573, *Calendar of state papers and manuscripts [. . .] in the archives and collections of Venice*, Vol. 7, nos. 550–1, pp. 488–9; [Fogaça] to Alba, 9 Jun. 1573, *CSP Spanish*, Vol.

2, no. 386, pp. 470–1; accounts for William's army, Gemeentearchief van Leiden, Archief der Secretarie 1253–1575, MS 1033, fols 12r, 43v.

13 De Guaras to Alva, 23, 26 and 30 June 1573, KL, nos. 2604–5, 2606, Vol. 6, pp. 784–86, 789.

14 Thompson, *Wars of Religion*, pp. 472–3, 484–5; William Drury to Earl of Rutland, 31 Mar. 1574, *HMC, Duke of Rutland MSS*, Vol. 1, p. 101; anon. newsletter, 5 May 1574, Universiteitsbibliotheek Leiden, MS Vulc. 104/13; Spicer, *French-Speaking Reformed Community*, p. 132.

15 Community of Flushing to Elizabeth I, 20 Apr. 1572, KL, no. 2391, Vol. 6, p. 4391, and to the Dutch Churches of England, 26 Apr. 1572, Hessels, Vol. 2, no. 112, pp. 397–99; Magistrates of Flushing to Elizabeth I and Lord Burghley, May 1572, KL, nos. 2406–7, Vol. 6, p. 410; Diedrich Sonoy (Minister of Enkhuizen) to the Dutch Church of London, 4 and 10 July 1752, Hessels, Vol. 2, nos. 119–20, pp. 420–25 (the latter letter refers to letters to the refugee communities of King's Lynn and Norwich which have not survived); Pettegree, *Foreign Protestant Communities*, pp. 253–5.

16 See Ramsay, *Queen's Merchants*, p. 176; Conyers Read, *Lord Burghley and Queen Elizabeth*, p. 73; Dop, "Eliza's Knights", pp. 131, 142–3; cf. Parker, *Spain and the Netherlands*, p. 212.

17 François de Sweveghem to Alba, 23 Apr. 1572, KL, no. 2393, Vol. 6, p. 395; anon. report from the Netherlands, 30 Apr. 1572, *ibid.*, no. 2398, VI, p. 403.

18 Antonio de Guaras to Alba, 12 May 1572, *CSP Spanish*, Vol. 2, no. 327, p. 390; anon. report from the Netherlands, 24 May 1572, KL, no. 2408, VI, p. 412; Herman Moded to the Dutch Church of London, 29 May 1572, Hessels, Vol. 3 Part 1, no. 195, pp. 166–7.

19 Dutch community of Ipswich to Dutch Church of London, 11 and 14 May 1572, Hessels, Vol. 2, nos. 114, 116, pp. 403–4, 408–9; Dutch community of Colchester to Dutch Church of London, 12 May 1572, *ibid.*, no. 115, pp. 405–6.

20 Herman Moded to the Dutch community of London, 5 Jun. 1572, Hessels, Vol. 3 Part 1, no. 197, p. 168.

21 Trim, "Mercenaries", p. 111.

22 See Hessels, Vol. 2, no. 123, pp. 438–42.

23 See de Sweveghem to Alba, 23 Apr. 1572, KL, no. 2393, Vol. 6, p. 395; Dutch community of Colchester to the Dutch Church of London, 12 May 1572, Hessels, Vol. 2, no. 115, p. 405; de Guaras to Alba, 18 May, and [Antonio Fogaça] to Alba, 22 Jul. 1572, *CSP Spanish*, Vol. 2, nos. 329, 339 pp. 391, 397; Thomas Morgan to Burghley, 16 Jun. 1572, KL, no. 2414, Vol. 6, p. 426; Williams, *Actions of the Lowe Countries*, p. 108; and see Trim, "Mercenaries", p. 111.

24 BL, Lansdowne MS 1204, fols 114r, 121v, 123r; Churchyard, *Lamentable and Pitifull Description*, pp. 51–2; Williams, *Actions of the Lowe Countries*, p. 104; Spicer, *French-Speaking Reformed Community*, pp. 134–7.

25 Printed in Hessels, Vol. 2, no. 112, p. 399.

26 Claude de Mondoucet (French ambassador in Brussels) to Charles IX, 27 Apr. 1572, BN, MS Fr. 16127, fol. 39r.

27 Williams, *Actions of the Lowe Countries*, p. 108.

28 Francis Walsingham to Burghley, 21 May [1572], in Digges (ed.), *Compleat Ambassador [...]*, p. 202; Williams, *Actions of the Lowe Countries*, pp. 83–4, 87; Mondoucet to Charles IX, 4 Jan. 1573, BN, MS Fr. 16127, fol. 126v; Churchyard, *A Generall Rehearsall*, sigs K2v-K4r, and *Lamentable and Pitifull Description*, pp. 51, 54; Blok (ed.), *Correspondentie*, p. 102.

29 KL, no. 2425, Vol. 6, p. 440; Devereux Papers, MS II, fol. 9r: the Devereux Papers are cited by permission of the Marquess of Bath, Longleat House, Warminster, Wiltshire.

30 Algemeen Rijksarchief, Den Haag [hereafter ARA], Collectie Ortell 73 (unfoliated); Trim, "Mercenaries", pp. 111–12.

31 De Guaras to Alba, 6 Jun. 1572, KL, no. 2412, Vol. 6, p. 424; Fogaça to Alba, 30 Aug. 1572, ibid., no. 2457, p. 503. See Spicer, *French-Speaking Reformed Community*, pp. 130–2.

32 Collinson, "John Field and Elizabethan Puritanism", p. 141; *idem*, "Elizabethan Puritans & Foreign Reformed Churches", pp. 528–55; *idem*, "England and International Calvinism, 1558–1640", pp. 204–9, 211–12.

33 De Guaras to Alba, 24 May 1572, *CSP Spanish*, Vol. 2, no. 330, pp. 391, 394; [Fogaça] to Alba, 17 and 18 Nov. 1572, *ibid.*, nos. 365, 368, pp. 441, 447.

34 [Fogaça] to Alba, 16 Feb. 1573, *ibid.*, no. 380, pp. 464–5.

35 Daniel Rogers to Abraham Ortell, 20 Oct. 1572, Hessels, Vol. 1, no. 42, p. 101.

36 Jan vander Beke to the Dutch community of London, 29 Dec. 1572, Hessels, Vol. 3 Part 1, no. 215, pp. 186–87; de Guaras to Alba, 16 Feb. 1573, *CSP Spanish*, Vol. 2, no. 379, p. 463; William of Orange to the Dutch Churches in England, 26 Feb. 1573, Hessels, Vol. 2, no. 125, pp. 447–53; and to the Dutch communities of Norwich, Thetford and Ipswich, 27 Feb. 1573, M. Gachard (ed.), *Correspondance de Guillaume le taciturne*, no. 534, 3 (Brussels, Leipzig & Ghent, 1851), pp. 73–4; the Magistrates of Flushing to the Dutch community of London, 7 Apr. 1573, Hessels, Vol. 3 Part 1, no. 238, p. 215; the Magistrates of Veere to the Dutch Church of London, 7 Jun. 1573, *ibid.*, no. 254, p.230; the Dutch community of Sandwich to the Dutch community of London, 18 Jun. 1573, *ibid.*, no. 255, p.231; the Dutch Church of Norwich to the Dutch Church of London, 27 Jun. 1573, *ibid.*, no. 257, pp. 232–3; William of Orange to the Dutch French and Italian Churches of London, 13 Dec. 1573, *ibid.*, Vol. 2, no. 129, pp. 472–5; and to the Dutch Church of London, 29 Dec. 1573, *ibid.*, no. 132, pp. 490–2. (These refer to military-related activity; the numerous cases of charitable assistance to communities in the Netherlands are excluded.)

37 E.g., William of Orange to Elizabeth I, 31 Mar. 1574, KL, no. 2710, Vol. 7, p. 97.

38 Parker, *Spain and the Netherlands*, p. 35.

39 E.g., William of Orange to Burghley, 16 Feb. 1573, BL, Lansdowne MSS 16, f. 34r.

40 Dresch (ed.), "Rekening van Maerten Ruychaver", pp. 98–9.

41 Lang (ed.), *Two Tudor Subsidy Assessments*, p. 199 (I owe this reference to Brett Usher); Pullison to Joachim Ortell, 12 May and 16 Jun. 1576, ARA, Collectie Ortell 54, unfoliated.

42 Dodd, "Mr. Myddelton the Merchant of Tower Street", p. 211; *HMC, 2nd Report*, p. 73.

43 J. Jernegan to Walsingham, 3 August (n.s.) 1583, *CSP Foreign*, Vol. 18, no. 43, p. 36.

44 Georges de Montmorency to Alexander of Parma, 1 Aug. 1585 [n.s.], Piot (ed.), *Corresponance du Cardinal de Granvelle*, Vol. 12, no. 81, p. 334; Grell, *Dutch Calvinists*, 28–9. See Trim, "Mercenaries", pp. 163–6.

45 Sir Robert Jermyn to William Davison, 25 Aug. 1585, Bodleian Library, Oxford, MS Tanner 78, fol. 73r.

46 Adams, "A Puritan Crusade?", p. 23; *idem* (ed.), *Household Accounts*, p. 196 fn. 414.

47 Wernham, *After the Armada*, p. 36.

48 BL, Lansdowne MSS 1218, fol. 114r-v; HMC, Salisbury MSS, Vol. 16, pp. 319, 321, 346, 375.

49 Privy Council to Lord Cobham and the Mayors of London and Norwich, 7 Apr. 1602, APC, n.s., Vol. 32, p. 487, "for the leavying of voluntaries out of the Dutch congregations in the several places": Cobham was Lord Warden of the Cinque Ports, which of course included Sandwich, Rye and Winchelsea.

50 Grell, *Dutch Calvinists*, p. 7; Goose, "The 'Dutch' in Colchester", pp. 265–71.

51 Trim, "Sir Thomas Bodley", p. 316; Oakley (ed.), *Actes du Consistoire*, Vol. 2, 1571–1577, pp. 76, 78.

52 Berry (ed.), *John Stubbs's 'Gaping Gulf'*, p. 138.

53 I am obliged to Mark Fissel for this information, which derives from his work in the Norwich archives.

54 Devereux (ed.), *Lives and Letters*, pp. 478, 485, 491; Devereux Papers, MS I, fol. 28r; BN, Fonds Clairambault 1907, fol. 133r.

55 PRO, SP 12/259, fol. 179r (I owe this reference to Paul Hammer); van Meteren's album amicorum, Bodleian Library, Oxford, MS Douce 68, fol. 42v. On van Meteren's circle, mostly comprising other Dutchmen resident in London, see van Dorsten, "'I. C. O'", pp. 8–20.

56 Carter, "Marriage Counselling", p. 94, citing Bodley to Burghley, PRO, SP 84/41, fol. 152. The registers of betrothals, marriages, citizenship, and court sentences held in the gemeentearchief of Leiden are printed in Tammel *et al.* (eds.), *Pilgrims and Other People*.

57 Browne to Walsingham, *CSP Foreign*, Vol. 21, iv, p. 37.

58 Cokayne, *Complete Baronetage*, pp. 61–2.

59 See John Chamberlain to Dudley Carleton, 28 Feb. 1603, McClure (ed.), *Letters of John Chamberlain*, Vol. 1, no. 61, p. 187; Cokayne, *Complete Peerage*, Vol. 3, p. 400; *DNB*, Vol. 8, p. 1275, 14, pp. 934–5; van Nierop, *Van Ridders tot Regenten*, p. 82; Wood (ed.), *Memorials of the Holles Family*, pp. 84–5, at 85; Koninklijke Bibliotheek, Den Haag, Handschriften, lias 132.G.27; ARA Collectie Aanwinsten 1098, fol. 82r; *HMC*, De L'Isle & Dudley MSS, Vol. 2, p. 520.

60 McGurk, "Wild Geese", p. 40.

61 Oakley (ed.), *Actes du Consistoire* , p. 87.

62 Rowse, *Simon Forman*, p. 52; Cokayne, *Complete Peerage*, Vol. 3, p. 400.

63 Sorlien (ed.), *Diary of John Manningham*, p. 86.

64 Tammel *et al.* (eds), *Pilgrims and Other People*, pp. 32, 241, 245.

65 Van Nierop, *Van Ridders tot Regenten*, pp. 82–4; Morgan to Christian Huygens, 27 Apr. 1589, ARA, Collectie Aanwinsten 593; Carter, p. 94; *List and Analysis of State Papers, Foreign Series, Elizabeth I*, no. 79, p. 101.

66 ARA, Collectie Aanwinsten 593. Morgan was not unique among English soldiers in Dutch pay, for though the Veres conducted all their correspondence with their Dutch paymasters in French, at least two other mercenary officers, Captain Edmund Bishop and Anthony Slingsby also wrote in Dutch: see Bishop to William Davison, 15 Apr. 1578, PRO, SP 83/6, fol. 19r; and Slingsby's petition to the States General, 1606, ARA, Archief van Johan van Oldenbarnevelt, no. 2979.

67 Galatians 3:28.

68 8 Oct. 1572, BL, Lansdowne MSS 15, fol. 199v.

69 Silver, *Paradoxes of Defense*: online edition available at:http://www.pbm.com/~lindahl/paradoxes.html.

70 Bradshaw, *Myld and Just Defence of Certeyne Arguments* . . . (1606), quoted by Collinson in "England 1558–1640", p. 213 and *Birthpangs of Protestant England*, p. 16, and by Alastair Duke, "Perspectives on European Calvinism", p. 1.

12

Alien Immigrants to England, One Hundred Years On

Lien Luu

The essays in this volume present the fruits of some exciting research undertaken in recent years on the first major wave of refugees to England. The movement, originating largely from the southern Netherlands, was a complex affair, comprising a series of emigrations across several generations, beginning in the 1560s and lasting until the early seventeenth century.[1] However, within this emigration it is possible to pinpoint two significant waves: one was precipitated by the pending arrival of the Duke of Alva in 1566–7; the other, by the fall of Antwerp in 1585. In the first wave, the refugees fled largely to England and Germany, while in the second exodus many also chose to settle in the Dutch Republic. The migration to England after 1585 was numerically smaller than the previous wave. These migrations from the southern Netherlands represented two of the four major waves of migration in early modern Europe, alongside the expulsion of the Jews in 1492 and the Huguenots after 1685.[2]

The arrival of these refugees in England had a far reaching impact on its culture and society for two reasons. First, their exodus involved the transplanting of whole communities or sections of the local economy, and there was little precedent for this type of sudden, targeted population transfer.[3] Second, the emigrants, with the skilled and educated over-represented in the exodus, came from the more advanced parts of Europe, which had long furnished England with manufactured goods to meet its material needs. Since the nineteenth century historical interest in immigration, influenced in part by the need to explain the industrial revolution in England, centred largely on the economic impact of these immigrants. In many standard economic history textbooks, immigrants were portrayed as harbingers of economic change and – as discussed in chapter one above – William Cunningham was a leading exponent of this thesis. Typical of this viewpoint is Ephraim Lipson who, in *The Economic History of England* (1934), claimed that each wave of immigration represented an economic landmark. According to Lipson, the immigration of the Flemings in the fourteenth century constituted the first industrial landmark in the industrial history of England, and the influx of the Dutch and Walloons in the sixteenth century and Huguenots in the seventeenth century the second and third landmarks. Their immigration, he argued, benefited many branches of the national economy. Hence in the sixteenth century, aliens introduced new industries such as the new draperies, fine linen, copper and brass, glassmaking, paper and cordage, while they also revived the silk industry and improved the art of dyeing. In the seventeenth century the Huguenots gave stimulus to a range of manufactures including silk, linen, hats, soap and white paper. Like Cunningham, Lipson saw a clear link between overseas immigration and the subsequent rise of Britain to industrial supremacy, and he concluded that:

> the settlement of aliens must be assigned a prominent place among the factors which have helped to build up the industrial supremacy of England. The infusion of new blood enriched and strengthened the national life, while the technical skill and knowledge of the industrial arts, possessed by the strangers within her gates, enabled this country to wrest from her rivals the secrets of important industries and become the workshop of the world.[4]

In the post-war years, as development issues came to dominate international agenda, historians became less interested in the industrial revolution and more concerned with the transfer of technology as a means of alleviating world poverty. As migration was regarded as the principal medium of technology transfer, historical interest shifted to an explanatory model of the factors that affected a successful diffusion of innovations and skills. In a pioneering article published in 1951, Scoville examined the different types of migration in the early modern period and assessed the relative effectiveness of each as a means of diffusion: the individual, the group and the minority. He regarded the last as the most effective means of diffusion because it carried with it a "whole set of institutions".[5] However, this failed to stimulate wider scholarly research and there are few detailed studies of how early modern migrations, such as the exodus from the southern Netherlands in the sixteenth century and the Huguenots in the seventeenth century, precipitated the diffusion of innovations and technologies.

In the 1960s, historical interest in immigrants shifted away from theoretical framework towards case studies of particular crafts. Prompted in part by dissatisfaction with generalisations about the contribution of immigrants commonly found in economic textbooks, this approach focused on an analysis of the contribution of immigrants to industries in which they were largely associated with, such as the new draperies and glassmaking. However, the heyday of early modern migration studies came in the late 1980s and 1990s, with the appearance of important works such as Gwynn's *Huguenot Heritage* (1985), to mark the bicentenary of the Revocation of the Edict of Nantes in 1685, Pettegree's *Foreign Protestant Communities* (1986) and Grell's *Dutch Calvinists in Tudor and Early Stuart England* (1989). Putting the foreign communities at the centre of historical research, these works explored their religious importance as well as the organisation and functioning of their communities. They also stimulated several important Ph.D. theses in the 1990s on sixteenth-century immigrant communities in Sandwich, Norwich, Southampton and London. These studies are highly significant because, with their focus on prosopography, they have opened up a previously blackbox view of the immigrant communities in early modern England.

The utilisation of records created by the foreign communities themselves is undoubtedly a key factor responsible for this shift in paradigm. Besides the use of traditional English sources such as the records of the national and local governments and guilds, historians have also used extensively other important sources. The archive of the Dutch Church of London, published by J. H. Hessels and cited in this volume, is a cornucopia, containing valuable information about the foreign communities including correspondence between various Churches in England, petitions sent by the Dutch Church to the Crown and Privy Council for protection against informers, funds raised for military campaigns, international charitable support and disciplinary measures against its members.[6] The French Church also kept good records, and historians have made good use of sources such as minutes of the Consistory and account books to reconstruct the lives of its members.[7] The use of overseas archival sources has also added another dimension to the study of immigrants in England. Especially valuable are the records of the Council of Troubles, a tribunal set up by the Duke of Alva in 1567 to investigate the culprits responsible for the disturbances of the previous summer. Suspected individuals were summoned by the Council to appear before a local magistrate to explain their involvement. Many of the politically active had of course fled the country and sentences were therefore handed down in their absence: some were banished, others condemned to death. Various lists such as summons lists, lists of names of those involved in the Troubles and sentences, are extremely useful for the study of migration since they often listed the names and occupations of those who had fled. The properties of those who had been banished, executed or failed to appear were confiscated by the state, and the inventories of confiscated goods are excellent sources for gauging the levels of material wealth of refugees.[8]

By drawing upon some of these excellent sources, this collection of essays presents fresh perspectives on the immigrant communities, exploring their multi-faceted nature as well as raising pertinent issues relating to the study of immigrants in general. The first concerns the question of terminology: what is the apt term to describe those who left their homelands and settled in another country? Are they immigrants, refugees or exiles? The editors have chosen the term "immigrant" as the title for this volume, but the use of such a general term conceals the distinctiveness of different groups. Some historians such as Heinz Schilling describe the flight of the refugees from the Netherlands in the sixteenth century and from France in the seventeenth century as part of a "confessional migration", others like Andrew Pettegree prefer "Protestant migration", while Grell calls the exodus a "diaspora". Although neat and convenient, the use of such terms is problematic because they imply that all newcomers had come for religious reasons. This was not true. In December 1573, for example, 26 per cent of aliens living in London were forced to confess on investigation that they had come "to seek a living" rather than for a presumed religious cause.[9] Linguistic labels, such as "Dutch", "Flemish" and "Walloon" have also been used to describe the arrivals, but these too are problematic. This is because, as Raymond Fagel has shown in chapter two, they mask the diverse regional differences among the incomers. The Walloons in Norwich, for example, were not the same as the Walloons in Southampton, because while the former came predominantly from Lille in Flanders, Hainaut, Artois, Cambrai and Brabant, the latter originated largely from Valenciennes, Tournai and Armentieres. Likewise, the Dutch in Sandwich were not the same as the Dutch in London: those in Sandwich originated from the Westkwartier, while the Dutch in London had come largely from Antwerp and Brussels. The labels historians use to refer to a particular immigrant group may not, then, be the same ones that the newcomers would themselves use to describe their identity.

The integration or assimilation of immigrants in English society is another pertinent issue attracting a lot of interest: the essays in this volume suggest several factors which might have affected their assimilation in early modern society. The legal status of immigrants was clearly a significant one. Unlike modern society where it is possible for immigrants to adopt a "British" identity, the legal classification of immigrants into "aliens", "denizens" and "naturalized subjects" in the early modern period created potential barriers to integration, a hierarchy of status among aliens and made them highly visible and vulnerable. Exclusion was another factor which hindered assimilation. Membership of livery companies was a crucial step to climbing the social ladder as it was a "class marker" but, as Ward has shown, many livery companies barred immigrants from entry into their ranks. The Weavers' Company was one exception, which sought to find a compromise between the need to be benevolent and to protect its members from competition by creating a special category called "foreign brethren". However, this caused considerable conflict between rulers of the company and its members, who saw strangers as threats to their livelihoods. As Ward has shown, the immigrants were often blamed for social problems, such as raising rents and the costs of living, spreading infection and causing overcrowding. This raises the thorny question of whether Englishmen were xenophobic. While recognising that in hard times immigrants provided useful scapegoats, Nigel Goose has rightly cautioned against the uncritical reliance on reports of foreign observers to gauge English attitudes, and emphasizes the lack of outbreaks of violence directed against them, in London and the provinces, throughout the period defined by the first refuge. English views, he argues, were ambivalent, coloured by religious, political and economic considerations and mutable over time, despite a growing sense of national identity that could easily shade off into arrogance. It was the lowest social groups in early modern England, just as today, who appear to have more commonly exhibited anti-alien sentiments, and there is great scope for further research into the degree to which this found expression in inter-personal violence.

Assimilation of immigrants may have been impeded by the perception of their settlement as transient. As Littleton has shown, the refugees were highly mobile, frequently travelling back and forth to the continent to conduct business, see families and friends, look for work, and fight religious wars. It is possible that some of them saw their time in England as at best a temporary and transient refuge. If that was the case, their sense of belonging and bonding with the new homeland was not fully cultivated. The essays also point to the blurred boundary between 'homeland' and 'exile': with many refugees constantly moving back and forth, they were living between the two. By the early seventeenth century the communities appear to have become more settled, as the high proportion in both London and the provinces now described as "born in the realm" suggests. Also on a positive note, Trim has shown in chapter eleven that ideological solidarity and the Calvinist religion did help transcend any hostile tendencies towards foreigners among Englishmen. Fighting alongside the Dutch and French, for example, reduced even common English soldiers' xenophobia and encouraged trans-ethnic marriages with Dutch women.

Impact is the other theme explored in this volume. As several essays have shown, the stranger churches were instrumental in sustaining the international Calvinist struggle against papistical tyranny, by providing material assistance to their brethren churches abroad, by training and supplying the churches on the continent with ministers and by giving charitable funds. But, as Spicer has shown in chapter five, the

Stranger Churches occupied another role: they were the heart of the community, a place of gathering, the hub of community religious life and the communal focal point. At the same time, as the physical embodiment of the foreign population, they could also form the focal point of opposition.

In chapter seven Goose demonstrated how the immigrants exerted a considerable impact on the English economy, an impact that was widely appreciated at the time and which underpinned the support and protection they received from both local and national authorities. Various aspects of industry, commerce, finance and agriculture benefited from foreign immigration and influence, with the most notable contribution taking the form of the introduction of new types of textile cloth. While giving due credit for the breadth of the foreign contribution, however, Goose argued that the importance of indigenous developments should also be appreciated, as well as the readiness with which the English adopted and adapted new methods, providing a corrective to the overly enthusiastic appreciation given by Cunningham a century ago. Immigrants also exerted a significant cultural impact, on book production, costumes and fashions, Delftware, fine art and luxury goods. According to Esser, immigrants were interested in the written word and possessed a high degree of literacy. Is this characteristic of all immigrants or only Protestant refugees? The answer is probably the former, because of the selective nature of migration. The hardships involved in the process of uprooting means that only the most energetic, risk-prone, literate and educated would undertake those risks.

Despite their importance, the first wave of immigrants is still commonly overshadowed in the literature by the second wave of immigrants – the Huguenots. The Dutch and Walloons do not appear to dominate popular perceptions of early modern immigration as much as the Huguenots. The latter left a much deeper imprint on English culture and society. This might be partly the product of their differing propensity for assimilation. The sixteenth-century immigrants may have assimilated less readily because, in the early years at least, some of them may never have had any intention of staying in England. Many had fled before the Duke of Alva arrived, and therefore did not suffer from persecution. The political situation on the Continent was also much more fluid, enabling many to move back and forth, and therefore they were prevented from anchoring socially in English soils. They were also much more socially divided because of linguistic differences, with the result that each group had their own church, hindering the development of a real sense of unity among them. The Huguenots, on the other hand, faced a very different situation. Some had suffered terror and torture and had a different relationship with their native homeland. Their hopes of return were bleak, and many had to accept the reality of establishing themselves permanently in England. Some took appropriate steps to preserve the memories of their French background and their traditions.[10]

In 1885, a formal commitment was made by the descendants of Huguenots to preserve their French heritage. In that year, the Huguenot Society was established "to promote the publication and interchange of Knowledge about Huguenots and to form a bond of fellowship of those who, whether or not of Huguenot descent, respect and admire the Huguenots and seek to perpetuate their memory".[11] The Society was instrumental in the promotion of scholarship concerning immigrants in the early modern period by publishing primary sources, establishing a library, making funds available to help with archival research and organizing conferences to mark anniversaries and publishing the proceedings. In 1985, the Society organised a conference to mark the 200th anniversary of the Revocation of the Edict of Nantes, and in 2000 a conference to celebrate the 450-year-old Charter granted by Edward VI in 1550. With the help of its quarterly journal, the *Proceedings*, the Huguenot Society has been able to disseminate much recent research. Thanks to the work of its members, especially the late Irene Scouloudi and Randolph Vigne (the editor of the *Proceedings*), the Society is active in promoting scholarship on early modern migrations. Yet despite progress in recent years, there is still a lack of historical studies, especially general works, on immigrants in Britain.[12] The scholarship remains very much fragmented and the problem lies in two areas. First, the study of foreign immigrants is still not part of mainstream British history and studies on migration in early modern Britain often make little or no reference to their arrival.[13] There is clearly a need to integrate foreign immigration with other migratory movements in early modern Britain. Second, a comprehensive and authoritative study of the settlement of foreign immigrants in Britain is still lacking. However, there is a general acceptance that foreigners have exerted a deep imprint on British history. This recognition prompted the production of a three-part documentary on the "Mongrel Nation" in 2003, examining the influences of successive waves of invaders, settlers and immigrants on the British landscape. A written companion to this programme might be useful in stimulating some general interest in early modern migration scholarship.[14] It is hoped that the present volume will make a contribution towards a deeper understanding and appreciation of the role played by immigrants in English society in the Tudor and early Stuart period, both in its own right, and by acting as a stimulus to further research.

Notes

1   Grell, *Dutch Calvinists*, pp. 99–100.
2   Israel, *Dutch Republic*, p. 308.
3   Pettegree, "Protestant Migration", pp. 457–8.
4   Lipson, *Economic History*, Vol. 3, pp. 56–7, 60–1.
5   Scoville, "Huguenots and the Diffusion of Technology".
6   Hessels, *Ecclesiae Londino-Batavae Archivum, Epistulae et Tractatus* (3 Vols, Cambridge, 1889–97).
7   Johnson (ed.), *Actes du Consistoire*; Oakley (ed.), *Actes du Consistoire*.
8   Jamees, *Inventaris van het archief van de Raad van Beroerten*. For summon lists, see AGR, Conseil des Troubles, MS 18–21 (summon lists); MS 155 (lists of names of those executed and banished from Valenciennes); and MS 6 (sentences). Some of these materials have been published by Verheyden in *Le Conseil des Troubles*. For inventories of confiscated goods see *Conseil des Troubles* MS 163–166; for Valenciennes see MS 315A and 315 bis; for Tournai see MS 328.
9   PRO SP12/84/1 f.433 printed in Kirk and Kirk, Part 2, p.156
10 Gwynn, *Huguenot Heritage*, pp. 169–70.
11 See www.huguenotsociety.org.uk.
12 Panayi, "The Immigrant Experience", pp. 71–5.
13 Clark and Souden (eds), *Migration and Society* and Whyte, *Migration and Society* focus on internal migration within Britain and on emigration to America. There is little or no focus on the foreign immigration in this period which may be linked to the other movements.
14 This is the title of a recent three-part documentary programme shown on the Discovery Channel in June 2003.

Consolidated Bibliography

An Act of Common Councell, prohibiting all strangers borne, and forrainers, to use any trades ... (1606).

The Accusation and Impeachment of William Laud, Archbishop of Canterbury, by the House of Commons, Harleian Miscellany, Vol. 4 (London, 1745), pp. 545–7.

Adams, S., (ed.), *Household Accounts and Disbursement Books of Robert Dudley, Earl of Leicester, 1558–1561, 1584–1586*, Camden Society 5th ser., Vol. 6 (Cambridge & London, 1995).

Adams, S., "A Puritan Crusade? The Composition of the Earl of Leicester's Expedition to the Netherlands, 1585–1586", in *The Dutch in Crisis, 1585–1588: People and Politics in Leicester's Time* (Leiden, 1988).

Addleshaw, G.W.O. and Etchells, F., *The Architectural Setting of Anglican Worship* (London, 1948).

Andrewes, J., "Industries in Kent, c.1500–1640", in Zell (ed.), *Early Modern Kent*, pp. 105–39.

Andrewes, J. and Zell, M., "The Population of Sandwich from the Accession of Elizabeth I to the Civil War", *Archaeologia Cantiana*, Vol. 122 (2002), 79–99.

Anon. (Andrew Marvell), *The Character of Holland* (London, 1665), *Harleian Miscellany*, Vol. 5, pp. 575–6.

Anon., *A Late Voyage to Holland* (1691), *Harleian Miscellany*, Vol. 2 (London, 1744), pp. 569–81.

Anon., *How to Advance the Trade of the Nation, and Employ the Poor, Harleian Miscellany*, Vol. 4 (London, 1745), pp. 366–70.

Anon., *Sir Walter Raleigh's Ghost: Or England's Forewarner, Harleian Miscellany*, Vol. 5 (London, 1745), pp. 52–65.

Anon., *The Apprentices of Londons Petition presented to the Honourable Court of Parliament* (London, 1641).

Anon., *The Heads of the Petition* (London, 1647).

Anon., *The Pacquet-Boat Advice: Or a Discourse Concerning the War with France* (1678), *Harleian Miscellany*, Vol. 2, pp. 380–7.

Anon., *The Petition of the Weamen of Middlesex Which they intended to have presented to the High Court of Parliament* (London, 1641).

Anon., *The Wicked Plots and Perfidious Practices of the Spaniards against the Seventeen Provinces of the Netherlands, Harleian Miscellany*, Vol. 2 (London, 1744), pp. 393–400.

Archer, I., "Responses to Alien Immig rants in London, c. 1400–1650", *Proceedings of the 1993 Prato Conference*, Vol. 18 (1994), pp. 755–74.

Archer, I., *The Pursuit of Stability: Social Relations in Elizabethan London* (Cambridge, 1991).

Arkell, T., Evans N., and Goose, N. (eds), *When Death Do Us Part: Understanding and Interpreting the Probate Evidence of Early Modern England* (Oxford, 2000).

Ashton, R., *The Crown and the Money Market 1603–1640* (Oxford, 1960).

Aston, A., "Segregation in Church", in W. Sheils and D. Wood (eds), *Women in the Church, Studies in Church History*, Vol. 27 (1990).

Augstein, H.F., *James Cowles Prichard's Anthropology: Remaking the Science of Man in Early Nineteenth-Century Britain* (Amsterdam, 1999).

Backhouse, M., "Guerrilla War and Banditry in the Sixteenth Century: the Wood Beggars in the Westkwartier of Flanders (1567–68)", *Archiv für Reformationsgeschichte*, Vol. 74 (1983).

Backhouse, M., "The Flemish Refugees in Sandwich (1561–1603)", in *Revolt and Emigration* (Dikkebus, 1988).

Backhouse, M., "The Strangers at Work in Sandwich: Native Envy of an Industrious Minority 1561–1603", *Immigrants and Minorities*, Vol. 10 (1991), pp. 70–99.

Backhouse, M., *The Flemish and Walloon Communities at Sandwich During the Reign of Elizabeth I (1561–1603)*, (Brussels, 1995).

Backhouse, M.F. (ed.), "Dokumenten Betreffende de Godsdiensttroebelen in het Westkwartier: Jan Comerlynck en Tien Zijner Gezellen voor de Ieperse Vierschaer 1568–69", *Handelingen van de Koninklijke Commissie voor Geschiedenis*, Vol. 138 (1972).

Backhouse, M.F., *The Flemish and Walloon Communities at Sandwich During the Reign of Elizabeth I (1561–1603)*, 3 Vols (Unpublished Ph.D. thesis, University of Southampton, 1991).

Bade, K.J., Emmer, P.C., Lucassen, L., and Oltmer, J., "Migration and Integration: a Conceptual Guideline for Authors of the Encyclopaedia of Migration, Integration and Minorities since the 17th Century: a European Encyclopaedia" (communication from Klaus Bade and Jochen Oltmer, July 2002).

Barbour, V., *Capitalism in Amsterdam in the 17th Century* (Ann Arbor, 1963).

Barnes, T.G., "The Prerogative and Environmental Control of London Building in the Early Seventeenth Century: The Lost Opportunity", *California Law Review*, Vol. 58 (1970), pp. 1332–63.

Barrington, R., "A Venetian Secretary in England: an Unpublished Diplomatic Report in the Biblioteca Marciana, Venice", *Historical Research*, Vol. 70 (1997).

Battles, F.L. (ed.), John Calvin, *Institutes of the Christian Religion* (Grand Rapids, 1975).

Beier, A.L., "Engine of Manufacture: the Trades of London", in A.L. Beier and R.A.P. Finlay (eds), *The Making of the Metropolis: London 1500–1700*, pp. 141–67.

Beier, A.L., "Social Problems in Elizabethan London", *Journal of Interdisciplinary History*, Vol. 9 (1978).

Beier, A.L. and Finlay, R.A.P. (eds), *The Making of the Metropolis: London 1500–1700* (London, 1986).

Bellamy, J. *et al.*, *Culture and Belief in Europe 1450–1600: The British Isles* (Milton Keynes, 1990).

Bense, J.F., *The Anglo-Dutch Relations from the Earliest Times to the Death of William the Third* (The Hague, 1924).

Bermingham, A. and Brewer, J. (eds), *The Consumption of Culture, 1600–1800: Image, Object, Text* (London, 1995).

Berry, L.E. (ed.), *John Stubbs's 'Gaping Gulf' with Letters and Other Relevant Documents* (Charlottesville, Virginia, 1968).

Bettey, J.H., "A Fruitless Quest for Wealth: The Mining of Alum and Copperas in Dorset c. 1568–1617", *Southern History*, Vol. 23 (2001), pp. 1–9.

Bindoff, S.T., Hurstfield, J. and Williams, C.H. (eds), *Elizabethan Government and Society: Essays Presented to Sir John Neale* (London, 1961).

Birch, T., *Memoirs of the Reign of Queen Elizabeth . . . from the Papers of Anthony Bacon* (London, 1754).

Black, J., *The British Abroad: The Grand Tour in the Eighteenth Century*, 2nd edn (Stroud, 1992).

Blockmans, W. and Prevenier W., *The Burgundian Netherlands* (Cambridge, 1985).

Blok, P.J. (ed.), *Correspondentie van en Betreffende Lodewijk van Nassau en Andere Onuitgegeven Documenten*, Werken van het Historisch Genootshcap te Utrecht, n.s., Vol. 47 (Utrecht, 1887).

Boersma, O. and Jelsma, A.J. (eds), *Acta van het Consistorie van de Nederlandse Gemeente te Londen, 1569–1585*, Rijks Geschiedkundige Publicatiën, Kleine serie, Vol. 76 (The Hague, 1993).

Boersma, O. and Jelsma, A.J., *Unity in Multiformity. The Minutes of the Coetus of London, 1575 and the Consistory Minutes of the Italian Church of London, 1570–1591, Publications of the Huguenot Society*, Vol. 59 (1997).

Boersma, O., *Vluchtig voorbeeld. De Nederlandse, Franse en Italiaanse vluchtelingenkerken in Londen 1568–1585* (Kampen, 1994).

Boersma, O., *Vluchtig Voorbeeld: de Nederlandse, Franse en Italiaanse Vluchtelingenkerken in Londen, 1568–1585* (Kampen, 1994).

Bolton, J.L. (ed.), *The Alien Population of London in the Fifteenth Century: the Subsidy Rolls of 1440 and 1483–84* (Stamford, 1998).

Boulton, J., *Neighbourhood and Society: A London Suburb in the Seventeenth Century* (Cambridge, 1987).

Bower, J., "Kent Towns, 1540–1640", in M. Zell (ed.), *Early Modern Kent 1540–1640*, pp. 141–76.

Bradley, S. and Pevsner, N., *The Buildings of England. London: The City Churches* (London, 1998).

Bradshaw, W., *A Myld and Just Defence of Certeyne Arguments . . .* (London, 1606).

Bratchel, M.E., "Regulation and Group-Consciousness in the Later History of London's Italian Merchant Colonies", *Journal of European Economic History*, Vol. 9 (1980).

Bratchel, M.E., "Alien Merchant Colonies in Sixteenth-Century England: Community Organization and Social Mores", *Journal of Medieval and Renaissance Studies*, Vol. 14 (1984).

Brettel, C.B. and Hollifield, J. (eds), *Migration Theory. Talking across Disciplines* (New York and London, 2000).

Brettel, C.B., "Theorizing Migration in Anthropology. The Social Construction of Networks, Identities, Communities and Globalspace", in Brettel and Hollifield (eds), *Migration Theory*, pp. 97–137.

Brewer, J. and Porter, R. (eds), *Consumption and the World of Goods* (London, 1993).

Brewer, T., *A Newe Ballad Composed in Commendation of the Societie or Companie of the Porters to the Tune of in Edenbrugh, Behold* (London, 1605).

Bridbury, A.R., *Economic Growth: England in the Later Middle Ages* (London, 1962).

Briels, J, *Zuid-Nederlandse Immigratie 1572–1630* (Haarlem, 1978).

Brigden, S., *London and the Reformation* (Oxford, 1989).

Britton, F., *London Delftware* (London, 1987).

Bruce, J. et al. (eds), *Calendar of State Papers Domestic Series*, 22 Vols. (London, 1858–93).

Bulteel, J., *A Relation of the Troubles of the Three Forraign Churches in Kent. Caused by the Injunctions of William Laud Archbishop of Canterbury Anno Dom. 1634* (London, 1645).

Burn, J.S., *The History of the French, Walloon, Dutch and other Protestant Refugees Settled in England* (London, 1846).

Burnet, G.B., *The Holy Communion in the Reformed Church of Scotland, 1560–1960* (Edinburgh, 1960).

Burt, R., "The International Diffusion of Technology During the Early Modern Period: the Case of the British Non-Ferrous Mining Industry", *Economic History Review*, Vol. 44 (1991), pp. 249–71.

Burton, R., *The Anatomy of Melancholy* (1621), in T.C. Faulkner, N.K. Kiessling and R.L. Blair (eds) 6 Vols (Oxford, 1989–2000).

Byford, M., "The Birth of a Protestant Town: the Process of Reformation in Tudor Colchester, 1530–80", in P. Collinson and J. Craig (eds), *The Reformation in English Towns 1500–1640* (Basingstoke, 1998), pp. 23–47.

Byford, M.S., "The Price of Protestantism. Assessing the Impact of Religious Change on Elizabethan Essex: the Cases of Heydon and Colchester, 1559–1594" (Unpublished DPhil. thesis, Oxford, 1988).

Carlin, N., "Liberty and Fraternities in the English Revolution: The Politics of London Artisans' Protests, 1635–1659", *International Review of Social History*, Vol. 39 (1994), pp. 223–54.

Carter, A.C., "Marriage Counselling in the Early Seventeenth Century: England and the Netherlands Compared", in J.A. Van Dorsten, *Ten Studies in Anglo-Dutch Relations*, PTBI, gen. ser., Vol. 5 (Leiden & London, 1974).

Chalklin, C.W., *Seventeenth-Century Kent* (London, 1965).

Chamberlayne, E., *Angliae Notitia, or the Present State of England*, 5th edn (London, 1671).

Chamberlayne, E., *Angliae Notitia, or the Present State of England*, 19th edn, *with Great Additions and Augmentations* (London, 1700).

Chamier, A.C. (ed.), *Les Actes des Colloques des Eglises Françaises et des Synodes des Eglises Etrangeres Réfugiées en Angleterre, 1581–1654, Publications of the Huguenot Society*, Vol. 2 (1890).

Chaney, E., *The Evolution of the Grand Tour. Anglo-Italian Cultural Relations since the Renaissance* (London, 1998).

Chapman, S.D., "The Genesis of the British Hosiery Industry 1600–1750", *Textile History*, Vol. 3 (1972), pp. 7–46.

Chartier, R. (ed.), *Les Usages de l'Imprimé (XVe–XIXe siècle)* (Paris, 1987).

Chartier, R., *L'Ordre des Livres, Lecteurs, Auteurs, Bibliothèques en Europe entre XIVe et XVIIIe Siècles* (Aix-en-Provence, 1992).

Churchyard, T., *A Generall Rehearsall of Warres* (London, 1579).

Churchyard, T., *A Lamentable and Pitifull Description of the Wofull Warres in Flaunders* (London, 1578).

Churchyard, T., *A Pleasant Discourse of Court and Wars with a Replication to Them Both* (London, 1596; repr. 1816).

Cipolla, C. (ed.), *The Fontana Economic History of Europe: the Sixteenth and Seventeenth Centuries* (Glasgow, 1974).

Cipolla, C., *Before the Industrial Revolution: European Society and Economy, 1000–1700* (London, 1976).

Clark, J.C.D., "Protestantism, Nationalism and National Identity, 1660–1832", *Historical Journal*, Vol. 43 (2000), pp. 249–76.

Clark, P. (ed.), *Country Towns in Pre-industrial England* (Leicester, 1981).

Clark, P. (ed.), *The Cambridge Urban History of Britain, Vol. II 1540–1840* (Cambridge, 2000).

Clark, P. and Murfin, L., *The History of Maidstone. The Making of a Modern County Town* (Stroud, 1995).

Clark, P. and Slack, P. (eds), *Crisis and Order in English Towns 1500–1700* (London, 1972).

Clark, P. and Slack, P., *English Towns in Transition 1500–1700* (Oxford, 1976).

Clark, P. and Souden, D. (eds), *Migration and Society in Early Modern England* (London, 1987).

Clark, P., "A Crisis Contained? The Condition of English Towns in the 1590s", in *idem* (ed.), *The European Crisis of the 1590s: Essays in Comparative History* (London, 1985), pp. 44–66.

Clark, P., "The Migrant in Kentish Towns", in Clark and Slack (eds), *Crisis and Order in English Towns 1500–1700*.

Clark, P., *English Provincial Society from the Reformation to the Revolution: Religion, Politics and Society in Kent 1500–1640* (Hassocks, 1977).

Clay, C.G.A., *Economic Expansion and Social Change: England 1500–1700*, 2 Vols (Cambridge, 1984).

Clifton, R., "Fear of Popery", in Russell (ed.), *Origins of the English Civil War*.

Cogswell, T., "England and the Spanish Match", in Cust and Hughes (eds), *Conflict in Early Stuart England*, pp. 107–33.

Cogswell, T., *The Blessed Revolution: English Politics and the Coming of War, 1621–1624* (Cambridge, 1989).

Cohen, M., "Manliness, Effeminacy and the French: Gender and the Construction of National Character in Eighteenth-Century England", in T. Hitchcock and M. Cohen (eds), *English Masculinities 1660–1800* (London, 1999), pp. 44–61.

Cohen, M., "The Grand Tour: Constructing the English Gentleman in Eighteenth-Century France", *History of Education*, Vol. 21 (1992), pp. 241–57.

Cokayne, G.E., *The Complete Baronetage* (repr., Stroud, 1993).

Cokayne, G.E., *The Complete Peerage of England, Scotland, Ireland, Great Britain and the United Kingdom, Extant, Extinct or Dormant*, 15 Vols (London, 1910–40).

Coleman, D.C., "Industrial Growth and Industrial Revolutions", *Economica*, Vol. 23 (1956).

Coleman, D.C., *The Economy of England 1450–1750* (Oxford, 1977).

Colley, L., *Britons: Forging the Nation 1707–1837* (London, 1992).

Collinson, C., "Enterprise and Experiment in the Elizabethan Iron Industry: the Career of Thomas Proctor", *Yorkshire Archaeological Journal*, Vol. 68 (1996), pp. 191–208.

Collinson, P., "England and International Calvinism, 1558–1640", in M. Prestwich (ed.), *International Calvinism 1541–1715* (Oxford, 1985).

Collinson, P., "Europe in Britain: Protestant Strangers and the English Reformation", in Vigne and Littleton (eds), *From Strangers to Citizens*, pp. 57–67.

Collinson, P., "John Field and Elizabethan Puritanism," in Bindoff, Hurstfield and Williams (eds), *Elizabethan Government and Society*.

Collinson, P., "The Elizabethan Puritans and the Foreign Reformed Churches in London", reprinted in Collinson, *Godly People* (first publ. *Proceedings of the Huguenot Society*, Vol. 20, 1964).

Collinson, P., *Godly People: Essays on English Protestantism and Puritanism* (London, 1983).

Collinson, P., *The Birthpangs of Protestant England: Religious and Cultural Change in the Sixteenth and Seventeenth Centuries* (Basingstoke, 1988).

Collinson, P., *The Elizabethan Puritan Movement* (Berkeley and Los Angeles, 1967).

Collinson, P., *The Religion of Protestants: The Church in English Society 1559–1625* (Oxford, 1982).

Consitt, F., *The London Weavers' Company* (Oxford, 1933).

Corfield, P., "A Provincial Capital in the Late Seventeenth Century: The Case of Norwich", in Clark and Slack (eds), *Crisis and Order in English Towns 1500–1700*, pp. 263–310.

Corfield, P., "East Anglia", in Clark (ed.), *The Cambridge Urban History of Britain, Vol. II 1540–1840* (Cambridge, 2000), pp. 31–8.

Cottret, B., *The Huguenots in England: Immigration and Settlement c.1550–1700* (Cambridge, 1991).

Coussemaker, C-E. de (ed.), *Troubles Religieux du XVIème Siècle dans la Flandre Maritime, 1560–70*, 4 Vols (Bruges, 1876).

Coward, B., *Social Change and Continuity in Early Modern England 1550–1750* (London, 1988).

Cowell, H. J., "The French-Walloon Church at Glastonbury 1550–1553", *Proceedings of the Huguenot Society*, Vol. 13 (1923–29), pp. 483–515.

Cracknell, B.E., *Canvey Island: the History of a Marshland Community*, Dept. English Local History, Occasional Papers No. 12 (Leicester, 1959).

Cramer, J.A. (ed.), *The Second Book of the Travels of Nicander Nucius, of Corcyra*, Camden Society Publications (London, 1841).

Crawford, D. (ed.), *Journals of Sir John Lauder Lord Fountainhall with His Observations on Public Affairs and Other Memoranda 1665–1676*, Scottish History Society (Edinburgh, 1900).

Crew, P.M., *Calvinist Preaching and Iconoclasm in the Netherlands, 1544–69* (Cambridge, 1978).

Cromwell, T., *History and Description of the Ancient Town and Borough of Colchester*, 2 Vols (London, 1825).

Cross, F.W., *History of the Walloon & Huguenot Church at Canterbury*, Publications of the Huguenot Society, Vol. 15 (London, 1898).

Cruso, J., *A Short Method for the Easie Resolving of Militarie Questions Propounded* (Cambridge, 1639).

Cruso, J., *Militaire Instructions for the Cavallrie* (Cambridge, 1632).

Cruso, J., *Uytbreydinge overn den Achsten Psalm Davids* (Amsterdam, 1642).

Cunningham, W., *Alien Immigrants to England* (London, 1897; 2nd edn, with an introduction by C. Wilson, London, 1969).

Cunningham, W., *Growth of English Industry and Commerce*, 2 Vols (1882).

Cust, R. and Hughes, A. (eds), *Conflict in Early Stuart England: Studies in Religion and Politics 1603–1642* (Harlow, 1989).

D. N., *Londons Looking-Glasse* (Saint-Omer, 1621).

D'Ewes, Sir Simonds, *A Compleat Journal of the Votes, Speeches and Debates, both of the House of Lords and House of Commons Throughout the Whole Reign of Queen Elizabeth* (Second edn, London, 1693).

Darby, G. (ed.), *The Origins and Development of the Dutch Revolt* (London and New York, 2001).

Darby, H.C., *The Draining of the Fens* (2nd edn, Cambridge, 1956).

Dasent, J.R. (ed.), *Acts of the Privy Council of England*, 32 Vols. (London, 1890–1907).

Davids, K. and Noordegraaf, L. (eds), *The Dutch Economy in the Golden Age* (Amsterdam, 1993).

Davids, K., "From De la Court to Vreede. Regulation and Self-Regulation in Dutch Economic Discourse from c. 1600 to the Napoleonic Era", *Journal of European Economic History*, Vol. 30 (2001), pp. 245–89.

Davies, D.W., *Dutch Influences on English Culture 1558–1625* (New York, 1964).

Davis, N.Z., "Rites of Violence", in Davis, *Society and Culture in Early Modern France* (Stanford, 1987).

Davis, R., *A Commercial Revolution: English Overseas Trade in the Seventeenth and Eighteenth Centuries* (London, 1967).

Davis, R., *English Overseas Trade 1500–1700* (London, 1973).

De Beer, E.S., "The Development of the Guide-Book until the Early Nineteenth Century", *The Journal of the British Archaeological Association*, 3rd Series, Vol. 15 (1952), pp. 35–46.

De Britaine, W., *The Dutch Usurpation, or a Brief View of the Behaviour of the States-General of the United Provinces, towards the Kings of Great-Britain*, Harleian Miscellany, Vol. 3 (London, 1745), pp. 1–16.

Den Blaauwen, A.L., *Dutch Silver 1580–1830* (1979).

De Vries, J. and Van der Woude, A., *The First Modern Economy: Success, Failure and the Perseverance of the Dutch Economy, 1500–1815* (Cambridge, 1997).

De Vries, J., "The Labour Market", in Davids and Noordegraaf (eds), *The Dutch Economy*, pp. 55–79.

Defoe, D., *A Tour Through the Whole Island of Great Britain* (1724–6) (Penguin edn, Harmondsworth, 1971).

Delafosse, M., "Les Corsaires Protestantes à La Rochelle (1570–1577)", *Bibliothèque de l'Ecole des Chartes*, Vol. 121 (1963).

Devereux, W.B. (ed.), *Lives and Letters of the Devereux, Earls of Essex, in the Reigns of Elizabeth, James I, and Charles I 1540–1646*, Vol. 2 (London, 1853).

Dickens, A.G., *Lollards and Protestants in the Diocese of York* (2nd edn, London 1982, first publ. 1959).

Dickens, A.G., *The English Reformation* (Fontana edn, London 1967, first publ. Batsford, 1964).

Dietz, B., "Antwerp and London: the Structure and Balance of Trade in the 1560s", in E.W. Ives and J. Knecht (eds), *Wealth and Power in Tudor England: Essays presented to S.T. Bindoff* (London, 1978).

Dietz, B., "Overseas Trade and Metropolitan Growth", in Beier and Finlay (eds), *London 1500–1700: the Making of the Metropolis*, pp. 115–40.

Digges, D. (ed.), *The Compleat Ambassador [. . .]* (London, 1655).

Dobson, R.B. (ed.), *The Peasants' Revolt of 1381* (London, 1970).

Dodd, A.H., "Mr. Myddelton the Merchant of Tower Street", in Bindoff, Hurstfield and Williams (eds), *Elizabethan Government and Society*.

Dolan, B., *Ladies of the Grand Tour* (London, 2001).

Dop, J.A., "Eliza's Knights: Soldiers, Poets and Puritans in the Netherlands 1572–1586" (Unpublished Ph.D. thesis, Leiden University, 1981).

Doran, S., *England and Europe in the Sixteenth Century* (Basingstoke, 1999).

Dresch, N.J.M. (ed.), "Rekening van Maerten Ruychaver, Thesaurier in het Noorder-Kwartier, 1572/1573", *Bijdragen en Mededeelingen van het Historisch Genootschap*, Vol. 49 (1928).

Du Boulay, F.R.H., *An Age of Ambition* (London, 1970).

Duffy, M., *The Englishman and the Foreigner: the English Satirical Print 1600–1832* (Cambridge, 1986).

Duke, A., "Martyrs with a Difference: Dutch Anabaptists Victims of Elizabethan Persecution", *Nederlands Archief voor Kerkgeschiedenis*, Vol. 80 (2000).

Duke, A., "Perspectives on European Calvinism", in A. Pettegree *et al.*, *Calvinism in Europe, 1540–1620* (Cambridge, 1994).

Duke, A., *Reformation and Revolt in the Netherlands* (London, 1990).

DuPlessis, R.S., "One Theory, Two Draperies, Three Provinces and a Multitude of Fabrics. The New Drapery of France, Flanders, Hainaut and the Tournaisis, *c.* 1500–1800", in Harte (ed.), *The New Draperies*.

Duplessis-Mornay, P., *Mémoires et Correspondance de Duplessis-Mornay* (ed.), P. Anguis, 12 Vols (Paris, 1824–5).

Durkin, G., "The Civic Government and Economy of Elizabethan Canterbury" (Unpublished Ph.D. thesis, University of Kent, 2001).

Duthie, R., "Introduction of Plants to Britain in the 16th and 17th Centuries by Strangers and Refugees", *Proceedings of the Huguenot Society*, Vol. 24 (1987), pp. 403–20.

Dyer, A., *Decline and Growth in English Towns 1400–1640* (Basingstoke and London, 1991).

Dyer, A.D., "Growth and Decay in English Towns", *Urban History Yearbook 1979* (Leicester, 1979), pp. 60–72.

Edwards, E., "Interpretations of the Influence of the Immigrant Population in Kent in the Sixteenth and Seventeenth Centuries", *Archaeologia Cantiana*, Vol. 122 (2002), pp. 275–92.

Elton, G.R., *The Tudor Constitution: Documents and Commentary* (Cambridge, 1982).

Emery, A., *Dartington Hall* (Oxford, 1970).

Eßer, R., "From the Hansa to the Present: Germans in Britain since the Middle Ages", in P. Panayi (ed.), *Germans in Britain Since 1500* (London, 1996).

Eßer, R., "The Norwich Strangers and the Sandwich Connection", WH info X afl.2, (1994), pp. 66–81.

Eßer, R., *Niederländische Exulanten im England des 16. und frühen 17. Jahrhunderts* (Berlin, 1996).

Evans, C., "A Skilled Workforce During the Transition to Industrial Society: Forgemen in the British Iron Trade", *Labour History Review*, Vol. 63 (1998), pp. 143–59.

Everitt, A., "The Marketing of Agricultural Produce", in Thirsk (ed.), *The Agrarian History of England and Wales Vol. IV 1540–1640*.

Evers, M., 'Religiones et Libertatis Ergo: Dutch Refugees in England and English Exiles in the Netherlands,' in *Refugees and Emigrants in the Dutch Republic and England: Papers of the Annual Symposium Held on 22 November* 1985 (Leiden, 1986), pp. 7–27.

Excavations in Norwich, 1971–78, part II, *East Anglian Archaeology*, Vol. 26 (1985).

Fagel, R., "The Netherlandish Presence in England Before the Coming of the Stranger Churches, 1480–1560", in Vigne and Littleton (eds), *From Strangers to Citizens*, pp. 7–16.

Falvey, H., "Crown Policy and Local Economic Context in the Berkhamsted Common Enclosure Dispute, 1618–42", *Rural History*, Vol. 12 (2001).

Finlay, R.A.P. and Shearer, B., "Population Growth and Suburban Expansion", in Beier and Finlay (eds), *The Making of the Metropolis: London 1500–1700*, pp. 37–59.

Finlay, R.A.P., *Population and Metropolis: The Demography of London 1580–1650* (Cambridge, 1981).

Firth, C.H. and Rait, R.S., *Acts and Ordinances of the Interregnum*, Vol. 1, 1642–9 (repr. Oxford, 1982).

Fisher, F.J. (ed.), *Essays in the Economic and Social History of Tudor and Stuart England* (Cambridge, 1961).

Fisher, F.J., "London's Export Trade in the Early Seventeenth Century", *Economic History Review*, Vol. 3 (1950), pp. 151–61.

Fisher, F.J., "Tawney's Century", in Fisher (ed.), *Essays in the Economic and Social History of Tudor and Stuart England*.

Fletcher, A, *Tudor Rebellions*, 2nd edn (London, 1973).

Foster, J., *Alumni Oxoniensis: The Members of the University of Oxford, 1500–1886*, 8 Vols. (Oxford, 1888–92).

French, H.R., "Social Status, Localism and the 'Middle Sort of People' in England 1620–1750", *Past & Present*, No. 166 (2000).

French, H.R., "The Search for the 'Middle Sort of People' in England", *Historical Journal*, Vol. 43 (2000).

French, M.J., "Privateering and the Revolt of the Netherlands: The *Watergeuzen* or Sea Beggars in Portsmouth, Gosport and the Isle of Wight 1570–71", *Proceedings of the Hampshire Field Club and Archaeological Society*, Vol. 47 (1991), pp. 171–80.

Fumerton, P., "London's Vagrant Economy: Making Space for 'Low' Subjectivity", in L.C. Orlin (ed.), *Material London, ca. 1600* (Philadelphia, 2000), pp. 206–25.

Fussell, G.E, "Low Countries' Influence on English Farming", *English Historical Review*, Vol. 74 (1959), pp. 611–22.

Gachard, M. (ed.), *Correspondance de Guillaume le Taciturne, Prince d'Orange*, Vol. 3 (Brussels, Leipzig & Ghent, 1851).

Gadd, I.A. and Wallis, P. (eds), *Guilds, Society and Economy in London 1450–1800* (London, 2002).

Gairdner, J. (ed.), *Three Fifteenth-Century Chronicles with Historical Memoranda by John Stowe, Camden Society Publications*, New Series ,Vol. 28 (London, 1880).

Galley, C., *The Demography of Early Modern Towns: York in the Sixteenth and Seventeenth Centuries* (Liverpool, 1998).

Games, A., *Migration and the Origins of the English Atlantic World* (Cambridge, Massachusetts, 1999).

Gentleman, T., *Englands Way to Win Wealth* (1614), *Harleian Miscellany*, Vol. 3 (London, 1745), pp. 378–91.

Godfray, H.M. (ed.), *Registre des Baptesmes, Mariages & Morts et Jeusnes de leglise wallonne . . . a Southampton, Publications of the Huguenot Society*, Vol. 4 (1890).

Godfrey, E.S., *The Development of English Glassmaking 1560–1640* (Oxford, 1975).

Goose, N. and Cooper, J., *Tudor and Stuart Colchester* (Chelmsford, 1998).

Goose, N. and Evans, N., "Wills as an Historical Source", in Arkell, Evans and Goose (eds), *When Death Do Us Part*, pp. 38–71.

Goose, N., "Economic and Social Aspects of Provincial Towns: a Comparative Study of Cambridge, Colchester and Reading c.1500–1700" (Unpublished Ph.D. thesis, University of Cambridge, 1984).

Goose, N., "Household Size and Structure in Early-Stuart Cambridge", *Social History*, Vol. 5 (1980), pp. 347–85.

Goose, N., "The 'Dutch' in Colchester: the Economic Influence of an Immigrant Community in the Sixteenth and Seventeenth Centuries", *Immigrants and Minorities*, Vol. 1 (1982), pp. 261–80.

Goose, N., "The Dutch in Colchester in the 16th and 17th Centuries: Opposition and Integration", in Vigne and Littleton (eds), *From Strangers to Citizens*, pp. 88–98.

Goose, N.R., "In Search of the Urban Variable: Towns and the English Economy, 1500–1650", *Economic History Review*, Vol. 39 (1986).

Goring, J., "Reformation and Reaction in Sussex, 1534–1559", *Sussex Archaeological Collections*, Vol. 134 (1996).

Goring, J.J., "Wealden Ironmasters in the Age of Elizabeth", in Ives, Knecht and Scarisbrick (eds), *Wealth and Power in Tudor England: Essays Presented to S.T. Bindoff*, pp. 204–23.

Gough, J.W., *The Rise of the Entrepreneur* (London, 1969).

Grabes, H. (ed.), *Writing the Early Modern English Nation: the Transformation of National Identity in Sixteenth- and Seventeenth-Century England* (Amsterdam and Atlanta, 2001).

Grassby, R., *The Business Community of Seventeenth Century England* (Cambridge, 1995).

Grell, O.P., "A Friendship Turned Sour: Puritans and Dutch Calvinists in East Anglia", in E. Leedham-Green (ed.), *Religious Dissent in East Anglia, 1603–1660* (Cambridge, 1991), pp. 45–61.

Grell, O.P. "A New Home or a Temporary Abode? Dutch and Walloon Exiles in England", in Grell, *Calvinist Exiles*, pp. 1–33.

Grell, O.P., "From Persecution to Integration: the Decline of the Anglo-Dutch Communities in England, 1648–1702", in Grell, *Calvinist Exiles*, pp. 120–46.

Grell, O.P., "From Uniformity to Tolerance: the Effects on the Dutch Church in London of Reverse Patterns in English Church Policy, 1634–1647", in Grell, *Calvinist Exiles*, pp. 74–97.

Grell, O.P., "Plague in Elizabethan and Stuart London: the Dutch Response", *Medical History*, Vol. 34 (1990).

Grell, O.P., "The French and Dutch Congregations in London in the Early Seventeenth Century", *Proceedings of the Huguenot Society*, Vol. 24 (1987), pp. 362–77, repr. in Grell, *Calvinist Exiles*, pp. 34–52.

Grell, O.P., *Cavlinist Exiles in Tudor and Stuart England* (Aldershot, 1997).

Grell, O.P., *Dutch Calvinists in Early Stuart London: the Dutch Church in Austin Friars 1603–1642* (Leiden, 1989).

Griffiths, P. *et al.*, "Population and Disease, Estrangement and Belonging", in Clark (ed.), *Cambridge Urban History*, pp. 195–233.

Griffiths, P., "Overlapping Circles: Imagining Criminal Communities in London, 1545–1645," in A. Shepard and P. Withington (eds), *Communities in Early Modern England: Networks, Place, Rhetoric* (Manchester, 2000), pp. 115–33.

Guy, J., *Tudor England* (Oxford, 1988).

Gwynn, R., *Huguenot Heritage. The History and Contribution of the Huguenots in Britain*, (2nd edn, Brighton, 2001, first publ. 1985).

Gwynn, R.D. (ed.), *A Calendar of the Letter Books of the French Church of London from the Civil War to the Restoration, 1643–1659, Publications of the Huguenot Society*, Vol. 54 (1979).

Haley, K.H.D., *An English Diplomat in the Low Countries. Sir William Temple and John De Witt, 1665–1672* (Oxford, 1986).

Haley, K.H.D., *The British and the Dutch: Political and Cultural Relations Through the Ages* (London, 1988).

Hall, K.F., *Things of Darkness: Economies of Race and Gender in Early Modern England* (New York, 1995).

Hamilton, G.H. (ed.), *Books of Examination and Depositions, 1570–1594, Southampton Record Society*, Vol. 16 (1914).

Harding, V., "Controlling a Complex Metropolis, 1650–1750: Politics, Parishes and Powers", *London Journal*, Vol. 26 (2001), pp. 29–37.

Harding, V., "The Population of London, 1550–1700: A Review of the Published Evidence", *London Journal*, Vol. 15 (1990), pp. 111–28.

Hardy, W.J., "Foreign Refugees at Rye", *Proceedings of the Huguenot Society*, Vol. 2 (1887–8), pp. 406–27, 567–87.

Hardy, W.J., "Foreign Settlers at Colchester and Halstead", *Proceedings of the Huguenot Society*, Vol. 2 (1887–88), pp. 182–96.

Harkness, D., "Maps, Spiders and Tulips: the Cole-Ortelius-L'Obel Family and the Practice of Science in Early Modern London", in Vigne and Littleton (eds), *From Strangers to Citizens*, pp. 184–96.

Harris, J., "Industrial Espionage in the Eighteenth Century", in Harris, *Essays in Industry and Technology*, pp. 164–75.

Harris, J., "Origins of the St Helens Glass Industry", in Harris, *Essays in Industry and Technology*, pp. 195–207.

Harris, J., "Saint-Gobin and Ravenhead", in Harris, *Essays in Industry and Technology*, pp. 34–77.

Harris, J., *Essays in Industry and Technology in the Eighteenth Century* (Hampshire UK, 1992).

Harris, L.E., *Vermuyden and the Fens. A Study of Sir Cornelius Vermuyden and the Great Level* (London, 1953).

Hart, M., "Freedom and Restrictions: State and Economy in the Dutch Republic, 1570–1670" in Davids and Noordegraaf (eds), *The Dutch Economy*, pp. 105–30.

Harte, N.B. (ed.), *The New Draperies in the Low Countries and England* (Oxford, 1997).

Hartlib, S., *A Discours of Husbandrie Used in Brabant and Flanders: Shewing the Wonderful Improvement of Land There; and Serving as a Pattern for Our Practice in this Commonwealth* (Second edn, London, 1652).

Hatcher, J., *Plague, Population and the English Economy 1348–1530* (London, 1977).

Heal, F. and O'Day, R. (eds), *Church and Society in England: Henry VIII to James I* (London, 1977).

Hearder, H. and Loyn, H.R. (eds), *British Government and Administrative Studies Presented to S.B. Chrimes* (Cardiff, 1974).

Hearn, K., "Insiders or Outsiders? Overseas-Born Artists at the Jacobean Court," in Vigne and Littleton (eds), *From Strangers to Citizens*, pp. 117–26.

Henning, B.D. (ed.), *The History of Parliament: The House of Commons, 1660–1690*, 3 Vols (London, 1983).

Hessels, J.H. (ed.), *Abrahami Ortelii, Geographi Antverpiensis et Virorum Eruditorum ad Eundem et ad Jacobum Colium Ortelianum, Epistulae* (Osnabrück, 1969).

Hessels, J.H. (ed.), *Ecclesiae Londino-Batavae Archivum. Epistulae et Tractatus*, 4 Vols (Cambridge, 1887–97).

Heywood, T., *The Famous and Remarkable History of Sir Richard Whittington* (London, 1656).

Hickman, D., "From Catholic to Protestant: the Changing Meaning of Testamentary Religious Provisions in Elizabethan London", in N. Tyacke (ed.), *England's Long Reformation 1500–1800* (London, 1998), pp. 117–39.

Higgs, L., "Wills and Religious Mentality in Tudor Colchester", *Essex Archaeology and History*, Vol. 22 (1991).

Higgs, L., *Godliness and Governance in Tudor Colchester* (Ann Arbor, Michigan, 1998).

Hill, C., *Intellectual Origins of the English Revolution* (Oxford, 1965).

Hindle, S., "Persuasion and Protest in the Caddington Common Enclosure Dispute, 1635–1639", *Past & Present*, No. 158 (1998).

Historical Manuscipts Commission, 2nd Report (London, 1874; repr., Liechtenstein, 1979).

Historical Manuscripts Commission Report, Duke of Rutland MSS, Vol. 1 (London, 1888).

Historical Manuscripts Commission, De L'Isle & Dudley MSS, Vol. 2 (London, 1936).

Historical Manuscripts Commission, Seventh Report of the Royal Commission on Historical Manuscripts: Report and Appendix (London, 1879).

Historical Manuscripts Commission, Sixth Report of the Royal Commission on Historical Manuscripts: Report and Appendix (London, 1877).

Hodgen, M.T., *Early Anthropology in the Sixteenth and Seventeenth Centuries* (Philadelphia, 1964).

Hoenselaars, A.J., *Images of Englishmen and Foreigners in the Drama of Shakespeare and his Contemporaries. A Study of Stage Characters and National Identity in English Renaissance Drama, 1558–1642* (Rutherford, Madison and Teaneck, 1992).

Holles, G., *Memorials of the Holles Family 1493–1656*, A.C. Wood (ed.), Camden Society 3rd ser., Vol. 55 (London, 1937).

Holmes, M., "Evil May Day, 1517: the Story of a Riot", *History Today*, Vol. 15 (1965), pp. 642–50.

Horn, D.B., *Great Britain and Europe in the Eighteenth Century* (Oxford, 1967).

Hovenden, R., *The Registers of the Walloon or Stranger's Church in Canterbury*, 3 Vols (Lymington, 1891–1898).

Howard, J.E., "Women, Foreigners, and the Regulation of Urban Space *in Westward Ho*," in L.C. Orlin, ed., *Material London, ca. 1600* (Philadelphia, 2000), pp. 150–67.

Howes, E. (ed.), *The Annales or Generall Chronicle of England, Begun First by Maister John Stow, and After Him Continued and Augmented. . .* (London, 1615).

Hudson, W. and Tingey, J.C., *The Records of the City of Norwich*, 2 Vols (London, 1906–10).

Huelin, G., *Think and Thank God. The Mercers' Company and its Contribution to the Church and Religious Life since the Reformation* (London, 1994).

Hume, I.N., *Early English Delftware from London to Virginia*, Colonial Williamsburg Occasional Papers in Archaeology, Vol. 2 (Williamsburg, 1977).

Hunt, W., *The Puritan Moment: the Coming of Revolution in an English County* (Cambridge, Massachusetts, 1983).

Israel, J.I., *The Dutch Republic: its Rise, Greatness, and Fall 1477–1806* (Oxford, 1995).

Ives, E.W., Knecht, R.J. and Scarisbrick, J.J. (eds), *Wealth and Power in Tudor England: Essays Presented to S.T. Bindoff* (London, 1978).

Jamees, A., *Inventaris van het archief van de Raad van Beroerten* (Brussels, 1980).

James I, *A Proclamation for Suppressing Insolent Abuses* (London, 1621).

Jansen, C., *Beschyvinghe vande Herlycke Arcus Triumphal ofte Eerepoorte vande Nederlantsche Natie Opgherecht in London* (Middelburg, 1604/1605).

Janssen, A.E.M., "A 'Trias Historica' on the Revolt of the Netherlands: Emmanuel van Meteren, Pieter Bor and Everhard van Reyd as Exponents of Contemporary Historiography", in A.C. Duke and.C.A. Tamse (eds), *Clio's Mirror. Historiography in Britain and the Netherlands* (Zutphen ,1985), pp. 9–30.

Johnson, E. (ed.), *Actes du Consistoire de l'Eglise Française de Threadneedle Street, London. Vol. I 1560–1565, Publications of the Huguenot Society*, Vol. 38 (1937).

Jones, D.W., "London Merchants and the Crisis of the 1690s", in P. Clark and P. Slack (eds), *Crisis and Order in English Towns 1500–1700*, pp. 311–55.

Jones, E.L., "Agricultural Conditions and Changes in Herefordshire, 1660–1815", in Jones, *Agriculture and the Industrial Revolution*, pp. 41–66.

Jones, E.L., *Agriculture and the Industrial Revolution* (Oxford, 1974).

Jones, J.R., *Britain and Europe in the Seventeenth Century* (London, 1966).

Jones, M.J., *British Nationality Law and Practice* (Oxford, 1947).

Journals of the House of Lords, 33 Vols (London, 1767–73).

Kahl, W., *The Development of London Livery Companies: an Historical Essay and a Select Bibliography* (Boston, Mass., 1960).

Kamen, H., *The Iron Century* (London, 1971).

Kaye, J.M. (ed.), *The Cartulary of God's House, Southampton*, 2 Vols, *Southampton Records Series*, Vols 19–20 (1976).

Kellett, J.R., "The Breakdown of Gild and Corporation Control over the Handicraft and Retail Trade in London", *Economic History Review*, Vol. 10 (1958), pp. 381–94.

Kermaingant, P. L. de, *L'Ambassade de France en Angleterre sous Henri IV* (Paris, 1886).

Kerridge, E., *Agrarian Problems in the Sixteenth Century and After* (London, 1969).

Kerridge, E., *Textile Manufactures in Early Modern England* (Manchester, 1985).

Kerridge, E., *The Agricultural Revolution* (London, 1967).

Kidd, C., "Protestantism, Constitutionalism and British Identity Under the Later Stuarts", in B. Bradshaw and P. Roberts (eds), *British Consciousness and Identity: the Making of Britain, 1533–1707* (Cambridge, 1998), pp, 321–42.

Kinder, A.G., *Casiodoro de Reina. Spanish Reformer of the Sixteenth Century* (London, 1975).

Kingsford, C.L. (ed.), John Stow, *A Survey of London*, 2 Vols (Oxford, 1971).

Kirk, R.E.G. and Kirk, E.F., *Returns of Aliens Dwelling in the City and Suburbs of London*, *Publications of the Huguenot Society*, Vol. 10, Parts 1–4 (1900–8).

Koenigsberger, H.G., *Monarchies, States Generals and Parliaments. The Netherlands in the Fifteenth and Sixteenth Centuries* (Cambridge, 2001).

Kümin, B.A. (ed.), *Reformations Old and New. Essays on the Socio-Economic Impact of Religious Change, c. 1470–1630* (Aldershot, 1996).

L'Abbé Le Blanc, *Letters on the English and French Nations*, 2 Vols (transl. London, 1747).

Lake, P., "Anti-Popery: the Structure of a Prejudice", in Cust and Hughes (eds), *Conflict in Early Stuart England. Studies in Religion and Politics 1603–1642*, pp. 72–106.

Lake, P., "The Laudian Style: Order, Uniformity and the Pursuit of the Beauty of Holiness in the 1630s", in K. Fincham (ed.), *The Early Stuart Church, 1603–1642* (Basingstoke, 1993).

Landes, D., *The Wealth and Poverty of Nations* (London, 1998).

Lang, R.G. (ed.), *Two Tudor Subsidy Assessment Rolls for the City of London: 1541 and 1582*, *London Record Society Publications*, Vol. 29 (London, 1993).

Langford, P., *A Polite and Commercial People: England 1727–1783* (Oxford, 1989).

Langford, P., *Englishness Identified: Manners and Character 1650–1850* (Oxford, 2000).

Laslett, P., *The World We Have Lost: Further Explored* (3rd edn, London, 1983).

Latham, R.C. and Matthews, W., *The Diary of Samuel Pepys*, 11 Vols (HarperCollins edn, London, 1995, first publ. 1971).

Laurence, A., "From the Cradle to the Grave: English Observation of Irish Social Customs in the Seventeenth Century", *The Seventeenth Century*, Vol. 3 (1988), pp. 63–84.

Le Moine, H.G.B., Moens, W.J.C. and Overend, G.H., "Huguenots in the Isle of Axholme", *Proceedings of the Huguenot Society*, Vol. 2 (1887–8).

Lemnius, L., *The Touchstone of Complexions* (1561), ed. T. Newton (London, 1581).

Lettenhove, K. de (ed.), *Relations Politiques des Pays-Bas et de l'Angleterre, sous le Règne de Philippe II*, 11 Vols (Brussels, 1882–1900).

Letts, M. (ed.), *Francis Mortoft: His Book, Being His Travels Through France and Italy 1658–1659*, Hakluyt Society, Series 2, Vol. 57 (London, 1925).

Letts, M. (ed.), *The Travels of Leo of Rozmital through Germany, Flanders, England, France, Spain, Portugal and Italy 1465–1467* (Cambridge, 1957).

Letts, M., *As the Foreigner Saw Us* (London, 1935).

Levine, D. and Wrightson, K., *The Making of an Industrial Society. Whickham, 1560–1725* (Oxford, 1991).

Lindeboom, J., *Austin Friars. History of the Dutch Reformed Church in London 1550–1950* (The Hague, 1950).

Lindley, K., *Popular Politics and Religion in Civil War London* (Aldershot, 1997).

Lipson, E., *The Economic History of England: The Age of Mercantilism*, Vol. 3 (4th edn, London 1947, First publ. 1931).

Littleton, C., "An Unpublished Letter from Robert de la Fontaine to Philippe Duplessis-Mornay", *Proceedings of the Huguenot Society*, Vol. 26 (1995), pp. 363–6.

Littleton, C., "Ecclesiastical Discipline in the French Church of London and the Creation of Community, 1560–1600", *Archiv für Reformationsgeschichte*, Vol. 92 (2001).

Littleton, C., "Social Interactions of Aliens in Late Elizabethan London: Evidence from the 1593 Return and the French Consistory 'Actes' ", in Vigne and Gibbs (eds), *The Strangers' Progress*, pp. 147–59.

Littleton, C., "The French Church of London in European Protestantism: the Role of Robert le Macon, dit de la Fontaine", *Proceedings of the Huguenot Society*, Vol. 26 (1994), pp. 45–57.

Littleton, C.G., "Geneva on Threadneedle Street: the French Church of London and its Congregation, 1560–1625" (Unpublished Ph.D. thesis, University of Michigan, 1996).

Lock, J., "'How Many Tercios Has the Pope?' The Spanish War and the Sublimation of Elizabethan Anti-Popery", *History*, Vol. 81 (1996), pp. 195–214.

Lough, J., "Two More British Travellers in the France of Louis XIV", *The Seventeenth Century*, Vol. 1 (1986), pp. 159–75.

Lough, J., *France Observed in the Seventeenth Century by British Travellers* (Stocksfield, 1984).

Lowe, B., "Religious Wars and the 'Common Peace': Anglican Anti-War Sentiment in Elizabethan England", *Albion*, Vol. 28 (1996), pp. 415–35.

Lucassen, L. and De Vries, B., "Leiden als Middelpunt van een Westeuropees Textiel-Migratiesysteem, 1586–1650", in *Tijdschrift voor Sociale Geschiedenis*, Vol. 22 (1996), pp. 138–67.

Luu, L.B., "French-Speaking Refugees and the Foundation of the London Silk Industry in the 16th Century", *Proceedings of the Huguenot Society*, Vol. 26 (1997), pp. 564–76.

Luu, L.B., "'Taking the Bread Out of Our Mouths': Xenophobia in Early Modern London", *Immigrants and Minorities*, Vol. 19 (2000), pp. 1–22.

Luu, L.B., "The Dutch and their Beer Brewing", in A. Kershen (ed.), *Food in the Migrant's Experience* (Ashgate, 2002), pp. 101–33.

Luu, L.B., *Immigrants and the Industries of London* (Ashgate, 2004).

Mackay, C. (ed.), *A Collection of Songs and Ballads Relative to the London Prentices and Other Trades*, Percy Society, Vol. 1 (London, 1841).

Mackie, E. (ed.), *The Commerce of Everyday Life. Selections from The Tatler and The Spectator* (Boston, 1998).

MacLeod, C., *Inventing the Industrial Revolution: the English Patent System, 1660–1800* (Cambridge, 1988).

Magen, B., *Die Wallonengemeinde in Canterbury Von Ihrer Gründung Bis Zum Jahre 1635* (Bern and Frankfurt, 1973).

Malfatti, C.V. (transl.), *Two Italian Accounts of Tudor England* (Barcelona, 1953).

Malster, L.W., "The Passing of a Norwich Church", *Norfolk Magazine* (1953), pp. 56–9.

Maltby, W.S., *The Black Legend in England: the Development of Anti-Spanish Sentiment 1558–1660* (Durham, North Carolina, 1971).

Manley, L. (ed.), *London in the Age of Shakespeare: An Anthology* (Pennsylvania and London, 1986).

Mann, J. de Le, *The Cloth Industry in the West of England from 1640 to 1880* (repr. Gloucester, 1987, first publ. 1971).

Manning, B., *The English People and the English Revolution* (2nd edn, Bookmarks, London, 1991).

Manning, R.B., *Village Revolts: Social Protest and Popular Disturbances in England, 1509–1640* (Oxford, 1988).

Martin, A.R., *Franciscan Architecture in England* (Manchester, 1937).

Martin, L., "The Rise of the New Draperies in Norwich, 1550–1622", in Harte (ed.), *The New Draperies*, pp. 245–74.

Mathias, P., *The Brewing Industry in England, 1700–1830* (Cambridge, 1959).

Mayhew, G., *Tudor Rye* (Falmer, 1987).

Mayhew, G.J., "The Progress of the Reformation in East Sussex 1530–1559: the Evidence from Wills", *Southern History*, Vol. 5 (1983).

McClure, N.E. (ed.), *The Letters of John Chamberlain*, 2 Vols., American Philosophical Society (Philadelphia, 1939).

McGurk, J., "Wild Geese: the Irish in European armies (sixteenth to eighteenth centuries)", in P. O'Sullivan (ed.), *The Irish World Wide: History, Heritage, Identity*, Vol. 1, *Patterns of Migration* (London & Washington, pbk edn, 1997).

McLuskie, K.E., *Dekker and Heywood: Professional Dramatists* (Basingstoke, 1994).

McRae, A., "The Peripatetic Muse: Internal Travel and the Cultural Production of Space in Pre-Revolutionary England," in G. MacLean, D. Landry and J. P. Ward (eds), *The Country and the City Revisited: England and the Politics of Culture, 1550–1850* (Cambridge, 1999), pp. 24–40.

Meij, J.C.A. de, *De Watergeuzen en de Nederlanden 1568–1572*, Verhandelingen der Koninklijke Nederlandse Akademie van Wetenschapen, n.s., Vol. 77, ii/Werken uitgeven door de Commissie voor Zeegeschiedenis, Vol. 14 (Amsterdam, 1972).

Meldrum, T., *Domestic Service and Gender 1660–1750: Life and Work in the London Household* (Harlow, 2000).

Mentzer, R.A., "The Reformed Churches of France and the Visual Arts", in P. Corby Finney (ed.), *Seeing Beyond the Word. Visual Arts and the Calvinist Tradition* (Grand Rapids, 1999).

Metcalf, B.D. (ed.), *Making Muslim Space in North America and Europe* (Berkeley, California, 1996).

Miller, A.C., *Sir Henry Killigrew: Elizabethan Soldier and Diplomat* (Leicester, 1963).

Miller, J., "Town Governments and Protestant Strangers 1560–1690", *Proceedings of the Huguenot Society*, Vol. 26 (1997), pp. 577–89.

Miller, J., *Popery and Politics in England 1660–1688* (Cambridge, 1973).

Miller, W. (ed.), *Francis Blomefield, The History of the City of Norwich (1734)*, 2 Vols (n.p., 1806).

Mingay, G.E., "Dr Kerridge's Agricultural Revolution: a Comment", *Agricultural History*, 43 (1969).

Mitchell, D. (ed.), *Goldsmiths, Silversmiths and Bankers. Innovation and the Transfer of Skill 1550–1750* (Stroud, 1995).

Mitchell, D.M., "'It will be easy to make money'. Merchant Strangers in London, 1580–1680", in C. Lesger and L. Noordegraaf (eds), *Entrepreneurs and Entrepreneurship in Early Modern Times: Merchants and Industrialists within the Orbit of the Dutch Staple Market*, Hollandse Historische Reeks, Vol. 24 (Haarlem, 1995), pp. 119–33.

Moens, W.J.C. (ed.), *Register of Baptisms at the Dutch Church at Colchester*, Huguenot Society Publications, Vol. 12 (London, 1905).

Moens, W.J.C. (ed.), *The Marriage, Baptismal, and Burial Registers, 1571 to 1874, and Monumental Inscriptions of the Dutch Reformed Church, Austin Friars, London* (Lymington, 1884).

Moens, W.J.C., *The Walloons and their Church at Norwich*, Pt 1 (Lymington 1887–88).

Molhuysen, P.C. *et al.* (eds), *Niuew Nederlandsch Biografisch Woordenboek*, 10 Vols (Leiden, 1911–37).

Morant, P., *The History and Antiquities of the County of Essex*, 2 Vols (London, 1768).

Morant, V., "The Settlement of Protestant Refugees in Maidstone during the Sixteenth Century", *Economic History Review*, Vol. 4 (1951), pp. 210–14.

Moreau, G., *Histoire du Protestantisme à Tournai jusqu'à la Veille de la Révolution des Pays-Bas* (Paris, 1962).

Moryson, Fynes, *An Itinerary, written by Fynes Moryson Gent, first in the Latin tongue and then translated by him into English: containing his ten yeeres travell through the twelve dominions of Germany, Bohmerland, Sweitzerland, Netherland, Denmarke, Poland, Italy, Turky, France, England, Scotland, and Ireland* (London, 1617).

Mosley, C., *Burke's Peerage & Baronetage* (London, 1999).

Muldrew, C., *The Economy of Obligation: The Culture of Credit and Social Relations in Early Modern England* (Basingstoke, 1998).

Musgrave, P., *The Early Modern European Economy* (Basingstoke, 1999).

Mutsaerts, L., *Rockin' Ramona* (The Hague, 1989).

Myers, O.M. (ed.), *The Coverley Papers* (Oxford, 1908).

Nef, J.U., "The Progress of Technology and the Growth of Large-Scale Industry in Great Britain, 1540–1640", *Economic History Review*, first series, Vol. 5 (1934).

Newman, G., *The Rise of English Nationalism: a Cultural History* (revised edn, 1997, first publ. 1987).

Noonan, K.M., "'The Cruell Pressure of an Enraged, Barbarous People': Irish and English Identity in Seventeenth-Century Policy and Propaganda", *The Historical Journal*, Vol. 41 (1998), pp. 151–77.

Oakley, A.M. (ed.), *Actes du Consistoire de l'Église Française de Threadneedle Street, Londres, Vol. II 1571–1577*, *Publications of the Huguenot Society of London*, Vol. 48 (1969).

Oakley, A.M., "The Canterbury Walloon Congregation from Elizabeth I to Laud", in Scouloudi (ed.), *Huguenots in Britain and their French Background, 1550–1800*, pp. 56–71.

Oakley, A.M., "Dispute over Austin Friars Church, 1573", *Proceedings of the Huguenot Society*, Vol. 21 (1970), pp. 492–8.

Oliver, P., *Music in Britain. Essays on Afro-American Contributions to Popular Music* (Milton Keynes, 1990).

Oppenheim, M. (ed.), *The Naval Tracts of Sir William Monson*, 5 Vols, Navy Records Society (1902–14), Vol. 5 (1914) [written c. 1624–36].

Ormrod, D., *The Dutch in London* (London, 1973).

Outhwaite, R.B., *Dearth, Public Policy and Social Disturbance in England, 1500–1800* (Basingstoke, 1991).

Overend, G.H., "Strangers at Dover, Part I, 1558–1644", *Proceedings of the Huguenot Society*, Vol. 3 (1888–1891), pp. 91–171.

Pablo, J. de, "L'Armée de Mer Huguenote pendant la Troisième Guerre de Religion", *Archiv für Reformationsgeschichte*, Vol. 47 (1956).

Page, W. (ed.), *Letters of Denization and Acts of Naturalization for Aliens in England 1509–1603* (Lymington, 1893).

Palliser, D., "Popular Reactions to the Reformation During the Year of Uncertainty 1530–70", in Heal and O'Day (eds), *Church and Society.*

Palliser, D., *The Age of Elizabeth: England under the Later Tudors 1547–1603* (London, 1983).

Palliser, D., *Tudor York* (Oxford, 1979).

Palliser, D.M., "The Role of Minorities and Immigrants in English Medieval Towns", in *Il Ruolo Economico Delle Minoranze in Europa Secc. XIII–XVIII*, Instituto Internazionale di Storia Economica 'F. Datini', Prato, Serie II, Vol. 31 (2000), p. 183.

Panayi, P., "The Immigrant Experience in London's History", *London Journal*, Vol. 14 (1989), pp. 71–5.

Parker, G., *Spain and the Netherlands, 1559–1659* (London, 1979).

Parker, G., *The Dutch Revolt* (Harmondsworth, 1979, first publ. 1977).

Parker, T.H.L., *Calvin's Preaching* (Edinburgh, 1992).

Patten, J., *English Towns 1500–1700* (Folkestone, 1978).

Patterson, W.B., *King James VI and I and the Reunion of Christendom* (Cambridge, 1997).

Peacham, H., *Coach and Sedan Pleasantly Disputing for Place and Precedence* (London, 1636).

Peacham, H., *The Art of Living in London* (London, 1642).

Pearl, V., *London and the Outbreak of the Puritan Revolution: City Government and National Politics, 1625–43* (Oxford, 1961).

Pennell, S., "'Great quantities of Gooseberry Pye and Baked Clod of Beef': Victualling and Eating Out in Early Modern London," in P. Griffiths and M.S.R. Jenner (eds), *Londinopolis: Essays in the Social and Cultural History of Early Modern London* (Manchester, 2000), pp. 228–49.

Peters, H., *Good Work for a Good Magistrate* (London, 1651, repr. Belfast, 1992).

Pettegree, A., "Protestant Migration During the Early Modern Period", in *Le Migrazioni in Europa secc. XIII–XVIII*, Instituto Internazionale di Storia Economica 'F. Datini', Prato, Serie II (1994).

Pettegree, A., "The Exile Churches during the *Wonderjaar*", in *Church, Change and Revolution: Transactions of the Fourth Anglo-Dutch Church History Colloquium*, ed. J. van den Berg and P. G. Hoftijzer, PTBI, n.s., Vol. 12 (Leiden, 1991).

Pettegree, A., "The Foreign Population of London in 1549", *Proceedings of the Huguenot Society*, Vol. 24 (1984).

Pettegree, A., "The Stranger Community in Marian London", *Proceedings of the Huguenot Society*, Vol. 24 (1987).

Pettegree, A., "'Thirty Years On': Progress Towards Integration amongst the Immigrant Population of Elizabethan London", in J. Chartres and D. Hey (eds), *English Rural Society, 1500–1800: Essays in Honour of Joan Thirsk* (Cambridge, 1990), pp. 297–312.

Pettegree, A., *Emden and the Dutch Revolt. Exile and the Development of a Reformed Protestantism* (Oxford, 1992).

Pettegree, A., *Foreign Protestant Communities in Sixteenth-Century London* (Oxford, 1986).

Pevsner, N. and B.Wilson, B., *The Buildings of England. Norfolk I: Norwich and North-East* (London, 1997).

Phythian-Adams, C. and Slack, P., "Urban Crisis or Urban Change?", in Phythian-Adams *et al.*, *The Traditional Community Under Stress* (Milton Keynes, 1977), pp. 5–29.

Phythian-Adams, C., "Dr Dyer's Urban Undulations", *Urban History Yearbook 1979* (Leicester, 1979), pp. 73–6.

Phythian-Adams, C., "Urban Decay in Late Medieval England", in P. Abrams and E.A. Wrigley (eds), *Towns in Societies* (Cambridge, 1978), pp. 159–69.

Pilgrim, J.E., "The Rise of the 'New Draperies' in Essex", *University of Birmingham Historical Journal*, Vol. 7 (1959–60), pp. 36–59.

Piot, C., *Corresponance du Cardinal de Granvelle, Vol. 12, 1586* (Brussels, 1896).

Plummer, A., *The Weavers' Company 1600–1970* (London, 1972).

Postan, M.M., *The Medieval Economy and Society: an Economic History of Britain 1100–1500* (London, 1972).

Pound, J., "The Social and Trade Structure of Norwich 1525–1575" (Unpublished Ph.D. thesis, University of Leicester, 1974).

Pound, J., *Tudor and Stuart Norwich* (Chichester, 1988).

Powell, A., *John Aubrey and His Friends* (revised edn, London, 1963, First publ. 1948).

Power, M.J., "A 'Crisis' Reconsidered: Social and Demographic Dislocation in London in the 1590s", *London Journal*, Vol. 12 (1986), pp. 134–45.

Power, M.J., "London and the Control of the 'Crisis' of the 1590s", *History*, Vol. 70 (1985), pp. 371–85.

Quick, J., *Synodicon in Gallia Reformata: or the Acts, Decisions, Decrees and Canons of those Famous National Councils of the Reformed Churches in France* (London, 1692).

Quinn, D.B., *The Elizabethans and the Irish* (New York, 1966).

Rabb, T.K., *Enterprise and Empire: Merchant and Gentry Involvement in the Expansion of England 1575–1630* (Cambridge, Massachusetts, 1967).

Ramsay, G.D., *The Queen's Merchants and the Revolt of the Netherlands* (Manchester, 1986).

Rappaport, S., *Worlds Within Worlds: Structures of Life in Sixteenth-Century London* (Cambridge, 1989).

Read, C., *Lord Burghley and Queen Elizabeth* (New York, 1960).

Redstone, V.B., "The Dutch and Huguenot Settlements of Ipswich", *Proceedings of the Huguenot Society*, Vol. 12 (1917–23), pp. 183–204.

Reed, M., "The Peasantry of Nineteenth-Century England: a Neglected Class?", *History Workshop*, No. 18 (1984).

Registres de la Compagnie des Pasteurs de Genève, 12 Vols (Geneva, 1962).

Ressinger, D.W. (ed.), *Memoirs of the Reverend Jacques Fontaine 1658–1728, Publications of the Huguenot Society*, New Series, Vol. 2 (Ashford, 1992).

Rimbault, E.F. (ed.), *The Miscellaneous Works in Prose and Verse of Sir Thomas Overbury, Knt* (London, 1856).

Robbins, C., "A Note on General Naturalization under the Later Stuarts", *Journal of Modern History*, Vol, 34 (1972).

Robertson, C., *"Il Gran Cardinale": Alessandro Farnese, Patron of the Arts* (New Haven, 1992).

Robertson, J., "The Adventures of Dick Whittington and the Social Construction of Elizabethan London," in Gadd and Wallis (eds), *Guilds, Society and Economy*, pp. 51–66.

Robertson, J., "Re-Writing the English Conquest of Jamaica in the Late Seventeenth Century", *English Historical Review*, Vol. 117 (2002), pp. 813–39.

Robson-Scott, W.D., *German Travellers in England 1400–1800* (Oxford, 1953).

Rockett, W., "The Structural Plan of Camden's Britannia", *Sixteenth Century Journal*, Vol. 26 (1995), pp. 829–41.

Roker, L.F., "The Dutch Fishing Community in Yarmouth", *East Anglia Magazine*, Vol. 30 (1971), pp. 306–8.

Rowse, A.L., *Simon Forman: Sex and Society in Shakespeare's Age* (London, 1974).

Ruddock, A.A., *Italian Merchants and Shipping in Southampton, 1270–1600, Southampton Records Series*, Vol. 1 (1951).

Russell, C. (ed.), *The Origins of the English Civil War* (London, 1973).

Russell, C., *The Crisis of Parliaments: English History 1509–1660* (Oxford, 1971).

Rutger, F. L. (ed.), *Acta van de Nederlandsche Synoden der Zestiende Eeuw*, Werken der Marnix-Vereeniging, Ser. 2, pt. 3 (Utrecht, 1889).

Ruytinck, S., *Gheschiedenissen ende Handelingen die Voornemelick aengaen de Nederduytsche Natie ende Gemeynten Wonende in Engelant ende in Bysonder Tot Londen*, ed. J. J. van Toorenbergen, Werken der Marnix-Vereeniging, Ser. 3, pt. 1 (Utrecht, 1873).

Rye, W.B., *England as Seen by Foreigners in the Days of Elizabeth and James the First* (London, 1865).

Schama, S., *The Embarrassment of Riches. An Interpretation of Dutch Culture in the Golden Age* (London, 1987).

Schepper, H. de, "The Burgundian-Habsburg Netherlands", in T.A. Brady jr., H.A. Oberman and J.D. Tracy (eds), *Handbook of European History 1400–1600* (Leiden, New York and Cologne, 1994), pp. 499–530.

Schickler, F. de, *Les Eglises du Refuge en Angleterre*, 3 Vols (Paris, 1892).

Scouloudi, I. (ed.), *Huguenots in Britain and their French Background, 1550–1800* (Basingstoke, 1987).

Scouloudi, I., "The Stranger Community in London 1558–1640", *Proceedings of the Huguenot Society*, Vol. 24 (1987).

Scouloudi, I., *Returns of Strangers in the Metropolis 1593, 1627, 1635, 1639: a Study of an Active Minority*, Huguenot Society of London, Vol. 57 (1985).

Scoville, W.C., "The Huguenots and the Diffusion of Technology", *Journal of Political Economy*, Vol. 60, pp. 294–311, 392–411.

Scoville, W.C., *The Persecution of Huguenots and French Economic Development, 1680–1720* (Berkeley, 1960).

Sessions, W.K. and Stoker, D., *The First Printers in Norwich from 1567 – Anthony de Solempne, Albert Christiansz & Johannes Paetz* (York, 1987).

Sharp, B., "Popular Political Opinion in England 1660–1685", *History of European Ideas*, Vol. 10 (1989), pp. 13–29.

Sharpe, P.A., *Population and Society in an East Devon Parish: Reproducing Colyton 1540–1840* (Exeter, 2002).

Sheils, W.J., "Religion in Provincial Towns: Innovation and Tradition", in Heal and O'Day (eds), *Church and Society*.

Shepherd, M.E., "The Small Owner in Cumbria c. 1840–1910: a Case Study from the Upper Eden Valley", *Northern History*, Vol. 35 (1999), pp. 161–84.

Shyllon, F., *Black People in Britain 1555–1833* (London, 1977).

Silver, G., *Paradoxes of Defense* (London, 1599), online edn at http://www.pbm.com/~lindahl/paradoxes.html.

Skipp, V., *Crisis and Development: an Ecological Case Study of the Forest of Arden 1570–1674* (Cambridge, 1978).

Slack, P., "Great and Good Towns 1540–1700", in Clark (ed.), *The Cambridge Urban History of Britain. Vol. II 1540–1800*, pp. 347–76.

Slack, P., *Poverty and Policy in Tudor and Stuart England* (London, 1988).

Slack, P., *The Impact of Plague in Tudor and Stuart England* (Oxford, 1985).

Sleigh-Johnson, N.V., "The Merchant Taylors Company of London 1580–1645, with Special Reference to Government and Politics" (unpubl. Ph.D. thesis, University of London, 1989).

Smiles, S., *The Huguenots: Their Settlements, Churches, and Industries, in England and Ireland* (London, 1880).

Smith, S.R., "The London Apprentices as Seventeenth-Century Adolescents", *Past & Present*, No. 61 (1973), pp. 149–61.

Smuts, M.R., "The Court and Its Neighborhood: Royal Policy and Urban Growth in the Early Stuart West End", *Journal of British Studies*, Vol. 30 (1910), pp. 117–49.

Sneyd, C.A. (ed.), *A Relation, or Rather a True Account, of the Island of England, Camden Society Publications* (London, 1847).

Solt, L.F., *Church and State in Early Modern England, 1509–1640* (Oxford, 1990).

Sorlien, R.P. (ed.), *The Diary of John Manningham of the Middle Temple 1602–1603* (Hanover, New Hampshire, 1976).

Spenceley, G.F.R., "The Origins of the English Pillow Lace Industry", *Agricultural History Review*, Vol. 21, Part II (1973), pp. 81–93.

Spicer, A., "'Accommodating of Thame Selfis to Heir the Worde': Preaching, Pews and Reformed Worship in Scotland, 1560–1638", *History*, Vol. 88 (2003).

Spicer, A., "'Qui est de Dieu oit la Parole de Dieu': the Huguenots and their Temples", in R.A. Mentzer and A. Spicer (eds), *Society and Culture in the Huguenot World, 1559–1685* (Cambridge, 2002).

Spicer, A., "A Process of Gradual Assimilation: the Exile Community in Southampton, 1567–1635", in Vigne and Gibbs (eds), *The Strangers' Progress*, pp. 186–98.

Spicer, A., "Continental Calvinism and its Churches – An Overview", *Aberdeen University Review*, Vol. 58 (2000).

Spicer, A., "Iconoclasm and Adaptation: The Reformation of the Churches in Scotland and the Netherlands", in D.Gaimster and R. Gilchrist, *The Archaeology of the Reformation* (2003), pp. 29–43.

Spicer, A., "Poor Relief and the Exile Communities", in Kümin (ed.), *Reformations Old and New*.

Spicer, A., "Profanation and Consecration: the Sanctity of the Scottish Kirks, 1560–1638" in W. Coster and A. Spicer (eds), *Sacred Space: the Redefinition of Sanctity in Post-Reformation Europe* (forthcoming, Cambridge University Press).

Spicer, A., "Reflections on Post-Reformation Rites of Consecration", in S. Hamilton and A. Spicer, *Defining the Holy: Sacred Spaces in Medieval and Early Modern Europe* (forthcoming).

Spicer, A., *The French-Speaking Reformed Community and their Church in Southampton 1567–c.1620*, Southampton Record Series, Vol. 39 (Stroud, 1997).

Spufford, M., *Contrasting Communities: English Villagers in the Sixteenth and Seventeenth Centuries* (Cambridge, 1974).

Statt, D., "The Birthright of an Englishman: the Practice of Naturalization and Denization of Immigrants under the Later Stuarts and Early Hanoverians", *Proceedings of the Huguenot Society*, Vol. 25 (1989).

Statt, D., *Foreigners and Englishmen. The Controversy over Immigration and Population, 1660–1760* (London, 1995).

Stell, C., "Puritan and Nonconformist Meetinghouses in England", in P. Corby Finney (ed.), *Seeing beyond the Word. Visual Arts and the Calvinist Tradition* (Grand Rapids, 1999).

Stephen, L. and Lee, S., *Dictionary of National Biography* (Oxford, 1917).

Stephens, W.B., "The Cloth Exports of the Provincial Ports, 1600–1640", *Economic History Review*, Vol. 22 (1969).

Stern, W.M., *The Porters of London* (Longmans, 1960).

Stoate, T.L., *Devon Lay Subsidy Rolls 1524–7* (Bristol, 1979).

Stone, L., "The Residential Development of the West End of London in the Seventeenth Century", in B.C. Malament (ed.), *After the Reformation: Essays in Honour of J. H. Hexter* (Manchester, 1980), pp. 167–212.

Stoye, J.W., *English Travellers Abroad 1604–1667: Their Influence in English Society and Politics* (London, 1952).

Strohm, C., "Discipline and Integration: Jan Laski's Church Order for the London Strangers' Church", in Vigne and Littleton (eds), *From Strangers to Citizens*, pp. 25–37.

Strype, J., *Annals of the Reformation*, 4 Vols (London, 1725–31).

Supple, B., *Commercial Crisis and Change in England 1600–1642* (Cambridge, 1970).

Swinden, H., *The History and Antiquities of the Ancient Burgh of Great Yarmouth in the County of Norfolk* (Norwich, 1772).

Tammel, J.W., *The Pilgrims and Other People from the British Isles in Leiden, 1576–1640* (Peel, 1989).

Tawney, R.H. and Power, E. (eds), *Tudor Economic Documents*, 3 Vols (London, 1924).

Tawney, R.H., "The Rise of the Gentry, 1558–1640", *Economic History Review*, 1st series, Vol. 11 (1941).

Tawney, R.H., *The Agrarian Problem in the Sixteenth Century* (London, 1912, repr. New York, 1967).

Taylor, H., "Trade, Neutrality and the 'English Road', 1630–1648", *Economic History Review*, Vol. 25 (1972), pp. 236–60.

Temple, R.C. (ed.), *The Travels of Peter Mundy in Europe and Asia 1608–1667, Vol. 4 Travels in Europe 1639–1647*, Hakluyt Society, Series 2, Vol. 55 (London, 1925).

Temple, R.C. (ed.), *The Travels of Peter Mundy, In Europe and Asia, 1608–1667, Vol. 1 Travels in Europe, 1608–1628*, The Hakluyt Society, Series 2, Vol. 17 (Cambridge, 1907).

Temple, Sir John, *The Irish Rebellion: or a History of the beginnings and the First Progress of the General Rebellion Raised within the Kingdom of Ireland, upon the three and twentieth day of October, 1641* (6th edn, Dublin, 1724, First publ. 1646.

Thirsk, J. (ed.), *The Agrarian History of England and Wales Vol. IV 1540–1640* (Cambridge, 1967).

Thirsk, J. (ed.), *The Agrarian History of England and Wales Vol. V 1640–1750, Part II Agrarian Change* (Cambridge, 1985).

Thirsk, J. and Cooper, J.P. (eds), *17th Century Economic Documents* (Oxford, 1972).

Thirsk, J., "Agriculture in Kent, 1540–1640", in Zell (ed.), *Early Modern Kent 1540–1640* (Woodbridge, 2000), pp. 75–103.

Thirsk, J., "Stamford in the Sixteenth and Seventeenth Centuries", in J. Thirsk, *The Rural Economy of England: Collected Essays* (Hambledon, London, 1984), pp. 309–25.

Thirsk, J., "The Fantastical Folly of Fashion: the English Stocking Knitting Industry, 1500–1700", reprinted in J. Thirsk, *The Rural Economy of England: Collected Essays* (London, 1984), pp. 235–57.

Thirsk, J., *Economic Policy and Projects. The Development of a Consumer Society in Early Modern England* (Oxford, 1978).

Thøfner, M., "Domina & Princeps Proprietaria. The Idea of Sovereignty in the Joyous Entries of the Archdukes Albert and the Infanta Isabella", in W. Thomas and L. Duerloo (eds), *Albert & Isabella 1598–1621* (Brepols, 1998), pp. 55–66.

Thomas, K., *Man and the Natural World: Changing Attitudes in England 1500–1800* (Penguin edn, Harmondsworth, 1984, First publ. 1983).

Thompson, E.P., "The Moral Economy of the English Crowd in the Eighteenth Century," reprinted in Thomspon, *Customs in Common: Studies in Traditional Popular Culture* (New York, 1993), pp. 185–258.

Thompson, J.W., *The Wars of Religion in France 1559–1576* (Chicago, 1909).

Thrupp, S., "A Survey of the Alien Population of England in 1440", *Speculum*, Vol. 32 (1957), pp. 262–72.

Thrupp, S., "Aliens in and Around London in the Fifteenth Century", in A.E. Hollander and W. Kellaway (eds), *Studies in London History: Essays Presented to P.E. Jones* (London, 1969), pp. 251–72.

Thurley, S., "The Stuart Kings, Oliver Cromwell and the Chapel Royal 1618–1685", *Architectural History*, Vol. 45 (2002).

Tilly, C., "Neuere Angloamerikanische Sozialgeschichte", in J. Eibach and G. Lottes (eds), *Kompass der Geschichtswissenschaft* (Göttingen, 2002), pp. 38–52.

Toorenenbergen, J.J. van (ed.), *Acten van de Colloquia der Nederlandsche Gemeenten in Engeland, 1575–1609*, Werken der Marnix-Vereeniging Ser. 2, pt. 1 (Utrecht, 1872).

Towner, J., "The Grand Tour: A Key Phase in the History of Tourism", *Annals of Tourism Research*, Vol. 12 (1985), pp. 297–333.

Towner, J., "The Grand Tour: Sources and a Methodology for an Historical Study of Tourism", *Tourism Management*, Vol. 5 (1984), pp. 215–22.

Trim, D.J.B., "Fighting 'Jacob's Wars'. The Employment of English and Welsh Mercenaries in the European Wars of Religion: France and the Netherlands, 1562–1610" (Unpublished Ph.D. thesis, University of London, 2003).

Trim, D.J.B., "Sir Thomas Bodley and the International Protestant Cause", *Bodleian Library Record*, Vol. 16 (1998).

Trim, D.J.B., "The 'Foundation-Stone of the British Army'? The Normandy Campaign of 1562", *Journal of the Society for Army Historical Research*, Vol. 77 (1999), pp. 71–87.

Trim, D.J.B., "The 'Secret War' of Elizabeth I: England and the Huguenots during the Early Wars of Religion", *Proceedings of the Huguenot Society*, Vol. 27 (1999), pp. 189–99.

Tsushima, J., "Melting into the Landscape: the Story of the 17th Century Walloons in the Fens", in Vigne and Littleton (eds), *From Strangers to Citizens*, pp. 106–13.

Turner, E., *An Introduction to English Silver from 1660* (London, HMSO, 1985).

Tyacke, N., "Puritanism, Arminianism and Counter-Revolution", in Russell (ed.), *Origins of the English Civil War*.

Ultee, M., "Review Article: the Riches of the Dutch Seventeenth Century", *The Seventeenth Century*, Vol. 3, No. 2 (1988), pp. 223–42.

Usher, B., "The Silent Community: Early Puritans and the Patronage of the Arts", in D. Wood (ed.), *The Church and the Arts, Studies in Church History*, Vol. 28 (Oxford, 1991), pp. 287–302.

Van Deursen, A.T., *Plain Lives in a Golden Age: Popular Culture, Religion and Society in Seventeenth-Century Holland* (Cambridge, 1991).

Van Dillen, J.G., *Bronnen tot de Geschiedenis van het Bedrijfsleven en het Gildewezen van Amsterdam*, Rijks Geschiedkundige Publicatië, Vol. 69 (1929).

Van Dorsten, J.A. " 'I. C. O'. The Rediscovery of a Modest Dutchman in London", in Van den Berg, J. and Hamilton, A., *The Anglo-Dutch Renaissance: Seven Essays*, PTBI, n.s., Vol. 10 (Leiden, 1988).

Van Houtte, J.A., *An Economic History of the Low Countries, 800–1800* (London, 1977).

Van Muyden, Madame (ed.), *A Foreign View of England in the Reigns of George I and George II. The Letters of Monsieur César de Saussure to his Family* (London, 1902).

Van Nierop, H.F.K., *Van Ridders tot Regenten: de Hollandse Adel in de Zestiende en de Eerste Helft van de Zeventiende Eeuw* (2nd edn, Amsterdam, 1990).

Van Toorenenbergen, J.J. (ed.), *Geschiedenissen ende Handlingen die Voornemelick Angaen de Nederduytsche Natie ende Gemeynten Woende in Engeland ende Bysonder Tot London* (Utrecht, 1873).

Vane, C.M., "The Walloon Community in Norwich: the First Hundred Years", *Proceedings of the Huguenot Society*, Vol. 24 (1984), pp. 129–40.

Venn, J. & Venn, J.A., *Alumni Cantabrigiensis. A Biographical List of all Known Students, Graduates and Holders of Office at the University of Cambridge*, 4 vols (Cambridge, 1922–27).

Verberckmoes, J., "Seventeenth-Century Low Countries Jests in International Perspective", in Hermans, T. and Salverda, R. (eds), *From Revolt to Riches: Culture and History of the Low Countries 1500–1700* (London, 1993).

Verheyden, A. L. E., "Le Protestantisme à Nieuport au XVIème siècle", *Bulletin de la Commission Royale de l'Histoire*, Vol. 116 (1951).

Verheyden, A.L.E., "Une Correspondance Inédite Addressée par des Familles Protestantes des Pays-Bas à leurs Coreligionnaires d'Angleterre (11 Novembre 1569–25 Février 1570)", *Bulletin de la Commission Royale d'Histoire*, Vol. 120 (1955), pp. 95–257.

Verheyden, A.L.E., *Le Conseil des Troubles. Liste des Condamnes 1567–1573* (Brussels, 1961).

Veryard, E., *An Account of Diverse Choice Remarks . . . Taken in a Journey Through the Low Countries, France, Italy and parts of Spain, with the Isles of Sicily and Malta, as also a Voyage to the Levant* (London, 1701).

Vigne, R. and Gibbs, G.C. (eds), *The Strangers' Progress: Integration and Disintegration of the Huguenot and Walloon Refugee Community, 1567–1889. Essays in Honour of Irene Scouloudi*, Proceedings of the Huguenot Society, Vol. 26 (London, 1995).

Vigne, R. and Littleton, C. (eds), *From Strangers to Citizens: the Integration of Immigrant Communities in Britain, Ireland and Colonial America, 1550–1750* (Brighton, 2001).

Walvin, J., *Black and White. The Negro and English Society 1555–1945* (London, 1973).

Ward, J.C., "The Reformation in Colchester, 1528–1558", *Essex Archaeology and History*, Vol. 15 (1983).

Ward, J.P., "Fictitious Shoemakers, Agitated Weavers and the Limits of Popular Xenophobia in Early Modern London", in Vigne and Littleton (eds), *From Strangers to Citizens*, pp. 80–7.

Ward, J.P., "Livery Companies and the World Beyond the Metropolis", in Gadd and Wallis (eds), *Guilds, Society and Economy*, pp. 175–8.

Ward, J.P., *Metropolitan Communities: Trade Guilds, Identities, and Change in Early Modern London* (Stanford, 1997).

Werbner, P., "Shaping the Earth in the Name of Allah: Zikr and the Sacralization of Space among British Muslims", in B.D. Metcalf (ed.) *Making Muslim Space in North America and Europe*, pp. 167–85.

Wernham, R.B., *After the Armada: Elizabethan England and the Struggle for Western Europe 1588–1595* (Oxford, 1984).

Whyte, I.D., *Migration and Society in Britain 1550–1830* (Basingstoke, 2000).

Williams, L., "The Crown and the Provincial Immigrant Communities", in Hearder and Loyn (eds), *British Government and Administrative Studies Presented to S.B. Chrimes*.

Williams, N.J., "Two Documents Concerning the New Draperies", *Economic History Review*, Vol. 4 (1952).

Williams, R., *The Actions of the Lowe Countries*, in J.X. Evans (ed.), *The Works of Roger Williams* (Oxford, 1972).

Wilson, C., *England's Apprenticeship 1601–1763* (2nd edn, London, 1984, First publ. 1965).

Winstanley, M., "Industrialization and the Small Farm: Family and Household Economy in Nineteenth-Century Lancashire", *Past & Present*, No. 152 (1996).

Wood, A., *The Politics of Social Conflict: The Peak Country, 1520–1770* (Cambridge, 1999).

Woods, W.J., "Publications Connected with the Dutch Church in Norwich", in N. Virgo and T. Williamson (eds), *Religious Dissent in East Anglia* (Norwich, 1993).

Wright, T., *Queen Elizabeth and Her Times*, 2 Vols (London, 1838).

Wright, T., *The History and Topography of the County of Essex*, 2 Vols (London, 1835).

Wrightson, K. and Levine, D., *Poverty and Piety in an English Village: Terling, 1525–1700* (2nd edn Oxford, 1995, First published 1979).

Wrightson, K., *Earthly Necessities: Economic Lives in Early Modern Britain* (New Haven and London, 2000).

Wrightson, K., *English Society 1580–1680* (London, 1982).

Wrigley, E.A. and Schofield, R.S., *The Population History of England 1541–1871: a Reconstruction* (London, 1981).

Wrigley, E.A., "A Simple Model of London's Importance in Changing English Society and Economy, 1650–1750", reprinted in Wrigley, *People, Cities and Wealth: The Transformation of Traditional Society* (Oxford, 1987), pp. 133–56.

Wrigley, E.A., "The Divergence of England: the Growth of the English Economy in the Seventeenth and Eighteenth centuries", *Transactions of the Royal Historical Society*, Vol. 10 (2000), pp. 117–41.

Wrigley, E.A., *Continuity, Chance and Change. The Character of the Industrial Revolution in England* (Cambridge, 1988).

Yule, G., "James VI and I: Furnishing the Churches in his Two Kingdoms", in A. Fletcher and P. Roberts (eds), *Religion, Culture and Society in Early Modern Britain* (Cambridge, 1994).

Yungblut, L.H., *Strangers Settled Here Amongst Us: Policies, Perceptions and the Presence of Aliens in Elizabethan England* (London, 1996).

Zell, M. (ed.), *Early Modern Kent 1540–1640* (Woodbridge, 2000).

Index

INDEX

Westkwartier, 52, 212, 225
Westmoreland, 142
Weston, Richard, 148–9
Westphalia, Treaty of (1648), 8
Whitehaven, 123
Whittington, Dick, 77, 85
Wilhelm, Christian, 170
William of Orange, 189, 212–13, 215
Willoughby, Lord, 217
wills, religious preambles of, 3, 5
Wilson, C., 152
Winchelsea, 17, 19, 27, 51, 216
Winchester, Bishop of, 214
Wivenhoe, 145
Wolley, Sir John, 67, 120, 138
Wood Beggars, the, 212
Wraye, Lady Anne, 63
Wren, Matthew, 101
Wright, T., 153
Wright, Thomas, 114

Wrightson, K., 10, 12, 155
Wrigley, E.A., 10

xenophobia, 110–35, 169, 206
    definitions of, 111–12
    limits of, 84–5, 211, 217
    see also English attitudes to immigrants

Yeoman, John, 65
York, City of, 3
Yorkshire, 3, 142–3, 151–3
Yungblut, L.H., 110

Zeeland, 24, 25, 42, 44, 47, 49, 52, 177, 179–80, 194, 213–15
Zucatto, Girolamo, 113
Zuider Zee, 201
Zutphen, 42, 48
Zwolle, 50